D1737036

THE FATHERS
OF THE CHURCH

A NEW TRANSLATION

VOLUME 30

THE FATHERS
OF THE CHURCH

A NEW TRANSLATION

SAINT AUGUSTINE

LETTERS

VOLUME IV (165-203)

Translated by

SISTER WILFRID PARSONS, S.N.D.

THE CATHOLIC UNIVERSITY OF AMERICA PRESS
Washington, D.C.

NIHIL OBSTAT:

JOHN M. A. FEARNS, S.T.D.

Censor Librorum

IMPRIMATUR:

✠ FRANCIS CARDINAL SPELLMAN

Archbishop of New York

November 21, 1955

Library of Congress Catalog Card No. 77-081344

ISBN 8132-0030-X

Copyright © 1955 by
THE CATHOLIC UNIVERSITY OF AMERICA PRESS, INC.

Second Printing 1977
Third Printing 1981

WRITINGS
OF
SAINT AUGUSTINE

VOLUME 12

CONTENTS

vii

INTRODUCTION

THE LETTERS INCLUDED in Volume 4 (165-203) cover
the years from 410 to the beginning of 420. The
long conflict with the Donatists was drawing to a
close; Letter 185 is the next to the last and much the most
important one on this bitter subject. It is addressed to the
tribune Boniface, afterward Count of Africa, and is one of
the longest of the letters. Augustine himself calls it a book:
Liber de correctione Donatistarum. Its importance lies in the
fact that it gives a fairly complete summary of the whole
controversy, by this time practically settled, and shows the
writer reluctantly convinced that the policy of *compelle
intrare* was the right one after all. At the same time, he was
invincibly opposed to harsh punishments for heretics.

But if the Donatist threat was dying out, the new and more
insidious danger of Pelagiansm was spreading in unsuspected
quarters, and during these ten years was to absorb more and
more of Augustine's time and effort. Two African synods, one
at Carthage and one at Milevis, had condemned the here-
siarch, and a report of this action was sent to Pope Innocent
I from each gathering (Letters 175-177). Though sent in
the name of a long list of bishops, each of these reports is

evidently the work of Augustine. The Pope answered them in Letters 181 and 182, giving the formal condemnation which had been requested.

Another aspect of the case is shown in Letter 179 to Bishop John of Jerusalem, who had not accepted the verdict of the Council of Carthage. Instead, he had held his own synod in 415 and had acquitted Pelagius. Augustine was thoroughly alarmed at this and wrote firmly but tactfully to Bishop John, protesting the acquittal, pointing out the evasive character of Pelagius, and suggesting certain questions which he should be required to answer unequivocally. The question of nature and grace recurs so frequently in letters of this period, even in letters not dealing specifically with this subject, that it is plain to see how deeply disturbed Augustine was at the spread of this deadly error. One of these is addressed to Juliana (188), daughter-in-law of Proba (cf. the earlier Letters 130 and 131), whose daughter Demetrias had consecrated herself to a life of virginity and had received some graceful congratulations in Letter 150. Learning that Pelagius had written a 'book' to Demetrias, the theme of which was that all her virtue was due to her own efforts and not to the grace of God, Augustine wrote a vigorous warning to mother and daughter.

St. Jerome appears in this series of letters, but the old fire is extinguished. He wrote to Marcellinus the tribune (165), who had asked him some questions on the origin of the soul, advising him to address himself to 'the holy and learned man, Augustine' for his answers, because he, Jerome was anxious to get to work on a promised commentary on Ezechiel. Augustine complied with the request and also sent a copy of his treatise (166) to Jerome by the hands of his young protege, Orosius. He also sent his treatise (167) on the words of St. James (2.10): 'Whoever shall keep the whole law but offend in one point is become guilty of all,' into which he introduces

some interesting parallels to Stoic teaching. In *Retractations*
2.45, Augustine gives evidence of the tact he had learned by
sad experience in his correspondence with Jerome. He says
of Letter 166: 'I only raised the question; I did not solve it.'
This was evidently because Jerome had written on the *Origin
of the Soul* in one of his works against Rufinus, and Augustine
did not want to seem to differ with him. Of Letter 167 he
says: 'I set forth what I thought might solve this question,'
and of both works he says: 'I did not publish these treatises
while Jerome was alive, because he might answer them at
some time and I should have had to publish them with his
reply. But after his death I published both.' Jerome had
acknowledged the receipt of the two treatises in Letter 172,
and had praised them, but excused himself from commenting
on them. Letter 202 was Jerome's last to Augustine. He
died the following year.

This problem of the origin of the soul, so closely connected
with the mystery of original sin, attacked by Pelagius, was
plainly one that preoccupied Augustine. In addition to the
treatise in which he set forth four theories on the time and
manner of the creation of the soul, without indicating his
preference for any of them, he wrote two letters to Optatus
(190 and 202A) reviewing the same material, and one to
Oceanus (180). His conclusion was that, no matter which
theory was the true one, it is of faith that everyone born of
Adam is under the curse of original sin, and no one is freed
from it except by rebirth in Christ.

A feeling of the imminent approach of the end of the world
recurred constantly in the early centuries of the Church, and
it was natural that it should be especially strong in an age
that had seen Rome fall for the first time to barbarian on-
slaught. Hesychius, Bishop of Salona, asked Augustine (198)
whether it might reasonably be inferred from Scripture that
the second coming of Christ was near at hand. The reply

was admirably prudent. In Letter 198 Augustine makes a careful analysis of the Scriptural passages cited and concludes that it is not profitable to inquire into the future, but that each one should so act as to be ready to receive Christ whenever He comes.

It was during this period that Augustine finished his treatise on *The Trinity,* begun in 400. He had intended to publish it as a whole after careful revision, because the nature of the subject requires the utmost precision of language. Unfortunately for him, some too zealous friend borrowed—or stole—the earlier books, and circulated them, which made the author set the whole project aside for several years. Finally, he yielded to pressure and completed the work, sending it to Aurelius, Archbishop of Cathage, with a covering letter (174) which he intended should be used as a preface.

He also wrote Letters 169 and 170 on this subject to Evodius and to Maximus, a physician. This latter communication gave rise to an amusing note to Peregrinus, in which we learn something of the difference between formal and informal letter writing. He and Alypius had written jointly to Maximus, a recent convert from Arianism, exhorting him to try to reclaim some of those whom he had led into error, and setting him clear on a point of doctrine concerning the Trinity. They had received no answer from him, so they wrote to his bishop, Peregrinus, asking him to find out how their letter had been received. They were afraid Maximus might have taken offense because their letter was written by hand, not dictated, and was on paper instead of parchment. They wanted him to know that they wrote to their dearest friends that way, even to bishops, because it was quicker and because paper was easier to hold in the hand while being read.

Letter 189 is addressed to Count Boniface, Roman Vicar of Africa, a man of strangely conflicting desires. He had aspirations to the higher life, but could descend to depths of revenge against a rival, which resulted in the summoning of the Vandals into Africa. A friend of his had suggested to Augustine that Boniface would appreciate some spiritual counsels, as he was under the apprehension that a soldier could not please God in the profession of arms. Augustine gives him the highest of all rules for a holy life: 'Thou shalt love the Lord thy God with thy whole heart,' and then proceeds to give some examples of soldiers who were pleasing to God. The list includes David, the good centurion of the Gospel, and the soldiers who had applied to John the Baptist for advice. All of these prove that the military life is not forbidden by God. A particularly fine aphorism which occurs here might be pondered with profit by modern military men: *'Non enim pax quaeritur ut bellum excitetur, sed bellum geritur ut pax acquiratur.'* On the whole, however, war is to be the result of necessity, not of choice; a promise made to an enemy must be kept; the warrior must be a peace-maker that he may be called the son of God. In his private life Augustine advises Boniface to observe chastity, sobriety, moderation, honesty; to forgive easily, to pray often. If he had practised all this he might have been another soldier-saint.

The letters of these years show on the whole a preoccupation with intellectual and doctrinal matters, and they probably represent the climax of Augustine's achievement. There is a conspicuous lack of mention of the merely mundane affairs which figure so frequently in earlier letters. It is possible that the bishop had by this time an assistant who could take such problems off his hands and leave him free to pursue his glorious career as the champion of Catholic truth.

LETTERS

165-203

Translated by

SISTER WILFRID PARSONS, S.N.D., Ph.D.
Emmanuel College
Boston, Mass.

165. Jerome gives greeting in Christ to the truly holy lords,
his sons, Marcellinus and Anapsychia, deserving
of every consideration of affection (c. 410)[1]

At last I have received the letter of your Unanimity from
Africa, and I am not ashamed of my boldness in harassing
you out of your silence by my frequent letters, because I did
it in order to deserve an answer and thus learn by no other
message than your own word, that you are safe and well. I
remember your 'little' question about the origin of the soul—
it is, rather, a question of great importance to the Church—
whether it slipped down from heaven, as the philosopher
Pythagoras,[2] all the Platonists, and Origen[3] think; or is an
emanation of the substance of God, as the Stoics, Mani, and
the Spanish heresy of Priscillian imagine; or is long preserved
in the treasury of God, as some churchmen are foolishly induced to believe; or is daily created by God and sent into
bodies, according to the words of Scripture: 'My Father
worketh until now and I work';[4] or, at least, is derived from

---

1 The tribune of Letters 128, 129, 133, 136, 138, 139, and 143, who was
  put to death by the heretics in 413. This letter was written not later
  than 410, but is listed here by Migne because Letter 166 is based on it.
2 End of 5th century B.C.
3 A.D. 185-255.
4 John 5.17.

3

a root-stock, as Tertullian,[5] Apollinaris,[6] and most of the Western scholars claim, holding that, as each body is born of another body, so the soul is born of a soul and has an origin like that of the lower animals. I know that I wrote my opinion of this long ago, in my treatises against Rufinus,[7] especially against that work which he dedicated to the bishop of the Church of Rome, Anastasius[8] of holy memory. In that work he tries to play on the simplicity of his hearers by a sly and crafty, but really stupid, confession, but he only made a mockery of his own faith, or, rather, his unfaith. I think your holy father, Oceanus,[9] has these works, for they were published long ago,[10] in refutation of the many calumnies in the book of Rufinus against us. In any case, you have with you a holy and learned man in Bishop Augustine who will be able to teach you by the living word, as they say, and will set forth his opinion, or rather mine in his words.

I have been wanting for a long time to go to work on the Book of Ezechiel, and thereby fulfill a promise frequently made to my eager readers, but I had hardly begun to dictate it when my mind was so disturbed by the sack of the Western provinces, and especially of the city of Rome, that, to use a common proverb, I hardly knew my own name, and I fell into a long silence, knowing that 'it is a time to weep.'[11] In this very year, after I had made a commentary on three books, there was such a sudden incursion of barbarians, whom your Vergil calls 'The far-wandering Barcaeans,'[12] and holy Scrip-

---

5 C. 150-211.
6 Flourished at end of 4th century; taught that Christ had no rational human mind.
7 An early friend but later bitter opponent of St. Jerome.
8 Pope from 399 to 402.
9 I.e., his spiritual father or director.
10 C. 403.
11 Eccle. 3.4.
12 Vergil, *Aeneid* 4.42,43.

ture describes in the words about Ismael: 'He shall dwell over against the face of all his brethren,'[13] that they overran the boundaries of Egypt, Palestine, Phoenicia, Syria, like a torrent carrying all before it, and it was only by the mercy of Christ that we were able to escape from their hands. But if it is true, as that illustrious orator said: 'In the midst of war the law is silent,'[14] how much more true is it of Scriptural studies, which need innumerable books, silence, frequenting of libraries, and, as an absolute requirement, safety and peace for dictating. So, I sent two books to my holy daughter, Fabiola,[15] and you can borrow copies of them, if you like, from her, for I was not able to copy out any others in these woeful times. When you read them and see the vestibule, you will easily be able to form an idea about the future nature of the house. But I believe that the mercy of God, which has helped us in the very difficult beginning of the above-mentioned work, will help through the parts near the end where the wars of Gog and Magog are described,[16] and also the very end where the building of the sacred and intricate temple with its parts and dimensions is set forth.[17]

Our holy brother, Oceanus, to whom you wished to be remembered, has such weight and erudition in the law of the Lord that he can instruct you without any request from us, and can explain my opinion about the rest of the questions on the Scriptures in a manner adapted to the ordinary mind. May Christ, our almighty God, keep you safe, truly holy lords, and may you flourish to an advanced age.

13 Cf. Gen. 16.12.
14 Cicero, *Pro Milone* 4.10.
15 One of the noble and scholarly Roman women who gathered around Jerome to study the Scriptures.
16 Ezech. 38-39.
17 Ezech. 40-48.

166. Augustine to Jerome[1] (415)

On the Origin of the Human Soul

Chapter 1

I have called upon and I continue to call upon our God 'who hath called us unto his kingdom and glory,'[2] that He may grant what I write to you, holy brother Jerome, to be fruitful to us, while I consult you on those points on which I am ignorant. Although you are much older than I am, it is as an old man that I consult you, for it seems to me that no age is too advanced to learn what needs learning, because, although it is more fitting for old men to teach than to learn, it is even more fitting to learn what they teach than to remain ignorant. There is nothing I feel more in all the perplexities which I endure in dealing with these difficult questions than the great distance there is between me and your Charity. The time that elapses between sending my letter and receiving yours is so great that the interval is not of days or of months, but of several years. If I could have my way I would have you with me daily, so that I could discuss whatever I wish with you. However, if I cannot have everything I want, there is no reason for my not doing what I can.

---

1 There is no formula of address. In *Retractations* 2.45, Augustine says of this letter: 'I wrote two books to the priest Jerome residing at Bethlehem; one on the origin of the human soul.'
2 1 Thess. 2.12.

Chapter 2

Just now Orosius[1] has come to me, a religious young man, a brother in the Catholic fold, in age a son, in dignity a fellow priest, alert of mind, ready of speech, burning with eagerness, longing to be a useful vessel in the house of the Lord,[2] in order to refute the false and pernicious teachings which have been much more deadly to the souls of Spaniards[3] than the sword of the barbarian has been to their bodies. He hastened from there, even from the shore of the ocean,[4] moved by the report that he might be able to learn from me whatever he wished of the topics in which he was interested. And he did gain something from his coming: first, not to put too much faith in what he heard of me; then I instructed the man as far as I could; I pointed out to him where he could learn what I could not give him, and encouraged him to go to you. Seeing that he took my advice or command willingly and obediently, I asked him to return from you by way of us when he traveled back to his own country. I have his promise, so I believe this opportunity has been granted me by the Lord to write you about the subjects on which I wish to be enlightened by you. I was looking around for someone to send to you, but it was not easy to find anyone endowed with reliability of conduct, readiness to obey and experience in traveling; so, when I found this young man, I did not doubt that he was just the one I had been asking of the Lord.

---

1 Born about 390 in Spain, came to Hippo in 414, spent some time with Jerome in Bethlehem, author of *Liber apologeticus* against the Pelagians, and *Adversus paganos, libri septem.*
2 2 Tim. 2.21.
3 The Priscillianist heresy.
4 I.e., the Atlantic. He came from Bracara in Galicia, in northwest Spain.

Chapter 3

Learn, then, what I ask you to solve, and do not refuse to discuss it. The question about the soul troubles many, among whom I confess I am found. I will set forth what I hold with certainty about the soul, and then I will add what I still wish to learn. The soul of man is immortal according to a certain mode of its own, for it is not in every respect like God, of whom it is said that 'He only hath immortality.'[1] Holy Scripture has many references to the death of the soul, among them this: 'Let the dead bury their dead.'[2] But, inasmuch as the soul, turned away from God, dies in such way that it does not entirely cease to exist according to its own nature, so it is found to be mortal under one aspect in such way that it is not unreasonably called immortal. The soul is not a part of God. If this were so, the soul would be entirely unchangeable and incorruptible. And if this were so, it would not degenerate into a worse state or advance to a better one, or begin to have something in itself which it did not have before, or cease to have what it had, as far as its affections are concerned. There is no need of external proof to show how different it is from this: one has only to look into himself to know it. It is useless for those who claim that the soul is a part of God to say that the defilement and vileness which we see in men of great wickedness, as well as the disease and weakness which we perceive in all men, come from the body, not from the soul. What difference does it make where the illness comes from, when there could not possibly be any illness if the soul were unchangeable? What

1 1 Tim. 6.16.
2 Matt. 8.22; Luke 9.60.

is truly unchangeable and incorruptible cannot be changed or corrupted by contact with anything whatsoever, otherwise not only Achilles, as the legends tell, but all flesh would be invulnerable so long as no accident befell it. Therefore, the soul is not unchangeable by nature but is subject to change in some way, for some cause, in some part. But it is forbidden to believe that God is anything else than truly and supremely unchangeable. Therefore, the soul is not a part of God.

Chapter 4

Although it is difficult to convince those who are slow of comprehension that the soul is also incorporeal, I confess that I am convinced of it. But I do not wish to make a useless difficulty over terms, nor deserve to bring one down upon myself, since when there is question of reality there is no need to quarrel over a word. Therefore, if the body is the whole substance or essence or whatever better term one can use to express what it is in itself, then the soul is a body. Likewise, if one chooses to call that alone incorporeal which is supremely unchangeable and everywhere wholly present, then the soul is a body, since of itself it is no such thing. Furthermore, if it is a characteristic of a body to occupy space with a certain length, width, and height, and for it to be so placed or moved that it fills a larger space with the larger part of itself, and a smaller space with a smaller part, and for the part to be less than the whole, then the soul is not a body. For, the soul extends through the whole body to which it imparts life, not by a distribution in space but by a certain life-giving impetus; it is wholly present in every smallest part, not less in smaller parts and more in larger ones, but in one place more conscious, in another less attentive, yet wholly present in each and all parts. Otherwise, it would not wholly feel, as it does, what is not felt by the whole body; for, when some part of the living flesh is touched by the slightest prick, although that spot is not only not the whole body but hardly seems to be in the body, the whole soul is conscious of it, even when what is felt does not run through the whole body but is felt only where it occurs. How, then, does it happen that the sensation which is not total reaches the whole soul, except that the soul is wholly there where the pain is, and does not leave the other parts of the body to be wholly present at that spot? Those parts are alive and the soul is present in them where nothing of the sort has happened. But, if it did happen there, and both sensations happened at the same time, the whole soul would be equally conscious of both. Therefore, it could not at the same time be wholly present in all and each several part of its body if it were distributed through the parts as we see bodies distributed in space, occupying less room with their smaller parts and more with their larger ones. Therefore, if the soul is to be called a body, it certainly is not a body like anything made of earth or water or air or light. Indeed, all of these are such that they are more extensive in larger space and smaller in lesser places, and none of them is wholly present in any part of itself; but, as there are parts of space, so they are occupied by parts of bodies. Hence, it is clear that, whether the soul is to be called corporeal or incorporeal, it has a special nature created of a more excellent substance than all these elements of earthly material, a nature which cannot be represented to the fancy by any of the corporeal images which we perceive through the senses, but is understood by the mind and apprehended by its life. I do not repeat these things, which are known to you, in order to teach you, but to make clear what I firmly believe about the soul, so that, when I come to the points on which I raise a question, no one may think that I have no views about the soul whether they are based on knowledge or faith.

Chapter 5

I am certain that the soul fell into sin, through no fault, no compulsion, on God's part, but by its own personal will, and that it cannot be delivered from 'the body of this death,'[1] either by the strength of its own will, as if this were sufficient for it, or by the death of the body itself, but by 'the grace of God by Jesus Christ our Lord';[2] and that there is no soul in the whole human race which does not need to be delivered by 'the mediator of God and men, the man Christ Jesus.'[3] Every soul that departs from the body, no matter at what age, without the grace of the Mediator and His sacrament is destined for punishment, and will receive back its body for punishment at the Last Judgment. But if, after the human generation which comes to it from Adam, the soul is regenerated in Christ and belongs to His fold, it will attain rest after the death of the body, and will receive back its body for its glory. These are the truths which I firmly believe about the soul.

Chapter 6

Now listen, please, to what I ask, and do not despise me, as I pray that He may not despise you who deigned to be despised for us. I ask when the soul contracted the guilt through which it is doomed to condemnation, even in the

---

1 Rom. 7.24.
2 Rom. 9.25.
3 1 Tim. 2.5.

case of an infant, prematurely dead, on whom the grace of
Christ was not conferred through the sacrament by which
even babies are baptized. You are not one of those who have
begun to babble new doctrines, saying that there is no guilt
inherited from Adam, which has to be remitted in the infant
by baptism. If I knew that you approved of this view, or,
rather, if I did not know that you do not approve of it, I
would never ask this of you nor think it something to be
asked. But I do believe that your opinion on this point is
consonant with the foundations of Catholic faith, as you
proved by refuting the idle prating of Jovinian,[1] by the
passage from the Book of Job: 'No one is clean in the sight
of God, nor is the infant whose life upon earth is but of one
day.'[2] Then you went on and said: 'We are held guilty after
the similitude of the transgression of Adam';[3] and your book
on the Prophet Jonas[4] asserts this with emphasis and clarity,
where you said that it was right for infants to be obliged to
fast because of original sin. Consequently, I think it is proper
for me to ask you when the soul contracted that guilt from
which it has to be delivered, even at that age, by the sacrament of Christian grace.

Chapter 7

A few years ago when I wrote some books on free will—
which have gone out into many hands and are possessed by
many more—I thought well to discuss four opinions about
the union of the soul and the body: Whether all subsequent
souls are propagated from that one which was given to the

---

1 *Adversus Jovinianum* 2.2 (*c.* 383), in Migne, *PL* 23.284.17-21. Jovinian
  held that salvation comes by faith alone without good works.
2 Job 14.4,5 (Septuagint).
3 Rom. 5.14.
4 *Comment. In Jonam* 3.5, in *PL* 25.1140.47-1141.4.

first man, or whether new ones are now created for each single person, or whether they exist somewhere and are sent down from heaven, or are spontaneously joined to bodies. I discussed them so that whichever one of them should prove to be true, it would not interfere with my purpose of opposing with all my might those who were trying to prove that nature was endowed with its own principle of evil in conflict with God. These were the Manichaeans, for I had not yet heard of the Priscillianists who babble blasphemies not much different from theirs. I did not add the fifth opinion—that the soul is a part of God—which you mentioned, so as not to omit any, in your letter to Marcellinus,[1] a man of religious memory and very dear to us in the charity of Christ, who had asked you about it. I did not add that one to my list because, first, when the question was asked, it was on the nature of the soul and not of its union with the body; and, second, because that view is held by those whom I was attacking, and I made it a special point to distinguish the sinless and inviolable nature of the Creator from the vices and corruption of the creature; because they contend that the very substance of the good God is, in part, derived from the substance of evil to which they attribute dominion and rulers, and they say that in that part it is corrupted, under subjection, and prone to the necessity of sinning. Leaving out this erroneous and heretical opinion, I am anxious to know which of the four remaining opinions is the preferred one. Whichever one is preferred, God forbid that it should be opposed to this tenet of faith, of which we are certain, that deliverance from the bond of sin is necessary for every soul, even in the tiny infant, and that there is no such deliverance except through Jesus Christ and Him crucified.

---

1 Letter 165.

Chapter 8

Therefore, to make a long story short, you certainly believe that God still creates separate souls for separate persons at birth. To forestall the objection to this opinion that God finished creating all living beings on the sixth day and rested on the seventh[1] you offer the testimony of the Gospel: 'My Father worketh until now.'[2] That is what you wrote to Marcellinus, and in your letter you were kind enough to speak very favorably of me, saying that he had me here in Africa, and that I could more easily explain that opinion to him. But, if I had been able to do it, he would not have appealed to you at such a distance, if, however, he really wrote that to you from Africa. I do not know when he wrote it; I only know that he was well aware of my hesitancy on this subject, and chose to do it without consulting me. But, even if he had consulted me, I would have encouraged him to write to you and would have been thankful for the favor conferred on all of us, if you had not preferred to write briefly rather than really to answer him. I suppose you did that so as not to waste your effort, since I was here and you thought I was sure of what he asked. And now you see that I wish that opinion to be mine, but I do not yet claim it.

Chapter 9

You have sent me pupils to learn the very thing I have not yet learned myself. Teach me, then, what I am to teach. Many keep asking me and I confess to them that I am ignorant of this, as well as of many other things. And, perhaps, although they respect me to my face, they say among them-

1 Gen. 2.2.
2 John 5.17.

selves: 'Art thou a master in Israel and knowest not these things?'[1] These words the Lord said to a man who was one of those who delighted to be called Rabbi (master), and probably his reason for coming to the true Master by night[2] was that he was accustomed to teach and he was ashamed to have to learn. But it gives me greater pleasure to listen to a master than to be listened to as a master, for I recall what He said to those whom He had chosen before the others: 'But be not you called Rabbi by men,' He said, 'for one is your Master, Christ.'[3] It was no other, not even Jethro, who taught Moses;[4] no other who first taught Cornelius through Peter;[5] no other who afterward taught Peter through Paul; for, by whomever truth is spoken, it is spoken through the bounty of Him who is truth itself.[7] And if we are still ignorant of these things, and we have not been able to find a solution either by prayer or reading or thought and reasoning, is not the reason, perhaps, to show not only with what charity we should teach but also with what humility we should learn from the learned?

Chapter 10

Teach me, then, I beg of you, what I am to teach; teach me what I am to hold, and tell me, if souls are individually created today for individuals at birth, when these souls commit sin in infants, so as to need remission of sin in the sacrament of Christ, since they sin in Adam from whom the flesh of sin is derived; or, if they do not sin, how can it be just of the

1 John 3.10.
2 John 3.1,2.
3 Matt. 23.8.
4 Exod. 18.14-23.
5 Acts 10.25-48.
6 Gal. 2.11-21.
7 John 14.6; 1 John 5.6.

Creator to bind them by another's sin, when they are joined to mortal bodies descended from him, so that damnation is their lot unless help is given them by the Church, yet it is not in their power to be helped by the grace of baptism? What kind of justice is it that so many thousands of souls should be damned because they departed from their bodies by death in infancy, without the grace of the Christian sacrament, if new souls, created separately by the will of the Creator, are joined to separate bodies at birth, with no previous sin of their own; souls which He created and gave to animate these bodies, when He certainly knew that each one of them by no fault of its own would leave the body without the baptism of Christ? Since, therefore, we cannot say of God that He either forces souls to become sinful or punishes the innocent, and we must necessarily assert that souls, even those of infants, which leave the body without the sacrament of Christ are subject to damnation, how are we to defend this opinion which holds that other souls do not come into being from that of the first man, but are thus created separately for separate bodies as that first one was?

Chapter 11

I think I can easily refute the other objections made against this opinion, as, for instance, that one which some seem to press, asking how God completed all His works on the sixth day and rested on the seventh, if He still creates new souls. If we answer by saying to them what you quoted from the Gospel in the above-mentioned letter: 'My Father worketh until now,' they reply that 'work' is used in the sense of carrying on what is established, not of setting up new creatures, and this they do in order not to contradict the passage from Genesis, where it is very plainly said that

God finished all His works. And where it is written that He rested, it surely means that He rested from creating new beings, not from ruling over them; that He had then made those things which had not previously existed and He rested from making them; that He had finished all the things which had not previously existed and He rested from making them; that He had finished all the things which He saw were to be made before they existed, so that afterwards, whatever He made, He should create and make, not as something which had not existed, but as something which came from what did previously exist. Thus it is proved that both are true: the saying 'He rested from His works' and the saying 'He worketh until now,' since the Gospel cannot contradict Genesis.

Chapter 12

Those who say this so that we may not believe that God creates new souls which did not then exist, as He created the first one, but creates them from that first one, which then existed, as from some fount or treasury which He then made, and lets them out, are easily answered that even on those six days God created many things from creatures previously created, as, birds and fish from the waters, trees, grass, animals from the earth. It is clear that He did then make things which were not in existence, for there was no bird, no fish, no tree, no animal, and it is easy to understand that He rested after creating these beings which had not existed and were created, that is, He ceased to create any more creatures which did not exist. But, now, if we reject the opinion that He sends down souls already existing in some fount or other, that He sprinkles them with something of Himself as if they were parts of Him, that they are derived from that first soul and are bound before they are joined to

flesh by fleshly sins committed previously, and if we say
that He creates new souls individually for each person at
birth, we are not saying that He makes something which did
not previously exist. For, on the sixth day He made man 'to
His image,'[1] which we naturally understand to be according
to the rational soul. And this He then did, not by establishing
something which did not exist, but by multiplying what did
exist. Hence it is true that He rested from creating things
which did not exist, and it is also true that He worketh
until now, not only by governing what He made, but also
by making more numerous not what He had not but what He
had already created. By this or by some other argument we get
out of this objection which is made to us about the rest of
God from His works, which might prevent us from believing
that new souls are now being created, not from that first one,
but like that one.

Chapter 13

When they say: 'Why does He make souls for those of
whom He knows that they are going to die soon?' we can
answer that in this way the sins of parents are either made
known or punished. With good reason we can leave all that
to His guidance, since we know that He gives a lovely and
ordered course to all things that pass with time, among which
are the birth and death of living creatures, but we cannot
see this, for if we could we should be comforted with indescribable sweetness. Not in vain did the Prophet say of
God what he had learned by divine revelation: 'Who bringeth
out their age by number.'[1] Therefore, music, that is, the

1 Gen. 1.26.

1 Isa. 40.26 (Septuagint).

science or perception of rhythm, is granted by the liberality of God to mortals having rational souls, to teach a great truth. Hence, if a man who is skilled in composing a song knows what lengths to assign to what tones, so that the melody flows and progresses with beauty by a succession of slow and rapid tones, how much more true is it that God permits no periods of time in the birth and death of His creatures—periods which are like the words and syllables in the measure of this temporal life—to proceed either more quickly or more slowly than the recognized and well-defined law of rhythm requires, in this wonderful song of succeeding events, for the wisdom through which He made all things is to be esteemed far above all the arts. When I apply this to the leaves of the tree and the number of our hairs,[2] how much more is it applicable to the rise and fall of man whose span of life is neither shortened nor prolonged beyond what God, the distributer of time, knows to be in harmony with the control of the universe!

Chapter 14

Some say that whatever begins to exist in time cannot be immortal, because 'All things are born and die, they increase and grow old,'[1] and thus they would compel the belief that the human soul is immortal only because it was created before all time, but this does not disturb our faith, for, to pass over other instances, the immortality of Christ's flesh began in time, yet 'He dieth now no more, death shall no more have dominion over him.'[2]

---

2 Matt. 10.30; Luke 12.7.

1 Sallust, *Jugurtha* 2.3.
2 Rom. 6.9.

Chapter 15

Regarding that instance which you brought up in your book against Rufinus,[1] that some are giving a wrong meaning to the statement that it seems unworthy of God to give souls to those conceived in adultery, and that from it they try to endow souls with merits of a life lived before their union with the flesh, to which, as to a penitentiary, they claim that it is just for them to be sentenced, I am not much impressed, for I can think of many ways of refuting this false claim. And you yourself made use of an exquisitely chosen comparison when you answered that there is no guilt in the sower when his wheat is carried off by stealth, but there is in the thief who stole the wheat; and there is no reason for the earth to refuse to cherish the seed in her bosom because the sower has scattered it with an unclean hand. Before I read that, the objection about adulterous conceptions had not caused me any difficulty in this question, because, as I see it, God usually brings much good even from our evils and our sins. If the creation of any living creature calls for unutterable praise to the Creator from the thoughtful man who devoutly considers it, how much more the creation of man above that of any living creature! But if the reason for its creation is sought, there is no quicker or better answer than that every creature of God is good, and what is more worthy of a good God than that He should create good things, which no one but God can create?

Chapter 16

These and other arguments according to my ability I advance, as best I can, against those who try to break down this opinion which holds that souls are created individually as

---

1 Jerome, *Apologia adversus libros Rufini* 3.28, in *PL* 23.478.35-47.

the first one was. But, when I come to the question of the sufferings of infants, believe me I am beset with great trouble, and I find no ready answer. I mean not only those sufferings which damnation brings after this life, and which must necessarily come upon those who leave the body without the grace of the Christian sacrament, but also those which are presented in this life to our grieving eyes, so numerous that time fails me rather than examples to recount them. They pine away with illness, they are racked with pains, they are tortured with hunger and thirst, they are weak of limb, they are deprived of their faculties, they are tormented by unclean spirits. Certainly, there must be a proof that they suffer all this justly, but without any evil cause on their part. It is not permissible to say either that these things happen without God's knowledge, or that He is unable to hinder those who cause them, or that He causes or permits them unjustly. Of irrational animals we say rightly that they are given over to be used by higher beings, even sinful ones, as we see in the Gospel, where the devils were allowed to use the swine for their intended purpose,[1] but how can we rightly say the same of man? He is an animal, but a rational though mortal one. There is a rational soul in his members which pays the penalty by such sufferings. God is good, God is just, God is almighty: only a madman doubts this. Therefore, a just cause must be assigned to these great sufferings which befall little children. Doubtless, when their elders suffer these afflictions, we are wont to say either that their goodness is being tested, as in the case of Job, or that their sins are being punished, as happened to Herod; and from the examples which God has willed to manifest it is granted men to make a conjecture about others which are hard to understand. But these are older people. Tell me what we are to answer about children, if there are no sins to be punished in them by such

---

1 Matt. 8.31,32; Mark 5.12,13; Luke 8.32,33.

sufferings, since there obviously is no virtue to be tested at that age.

Chapter 17

But what shall I say about the variety of their mental endowment? This lies hidden in children, of course, but its development as they grow older appears as a consequence of their natural mentality, as it was from the beginning. Some are so slow and so forgetful that they cannot even learn the first rudiments of language, while some are so unintelligent that they are not many removes from animals, and these are commonly called morons.[1] Perhaps the answer is that their bodies cause this. But, according to this opinion which we wish to uphold, did the soul choose its body, and then commit some wrong by being mistaken in its choice? Or, when it was forced by the necessity of birth to enter a body, could it find no other because crowds of souls took possession of other bodies before it could get them, and, like people hunting for a place at the public games, did it take, not the one it wanted, but the one it could get? Is it possible for us to say such things, or should we even think them? Tell me, then, what we ought to think and say, so that the theory of new souls, created individually for each body, may be confirmed for us.

Chapter 18

It is a fact that I had something to say about the sufferings which children endure in this life, if not about their mentality, in my books on free will.[1] To let you know what it is, and

---

1 *moriones.*

1 *De libero arbitrio* 3.68.

why it does not meet my difficulty in the question we have at hand, I shall quote an excerpt from Book 3 in this letter. It goes like this: 'In the case of bodily sufferings endured by children too young to commit sin, if the souls which animate them had no existence before they became men, a greater complaint, and in a sense, a compassionate one, is offered when someone says: "What wrong have they done that they should suffer so?" As if there could be any merit in innocence before it is able to do wrong! But when God accomplishes some good by the correction of older persons, scourging them by the death or suffering of the children who are dear to them, why should these things not happen, since, in those who suffer them, they are as if they had never been, once they are past, and those on whose account they have happened will either be better, if they are converted by these temporal trials, and will resolve to lead a better life; or they will have no defense against condemnation at the last judgment, if they have refused to turn their desires away from this life of anguish toward eternal life. Who knows what reward, in the secret of His judgments, God has in store for these little ones, whose sufferings have served to break down the hardness of their elders or to test their faith or to prove their mercy; who knows what these little ones will receive, for, although they have done no good deed, neither have they sinned, yet they have suffered? When Herod sought to kill the Lord Jesus Christ, and the Innocents were put to death, it is not without reason that the Church receives and honors them among the martyrs.'

Chapter 19

That is what I said when I wanted to strengthen this very opinion which is now in question. For, as I mentioned a short time ago, I was striving to show that, whichever of

those four opinions should prove to be true, the blameless
substance of the Creator is absolutely removed from any
participation in our sins. Therefore, if any one of them
could be truthfully refuted and rejected, it would lie outside
the scope of the intention which I then had, since, after all
had been discussed with careful argument, whichever of them
should prevail over the others, I would be on the safe side,
because I had proved that according to each one of them
the point I was making remained irrefutable. But now I
want, if possible, to choose one clear argument from all of
them, because, as I look more carefully at the words which
I have quoted from my book, I do not see that I have a strong,
unshakeable defense of this point which we are now treating.

Chapter 20

What I said above is a sort of support for this: 'Who knows
what good reward, in the secret of His judgments, God has
in store for these little ones whose sufferings have served to
break down the hardness of their elders, or to test faith, or
to prove their mercy; who knows what these little ones will
receive?' But I see that this could also be said, not unreasonably, of those who either unknowingly suffer something similar
for the name of Christ and the true religion, or have now
been immersed in the sacrament of Christ, because they
cannot be delivered from damnation unless they belong to the
fold of the one Mediator; and so that reward could be given
to them also for the evils which they suffer in the manifold
afflictions of this life. But now, since that difficulty cannot be
solved unless an answer is also found to this one about the
children who die, after bitter torments, without the sacrament
which admits them to the society of Christians, what reward
can be imagined in their case when they are over and above

foredoomed to damnation? It is true I made some answer about the baptism of infants in that same book, not an adequate one, perhaps, but one that seemed sufficient for the scope of the work, which is useful for those who do not know or do not yet possess the faith, but I did not then think fit to say anything about the damnation of those infants who depart this life without baptism because that question was not at issue, as it now is.

Chapter 21

But to pass over and make little of those sufferings which last but a short time and, once over, are not repeated, can we make little of this: 'By one man came death and by one man the resurrection of the dead; for as in Adam all die, so also in Christ all shall be made alive'?[1] By this divine and direct statement of the Apostle it is quite unequivocally clear that no one enters into death except through Adam and no one into eternal life except through Christ. This is the meaning of that repeated 'all,' because as all men belong to Adam through their first, that is, their carnal birth, so all men who belong to Christ come to the second or spiritual birth. Therefore, he says 'all' in both places because as all who die die only in Adam, so all who will be made alive will not be made alive except in Christ. Therefore, we must detest as the bane of our common faith the one who tells us that anyone can be made alive at the resurrection of the dead otherwise than in Christ. Likewise, if anyone shall say that even infants who depart life without sharing in this sacrament shall be made alive in Christ, he certainly goes counter to the teaching of the Apostle and condemns the whole Church, which is in great haste to baptize infants, because of the unquestioned belief that otherwise they cannot possibly be made alive in Christ. And of

---

1 1 Cor. 15.21,22.

those who are not made alive in Christ we must conclude
that they remain under that condemnation of which the
Apostle speaks: 'By the offense of one unto all men to condemnation.'[2] The whole Church believes that infants are subject to this condemnation at birth, and you yourself have
expressed it with truest faith in your argument against
Jovinian, and in your commentary on Jonas, as I mentioned
awhile ago, and, I believe in other passages of your works
which I have either not read or do not at present recall.
Therefore, I am seeking for the reason of this sentence of
damnation against infants, because I do not see any sin on
their souls at that age, if new souls are created individually,
nor do I believe that any soul is condemned by God in which
He does not see sin.

Chapter 22

Are we, then, to say, perhaps, that only the flesh of the
child is sinful, that a new soul is created for him and that
this soul, by living according to the commandments of God
with the help of Christ's grace, can purchase the reward of
incorruption even for the subdued and conquered flesh? Or
shall we say that as the soul is not yet able to achieve this
in the child, but, if it receives the sacrament of Christ, it
gains for its body by this grace what it could not gain by
those modes of action; but, if the soul departs without that
sacrament, it will itself be in eternal life from which no sin
has been able to separate it, yet its body will not rise in Christ
because it had not received His sacrament before death?

---

2 Rom. 5.18.

Chapter 23

I have never heard or read this opinion, but I have clearly heard and 'I have believed therefore I have spoken,'[1] that 'the hour cometh wherein all that are in the graves shall hear the voice of the Son of God, and they that have done good things shall come forth unto the resurrection of life.'[2] This is the life of which it is said: 'and by one man the resurrection of the dead'; this is the life by which 'all shall be made alive in Christ';[3] 'but they that have done evil shall come forth unto the resurrection of judgment.'[4] What, then, are we to think of those infants who have been stripped of their bodies without baptism, before they were able to do either good or evil? Nothing is said about such in these passages. If their flesh will not rise because they have done neither good nor evil, then the bodies of those who have died at that early age after receiving the grace of baptism will not rise either, because they have not been able to do either good or evil. And if they rise among the saints, that is, among those who have done good, among whom will the others rise if not with those who have done evil? Otherwise, we should have to believe that some human souls will not receive their bodies either at the resurrection of life or at the resurrection of judgment. This opinion is repellent by its very novelty even before it is refuted. Moreover, who could bear it if those who hurry their children to baptism believe that they hurry them for the sake of their bodies, not their souls? Blessed Cyprian, indeed, was not setting up some new decree, but affirming the most solid belief of the Church in order to correct some who thought that a child should not be baptized

---

1 Ps. 115.1.
2 John 5.28,29.
3 1 Cor. 15.21,22.
4 John 5.29.

sooner than the eighth day after birth, when he said that it
was not the body but the soul that was to be saved from
destruction. He also agreed with some of his fellow bishops
that a child could be validly baptized almost at the instant
of birth.[5]

Chapter 24

Let each one think what he likes contrary to any of
Cyprian's opinions, but let no one hold any opinion contrary
to the most evident belief of the Apostle who teaches that
from one man's offense all are subject to condemnation, and
from this condemnation there is no deliverance except 'the
grace of God by Jesus Christ our Lord,'[1] in whom alone all
are made alive who are to be made alive. Let no one think,
contrary to this absolutely fundamental custom of the Church,
that children are rushed to baptism for the welfare of their
bodies only, because, if that were true, the dead also could
be brought to be baptized.

Chapter 25

This being granted, a reason must be sought and given why
souls which are newly created for each one at birth are
damned if the children die without the sacrament of Christ.
Holy Scripture and holy Church both testify that they are
damned if they depart thus from the body. Consequently, if
that opinion about the creation of new souls is not opposed
to this fundamental belief, let it be mine; if it is opposed, let
it not be yours.

5 Cyprian, *Epistolae* 64.2-6 (ed. Hartel, pp. 718-721).

1 Rom. 7.25.

Chapter 26

I do not want anyone to tell me that this view should be supported by the passage: 'Who formed the spirit of man in him,'[1] and 'Who made the heart of every one of them.'[2] Something supremely strong and invincible is needed to force me to believe that God condemns any souls without any guilt of theirs. It is either as great a thing, or it is, perhaps, greater, to create as to form, yet it is written: 'Create a clean heart in me, O God.'[3] This is no argument for thinking that the soul in this passage prays to be made before it had any being. As, therefore, while now existing, it is created by the renewal of its justice, so, while now existing, it is formed by the shaping force of doctrine. That other passage in Ecclesiastes: 'Then the dust shall return into its earth as it was, and the spirit shall return to the Lord who gave it,'[4] does not confirm the opinion which we wish to hold; it is rather on the side of those who think that all souls were created together; 'For,' they say, 'as the dust returns into its earth as it was, and the flesh, which is here meant, does not return to the man from whom it originally came but to the earth from which the first man was made, so also the spirit, derived from his spirit, does not return to him but to the Lord who gave it to him.' However, inasmuch as this testimony favors them but does not seem to be entirely opposed to the theory which I wish to defend, I thought that your Prudence should be warned, at least this far, that you would not try to extricate me from this dilemma by such testimony. For, although no one by wishing can make a thing true which is not true, still, if it were possible, I would wish

---

1 Zach. 12.1.
2 Ps. 32.15.
3 Ps. 50.12.
4 Eccle. 12.7.

that this theory might be true, as I wish that, if it is true, you may defend it brilliantly and invincibly.

Chapter 27

But there is a difficulty which pursues those who hold that souls, already in existence and prepared by God from the beginning of His divine works, are sent down into bodies. This same question can be put to them: If innocent souls go obediently where they are sent, why are they punished in children whose lives end without baptism? Exactly this same difficulty is found in both theories. Those who assert that souls are assigned individually to bodies according to the merits of a former life imagine that they escape this objection more easily. They think this is what it is to die in Adam, namely, to pay the penalty in the flesh which is derived from Adam, but they say that the grace of Christ delivers 'both little and great'[1] from this guilt. In saying that the grace of Christ delivers the little with the great from the guilt of sin they are indeed speaking rightly, truly, and infallibly. But that souls sin in another previous life and are therefore thrust down into fleshly prisons I do not believe, I do not agree to, I do not accept, because, first of all, I do not know a more revolting opinion than that these souls should make some indefinite number of trips through an indefinite number of cycles of ages only to return again to that burden of corrupt flesh to pay the penalty of torment; and, second, how could there be anyone who died in the state of grace about whom we should have to be anxious lest—if what they say is true— even in the bosom of Abraham he might commit sin after leaving the body if he could do so before entering it? Finally,

---

1 Ps. 113.13.

there is a great difference between sinning in Adam, as the Apostle says: 'In whom all sinned,'[2] and sinning out of Adam somewhere or other, and for that reason being thrust down in Adam, that is, into the flesh which is derived from Adam, as into a prison. The opinion that all souls come from the first soul is one I do not wish to discuss, unless it should be necessary, and how I wish that the one we are now debating may be so well upheld by you that the other may not require discussion! Although I desire, I ask, I pray with ardent longings that the Lord may make use of you to remove my ignorance in this matter, still, if I do not deserve this, which God forbid, I shall ask patience of the Lord our God in whom I have such faith that I should not murmur against Him if He refuses to open to me when I knock.[3] I shall recall the saying of the Apostle: 'I have many things to say to you but you cannot bear them now.'[4] As far as in me lies may I apply this to myself, and may I not knowingly be offended at being deemed unworthy, lest by this very fact I be proved more unworthy. There are many other points on which I am likewise ignorant—too many to recall or recount —and I would try to bear my ignorance on this one if I did not fear that some one of those opinions might be contrary to what we hold with strongest faith, and might creep into unwary minds. But, before I know which one of them is to be preferred, I protest that I hold confidently that the one which is true is not opposed to the firm and fundamental faith by which the Church of Christ believes that the children of men just born cannot be delivered from damnation except through the grace of the name of Christ which He has entrusted to us in His sacraments.

---

2 Rom. 5.12.
3 Matt. 7.7,8; Luke 11.9,10.
4 John 16.12.

167. Augustine to Jerome[1] *(Spring, 415)*

On the Passage from the Apostle James: 'Whosoever shall keep the whole law,' *etc.*

Chapter 1

When I had finished my letter to you, brother Jerome, revered by me in Christ, with my inquiry about the human soul—whether new ones are now created for each one at birth, and when they contract the debt of sin which we do not doubt must be canceled by the sacrament of Christ's grace, even in newborn infants—I found my letter had lengthened into a sizable volume, so I decided against loading it with another question. But, the more pressing a difficulty is, the more we are bound not to pass it by. Therefore, I ask and beg you by the Lord to explain for me something which I think will benefit many, or, if you have an explanation done either by you or by somebody else, to send it to me; namely, how we are to understand those words in the Epistle of the Apostle James: 'Whosoever shall keep the whole law but offend in one point is become guilty of all.'[2] This is a matter of such great importance that I regret profoundly not having written you about it long ago.

---

1 Cf. *Retractations* 2.45: 'I also wrote two books to the priest Jerome, residing at Bethlehem, of which the second was on the passage from the Apostle James: "Whoever shall keep the whole law," etc.'
2 James 2.10.

Chapter 2

We have to think about leading our present life so as to attain eternal life, not about examining how completely the past is buried in oblivion, such as that question which I thought it necessary to ask about the soul. That question keeps coming back. There is a cleverly told story which fits this case neatly. Someone once fell into a well where the water was deep enough to hold him up so that he did not drown, but not enough to choke him so that he could not speak. A bystander came over when he saw him and asked sympathetically: 'How did you fall in?' He answered: 'Please find some way of getting me out and never mind how I fell in.' Thus, as we confess and hold by our Catholic faith that the soul, even of the little infant, has to be delivered from sin, as from a well, by the grace of Christ, it is enough for him that we know how he may be saved, even if we never find out how he came into that evil state. But I thought it wise to raise the question lest we unwittingly hold one of those opinions about the soul joining the body which might forthwith go counter to the necessity of deliverance for the soul of the child by denying that he is in that state. I cling to this most firmly: that the soul of the child can be freed from the guilt of sin in no other way than by the 'grace of God by Jesus Christ our Lord.'[1] If we can discover the cause and origin of that evil, we shall be better prepared and equipped to refute the idle prating of pettifoggers—I do not call them debaters. However, if we cannot discover it, we should not grow slothful in the exercise of mercy because the origin of the misery is hidden from us. By not ignoring our own ignorance we shall be more secure against those who imagine they know what they do not know. There is a difference between what it is evil not to know and what cannot be known, or what it is

1 Rom. 7.25.

not necessary to know, or what has no bearing on the way of life we seek. But this question which I am now asking about the Epistle of the Apostle James involves our conduct in the life which we are now leading and which we wish to live so as to please God.

Chapter 3

I ask you, then, how to interpret 'Whosoever shall keep the law but offend in one point is become guilty of all.' Is it possible that he who has committed theft, nay, he who has said to the rich man: 'Sit thou here,' but to the poor man: 'Stand thou there,'[1] is guilty of murder and adultery and sacrilege? If that is not so, how has he that has offended in one point become guilty of all? Or is what I said about the rich and the poor man not included in the things of which if a man offend in one he is guilty of all? But we must recall the source of that statement, what preceding words led up to it, and in what connection it was uttered. He says: 'My brethren, have not the faith of our Lord Jesus Christ of glory with respect of persons. For if there shall come into your assembly a man having a golden ring, in fine apparel, and there shall come in also a poor man in mean attire, and you have respect to him that is clothed with the fine apparel and shall say to him: Sit thou here well; but say to the poor man: Stand thou there: or Sit under my footstool: do you not judge within yourselves and are become judges of unjust thoughts? Hearken, my dearest brethren: hath not God chosen the poor in this world, rich in faith and heirs of the kingdom which God hath promised to them that love him? But you have dishonored the poor man,'[2] because of him to whom it is said 'Stand thou there,' while to the man with the

---

1 James 2.3.
2 James 2.1-6.

golden ring it was said: 'Sit thou here well.' Then he follows up that statement, developing it more fully and explaining it by saying: 'Do not the rich oppress you by might, and do not they draw you before the judgment seats? Do not they blaspheme the good name that is invoked upon you? If then you fulfil the royal law according to the Scriptures: Thou shalt love thy neighbor as thyself: you do well, but if you have respect to persons, you commit sin, being reproved by the law as transgressors.'[3] See how he calls those transgressors who say to the rich man: 'Sit thou here,' and to the poor man: 'Stand thou there.' And lest they think it an insignificant sin to transgress the law in this one point, he goes on and adds: 'But whosoever shall keep the whole law but offend in one point is become guilty of all. For he that said: Thou shalt not commit adultery, said also: Thou shalt not kill. Now if thou do not kill but commit adultery thou art become a transgressor of the law,'[4] because he had also said: 'Being reproved by the law as transgressors.' This being established, the conclusion seems to be, unless another meaning can be shown for it, that the one who said to the rich man: 'Sit thou here,' and to the poor one: 'Stand thou there,' offering greater deference to the former than to the latter, is an idolater, a blasphemer, an adulterer, and a murderer; not to run through the whole list, which would take too long, he is to be judged guilty of every crime, and thus, offending in one point, he is become guilty of all.

Chapter 4

On the other hand, he who has one virtue has them all, and he who does not have a particular one has none. If

---

3 James 2.6-9.
4 James 10.11.

this is true, that statement is proved. But I want an explanation, not an assent, for that principle which in itself is more weighty for us than the authority of all the philosophers. If it is really true to say that of virtues and vices, it does not follow that therefore all sins are equal. I might conceivably be wrong, but if my memory serves me well in something I barely remember, all the philosophers accept that dictum about the inseparability of virtues, by saying that the same virtues are necessary for right living. But the Stoics are the only ones who dared to argue for the equality of sins and this they did against all human experience. Your adversary, Jovinian, was a Stoic in following that opinion, but an Epicurean in grasping at and constantly defending pleasure, and you refuted him brilliantly from the holy Scriptures.[1] In that most delightful and most luminous work of yours, it is quite clear that neither the authors on our side, nor Truth Itself which spoke through them, accepted the view that all sins are equal. How it can happen that even if this is true of virtues we are not thereby obliged to admit the equality of sins, I shall try to expound to the best of my ability, with the help of the Lord; if I succeed, you will approve; where I am lacking in my argument, you will supply.

Chapter 5

Those who hold that he who has one virtue has them all, and that all are lacking to him who lacks one particular one, use this argument: that prudence can be neither cowardly, nor unjust, nor intemperate, for if it is any of these it will not be prudence. On the other hand, if it is brave and just and temperate, it will be prudence; therefore, wherever it is found it has the other virtues with it. Thus, also fortitude

---

1 Jerome, *Adversus Jovinianum* 2.21-34, in *PL* 23.

cannot be imprudent or intemperate or unjust; likewise, temperance must necessarily be prudent, brave, and just, as justice will not be present if it is not prudent, brave, and temperate. Therefore, wherever any of these virtues is truly present, the others are likewise there; where the others are lacking, the one is not a true virtue, even though in some ways it seems like one.

Chapter 6

There are, as you know, certain vices forming contraries to the virtues by a clear distinction, as, imprudence to prudence; but there are also some which are only contrary because they are vices, but which have a sort of deceptive resemblance to virtues, as when we set against prudence, not imprudence, but craftiness. I am now speaking of that craftiness which is more commonly understood and expressed in an evil sense, not as our Scripture ordinarily uses it, which often gives it a good meaning; hence we have: 'Wise as serpents,'[1] and 'to give subtlety to little ones.'[2] We admit that the most fluent author of the Roman tongue among the ancients said: 'One did not have to be on guard against trickery in him, nor was he lacking in subtlety,'[3] giving *astutiam* a good meaning; but among them that usage is extremely rare, though most common among our writers. Likewise, among the subdivisions of temperance, prodigality is clearly contrary to thrift, but what, in everyday speech, is called niggardliness is obviously a vice, not like thrift by nature, but having a deceptive resemblance to it. In the same way, injustice is contrary to justice by an evident antithesis, whereas the craving for vengeance puts on a show of justice but is a vice. Slothfulness is clearly the

---

1 Matt. 10.16. The adjective used is *astuti* (from *astutiam*), translated as 'craftiness.'
2 Prov. 1.4. *Astutia* is here 'subtlety.'
3 Sallust, *Catiline* 5.3.

opposite of fortitude; hardihood differs from it by nature but counterfeits its appearance. Constancy is an essential part of virtue; inconstancy is completely different and forms an undeniable contrary, but stubbornness aims at being called constancy and is not constancy, because the one is a virtue, the other a vice.

Chapter 7

Let us take an example to illustrate the rest of this subject so as not to have to repeat the same things over and over. Those who had the opportunity of knowing Catiline have written of him that 'he was able to endure hunger, cold, and lack of sleep to an unbelievable degree,'[1] and for this reason it seemed to himself as well as to his followers that he was endowed with great fortitude. But, this fortitude was not prudent: it took evil for good; it was not temperate because it was defiled with base excesses; it was not just for he conspired against his country. Therefore, in him it was not fortitude, but hardihood, that put on the name of fortitude to lead fools astray. If it had been fortitude it would not have been a vice but a virtue; if it had been a virtue it would never have been abandoned by the other virtues which are, so to speak, its inseparable companions.

Chapter 8

Thus, when the question is raised about vices, whether they are all equally present when one is present, or whether none is present when a particular one is lacking, it is a difficult task to prove it, because two vices are usually the opposites of one virtue: the manifest contrary and the one which

1 Sallust, *Catiline* 5.3.

masquerades under the appearance of similarity. Thus, also, it is easily seen that Catiline did not have fortitude, because he did not have the other virtues with it, but we can hardly be convinced that it was slothfulness which practised that endurance and tolerance of such extreme discomforts 'to an unbelievable degree.' But, perhaps, if we examine more closely, that hardness will appear as slothfulness because he had neglected the effort of the pursuit of good through which true fortitude is attained. Nevertheless, as those who are not timid are bold and, on the other hand, those who lack boldness are timid—and here there is vice on both sides—whereas he who is strong in true virtue neither rashly dares nor unreasonably fears, we are forced to admit that vices are more numerous than virtues.

Chapter 9

Sometimes, indeed, one vice is driven out by another, as love of money by love of praise; sometimes one yields and gives place to several, as when a man who has been a drunkard has learned to drink with moderation through miserliness and ambition. Therefore, it is possible for vices to to give place, not to virtues but to successive vices, because there are more of them. But, when one virtue has entered, bringing the others with it, at once all the vices which were present leave; not that all the vices were present, but sometimes as many, sometimes more, vices yield place to fewer virtues or fewer give way to more.

Chapter 10

Whether this is really the case is something we must look into with great care. When we say that he who has one virtue has them all and he who lacks any particular one has none, we are not making a statement on divine authority. This is the result of men's thought—men of great ability, deep study and leisure, it is true, but still men. But I do not know how I can deny that even a woman—to say nothing of man from whom virtue[1] takes its name—who keeps marital faith with her husband, if she does this because of the commandment and promise of God and is faithful to Him first of all, has chastity; nor would I say that it is a non-existent or insignificant virtue, and the same is true of the husband who keeps faith with his wife. Yet there are many such, none of whom I would say are without some sin, and certainly that sin, whatever it is, comes from some vice. We deduce that conjugal chastity in God-fearing men and women is unquestionably a virtue—for it is something and it is not a vice —but it does not have all the virtues with it. If they were all present there would be no vice; if no vice, absolutely no sin; but who is without some sin? Who, then, is without any vice, that is, the very stock and root, so to speak, of sin, when he who leaned upon the Lord's bosom[2] cried out: 'if we say that we have no sin we deceive ourselves, and the truth is not in us'?[3] This does not have to be developed further for you, but I am saying it for the sake of others who will read it. For you, indeed, in that same brilliant work against Jovinian[4] have proved it exhaustively from the holy Scriptures, when you quoted from this very Epistle, part of which we are now seeking to understand, the following: 'For in many things we all offend.'[5] When the Apostle of Christ spoke, he did not say: 'You offend,' but 'We offend,' and when he says in this passage: 'Whosoever shall keep the whole law, but offend in one point, is become guilty of all,' he is there speaking of many, not of one; he says that all offend, not merely some.

---

1 *Virtus;* literally, 'manliness,' from *vir* ('man').
2 John 13.25; 21.20.
3 1 John 1.8.
4 Jerome, *Adversus Jovinianum* 2.2, in *PL* 23.
5 James 2.10.

Chapter 11

But God forbid that any of the faithful should think that so many thousands of the servants of God have no virtue when they say that they have sin, lest they deceive themselves and truth should not be in them, because wisdom is a great virtue. 'But he said to man: Behold piety, that is wisdom.'[1] God forbid that we should say of so many deeply pious and faithful men of God that they have not piety, which the Greeks call *eusébeian*,[2] or, more exactly and completely, *theosébeian*.[3] For, what is piety but the worship of God? What is the source of that worship if not charity? For, 'charity from a pure heart and a good conscience and an unfeigned faith' is also a true virtue, because it is 'the end of the commandment.'[4] Rightly is it said to be 'strong as death,'[5] either because no one overcomes it as no one overcomes death, or because in this life the measure of charity is unto death, as the Lord said: 'Greater love than this no man hath that a man lay down his life for his friends,'[6] or, rather, because as death tears the soul away from the senses of the flesh, so charity tears it away from carnal passions. Knowledge is its handmaid when it is useful, for without charity 'knowledge puffeth up,'[7] but, in the measure that charity fills the heart by edification, knowledge finds there nothing empty to puff up. Moreover, the sacred writer showed that knowledge is useful by defining it, when he said: 'Behold piety, that is wisdom,' and he straightway continued: 'To depart from evil, that is wisdom.'[8] Why, then, do we not say that he who

---

1 Cf. Job 28.28.
2 I.e., reverence toward the gods.
3 I.e., worship or fear of God.
4 1 Tim. 1.5.
5 Cant. 8.6.
6 John 15.13.
7 1 Cor. 8.1.
8 Job 28.28.

has this virtue has them all, since 'love is the fulfilling of the law'?[9] Or is it true that, the more charity a man has, the more he is endowed with virtue, because charity is itself a virtue; and the less virtue he has the more vice there is in him? Therefore, where charity is full and perfect there will be no remains of vice.

Chapter 12

For that reason it seems to me that the Stoics are wrong in refusing to admit that the man who is increasing in wisdom has any wisdom at all, and insisting that he has it only when he is absolutely perfect in it; not that they refuse to admit the increase, but for them he is not wise in any degree unless he suddenly springs forth into the free air of wisdom after coming up and, as it were, emerging from the depths of the sea. Just as it makes no difference, if you want to drown a man, whether the water is many feet deep over him or only a hand's breadth or a finger's breadth, so, for them, those who are making progress are like men coming up from the depths of the sea into the air, but, unless they have entirely escaped from total folly by emerging and coming forth from the oppressive waters, they have no virtue and they are not wise; whereas, when they have escaped, they at once have complete wisdom, and no folly is left from which any sin could arise.

Chapter 13

This comparison in which folly is represented as water and wisdom as air, so that the soul coming up from the choking depths of folly into wisdom is suddenly able to breathe, does not seem to me compatible with the authority of our Scrip-

---

9 Rom. 13.10.

tures; that other comparison is better, where vice or folly is likened to darkness, virtue or wisdom to light, in so far, of course, as resemblance drawn from corporeal sources can be applied to intellectual concepts. Wisdom does not come suddenly, in the manner of one rising from water into air who is able to breathe as much as he needs as soon as he has reached the top of the waves; it comes, rather, by degrees, in the manner of one advancing from darkness into light and being gradually illumined as he progresses. Until this is fully accomplished we say that he is like someone emerging from a very dark cave into the proximity of light, who is illumined more and more as he approches the exit, and that the light he has comes from the brightness toward which he is advancing, but the darkness still about him is from the blackness out of which he is coming. Thus: 'In the sight of God shall no man living be justified,'[1] yet 'the just man liveth by faith.'[2] The saints are clad in justice,[3] one more, another less; yet no one lives here without sin. In this, also, one more, another less, but he is best who has least sin.

Chapter 14

But what am I about? I am forgetting to whom I am speaking; I have been making myself out to be a teacher after proposing something which I wished to learn from you. It was because the question of the equality of sins came up in the matter I was treating that I decided to set forth my opinion for you to examine. Now I will bring it to a conclusion soon because, although it is true that he who has one virtue has them all, while he who lacks a particular one has none, it is not equally true that sins are equal, because where

---

1 Ps. 142.2.
2 Hab. 2.4; Rom. 1.17; Gal. 3.11; Heb. 10.38.
3 Job 29.14.

there is no virtue there is nothing upright, yet a thing may be more or less crooked, more or less twisted. However, I think it more likely and more in accord with the sacred writings that the movements of the soul are like the members of the body, not that they are seen in different places, but they are felt in the affections, and one has more light, another less, while another lacks light entirely and is enveloped in its inhibition as in darkness. In like manner, according as a man is moved by the enlightenment of devout love, more in one act, less in another, he can be said to have one virtue, not to have another, or to have yet another in greater or less degree. We can rightly say: 'There is greater charity in this man than in that one,' and 'there is some in him, none at all in that one,' and this applies to charity which is piety. We can also say of one and the same man that he has more modesty than patience, and, if he makes progress, more today than yesterday, and that as yet he has no continence but he has no slight kindness.

Chapter 15

And now, to summarize briefly and comprehensively the idea I have of the virtue which belongs to right living: that virtue is charity by means of which we love what we should love. This is greater in some, less in others, lacking in still others; its fullest measure, beyond which there is no increase, is found in no one as long as he lives the life of man. As long as it is subject to increase, the defect by which it is less than it ought to be is accounted as vice; by reason of this vice 'There is no just man upon earth, that will do good and sin not';[1] because of this vice, 'No man living shall be justified in the sight of God';[2] because of this vice, 'If we

---

1 Eccle. 7.21; 3 Kings 8.46.
2 Ps. 142.2.

say that we have no sin we deceive ourselves and the truth is not in us';[3] because of it, also, however much progress we have made, we still have to say: 'Forgive us our debts,'[4] even though in baptism all our words, deeds, thoughts have been forgiven. Therefore, he who sees rightly sees where and when and whence that perfection is to be hoped for, to which no addition is possible. But, if there were no commandments, there would certainly be no norm by which a man might look into himself and see what he should avoid, what he should strive after, what he should rejoice in, what he should pray for. Commandments, then, are highly useful, if only because free will is thereby given the opportunity of doing greater honor to the grace of God.

Chapter 16

If all that is so, how does it happen that he who keeps the whole law is guilty of all if he offends in one point? Is it perhaps because 'Love is the fulfilling of the law'[1] by which God and the neighbor are loved, on which commandments 'dependeth the whole law and the prophets,'[2] that he is deservedly guilty of all who has acted against that virtue on which all depends? For, no one sins except by acting contrary to charity, because 'Thou shalt not commit adultery, thou shalt not kill, thou shalt not covet, and if there be any other commandment it is comprised in this word: Thou shalt love thy neighbor as thyself. The love of our neighbor worketh

---

3 1 John 1.8.
4 Matt. 6.12; Luke 11.4.

---

1 Rom. 13.10.
2 Matt. 22.40.

no evil. Love therefore is the fulfilling of the law.'[3] However, no one loves his neighbor unless he loves God, and, by loving him as himself to the limit of his ability, he pours out his love on him so that he, too, may love God. But, if he does not love God, he loves neither himself nor his neighbor. In this way, whoever shall keep the whole law but offend in one point becomes guilty of all because he acts against charity on which the whole law depends. Thus, he becomes guilty of all by acting against that virtue on which all depends.

Chapter 17

Why, then, cannot we say that sins are equal? It might be because he who sins more grievously deals a greater blow to charity, while he who sins more lightly wounds it less; the one who sins more grievously or more frequently is more culpable, the one who sins more lightly or less often is less guilty. Obviously, the guilt would be greater or less according as the sin has been greater or less; yet, if he has offended in one point, he becomes guilty of all, because he has violated charity on which all depends. If this is true, it explains what a man of even apostolic grace says: 'In many things we all offend,' for we do offend, one more grievously, another more lightly; and to measure how much more or less anyone sins we say that, the less he loves God and his neighbor, the more prone he is to commit sin; on the other hand, the greater his love of God and his neighbor, the less he is likely to commit sin; whoever has less charity has more sinfulness, but he who is perfect in charity has no remains of weakness.

---

3 Rom. 13.9,10.

Chapter 18

Yet, certainly, as I look at it, it is not to be deemed a light sin to have the faith of our Lord Jesus Christ with respect of persons, if we apply that difference of sitting and standing to ecclesiastical dignities. Who could bear to have a rich man chosen to a seat of honor in the Church while a more learned and holier one is passed over because he is poor? And if we speak of everyday seating arrangements, does he not commit this sin, if it is a sin, when he judges within himself, from appearances, that a rich man is a better man? The Apostle seems to have meant this when he said: 'Do you not judge within yourselves and are become judges of unjust thoughts?'[1]

Chapter 19

Therefore, the law of charity is the law of liberty, of which he says: 'If then you fulfil the royal law according to the Scriptures: Thou shalt love thy neighbor as thyself, you do well, but if you have respect to persons you commit sin, being reproved by the law as transgressors.'[1] And after that sentence, so very difficult to understand, on which I have said all that I think needs saying, he mentions that same law of liberty in the words: 'So speak ye, and so do, as being to be judged by the law of liberty.' And since, as I said awhile ago, 'in many things we all offend,' he suggests the Lord's remedy to be used as a daily medicine for daily wounds, even slight ones, for he says: 'Judgment without mercy to him that hath not done mercy.'[2] On this point, also, the Lord said: 'Forgive and you shall be forgiven; give and it shall be given to you';[3]

---

1 James 2.4.

---

1 James 2.8,9.
2 James 2.12.13.
3 Luke 6.37,38.

but 'Mercy exalteth itself above judgment.'⁴ It does not say: 'Mercy overcomes judgment,' for it is not in conflict with it, but 'exalteth itself' because more are won over by mercy, and by mercy it means those who have shown mercy. 'Blessed are the merciful because God will be merciful to them.'⁵

Chapter 20

Obviously, it is just that those who have pardoned should receive pardon and that it should be given to those who give. It is natural that there should be in God both mercy for him that judges and judgment for him that shows mercy. That is why we say to Him: 'Mercy and judgment I will sing to thee, O Lord.'¹ Whoever, presuming on his own justice, expects judgment with mercy as if he were secure provokes the most just anger, of which the Psalmist said in fear: 'Enter not into judgment with thy servant.'² Therefore, God says to His perverse people: 'Why will you contend with me in judgment?'³ For, when 'the just king shall sit on his throne, who will boast that he has a chaste heart, or who will boast that he is pure of sin?'⁴ What hope is there, then, unless 'mercy exalteth itself above judgment, ' but only toward those who have shown mercy by saying sincerely: 'Forgive us as we forgive,' and by giving without protest? 'For God loveth a cheerful giver.'⁵ Finally, in order to comfort those in whom the former sentence had roused extreme fear, St. James in the sequence to that passage speaks of the works

4 James 2.13.
5 Cf. Matt. 5.7.

1 Ps. 100.1.
2 Ps. 142.2.
3 Jer. 2.29.
4 Prov. 20.8,9 (Septuagint).
5 2 Cor. 9.7.

of mercy, when he points out how even daily sins, without which there is no living in this world, are expiated by daily remedies. Without these, man who becomes guilty of all by offending in one point, and by offending in many—'because in many things we all offend'—would drag with him to the judgment seat of the great Judge a mighty load of guilt, gathered up bit by bit, and would not find the mercy which he had not shown, but by forgiving and giving he deserves to have his debts forgiven and the promised reward given to him.

Chapter 21

I have spoken at length, and probably I have bored you by repeating arguments which you accept but which you do not expect to learn because you have been accustomed to teach them. If there is anything in them regarding their content—for I am not concerned about the language in which they are expressed—but if there is anything in them which offends your learning, I beg you in your answer to warn me of it, and to take the trouble to correct me. Unhappy is he who does not worthily honor such great and holy labors as are those of your studies, and give thanks for them to the Lord our God, by whose gift you are what you are! Therefore, since I ought to be more ready to learn from anyone at all what I am so useless as not to know rather than eager to teach anyone at all what I do know, how much more reason have I to beg to be indebted to your Charity, by whose learning, in the name and with the help of the Lord, ecclesiastical literature in the Latin tongue has been advanced as it could never have been before! Especially do I ask you by the Lord, if your Charity knows of a better way of interpreting that sentence: 'Whosoever shall keep the whole law but offend in one point is become guilty of all,' be so kind as to share it with us.

168. Timasius and James[1] give greeting in the Lord to the
truly blessed lord, their deservedly revered father,
Bishop Augustine (415)

The grace of God, administered by your word, has so
refreshed and revived us that we can appropriately say: 'He
sent his word and healed them,'[2] blessed lord, deservedly
revered father. Certainly we find that your Holiness has
rendered the text of that same book,[3] so redolent of your
careful attention, that we were in admiration of the answers
contained in it, down to the last page, whether in those points
which it befits a Christian to refute, detest, and avoid, or in
those in which it is shown that the objector[4] was not so far
wrong, although, by some clever twist or other, even in those
passages he believed that the grace of God was to be passed
over. But we have one regret in this favor you have done us,
that so sublime a gift of the grace of God should be so late
in shedding its light, because it happens that some are absent
whose blindness has need of the illumination of so shining a
truth, but we trust by the mercy of God that this same grace
may come to them, however late, since 'He will have all men
to be saved and to come to the knowledge of the truth.'[5] As
for us, taught as we have been long since by the spirit of
charity which is in you, we have cast off our attachment to
that error, and we now return thanks that we have learned
how to reveal to others what we have previously believed,
because the fruitful words of your Holiness have opened the
way and made it easy for us.

May the mercy of our God ever glorify your Blessedness
and make you mindful of us.[6]

---

1 Converts of Augustine's; probably members of a group of monks. Cf.
  Letter 179 n. 2.
2 Ps. 106.20.
3 *On Nature and Grace.*
4 Pelagius, against whom the book was written.
5 1 Tim. 2.4.
6 In another handwriting.

169. Augustine, bishop, to Evodius,[1] bishop (End of 415)

If your Holiness is so anxious to know what subjects keep me most occupied, from which I am unwilling to be diverted to something else, send someone to describe them to you. Several, which I began this year before Easter, at the approach of Lent, are now completed. I have added two more to my three books on the City of God against His enemies the demon-worshipers, and in these five books I think I have made out a rather good argument against those who think the gods are to be worshiped for the sake of happiness in this life, and who are hostile to the very name of Christian because they believe we are the obstacle to that happiness. Besides, it must be said, as we promised in Book 1, that it is also against those who think the worship of their gods necessary for the life after death, and that is the life for the sake of which we are Christians. I have also dictated some sizable volumes containing a commentary on three Psalms: 67, 71, and 77. The others, not yet dictated, or even composed, are urgently looked for and demanded of me. I do not want to be called off from these or slowed down by any flank attack of any other questions, and so I have no desire to give my attention to the books on the Trinity which I have had on hand for a long time, but have not yet finished, because they are too exacting a work, and I think they are comprehensible to few. Therefore, the other works which I hope will be useful to more people are more pressing.

The passage, 'If any man know not he shall not be known,'[2] does not mean, as you write, that the Apostle spoke in this matter as if that punishment would be inflicted on anyone whose mind is not keen enough to perceive the ineffable unity of the Trinity, as memory, intellect, and will are perceived

---

1 There is no formal address. Evodius was his boyhood friend.
2 1 Cor. 14.38.

in our mind. The Apostle is here speaking of something else. Read it and you will see that he was saying such things as would serve to strengthen the faith or morals of many, not such as would appeal to the understanding of a few, a limited understanding, restricted, the only kind one can find in this life. He was dealing with such topics as these: that prophecy should be preferred to tongues; that their meetings should be carried on without disturbance, as if the spirit of prophecy forced even the unwilling to speak; that women should keep silence in church; 'that all things be done decently and according to order.'[3] When he had settled these points, he said: 'If any seem to be a prophet or spiritual, let him know the things that I wrote to you, that it is the commandment of the Lord. But if any man know not, he shall not be known';[4] by these words restraining the turbulent and recalling them to peaceful order, especially those who were more ready to dissent because they seemed to surpass the rest in spirituality, whose pride disturbed everything. 'If therefore any seem to be a prophet or spiritual, let him know,' says the Apostle, 'the thing I write to you, because it is the commandment of the Lord.' 'If any seem to be,' and obviously is not, for he who is knows beyond doubt and has no need of warning or exhortation, because 'he judgeth all things and is judged by no man.'[5] Therefore, those who make dissensions and disturbances in the Church are the ones who seem to be what they are not. He teaches these to know that it is the commandment of the Lord because 'He is not the God of dissension but of peace.'[6] But, 'if any man know not, he shall not be known,' that is, he shall be cast off, for, if you are speaking of knowledge, God is not without knowl-

---

3 1 Cor. 14.34-40.
4 1 Cor. 14.37-39.
5 1 Cor. 2.15.
6 1 Cor. 14.33.

edge of those to whom He will say: 'I know you not.'[7] His rejection is indicated by that word.

But when the Lord says: 'Blessed are the clean of heart for they shall see God,'[8] and that vision is thereby promised at the end as our reward, we have no reason to fear that we shall then hear the word: 'if any man know not, he shall not be known,' because we are now unable to see what we believe about the nature of God. 'For seeing that in the wisdom of God the world by wisdom knew not God, it pleased God by the foolishness of our preaching to save them that believe.'[9] This foolishness of preaching and 'foolishness of God which is wiser than men'[10] draws many to salvation, and so, not only those who are not yet able to perceive with sure understanding the nature of God which they hold by faith, but also those who do not yet distinguish in their own mind incorporeal substance from the common nature of the body, and do not know how to live, know, and will, are still not deprived of salvation which that foolishness of preaching bestows on the faithful.

For, if Christ died for those only who are able to discern these truths with sure understanding, our labor in the Church is almost worthless. But if, as truth holds, the believers among the peoples run to their Physician in their sickness to be healed by Christ, and Him crucified, so that 'where sin abounded grace might more abound,'[11] it happens in marvellous ways, 'through the depth of the riches of the wisdom and of the knowledge of God,' and by 'his unsearchable judgments'[12] that some, because they can distinguish incorporeal from corporeal things, seem great to themselves, mock at the

---

7 Matt. 7.23; Luke 13.25,27.
8 Matt. 5.8.
9 1 Cor. 1.21.
10 1 Cor. 1.25.
11 Cf. Rom. 5.20.
12 Cf. Rom. 11.33.

foolishness of the preaching through which they believed and
were saved, and wander far from the one way which alone
leads to eternal life. On the other hand, many who glory in
the cross of Christ and do not withdraw from that same way,
though ignorant of those points which are so subtlely debated,
because not one little one perishes for whom He died,[13]
attain to that same eternity, truth, charity, that is, to a fixed,
sure, and complete happiness where all things are clear to
those who remain faithful, who see, and who love.

Therefore, let us believe with firm piety in one God, Father
and Son and Holy Spirit, in such wise that the Son is not
believed to be the same Person as the Father, or the Father
the same as the Son, or the Father and the Son the same as
the Spirit of both. And let it not be thought that there is any
separation of time or place in this Trinity, but that these
three are equal and co-eternal and entirely of one nature; or
that one creature was created by the Father, another by the
Son, another by the Holy Spirit, but that all created things,
all and each one of them that have been or are being created
exist by the creative power of the Trinity. Nor must we think
that anyone is saved by the Father without the Son and the
Holy Spirit, or by the Son without the Father and the Holy
Spirit, or by the Holy Spirit without the Father and the
Son, but by the Father and the Son and the Holy Spirit, one
true and only God, truly immortal, that is, entirely unchangeable. In the Scripture many details are mentioned separately
of the Persons individually, such as cannot be said of them
jointly, even though they are inseparably together, as when
they are made manifest by corporeal sounds; and so in
certain passages of Scripture and through certain created
beings they are shown separately and successively, as the
Father in the voice which was heard: 'Thou art my Son,'[14]

---

13 Matt. 18.14; John 17.12.
14 Mark 1.11; Luke 3.22; Ps. 2.7; Matt. 3.17.

and the Son in the human nature which He took from the Virgin,[15] and the Holy Spirit in the physical appearance of a dove.[16] These are mentioned separately, it is true, but they do not prove that the Three are separated.

To understand this to some extent, we take the example of our memory, our understanding, our will. Although we list these separately, individually, and in their separate times, yet there is nothing we do or say which proceeds from one of them without the other two. However, we are not to think that these three faculties are compared to the Trinity so as to resemble it at every point, for a comparison is never given such importance in an argument that it exactly fits the thing to which it is compared. Besides, when can any likeness in a created being be applied to the Creator? In the first place, that comparison lacks resemblance because those three faculties—memory, understanding, will—are in the mind, the mind is not identical with the three of them; whereas the Trinity is not in God, it is God. Therein we admire His marvellous simplicity because in the nature of God being is not different from understanding or anything else we might say of Him; the mind, however, exists even without the understanding because its being is not identical with its understanding. In the second place, who would dare to say that the Father does not understand through Himself but through the Son, as the memory does not understand through itself, but through the understanding, or, rather, the mind itself, in which these faculties exist, understands only through the understanding, as it remembers only through the memory, and wills only through the will? Thus far, then, that comparison is applied to make us understand in some way how, when mention is made of the separate names by which these faculties of the mind are made known, each single name is

---

15 Matt. 1.23,25; Luke 2.7.
16 Matt. 3.16; Mark 1.10; Luke 3.22; John 1.22.

used of their joint action, as when we speak of remembering
and understanding and willing; but there is no created being,
by which the Father alone or the Son alone or the Holy
Spirit alone is made known, which is not the work of the
Trinity together, since its action is indivisible. Thus, neither
the voice of the Father, nor the soul and body of the Son,
nor the dove of the Holy Spirit is brought about in any other
way than by the common action of the same Trinity.

For, certainly, the sound of the voice which at once ceased
to be is not a fitting likeness to the unity of the person of the
Father, nor does the corporeal appearance of the dove resemble the unity of the person of the Holy Spirit, for it, also,
like that luminous cloud which overshadowed the Saviour
on the mountain with the three disciples,[17] or, rather, like
that fire which manifested the presence of the Holy Spirit,[18]
ceased to be as soon as its purpose had been fulfilled. But
man alone, because all the wonders took place to deliver
human nature, was assimilated to the unity of the person of
the Word of God, that is, the only Son of God, by His
marvellous and unique incarnation, yet the Word remained
unchangeable in His nature in which nothing complex is
to be supposed which could support any image of the human
mind. It is true, we read: 'The spirit of wisdom is manifold,'[19]
but it is also rightly called simple: manifold because there are
many things which it has, but simple because what it has is
nothing other than what it is, as the Son is said to 'have life
in himself'[20] and is Himself the same life.[21] It is man that
draws near to the Word, not the Word that by any change
draws near to man. Thus, He is called the Son of God and
God made man at the same time. Consequently, the same

---

17 Matt. 17.5; Mark 9.6; Luke 9.24.
18 Acts 2.3.
19 Wisd. 7.22.
20 John 5.26.
21 John 14.6.

Son of God is unchangeable and co-eternal with the Father in the Word alone; and the Son of God was buried, but in the flesh alone.

Therefore, in what is said of the Son of God the choice of words must be guided by the meaning intended. The number of Persons was not increased by the assuming of human nature, but the Trinity remained the same. Just as in any man, except the one who was uniquely assumed by the Word, soul and body form one person, so in Christ the Word and man form one Person. And just as a man is called, for instance, a philosopher—though this refers uniquely to his mind, and it is not an illogical but a highly appropriate and customary form of speech to say of him that a philosopher was killed, a philosopher died, a philosopher was buried, although all this affects him only in the body and not in what makes him a philosopher—so it must be held certain that Christ who is God, the Son of God, the Lord of glory, and any other titles that may be given to Him, is rightly said to be a crucified God, although He suffered this only according to the flesh and not according to His nature as Lord of glory.

But the sound of that voice and the corporeal appearance of the dove, and the 'parted tongues as it were of fire that sat upon every one of them,'[22] like those terrible manifestations that happened on Mount Sinai[23] and that pillar of cloud by day and of fire by night,[24] were performed and carried out as figurative acts. Now, in these matters, special care must be taken lest anyone believe that the nature of God, either the Father, the Son, or the Holy Spirit, is subject to change or transformation. And let no one be troubled because sometimes the sign receives the name of the thing signified. Thus, the Holy Spirit is said to have descended on Christ in the cor-

22 Acts 2.3.
23 Exod. 19.18.
24 Exod. 13.21.

poreal appearance, as it were, of a dove and to have remained upon Him; thus, also, the rock is called Christ because
it signifies Christ.[25]

But I am surprised that you think it possible for the sound
of that voice which said: 'Thou art my Son,'[26] to be produced
by the divine will acting on physical nature without the
agency of a living being, and you do not think it possible
for the physical appearance of any living creature and of
movement like that of life to be produced by the divine will
in the same way without the agency of any animal life-
principle. If created nature obeys God without the action of
a vivifying soul, so that sounds are uttered such as are
usually uttered by a living body, and the form of articulate
speech is brought to the ears, why should it not obey Him
so that without the agency of a vivifying soul the form and
movement of a bird should be presented to the sight by the
same power of the Creator? Can this be the privilege of the
sense of hearing but not of sight, although both sense im-
pressions are formed from the matter of the body which lies
near—both what sounds in the ears and what appears to the
sight, both the syllables of the voice and the outline of the
physical shape, both audible and visible movement—so that
it should be both a true body which is perceived by a bodily
sense and at the same time nothing more than what is
perceived by a bodily sense? The soul is not perceived by any
bodily sense, nor is it seen in any living being. Therefore,
there is no need to inquire how the corporeal appearance of
the dove was produced, just as we do not inquire how the
words of an articulate body produce their sound. For, if it
were possible for a soul not to be the medium by which a
voice is said to have been made audible and not as a voice
usually is, how much more possible was it when the dove was

25 1 Cor. 10.4.
26 Matt. 3.16-17; Mark 1.10,11; Luke 3.22.

spoken of that this word should signify merely a physical appearance presented to the eyes without the actual nature of a living creature! These words, also, were said in that sense: 'And suddenly there came a sound from heaven as of a mighty wind coming, and there appeared to them parted tongues as it were of fire,'[27] where a certain phenomenon is said to be 'as of a wind' and 'as it were' a visible fire, like the natural fire with its customary nature, but it does not seem to mean that natural fire of the customary kind was produced.

If a more subtle reasoning or a more thorough investigation into this matter shows that the nature which is not susceptible of motion in either time or space undergoes no motion except through a nature which can move in time only but not in space, the conclusion will be that all those phenomena were brought about through the agency of a living creature, as, for example, by angels. Hence, it would take too long and there is no need to discuss it more in detail. In addition, there are visions which appear to the mind as if to the bodily senses, not only to people in sleep or out of their minds, but sometimes to people of sane mind and wide awake; they are not caused by the deceit of mocking demons but by some spiritual revelation which acts through incorporeal forms resembling bodies. These cannot be distinguished at all unless they are more fully revealed by divine assistance and discerned by the understanding of the mind, and this is scarcely ever the case while they are happening, but occurs for the most part after they have disappeared. This being so, whether they have a corporeal nature or merely a corporeal appearance but a spiritual nature in which they appear to our mind as to the bodily senses, since sacred Scripture relates these things, we ought not to judge rashly of which sort these two are, or whether they are produced by the agency of a living

---

27 Acts 2.2,3.

creature if they occur in bodily form, so long as we either believe without any doubt or accept with such understanding as we have that the invisible and immutable nature of the Creator, that is, of the supreme and ineffable Trinity, is both far removed and distinct from the senses of mortal flesh, and from all change into something either better or worse or into anything else at all.

You see, in spite of my being so very busy, how lengthily I have been able to write you these thoughts on your two questions, that is, about the Trinity and the dove, the form under which the Holy Spirit was seen, not in His own nature but under a symbolical appearance, just as the Son of God was not crucified by the Jews in His own begotten nature of which the Father says: 'Before the day-star I begot thee,'[28] but in the human nature which He took in the womb of the Virgin. I thought better not to treat of all the objections which you put into your letter, but these two on which you wanted to hear from me I think I have answered fully enough to obey your Charity, though not enough, perhaps, for your insatiable desire.

In addition to those two books which, as I said above, I added to the other three, and the commentary on the three Psalms, I have also written a book to the holy priest Jerome on the origin of the soul, advising him how to defend that opinion which he had written as his own to Marcellinus of religious memory; that new, individual souls are created at birth, so that the fundamental belief of the Church may not be shaken, by which we steadfastly believe that 'in Adam all die'[29] and, unless they are redeemed by the grace of Christ, which is effected through His sacrament conferred even on infants, are doomed to condemnation. I also wrote him another one asking how he thought we should interpret what

28 Ps. 109.3.
29 1 Cor. 15.22.

is written in the Epistle of James: 'Whosoever shall keep the whole law but offend in one point, is become guilty of all.'[30] But in this one I said what I thought, whereas in the other one on the origin of the soul I only asked, in a sort of tentative argument, what he thought. I did not want to lose the opportunity of sending them by a certain very holy and very studious young man, the priest Orosius, who came to us from faraway Spain, that is, from the Atlantic coast, with the sole incentive of learning the holy Scriptures. I persuaded him to go to Jerome. In one small book, as briefly and clearly as I could, I gave this same Orosius the answers to several questions on the Priscillianist heresy and on certain of Origen's opinions, not accepted by the Church, which troubled him. And I wrote an especially long book against the Pelagian heresy at the request of several of the brethren who had been impressed by his deadly doctrine against the grace of Christ. If you want to have all these, send someone to transcribe them for you, but leave me free to study and to dictate works which are needful for many and which I think should have the right of way over your inquiries on matters of interest to few.

170. *Alypius and Augustine give greeting in the Lord to the excellent and deservedly honored lord, their religious brother, Maximus*[1] *(c. 415)*

When we were inquiring of our holy brother and fellow bishop, Peregrinus,[2] about your health—not your physical health only, but especially your spiritual health—and that of your household, his answers about you gave us pleasure, but

---

30 James 2.10.

---

1 A physician, recently converted from Arianism.
2 Cf. Letter 139. He became a bishop in 413, but his see is not named.

we were sad to hear of your household that they have not yet experienced a salutary conversion or joined the Catholic Church. As we had hoped that this would soon happen, we deeply regret that it has not yet come to pass, excellent lord, deservedly honored and religious brother.

Therefore, we greet your Charity in the peace of the Lord, and we enjoin on you and beg of you not to delay teaching them what you have learned, namely, that to the one God alone do we owe the worship which is called *latreía* in Greek. That same word is found in the Law, where it is written: 'The Lord thy God shalt thou adore and him only shalt thou serve.'[3] If we spoke of Him as God the Father only, we should be answered: 'Then the worship of *latreía* is now owed to the Son,' which it is forbidden to say. But if it is owed, how, then, is it owed to God alone if it is owed to the Father and the Son, unless the one God to whom we are commanded to give the worship of *latreía* is so named the only God as to mean the Father and the Son and, certainly, the Holy Spirit as well? Of Him doubtless the Apostle says: 'Know you not that your bodies are the temple of the Holy Spirit who is in you, whom you have from God, and you are not your own? For you are bought with a great price. Glorify God, therefore, in your body.'[4] Of what God but the Holy Spirit did he say that our bodies are the temple? Therefore, *latreía* is owed to the Holy Spirit. For, if we were commanded to build Him a temple of wood and stone as Solomon did, by this very building of a temple we should prove that we offered Him worship; how much more, then, do we owe Him worship, we who do not build Him a temple but are his temple!

Thus, if the worship of *latreía* is owed to the Father and to the Son and to the Holy Spirit and is paid by us, as it is said: 'The Lord thy God shalt thou adore and him only shalt thou

---

3 Deut. 6.13; Matt. 4.10.
4 1 Cor. 6.19,20.

serve,' without any doubt the Lord our God to whom alone
we owe worship of *latreía* is not the Father alone, or the Son
alone, or the Holy Spirit alone, but the Trinity Itself, one
only God, Father, and Son and Holy Spirit; but not in such
wise as that the Father should be the same as the Son, or the
Holy Spirit the same as the Father or the Son, since in that
Trinity the Father is Father of the Son alone, and the Son is
Son of the Father alone, but the Holy Spirit is the Spirit of
the Father and the Son. By reason of its one and the same
nature and inseparable life the Trinity is understood—as
far as can be understood by man, with faith leading the way—
as one Lord our God, of whom it is said: 'The Lord thy
God shalt thou adore and him only shalt thou serve,' of
whom the Apostle spoke when he said: 'For of him and by
him and in him are all things: to him be glory forever.'[5]

But the only-begotten Son does not come of God the
Father as the whole of creation came from Him, which He
created from nothing. He begot the Son of His own substance, He did not make Him out of nothing; He did not
beget Him in time, through whom He instituted all time, for,
as the flame is not antecedent to the brightness which it
produces, so the Father has never been without the Son.
Indeed, He is the wisdom of the Father, of whom it is
written: 'The brightness of eternal light.'[6] Therefore, there
is no doubt that wisdom is co-eternal with the light whose
brightness it is, that is, with God the Father, and therefore,
also, as in the beginning God made heaven and earth, not
so, in the beginning, did He make the Word, but 'In the
beginning was the Word.'[7] The Holy Spirit was not made,
either, as creation was from nothing, but as He proceeds

5 Rom. 11.36.
6 Wisd. 7.26.
7 John 1.1.

from the Father and the Son, so He was not created by the Son or by the Father.

This Trinity is of one and the same nature and substance, not less in each Person than in all, or more in all than in each; and as much in the Father alone or in the Son alone as in the Father and the Son together, and as much in the Holy Spirit alone as in the Father and the Son and the Holy Spirit together. And the Father did not diminish Himself in order to have a Son of Himself, but He begot Him as another self so as to remain whole in Himself, and to be as great in the Son as He is alone. Likewise, the Holy Spirit, a whole Person from a whole Person, does not precede Him from whom He proceeds, but is as much with Him as He is from Him; He does not diminish Him by proceeding from Him or increase Him by remaining with Him. All these Persons are not confusedly one or separately three, but because they are one they are three, and because they are three they are one. Moreover, as He has granted to the many hearts of His faithful to be one heart,[8] how much more does He reserve for Himself that these three Persons should be all and singly God and at the same time that they should be one God, not three gods. This is the Lord our God who is served with universal devotion, to whom alone the worship of *latreía* is due.

Since of His bounty He has granted to things which are born in time that each thing should beget offspring of its own substance, see how impious it is to say that He did not beget what He is, when man, by His gift, begets what he is, that is, man, not of another nature but of the same as his own, although He does not beget the Father of His Son which is Himself. These terms indicate analogy not nature, and, therefore, when applied to something they have a

8 Acts 4.32.

relative sense, sometimes identical, sometimes different. They have a meaning of identity, of course, when brother is compared to brother, friend to friend, neighbor to neighbor, kindred to kindred, and other like cases which could be drawn out to infinity if one wished to run through all of them. In these cases this one is to that one what that one is to this one. But they are different in comparisons of father to son, son to father, father-in-law to son-in-law, son-in-law to father-in-law, master to slave, slave to master: in these this one is not to that one what that one is to this one, although both are men. This comparison of diverse objects is not made in terms of their nature, since, as you notice, what one of the pair is to the other is not in the formula of this one is to that one as that one is to this one, because one is the father, the other the son; or one the father-in-law, the other the son-in-law; or one the master, the other the slave. But, if you notice what each one is to himself or in himself, one is the same as the other because one is man as the other is. Consequently, your Prudence understands the illogical contention of those from whose error the Lord has delivered you, which states that the nature of God the Father must be different from the nature of God the Son, because one is the Father, the other the Son, and therefore the Father did not beget what He is Himself, since He did not beget the Father of the Son which He is Himself. Anyone can see that those terms do not denote their natures in themselves, but the Person of each toward the other.

They also promote an error like this when they say that the Son is of another nature and of different substance because the Father does not derive His Godhead from another but the Son derives His from God the Father. Here, however, it is not a question of substance, but of origin; that is, not what each one is, but whence He is or is not. We do not say that Abel and Adam were not of the same nature and substance because the former had had human nature from the latter, but the latter had his from no man. If, then, we consider the nature of both, Abel was a man, Adam was a man; but, if we consider their origin, Abel descended from the first man, Adam from no man. Thus, in God the Father and God the Son, if we consider the nature of both, each one is God, but one is not more God than the other; if we consider their origin, the Father is God from whom the Son is God, but there is no god previous to God the Father.

Those who try to reply to this make a vain effort when they say: 'But man begets with sufferings; God begot His Son without suffering.' This does not help them at all, but it helps us greatly. For, if God granted to temporal and passible things to beget what they are, how much more did He who is eternal and impassible beget no other than He is Himself: one Father an only Son, to our unutterable wonder, since He begot Him with no suffering on His part, and with such complete equality to Himself that the Son does not excel Him either in power or in age! All He has and can do He attributes to His Father, not to Himself, because He is not of Himself but of the Father. For, He is equal to the Father and this also He received from the Father, but He did not so receive His being equal as if He had previously been unequal and was born equal, but, as He is always born, so He is always equal. Therefore, He did not beget one unequal and add equality to Him at birth, but He gave it to Him in begetting Him because He begot Him equal, not unequal. Therefore, being in the form of God, it was not robbery in Him to be equal to God;[9] since He assumed this at birth, He did not presume it by pride.

His reason for saying that the Father is greater[10] is that

---

9 Phil. 2.6.
10 John 14.28.

'He emptied himself, taking the form of a servant,'[11] without losing that of God. Because of this form of servant, He not only became less than the Father but also less than Himself and the Holy Spirit; not only less than this most high Trinity, but He was even made 'a little lower than the angels.'[12] He was also lower than man, because as a boy He was subject to His parents.[13] And so it was because of this form of the servant which He took by emptying Himself when the fullness of time was come that He said: 'The Father is greater than I,'[14] but it was because of that form of God which He did not lose by emptying Himself that He said: 'I and the Father are one.'[15] It is clear that He became man while remaining God, for man was assumed by God; God was not consumed in man. Therefore, it is perfectly reasonable to say both that Christ as man is less than the Father and that Christ as God is equal to the Father and is equally God.

Since, then, we rejoice that you have joined the right and Catholic faith in our presence, to the great exultation of the people of God, why are we still sad at your slothfulness toward your household? We beg you by the mercy of Christ and by His help to remove this grief from our hearts. We cannot believe that your influence has so much weight in supporting the obstinacy of your dependents and none at all in inducing their conversion. Or do they perhaps despise you because you have become a member of the Catholic Church at your age, when they ought rather admire and respect you because you overcame a very old error when your youth was growing old? God forbid that they who agreed with you in your departure from truth should now resist you when you

11 Phil. 2.7.
12 Heb. 2.9.
13 Luke 2.51.
14 John 14.28.
15 John 10.30.

speak the truth; God forbid that they who delighted to share your error should now refuse to accept your correct views. Pray for them, plead with them; nay, bring them with you into the house of God, since they are with you in your own house. You should feel shame and regret at coming to the house of God without those who are accustomed to meet in your house, especially as your Catholic Mother asks you to give some of them back, she asks them back. She asks for those whom she finds with you, but she asks back those whom she lost through you. Do not let her suffer in her losses, rather let her rejoice in her gains. Let her gain the sons whom she does not yet have, not mourn those whom she once had. We pray to God that you may do what we urge, and we hope of His mercy that our heart may be filled with joy and 'our tongue with gladness,'[16] at the letter of our holy brother and fellow bishop, Peregrinus, and the speedy answer of your Charity on this matter.

171. Alypius and Augustine give greeting in the Lord to the most happy lord, their esteemed and very dear brother and fellow bishop, Peregrinus (c. 415)

We sent a letter to our honored brother, Maximus,[1] in the belief that he would be glad to receive it. Please write back at the first opportunity you can find and tell us whether we did any good. Let him know that we are in the habit of writing long letters to our intimate friends, not only laymen but even bishops, in the same form[2] in which we wrote to

---

16 Ps. 125.2.

---

1 Cf. Letter 170.
2 The custom of the time required ceremonious letters to be written in one's own hand on parchment, where as letters to equals or inferiors were dictated and written on paper, as this letter was. Augustine feared that Maximus might have taken offense at his lack of formality.

him. We do this to speed up our correspondence, and besides, paper is more comfortable to hold when reading. Perhaps, as he is not acquainted with this custom of ours, he might think he has been slighted.

171A.[1] *Augustine to Maximus (c. 415)*

You should regulate your life and conduct by the commandments of God, which we have received to enable us to lead a good life, beginning with a religious fear, for 'the fear of the Lord is the beginning of wisdom,'[2] whereby human pride is broken down and weakened. Secondly, with a mild and gentle piety you should refrain from objecting to passages of the holy Scriptures which you do not yet understand and which seem to the uninstructed devoid of sense and self-contradictory, and you should not try to impose your ideas on the meaning of the holy books, but submit and hold your mind in check, rather than savagely attack its hidden meaning. Thirdly, when your human weakness begins to be revealed to you in the course of your self-knowledge, and you learn how low a place you occupy, what penal bonds of mortality you drag around with you, son of Adam that you are, and how far you are from the Lord[3] in your sojourning, and when you 'see another law in your members fighting against the law of your mind and captivating you in the law of sin that is in your members,' and you cry out: 'Unhappy man that I am, who shall deliver me from the body of this death?' let the 'grace of God by Jesus Christ our Lord,'[4] who promises you

---

1 This fragment on the seven stages of the spiritual life, without title or address, was found as a quotation in the *Commentaries* of Primasius *on the Apocalypse* (Primasius 1.2.5; *PL* 48.828.20).
2 Ps. 110.10; Prov. 1.7.
3 2 Cor. 5.6.
4 Rom. 7.23-25.

that deliverance, be your comfort in your grief. In the fourth place, desire to fulfill justice much more eagerly and ardently than carnal pleasures are usually desired by evil men, with this difference, that in such desire the ardor is peaceful and the flame safer because it rests on the hope of divine help. In that fourth stage of life there is constant application to prayer, that the fullness of justice may be granted to those who hunger and thirst for it.[5] In that stage it is not burdensome, it is rather a delight, to refrain from every pleasure of corruption, whether one's own or another's, either by struggling against it or by actively opposing it. That this heavenly help may be more readily granted, a fifth stage is added, setting forth the counsel of mercy, that, as far as you are able, you succor the needy, desiring to be helped by the Almighty in what you are not able to do. The practice of mercy is twofold: when vengeance is sacrificed and when compassion is shown. The Lord included both of these in His brief sentence: 'Forgive and you shall be forgiven, give and it shall be given to you.'[6] This work has the effect of purifying the heart, so that, even under the limitations of this life, we are enabled with pure mind to see the immutable substance of God. For there is something holding us back, which has to be loosed so that our sight may break through to the light. In connection with this the Lord said: 'Give alms and behold all things are clean to you.'[7] Therefore, the next and sixth step is that cleansing of the heart.

But, in order that an upright and pure gaze may be turned to the true light, none of the good and praiseworthy deeds which we do, none of the truths which we keenly and profoundly discern, is to have the intention of pleasing men or satisfying the needs of the body. God wishes to be worshiped

---

5 Matt. 5.6.
6 Luke 6.37,38.
7 Luke 11.41.

for Himself alone, for nothing outside Himself should be a motive for seeking Him. When by the stages of a good life we have come to that purity of mind, whether slowly or speedily, then let us dare to say that we are able to make some contact of mind with the unity of the supreme and ineffable Trinity, where there will be the deepest peace, because there is nothing more to hope for, when men become sons of God, remade according to the likeness of His nature, enjoying the immutability of their Father. For the first stage is: 'Blessed are the poor in spirit,' when they fear God; the second: 'Blessed are the meek,' when there is a docile piety; the third: 'Blessed are they that mourn,' when they know their own weakness; the fourth: 'Blessed are they that hunger and thirst after justice,' when strong effort keeps their passions under control; the fifth: 'Blessed are the merciful, for God will have mercy on them,' which is the counsel of helping that you may deserve to be helped. Then we come to the sixth stage, in which it is said: 'Blessed are the clean of heart for they shall see God,'[8] in which the mind cannot be kept pure and fit to understand the Trinity, in however slight a degree, unless we give up the craving for human praise even when we perform praiseworthy deeds. Thereafter, we come, by the seventh stage, to the tranquility of that peace which the world cannot give. This is brought about by those four virtues which the philosophers of old were able to strive for with commendable industry: namely, prudence, fortitude, temperance and justice; and if we add to them these three, faith, hope and charity, needed for the perfect practice of religion, we attain at once the number seven. With reason do we take care not to neglect these, without which we know that it is impossible for anyone to worship God or to please Him.

8 Matt. 5.3-8; Luke 6.20,21; Isa. 11.2,3.
9 Matt. 5.9; John 14.27.

172. Jerome gives greeting in the Lord to Augustine, truly holy lord and pope revered by me with all affection (c. 416)

At your bidding and because of his own worth, I have welcomed the priest Orosius[1] as my honored brother and the son of your Worthiness. But I have been going through a difficult time when it has been better for me to keep silent than to speak; consequently, my studies have fallen off and, like Appius,[2] my speech has been a snarl. So I have not been able to seize this occasion to answer the two books[3] which you dedicated to my name, learned books and brilliant, with the full splendor of eloquence; not that I think there is anything to criticize in them, but according to the blessed Apostle: 'Let every man abound in his own sense, one after this manner, another after that.'[4] Certainly, you have set forth and discussed with your profound mind all that can be said, drawing from the fount of sacred Scripture. But I ask your Reverence to leave me for a while to the praise of your genius. You and I carry on discussion with the intention of learning, but the envious and, especially, the heretics, if they see us holding different opinions, will conclude falsely that this comes from ill feeling between us. It is my fixed determination to love you, support you, cherish you, marvel at you, and defend your opinions as my own. Certainly, in the dialogue[5] which I published recently I made mention of your Blessedness, as was fitting; let us, then, make a greater effort to uproot this most baneful heresy from the Churches, a heresy which is always pretending to repent so as to have

---

1 This letter was probably brought back by him in the spring of 416.
2 Cf. Sallust, *Fragmenta Historiae* 2.37 (ed. Dietsch).
3 Letters 166 and 167.
4 Rom. 14.5; 1 Cor. 7.7.
5 *Libri adversus Pelagianos* 3.19 (*PL* 23.588-590).

the chance of teaching in the Churches, because, if it came out into the full light of day, it would be driven out and would die.

Your holy and venerable daughters, Eustochium and Paula,[6] are progressing in a manner worthy of their own rank and your encouragment, and they send special greetings to your Blessedness, as do all the brotherhood who strive with us to serve the Lord our Saviour. Last year we sent the holy priest Firmus to Ravenna on business connected with them, and afterward to Sicily and Africa. We think he is now delaying in some part of Africa. I pray you, give my greetings to the saints who belong to your household. I have addressed a letter to the holy priest Firmus; if it reaches you, be so kind as to direct it to him. May Christ keep you safe and mindful of me, truly holy lord and blessed pope.

We suffer in this province from a great scarcity of copyists of the Latin tongue, and therefore we cannot fulfill your behests, especially in regard to the edition of the Septuagint which is marked with asterisks and obelisks;[7] besides, we have lost a large part of our earlier work through someone's dishonesty.

173. Augustine, Bishop of the Catholic Church, to Donatus,[1] priest of the Donatist sect (c. 416)

If you could see the grief of my heart and my anxiety for your salvation, perhaps you would 'take pity on your own soul, pleasing God'[2] by listening to the word that is His, not

---

6 Two of the noble Roman ladies who followed Jerome to Bethlehem and there led a religious life. Paula was the mother of Eustochium.
7 Cf. Letter 71.

1 Donatist priest of Mutugenna in the diocese of Hippo. Brought forcibly into a church, he attempted to commit suicide.
2 Eccli. 30.24.

ours, and by not shutting your heart to the Scriptures which
you have committed to memory. You are angered because
you are brought by force to salvation, while yours have
dragged so many of ours to destruction. We have no other
wish for you than that you should be caught, brought in, and
saved from perishing. The inconsiderable bodily injury which
you suffered was self-inflicted, through your refusal to use
the horse that was immediately brought to you, and your
having fallen heavily to the ground, for it is a fact that the
other, who was brought in with you as your companion,
came unharmed because he did not act that way.

But you think that this should not have happened to you
because you believe that no one should be forced to do good.
See what the Apostle said: 'If a man desire the office of a
bishop, he desireth a good work,'[3] yet how many are forced
against their will to undertake the episcopacy; they are
dragged in, they are imprisoned, they are kept under guard;
they suffer all this unwillingly until there arises in them a
will to undertake this good work. With much greater reason
should you be dragged away from the baneful error in which
you are your own enemies, and led to the knowledge and
embrace of truth, not only that you may receive honor in
safety but that you may not come to an evil end. You say
that God gave man free will and therefore he should not be
forced ever to do good. Why, then, are those of whom I
have just spoken forced to do good? Note well a point you
do not want to consider. The good will is subject to merciful
compulsion in order that the bad will of man may receive right
guidance. Surely, everyone knows that no man is damned
unless he deserves it by his evil will, and no one is saved
unless he has a good will. Therefore, those we love are not
to be cruelly abandoned without restriction to their own evil

---

3 1 Tim. 3.1.

will, but, when possible, they are to be restrained from doing evil and forced to do good.

If an evil will is always to be left to its own freedom, why were the rebellious and querulous Israelites restrained from evil by such harsh scourges and compelled to enter the land of promise?[4] If the evil will is always to be left to its own freedom, why was Paul not allowed the use of his altogether perverted will to persecute the Church? Why was he thrown prostrate in order to be blinded, and blinded in order to be transformed, and transformed in order to become an apostle, and made an apostle in order to endure for the truth the same sufferings he had inflicted while in error?[5] If the evil will is always to be left to its own freedom, why is the father admonished in the holy Scriptures not only to correct his headstrong son with rebukes, but also to beat his sides in order that he may be brought under good discipline, tamed and directed into the right way?[6] And in the same sense it says: 'But thou shalt beat him with the rod and deliver his soul from hell.'[7] If the evil will is always to be left to its own freedom, why are careless shepherds rebuked, and why is it said to them: 'The wandering sheep you have not called back, that which was lost you have not sought'?[8] You, too, are the sheep of Christ, you bear the Lord's mark which you have received in His sacrament, but you have gone astray and become lost. It should not cause you displeasure that we call back the strays and seek the lost; it is better for us to do the will of the Lord when He urges us to force you to return to His sheepfold than to yield to the will of the straying sheep, and allow them to be lost. Do not then say what I hear you constantly saying: 'But I want to go astray, I want to be

---

4 Exod. 15.22-27.
5 Acts 9.1-9.
6 Eccli. 30.12.
7 Cf. Prov. 23.14.

lost that way,' it is better for us not to allow you to do this at all, as far as in us lies.

When, recently, you jumped into a well in order to die there, you certainly did this of your own free will, but how cruel the servants of God would have been had they abandoned you to your evil will and had not delivered you from that death! Yet you threw yourself into the water deliberately in order to die there, and they pulled you out of the water against your will so that you might not die there; you acted according to your own evil will to your own destruction; they acted against your will to save you. If, then, that bodily welfare is to be so safeguarded that it is preserved even in those who do not want it by those who love them, how much more is that spiritual welfare to be preserved since by its loss eternal death is feared! Yet, you would have remained in that death which you wanted to inflict on yourself, not for time but for eternity, because even if you were being forced to some evil deed instead of to salvation, to the peace of the Church, to the unity of the body of Christ, to holy and indivisible charity, you had no right to try to kill yourself.

Examine the divine Scriptures and scrutinize them as closely as you can, and see whether this was ever done by any of the good and faithful souls, even though they suffered great trials at the hands of those who were trying to drive them to eternal destruction, not to eternal life, to which you are being forced. I have heard that you said the Apostle Paul meant that this was lawful when he said: 'If I should deliver my body to be burned.'[9] Probably because he was listing all kinds of good things which are worth nothing without charity, such as tongues of men and angels, and all mysteries, and all knowledge, and all prophecy, and all faith so as to move mountains, and distribution of his goods to

8 Cf. Ezech. 34.4.
9 1 Cor. 13.3.

the poor,[10] you thought he included among good things the taking of one's own life. But notice carefully and understand in what sense Scripture says that anyone should deliver his body to be burned: not, certainly, that he should jump into the fire when harassed by a pursuing enemy, but that, when a choice is offered him of either doing wrong or suffering wrong, he chooses not to do wrong rather than not to suffer wrong. In this case he delivers his body into the power of the slayer, as those three men did who were being forced to adore the golden statue, and who were threatened by the one who was forcing them with the furnace of burning fire if they did not do it.[11] They refused to adore the idol, but they did not cast themselves into the fire, yet it is written of them: 'They delivered up their bodies that they might not serve nor adore any god but their own God.'[12] This is what the Apostle means by 'If I deliver my body to be burned.'

But notice what follows: 'If I have not charity it profiteth me nothing.'[13] You are called to that charity; you will not be allowed to perish away from that charity, and you think it profits you something if you hurl yourself to destruction, whereas it would profit you nothing if another put you to death as an enemy of charity. Even if you were burned alive for the name of Christ, you would suffer the punishment of eternal torment if you persisted in remaining outside the Church, separated from the edifice of unity and the bond of charity. This is the sense in which the Apostle said: 'And if I should deliver my body to be burned and have not charity it profiteth me nothing.' Bring your mind back to sane conclusions and serious thoughts, examine carefully whether you are being summoned to error and impiety; be willing to

10 1 Cor. 13.1-3.
11 Dan. 3.13-21.
12 Dan. 3.95.
13 1 Cor. 13.3.

suffer some inconvenience for the truth. If, instead, you are living in error and impiety, and truth and piety are on the side to which you are called, because Christian unity and the grace of the Holy Spirit are there, why do you still try to be an enemy to yourself?

For this reason the mercy of God provided your bishops and us with an opportunity of meeting at Carthage in such a well-attended, even crowded, conference, and of carrying on a discussion in a really orderly manner about this dissension of ours. The record of it has been written up; our signatures are in evidence. Read it or have it read to you, and then choose which side you prefer. I have heard that you said you could deal with us on the basis of that record if we would suppress the words of your bishops where they said: 'One case does not bring guilt on another nor one person on another.'[14] You want us to suppress those words in which truth itself spoke through them without their knowledge. You will say that on this point they were wrong, and that they stumbled into a false position through inadvertence, but we say that here they spoke truly, and we prove this with the greatest of ease from your own case. For, if you do not allow that your bishops, chosen from the entire Donatist sect to represent the whole group, with the understanding that whatever action they took would be ratified and accepted by the rest should prejudice your case by what you judge to have been rashly and incorrectly spoken, by this very fact the truth of their statement stands out that 'one case does not prejudice another nor one person another.' And here you ought to recognize that if you do not wish the person of so many of your bishops, represented by those seven,[15] to bring blame on the person of Donatus, priest of Mutugenna, how

---

14 Cf. Letter 141.
15 At the Conference of Carthage in 411, seven bishops were chosen to speak for each side.

much less should the person of Caecilian,[16] even if some defect
had been found in him, bring blame on the whole unity of
Christ, which is not confined to the single hamlet of Mutugenna, but is spread throughout the entire world!

But see, we do what you wanted. We deal with you as if
your bishops had not said: 'One case does not prejudice
another nor one person another.' It is your turn to find out
what they ought to have said in answer to the objection of the
case and person of Primian,[17] who at first joined the others
in condeming his accusers and then received the condemned
and accursed back to their former dignity. The baptism, too,
which 'dead men' had given—for it was then that the famous
statement was made that 'the shores are full of dead men'[18]—
was recognized and accepted by him instead of being scorned
and repudiated. Thus he cut the ground from under the
wrong interpretation your people are wont to give to the
words: 'He that washeth himself after touching the dead,
what doth his washing avail?'[19] Thus, if they had not said:
'One case does not prejudice another nor one person another,'
they would share in the guilt of Primian's case, but as they
have said it they have freed the Church of any implication
in the case of Caecilian, as we have always maintained.

But read the rest of the record, examine the rest of it.
See whether they have succeeded in proving any wrong-doing
against Caecilian himself, from whose person they tried to
bring blame on the Church. See whether, instead, they have
not done much for him, whether they have not altogether
strengthened and supported his case by the many extracts

---

16 His contested consecration was the starting point of the Donatist
   schism; cf. Letter 43 n. 5.
17 Cf. Letter 43 n. 52.
18 Cf. Exod. 14.31. The Donatists called the Christians 'dead men' because
   to them Catholics were deprived of Christian life. In *Contra
   Gaudentium* 1.54 (*PL* 43.740) Augustine gives this sentence in full.
19 Eccli. 34.30. The Donatists used this text to prove their case for rebaptism.

which they offered and read, to their own detriment. Read
them or have them read to you. Consider them all, examine
them carefully, and choose which side you will follow:
Whether you will rejoice with us in the peace of Christ, in
the unity of the Catholic Church, in the love of brothers, or
whether you will side with wicked dissension in support of
the Donatist sect with its accursed separation, and even so
endure yet longer the importunity of our love for you.

I hear that you often repeat and call attention to the
passage in the Gospel where it is written that the seventy
disciples went back from the Lord, and were left to their own
choice in their evil and impious separation; and to the
twelve who stayed with Him He said: 'Will you also go
away?'[20] You fail to notice that the Church then was just
beginning to put out young shoots and that as yet there was
no fulfillment of that prophecy: 'And all the kings of the
earth shall adore him; all nations shall serve him.'[21] Surely,
the more complete the fulfillment, the greater the authority
exercised by the Church, not only to invite but to compel
men to goodness. This is what the Lord wished to convey by
that incident, for, in spite of possessing full power, He chose,
instead, to commend humility. He showed this quite clearly
in the parable of the wedding feast, in which, after the
invited guests had been notified and had refused to come,
the servant was told: 'Go out into the streets and lanes of
the city and bring in hither the poor and the feeble and the
blind and the lame. And the servant said to his lord: It is
done as thou hast commanded and yet there is room. And
the lord said to the servant: Go out into the highways and
hedges and compel them to come in that my house may be
filled.'[22] Notice how of the first to come it says: 'Bring them

20 John 6.67,68. The Gospel does not say 'the seventy,' but 'many' went
   away.
21 Ps. 71.11.
22 Luke 14.21-23.

in'—it does not say 'compel'—thus indicating the beginnings
of the Church while it was still growing to the point where it
might have the strength to compel. Accordingly, since it was
fitting that when the Church had been strengthened with His
strength and greatness, men should be compelled to come in
to the feast, the words were afterward added: 'It is done as
thou hast commanded and yet there is room,' and he said:
'Go out into the highways and hedges and compel them to
come in.' Therefore, if you had been walking peacefully outside this banquet of the unity of holy Church, we should
have found you as if in the highways, but now, because of
the many evil cruelties which you have perpetrated against
our people, we find you, as it were, in the hedges, as if you
were full of sharp thorns, and we compel you to come in.
He who is compelled is forced to go where he does not wish
to go, but when he has entered he shares willingly in the
banquet. Therefore, you must restrain that wicked and
rebellious mind of yours so that, in the true Church of Christ,
you may find the life-giving banquet.

173A.[1] *Augustine to the beloved lords, his holy brothers, and
fellow priests and deacons, Deogratias*[2] *and Theo-
dore,*[3] *and their companion-brother, Titianus
(c. 416)*

Although you have not written to me, I have learned from
a trustworthy and faithful messenger that you wish me to
write you, without any of that uncertainty and obscurity
which is incomprehensible to slower minds, how the Holy
Spirit is proved to be God. But your Brotherhood must

---

1 This letter, not in Migne, was published by Goldbacher from a single
copy.
2 Cf. Letter 102.
3 Cf. Letters 61 and 107.

realize that of all the passages from holy Scripture which I can recall on this point, I do not know any that will convince you by the authority of revealed writings that the Holy Spirit is God, since you are not convinced by what the Apostle says: 'Know you not that your bodies are the temple of the Holy Spirit who is in you, whom you have from God, and you are not your own? For you are bought with a great price. Glorify and bear God in your body.'[4] However, by reasoning, such as can be used by man or by such a man as we are, the proof of this doctrine is worked out by an intricate process. Whoever yields assent to the supreme authority of divine Scripture should first examine these words: 'The Lord thy God shalt thou adore and him only shalt thou serve.'[5] In Greek, the expression used does not signify the service owed to human masters, but that which is offered to God, called *latreía*. Thus, idolatry is rightly condemned because the *latreía* which is due to the true God alone is offered to idols. It does not say: 'Thou shalt adore only the Lord thy God,' but it says: 'And him only shalt thou serve.' It uses the word 'only' with 'thou shalt serve', meaning, no doubt, that service which is called *latreía*. To this service belong temple, sacrifice, priest and other like attributes. Consequently, the Apostle would certainly not say that our body is the temple of the Holy Spirit if that service, called *latreía,* were not His due. But such service would not be His due if He were not God to whom it is due, especially as the Apostle says that our bodies are the members of Christ,[6] and those who deny that the Holy Spirit is God or who claim that Christ is greater than the Holy Spirit[7] do not deny that Christ is God. How, then,

---

4 1 Cor. 6.19,20.
5 Deut. 6.13; Matt. 4.10.
6 1 Cor. 6.15; 12.27.
7 A group of semi-Arians or Pneumatomachians under Macedonius were condemned for this error at Constantinople in 381.

could the members of the greater be the temple of the lesser? This argument proves incontestably not only that the Holy Spirit is God, because a temple cannot be rightly and religiously dedicated to anyone but God, but it also shows that He is necessarily one God with the Father and the Son, because the Trinity is one God. Since the dedication of a temple is part of that service which is called *latreía*, and since it is written: 'The Lord thy God shalt thou adore and him only shalt thou serve,' that is, offer Him *latreía*, it follows that as *latreía* is rightly offered to God, and *latreía* is offered to him to whom a temple is offered, then there is only one God to whom *latreía* is due, and that one God is, beyond doubt, the Father and the Son and the Holy Spirit. And this is what is meant by: 'Glorify God in your body,' of which it says: 'Your bodies are the temple of the Holy Spirit who is in you, whom you have from God.'

I have chosen to dictate this in great haste rather than use some pretext to prolong the desire of your Charity. If you think it is inconclusive, keep yourselves in readiness to read the books on the Trinity[8] which I am now preparing to publish in the name of the Lord; perhaps they may convince you where this brief letter cannot.

174. Augustine gives greeting in the Lord to Pope Aurelius,[1] most blessed lord, holy brother and fellow priest, revered with most sincere affection (c. 416)

In my youth I began a work on the Trinity,[2] the supreme

8 *De Trinitate*, begun in 398, probably finished in 418-419.

1 Archbishop of Carthage, primate of all Africa. Bishops generally were called pope until the ninth century.
2 A thirteenth book was added later to the original twelve.

and true God; I have finished it in my old age. Indeed, I had laid the work aside after discovering that it had been carried off prematurely or purloined from me, before I had finished it or revised and corrected it as I had planned. I had intended to publish it as a whole, not in separate books, for the reason that the subsequent books are linked to the preceding ones by a continuous development of the argument. Since my intention could not be carried out because of the persons who had secured access to the books before I wished it, I left off my interrupted dictation, thinking to make a complaint of this in some of my other writings, so that those who could might know that the said books had not been published by me but filched from me before I deemed them worthy of publication under my name. Now, however, under the insistent demands of many brethren and the compulsion of your bidding, I have devoted myself, with the Lord's help, to the laborious task of finishing them. They are not corrected as I should wish, but as best I could, so that the whole work might not differ too much from the parts which have for some time been circulating surreptitiously. I send it now to your Reverence by my son and very dear fellow deacon, and I give my permission for it to be read, heard, and copied by any who wish. If I had been able to carry out my original plan, it would have been much smoother and clearer, though the statements would have been the same; always, of course, as far as my ability and the difficulty of explaining such matters would allow. There are some persons who have the first four or, rather, five books without the introductions, and the twelfth without most of the last part. If they come to know of this edition they will make the corrections, provided they have the good will and the ability. I ask earnestly that you order this letter to be used as a preface, separated from but at the head of those same books. Pray for me.

*175. We who were present at the Council of Carthage send
greetings to the most blessed Lord, our honored
and saintly brother, Pope Innocent:[1] to wit:[2]
Aurelius, Numidius, Rusticanus, Fidentius, Eva-
grius, Antoninus, Palatinus, Adeodatus, Vincent,
Publian, Theasius, Tutus, Pannonius, Victor,
Restitutus, [another] Restitutus, Rusticus, Fortu-
natian, Ampelius, Avivius, Felix, Donatian,
Adeodatus, Octavius, Serotinus, Maiorinus,
Postumian, Crispulus, Victor, [another] Victor,
Leucius, Marianus, Fructuosus, Faustinian,
Quodvultdeus, Candorius, Maximus, Megarius,
Rusticus, Rufinian, Proculus, Thomas, Januarius,
Octavian, Praetextatus, Sixtus, [another] Quod-
vultdeus, Pentadius, [still another] Quodvultdeus,
Cyprian, Servilius, Pelagius, Marcellus, Venan-
tius, Didymus, Saturnian, Bazacenus, Germanus,
Germanian, Juventius, Candidus, [another]
Cyprian, Aemilian, Romanus, Africanus, and
Marcellinus (c. 416)*

After we had gathered in solemn conclave in the church at
Carthage, according to our custom, and were holding a synod
on various subjects, our fellow priest Orosius[3] brought us a
letter from our holy brothers and fellow priests, Heros and
Lazarus,[4] the substance of which we have decided to append
to this. After reading it, we make known that Pelagius and

---

1 Pope Innocent I.
2 These sixty-eight were all African bishops. Although Augustine is not
named in the list, this report is attributed to him.
3 Cf. Letter 166 n. 3.
4 Bishops of Arles and of Aix, respectively. These Gallic bishops were
driven from their sees and went to Palestine, where they had given to
Eulogius, primate of Caesarea, a treatise against Pelagius and Caelestius.

Caelestius[5] are the originators of an accursed error, which is a subject of anathema to all of us. As a consequence, we asked for a review of the disturbance raised under the name of Caelestius here in the church at Carthage about five years ago. When the report had been read, as your Holiness will be able to note from the documents appended, although there was clearly an undisputed verdict by the bishop's court at that time, by which this great sore seemed to have been cut out from the Church, we have decreed, after general deliberation, that the authors of opinions of this kind, even though the said Caelestius attained to the priesthood afterward, should be subject to anathema unless they have previously and openly anathematized these teachings. Thus, if their own recovery cannot be brought about, at least those who have been or can be deceived by them might be cured by the publication of this sentence against them.

Consequently, Lord and Brother, we have thought it best to transmit this report to your holy Charity, that the authority of the Apostolic See may be added to the decisions of our insignificance, in order to safeguard the welfare of many and to correct the perversity of some. In their detestable disputations these latter argue for freedom of will, or, rather, they elevate it to proud and sacrilegious heights, leaving no scope for the grace of God, which makes us Christians, which, in fact, makes the action of our will truly free, by delivering us from subjection to our carnal passions, according to the Lord's words: 'If the son shall make you free, you shall be free indeed';[6] and this is the help which faith asks and obtains in Christ Jesus our Lord. They affirm, as we have learned from brethren who have gone so far as to read their books, that the grace of God is to be reduced to the extent that

---

5 Cf. Letter 157 n. 71.
6 1 John 8.36.

He is supposed to have made and created the nature of man such that he is able by his own will to fulfill the law of God, whether written by nature in his heart, or given to him in books, but that this law also belongs to grace because God has given it to men as a help.[7]

But they refuse either to acknowledge fully or to oppose openly that grace by which, as it is written, we are Christians; which the Apostle preaches in the words: 'I am delighted with the law of God according to the inward man, but I see another law in my members fighting against the law of my mind and captivating me in the law of sin, that is in my members. Unhappy man that I am, who shall deliver me from the body of this death? The grace of God by Jesus Christ our Lord.'[8] But this is what they do when they constantly try to convince sensual men who 'perceive not the things that are of the spirit of God,'[9] that human nature alone can suffice to perform good works perfectly and to fulfill the commandments of God. They pay no attention to what is written: 'The Spirit helpeth our infirmity,' and 'It is not of him that willeth nor of him that runneth, but of God that showeth mercy,' and that 'We are one body in Christ, and every one members one of another, having different gifts according to the grace that is given us,'[10] and 'By the grace of God I am what I am and his grace in me hath not been void; but I have labored more abundantly than all they, yet not I but the grace of God with me,' and 'Thanks be to God who hath given us the victory through our Lord Jesus Christ,'[11] and 'Not that we are sufficient to think anything as of our-

7 Isa. 8.20 (Septuagint).
8 Rom. 7.22-25.
9 1 Cor. 2.14.
10 Rom. 8.26; 9.16; 12.5.6.
11 1 Cor. 15.10,57.

selves, but our sufficiency is from God,' and 'We have this treasure in earthen vessels; that the excellency may be of the power of God and not of us,'[12] and other pasages so innumerable that a volume could not contain them if we were to try to cull them from all the Scriptures. We fear we may seem to have been forward in citing these passages to you, which you have greater reason to preach from the Apostolic See; but we do it because we suffer frequently from those who are bold enough to rise up against us, in proportion to our feebleness, however much any of us may be considered more adept in preaching the word of God.

If your Reverence has believed that Pelagius was justly acquitted of heresy by the action of the bishops which was accomplished in the East,[13] it still remains urgent that his false doctrine, which now has many supporters scattered in various places, ought to be anathematized by the authority of the Apostolic See. Let your Holiness have compassion on us in your pastoral heart, and consider what a baneful and deadly thing it is for the sheep of Christ that a necessary consequence of their sacrilegious argument is that we ought not to pray lest we enter into temptation, as the Lord warned His disciples,[14] and set forth in the prayer which He taught,[15] or lest our faith fail as He testified that He had prayed for the Apostle Peter.[16] For, if these things are placed in our power through the capability of nature and the freedom of the will, anyone can see that it is useless to ask them of the Lord, and deceitful to pray, when we ask in prayer for what our nature so constituted possesses by its adequate strength.

12 2 Cor. 3.5; 4.7.
13 He had been acquitted by two assemblies of bishops in 415, one at Jerusalem, one at Diospolis. This acquittal had been conditonal on a denial of the errors condemned at Cathage in 411.
14 Matt. 26.41; Mark 14.38; Luke 22.46.
15 Matt. 6.13; Luke 11.4.
16 Luke 22.32.

In that case, the Lord Jesus ought not to have said: 'Watch and pray,' but only 'Watch, lest ye enter into temptation,' nor should He have said to the blessed chief of the Apostles: 'I have prayed for thee,' but 'I warn thee, or command thee, or enjoin on thee that thy faith fail not.'

That claim of theirs is opposed to our acts of blessing, and makes us seem to speak idle words over the people when we ask anything of the Lord for them, as, that they may please Him by living righteously and piously, or those graces which the Apostle asked in prayer for the faithful, saying: 'I bow my knees to the Father of our Lord Jesus Christ, of whom all paternity in heaven and earth is named; that he would grant you according to the riches of his glory to be strengthened by his Spirit with might.'[17] If, then, we wished to bless the people by saying: 'Grant them, O Lord, to be strengthened by thy Spirit with might,' the teaching of these heretics will gainsay us by claiming that our free will is denied by asking from God what is in our own power; if we wish to be strengthened with might, they say, we can do it by that capacity of our nature which we do not receive now, but did receive when we were created.

They also say that little children do not have to be baptized to secure salvation, and thus, by this deadly doctrine, they bring eternal death upon them by promising that even though not baptized they will have everlasting life, because they do not belong to those of whom the Lord said: 'For the Son of man is come to seek and to save that which was lost.'[18] They say that infants had not been lost, that there was nothing in them requiring salvation or redemption at such a price, because there was nothing depraved in them, nothing that held them captive under the power of the Devil, and that

---

17 Eph. 3.14-16.
18 Luke 19.10; Matt. 18.11.

what we read about blood shed for the remission of sins[19] does not apply to them. It is true that Caelestius admitted in the church at Carthage that according to his book the redemption of children, also, was accomplished by the baptism of Christ, but many of those who appear to be or to have been his disciples do not cease to proclaim these wicked theories, striving thereby, to the utmost of their power, to overturn the foundations of the Christian faith. Hence, even if Pelagius and Caelestius have been converted, or say that they never held those views, and that none of the writings produced against them is theirs, and there is no reason to convict them of lying, nevertheless, speaking generally, if anyone holds as dogma and asserts that human nature is able to get the better of its own sins and carry out the commandments of God, and is thereby discovered to be an enemy of the grace of God which is so clearly proclaimed in the utterances of the saints, and if anyone affirms that little children are not delivered from perdition by the baptism of Christ, thereby receiving eternal salvation, let him be anathema. Whatever other charges are brought against them, your Reverence will, no doubt, pass this judgment, after you have examined the report of the action taken by the bishops in the same case in the East. We shall then all rejoice in the mercy of God. Pray for us, blessed lord and pope.

---

19 Matt. 26.28.

*176. To the most holy Pope Innocent, deservedly revered and
     honored in Christ we, the following,*[1] *send greet-
     ings in the Lord from the Council of Milevis, to
     wit: the venerable Silvanus, Valentine, Aurelius,
     Donatus, Restitutus, Lucian, Alypius, Augustine,
     Placentius, Severus, Fortunatus, Possidius, No-
     vatus, Secundus, Maurentius, Leo, Faustinian,
     Cresconius, Melchus, Litorius, Fortunatus, Do-
     natus, Pontician, Saturninus, Cresconius, Hono-
     rius, Cresconius, Lucius, Adeodatus, Processus,
     Secundus, Felix, Asiaticus, Rufinus, Faustinus,
     Servus, Terence, Cresconius, Sperantius, Quadra-
     tus, Lucillus, Sabinus, Faustinus, Cresconius,
     Victor, Gigantius, Possidonius, Antoninus, Inno-
     cent, Felix, Antoninus, Victor, Honoratus,
     Donatus, Peter, Praesidius, Cresconius, Lam-
     padius, Delphinus (c. 416)*

Whereas, by a particular gift of His grace the Lord has
placed you in the Apostolic See and has given to our times
a man like you to reign over us, it would be more possible
for us to be charged with the guilt of negligence if we
failed to report to your Reverence matters which need to be
made known for the benefit of the Church than for you to
receive such suggestions coldly or negligently, we therefore
beg you to deign to apply your pastoral care to the great
perils of the weak members of Christ.

A new heresy is trying to break out, indeed a most ruinous
one, through the effort of the enemies of the grace of Christ,
who seek by their wicked arguments to deprive us even of
the Lord's Prayer. For, although the Lord taught us to say:
'Forgive us our debts as we also forgive our debtors,' they
say that it is possible for man in this life, by a knowledge

---

1 The order of bishops appears to be by seniority.

of the commandments of God, without the help of the Saviour's grace, to attain to such perfection of holiness, by the sole force of free will, that it is not even necessary to say: 'Forgive us our debts.' In that case, the words that follow: 'Lead us not into temptation,'[2] are not to be taken in the sense that we ought to ask for divine help lest we be tempted to fall into sin, but that this is in our own power, and the will of man alone suffices to fulfill it. If all this were in the power of man, it would make a liar of the Apostle when he says: 'It is not of him that willeth nor of him that runneth, but of God that showeth mercy,'[3] and 'God is faithful who will not suffer you to be tempted above that which you are able, but will make also with temptation issue, that you may be able to bear it.'[4] It would also make the Lord a liar when He said to the Apostle Peter: 'I have prayed for thee that thy faith fail not'[5] and 'Watch and pray lest ye enter into temptation.'[6] They claim, also, that little children will possess eternal life without the sacramental waters of Christian grace, thus, with anything but Christian boldness, making void what the Apostle says: 'By one man sin entered into the world, and by sin death, and so death passed upon all men in whom all have sinned,'[7] and in another passage: 'As in Adam all die, so also in Christ all shall be made alive.'[8]

We pass over, then, their many other contentions in which they go contrary to the holy Scriptures, and we single out, for the present, these two by which they try to undermine everything that makes us Christian, everything that is the support of faithful hearts, namely, that we are not to ask God to be our helper against the evil of sin and in our

2 Matt. 6.12,13; Luke 11.4.
3 Rom. 9.16.
4 1 Cor. 10.13.
5 Luke 22.32.
6 Matt. 26.41; Mark 14.38; Luke 22.40.
7 Rom. 5.12.
8 1 Cor. 15.22.

practice of goodness, and that the sacrament of Christian grace is not to be conferred on babies to enable them to attain eternal life. In making these errors known to your apostolic heart, we have no need to say much or to enlarge upon this great impiety by our words, since without doubt they move you so deeply that you could not possibly neglect to correct them, lest they creep in more widely and infect or, rather, destroy many souls, turning them in the name of Christ away from the grace of Christ.

Pelagius and Caelestius are named as the originators of this destructive error, and we would rather see them cured of it in the Church than cut off from the Church through despair of saving them, unless some necessity presses. It is reported that one of them, Caelestius, even attained to the priesthood in Asia, but your Holiness has probably been better informed by the Church at Carthage on the action taken in his regard a few years ago. Pelagius, however, as we learn from letters sent by some of our brethren, is established at Jerusalem and is said to lead many astray. But many more, who have been able to examine more carefully into the meaning of his teaching, are actively opposing him in defense of the grace of Christ and the truth of the Catholic faith; in the vanguard of these is your holy son, our brother and fellow priest, Jerome.

Trusting in the merciful help of the Lord our God, which deigns to guide you in your plans and hear you in your prayers, we think that those who hold these distorted and dangerous views will readily submit to the authority of your Holiness, which is derived from the authority of the holy Scriptures, so that we may congratulate you on their conversion rather than grieve over their loss, most holy lord. But, no matter what choice they make, your Reverence surely sees that immediate and speedy provision must be made for the others whom they are able to trap in their snares in great numbers if this is not made known to them.

We are addressing this written report to your Holiness from the Council of Numidia, imitating the Church at Carthage and our brother bishops of the Carthaginian province, having heard that they have written on this matter to the Apostolic See which you so blessedly adorn.

May you increase in the grace of the Lord and be mindful of us, most holy lord, honored and saintly Pope, worthy of our veneration in Christ.[9]

177. Aurelius, Alypius, Augustine, Evodius, and Possidius give greeting to the most holy lord, Pope Innocent, their deservedly honored brother (c. 416)

We have sent your Holiness letters from the two councils of the province of Carthage and of Numidia, signed by a large number of bishops. These letters condemn the enemies of the grace of Christ, who trust in their own virtue and say, in effect, to their Creator: 'You have made us men, but we have made ourselves good.' They say that human nature is free, so that they look for no liberator; and safe, so that they consider a saviour superfluous; they claim that this nature is so strong of its own strength, acquired once and for all at the moment of creation, without any helping grace from Him who created it, that it can subdue and extinguish all passions and overcome all temptations. 'Many are they who rise up against us and say to our soul: There is no salvation for him in his God.'[1] But the family of Christ, which says: 'When I am weak, then I am strong,'[2] and to which the Lord says: 'I am thy salvation,'[3] its heart quivering with fear and trembling,

---

9 In another handwriting.

1 Cf. Ps. 3.2,3.
2 2 Cor. 12.10.
3 Ps. 34.3.

awaits the help of the Lord even through the charity of
your Reverence.

We hear that there are many in the city of Rome, where
he lived for a long time, who take his side for various reasons;
some, indeed, because they are said to have convinced you
on such points, but many more who do not believe that he
held such views, especially as great publicity has been given
to ecclesiastical decisions in the East, where he is staying, by
which they think he has been cleared. But, if the bishops in
the East did indeed pronounce him a Catholic, we must
believe that it was done only because he said that he admitted
the grace of God and said that man can live a good life by
his own will and effort, yet not so as to deny the help of
God's grace. By these words the Catholic bishops could have
understood no other grace of God except that of which they
are accustomed to read in the books of God and to preach to
the people of God, the same, obviously, of which the Apostle
says: 'I cast not away the grace of God, for if justice be by
the law, then Christ died in vain,'[4] the same grace, beyond
doubt, by which we are justified from sin and saved from
weakness, but not that grace in our own will with which we
were created. For, if those bishops had understood him to
mean that grace which we possess in common with the
wicked, with those who share human nature with us, and
to deny the grace by which we are Christians and sons of
God, what Catholic prelate could have borne the sight of
him, much less have listened to him with patience? Therefore,
the judges are not to be blamed because they heard the
term grace according to Church usage without knowing what
meaning such men usually scatter through their books or
repeat in the hearing of their followers.

It is not a question of Pelagius alone, because it may be
that he has been converted—and may it be so!—but of so

4 Gal. 2.21.

many who argue noisily, dragging down weak and untutored souls as their conquest, wearing out those who are strong and well grounded in the faith by their very persistence until everything is full of them. Therefore, he ought either to be summoned to Rome and carefully questioned on the kind of grace he admitted, if he did admit it, whether it is the grace by which men are helped not to sin and to lead a good life, or this matter should be taken up with him by letter. And if you find that he says grace is what ecclesiastical and apostolic truth teach that it is, then he should be absolved by the Church without any scruple, without any lurking ambiguity, and that is really the time to rejoice at his being cleared.

For, if he says that grace is free will, or grace is forgiveness of sin, or grace is the commandment of the Law, he mentions nothing of what belongs to the overcoming of concupiscence and temptation, through the help furnished by the Holy Spirit, 'Whom he hath poured forth upon us abundantly,'[5] 'Who ascended into heaven and led captivity captive; he gave gifts to men.'[6] Hence we pray that we may be able to overcome the temptation to sin, that 'the Spirit of God,' of whom we have received the pledge, 'may help our infirmity.'[7] But when a man says in prayer: 'Lead us not into temptation,' he certainly does not pray to be a man, which he is by nature; he does not pray to possess free will, which he received when his nature itself was created; he does not pray for the forgiveness of sin, because in a previous phrase the prayer says: 'Forgive us our debts,' nor does he pray to receive the commandment; he manifestly does pray to fulfill the commandment. If he is led into temptation, that is, fails under temptation, it is plain that he commits sin, which is against

5 Titus 3.6.
6 Eph. 4.8; Ps. 67.19.
7 Cf. 2 Cor. 1.22; 5.5; Rom. 8.26.

the commandment. He prays, therefore, not to commit sin, that is, not to do any evil; that is what the Apostle asks in prayer for the Corinthians when he says: 'Now we pray the Lord that you may do no evil.'[8] From this it is quite clear that, although the freedom of the will is called into play in refraining from sin, that is, in doing no evil, its power is not efficacious unless there is help for its weakness. Therefore, the Lord's prayer itself is the clearest testimony of grace. Let him admit this and we will rejoice over him as being either in the right or set right.

There has to be a distinction between the Law and grace. The Law knows how to command; grace, how to help. The Law would not command if there were no free will, nor would grace help if the will were sufficient. We are commanded to have understanding when the Scripture says: 'Do not become like the horse and the mule that have no understanding,'[9] yet we pray to have understanding when it says: 'Give me understanding that I may learn thy commandments.'[10] We are commanded to have wisdom when it says: 'You fools, be wise at last,'[11] but we pray to have wisdom when it says: 'If any of you want wisdom, let him ask of God who giveth to all men abundantly and upbraideth not.'[12] We are commanded to have continence when it says: 'Let your loins be girt,'[13] but we pray to have continence when it says: 'As I knew that no one could be continent except God gave it, and this also was a point of wisdom to know whose gift it was, I went to the Lord and besought him.'[14] Finally, not to be too lengthy in listing all

---

8 Cf. 2 Cor. 13.7.
9 Ps. 31.9.
10 Cf. Ps. 118.125.
11 Ps. 93.8.
12 James 1.5.
13 Luke 12.35. Goldbacher indicates a lacuna at this point.
14 Wisd. 8.21.

the rest, we are commanded not to do evil when it says:
'Decline from evil,'[15] but we pray not to do evil when it
says: 'We pray the Lord that you do no evil.'[16] We are
commanded to do good when it says: 'Decline from evil and
do good,'[17] but we pray to do good when it says: 'We cease
not to pray for you, asking,'[18] and among other things that
he asks he mentions: 'That you may walk worthy of God
in all things pleasing, in every good work and good word.'[18]
As then we acknowledge the part played by the will when
these commands are given, so let him acknowledge the part
played by grace when these petitions are offered.

We are sending your Reverence a book given to us by
certain religious and honorable young men, servants of God,
whose names we do not withhold—they are called Timasius
and James[19]—and, as we have heard and as you also deign
to know, gave up the hope which they had in the world on
the urging of the said Pelagius, and are now serving God in
continence. When, some time ago, they were at length freed
from their erroneous opinion through some little service of
ours, by the Lord's inspiration, they produced the same book,
saying it was the work of Pelagius,[20] and they earnestly begged
that it might be answered. This has been done; the answer
itself has been sent to them as a reply to their letter; they
have written back thanking us. We are sending you both the
answer and the request which drew the answer, and, not to
cause you too much trouble, we have marked out the passages
which we beg you not to refuse to examine. They show how,
when the objection had been made to him that he was denying the grace of God, he answered in such a way as not to

15 Ps. 36.27.
16 2 Cor. 13.7.
17 Ps. 36.27.
18 Cf. Col. 1.9,10.
19 Cf. Letter 168.
20 De natura. Augustine's reply was De natura et gratia.

admit its existence except as the nature with which God created us.

However, if he says that the book is not his, that the above-mentioned passages in the book are not his, we do not continue the argument; let him solemnly repudiate them and openly confess that grace which Christian doctrine proves and preaches as the intimate possession of Christians, which is not nature, but that by which nature is saved and helped, not by teaching resounding in its ears, or by any visible assistance, as if it were something planted and watered from without, but by the inner action of the Spirit, and His hidden mercy, as God 'Who giveth the increase'[21] is wont to act. If, by some unobjectionable reasoning, the grace of God is identified with the favor of our creation, by which we escape from nothingness, by which we are something more than a corpse which is not alive, a tree which has no consciousness, or a sheep which has no understanding, by which we become men with being and life and consciousness and understanding, able to give thanks for this great benefit to our Creator, and if in that sense it might be called grace because it is not granted through the merits of any previous actions, but by the unsolicited goodness of God, still there is another grace by which we are predestined to be called, justified, and endowed with glory, which makes us able to say: 'If God be for us, who is against us? He that spared not even his own Son but delivered him up for all of us.'[22]

This is the grace that was being called into question when those whom Pelagius had offended and disturbed told him that he was making war on grace by the arguments in which he asserted that human nature, through its own free will, was sufficiently strong, not only to carry out the divine commandments but even to fulfill them perfectly. But the teach-

---

21 1 Cor. 3.7.
22 Rom. 8.31,32.

ing of the Apostles gives the name of grace to that gift by which we are saved and justified through our faith in Christ, and of this it is written: 'I cast not away the grace of God, for if justice be by the law, then Christ died in vain.'[23] Of this grace it is written: 'You are made void of Christ you who are justified in the law; you are fallen from grace.'[24] Of this grace it is written: 'And if by grace it is not now by works; otherwise grace is no more grace.'[25] This is the grace of which it is written: 'Now to him that worketh, the reward is not reckoned according to grace but according to debt. But to him that worketh not yet believeth in him that justifieth the ungodly, his faith is reputed to justice.'[26] There are many other passages which you can recall for yourself, with your prudent understanding and your well-known gift of expression. As to that other grace by which we are created as human beings, even though we understand that it may reasonably be called grace, it would be surprising if we found it so used in any of the authentic writings of the Prophets, of the Gospel, or of the Apostles.

Therefore, since the request has been made to him in regard to this grace so well known to the Christian and Catholic faithful that he cease to attack it, why, when the same person acting as objector reproached him with that passage in his book, so that he might answer it and clear himself, did he answer only that the nature of created man shows forth the grace of the Creator? Why did he say that this nature, without sin, can fulfill justice by its free will, with the help of divine grace which God gave to man as part of the endowment of his nature? A proper answer to him would be: 'Then is the scandal of the cross made void,'[27]

---

23 Gal. 2.21.
24 Gal. 5.4.
25 Rom. 11.6.
26 Rom. 4.4,5.
27 Gal. 5.1.

'then Christ died in vain.'[28] For, if He had not died for our sins and risen for our justification,[29] if he had not ascended on high, taking captivity captive, if he had not given gifts to men,[30] then that endowment of nature which he defends would not exist in man.

But, perhaps there was no commandment of God and that is why Christ died. On the contrary, there was a commandment and it was 'holy and just and good.'[31] Long before Christ it had been said: 'Thou shalt not covet';[32] long before, it had been said: 'Thou shalt love thy neighbor as thyself,'[33] a phrase which, as the Apostle says, expresses the fulfillment of the whole Law.[34] And as no one loves himself unless he loves God, the Lord says that the whole Law and the Prophets depend on these two commandments.[35] But these two commandments had long before been given to man from on high. Perhaps the eternal reward of justice had not yet been made. Pelagius himself does not say this, for he wrote in his letter that the kingdom of heaven had been promised in the Old Testament. If then, it was possible for human nature, through its free will, to attain to perfect justice, if the commandment of God's Law, holy, just, and good, was already in existence, if the promise of eternal reward had already been made, then Christ died in vain.

Therefore, justice does not come through the Law, nor through the innate power of human nature, but by faith and the gift of God through our Lord Jesus Christ, the one Mediator of God and men,[36] and if, in the fullness of time,[37]

28 Gal. 2.21.
29 Rom. 4.25.
30 Eph. 4.8; Ps. 67.19.
31 Rom. 7.12.
32 Exod. 20.17.
33 Lev. 19.18.
34 Rom. 13.8,9.
35 Matt. 22.37-40.
36 1 Tim. 2.5.
37 Gal. 4.4.

He had not died for our sins and risen again for our justification, it is clear that the faith of the men of old would have been made void and so would ours. But, if faith were made void, what justice would remain to man since the just man lives by faith?[38] 'Wherefore as by one man sin entered into the world, and by sin death, and so death passed upon all men in whom all have sinned,'[39] it is not to be doubted that no one ever has been or is now delivered by his own power from the body of this death, where another law fights against the law of the mind,[40] because that power was lost and is in need of a redeemer, it was wounded and is in need of a saviour. What did deliver him was the grace of God through faith in the one Mediator of God and men, the man Christ Jesus, who being God made man and continuing to be God, was made man and remade what He Himself had made.

I think Pelagius overlooks the fact that faith in Christ which afterwards came to be revealed was hidden in the times of our fathers, yet they were redeemed by the grace of God, and so are all the members of the human race in all times who, by a secret, irrefragable decree of God, are capable of being redeemed. Hence, the Apostle says: 'Having the same spirit of faith'—no doubt the same as they had—'as it is written: I believed for which cause I have spoken: we also believe for which cause we speak also.'[41] For that reason the Mediator himself said: 'Abraham desired to see my day, he saw it and was glad';[42] so, too, Melchisedech, offering the sacrament of the Lord's table, knew that he prefigured Christ's eternal priesthood.[43]

---

38 Hab. 2.4; Rom. 1.17; Gal. 3.11; Heb. 10.38.
39 Rom. 5.12.
40 Rom. 7.23,24.
41 2 Cor. 4.13; Ps. 115.10.
42 John 8.56.
43 Gen. 14.18.

Now that the Law has been given in writing, which the Apostle says entered in that sin might abound,[44] and of which he said: 'If therefore the inheritance be of the law, it is no more of promise; but God gave it to Abraham by promise. Why then was the law? It was set because of transgression, until the seed should come to whom he made the promise, being ordained by angels in the hand of a mediator. Now a mediator is not of one, but God is one. Was the law then against the promises of God? God forbid. For if there had been a law given which could give life, verily justice should have been by the law. But the Scripture hath concluded all under sin, that the promise by the faith of Jesus Christ might be given to them that believe,'[45] is it not quite clear that what the Law accomplished was to make sin known and to increase transgression—'for where there is no law, neither is there transgression.'[46] Thus, against the victory of sin there would be recourse to divine grace which is contained in the promises; thus, the Law would not be against the promises of God, because through it comes knowledge of sin, and abundance of sin from transgression of the Law, that thereby men may seek their deliverance through the promises of God, that is, the grace of God. Thus, there would be the beginning of justice in man, yet not his own but God's, given him by the gift of God.

But even now there are some, as there were then among the Jews, of whom it is said: 'Not knowing the justice of God and seeking to establish their own, they have not submitted themselves to the justice of God.'[47] No doubt they think they are justified by the Law, and that their own free will enables them to keep it. This means that their justice is derived from

44 Rom. 8.20.
45 Gal. 3.18-22.
46 Rom. 4.15.
47 Rom. 10.3.

their own human nature, not given by divine grace, which
is the reason of its being called the justice of God. Again on
this subject it is written: 'For by the law is the knowledge of
sin. But now without the law the justice of God is made
manifest, being witnessed by the law and the prophets.'[48]
When he says 'made manifest' he shows that it then existed
but was like that dew which Gideon asked; then it was not
visible on the fleece, but now it is made manifest on the
ground around.[49] Since, then, the Law without grace could
not have been the death of sin but its strength—as it is
written: 'The sting of death is sin and the strength of sin
is the law'[50]—as many flee for refuge from the face of sin
enthroned to grace, lying manifest, as it were, on the ground,
so at that time few fled to it for refuge, invisible as it were,
on the fleece. Indeed, this division of times belongs to the
depth of the riches of the wisdom and of the knowledge of
God, of which it is said: 'How incomprehensible are his
judgments and how unsearchable his ways!'[51]

Therefore, if it was not the innate power of a nature, weak
and needy and depraved and sold into the slavery of sin, that
justified the godly patriarchs who lived by faith before the
time of the Law or at the very time of the Law, and if it
was the grace of God which justified them by faith, and
which, coming into the open by revelation, does still justify
men, let Pelagius solemnly repudiate the writings in which
he argues against it, through ignorance if not through
obstinacy, defending the innate power of nature to win the
victory over sin and to fulfill the commandments. On the
other hand, if he says that the writings are not his, or that
they have been inserted into his by his enemies, let him still

---

48 Rom. 3.20,21.
49 Judges 6.36-40.
50 1 Cor. 15.56.
51 Rom. 11.33.

pronounce anathema against what he says is not his, and
let him condemn it, in obedience to the paternal exhortation
and authority of your Holiness. If he is willing to do that,
let him learn how to remove from the Church a scandal so
burdensome and so dangerous to himself, a scandal which
his hearers and his misguided lovers spread around unceas-
ingly in every direction. For, if they knew that the same
book which they think or know is his had been anathematized and condemned by him, in submission to the
authority of the Catholic bishops and especially of your
Holiness, which we are very certain has great weight with
him, we think they would not dare to go on speaking against
the grace of God, which was revealed through the Passion and
Resurrection of Christ, but they would cease to trouble the
hearts of simple and faithful Christians; or, rather, with the
help of the Lord's mercy, together with our joint forces and
your prayers, burning with charity and piety, they would
trust in that same grace, not in their own strength, for their
eternal happiness as well as for their justice and holiness in
this life. A letter has been written to him by one of us, to
whom he had addressed some writings in his own defense,
sending them by a certain deacon from the East, but a
citizen of Hippo,[52] but we have thought it better in our
judgment to forward it to your Blessedness, asking that you
would deign to send it to him yourself. In that way he will
not disdain to read it, having regard rather to the sender
than to the writer.

As to what they say of the ability of man to remain sinless
and to keep the commandments of God with ease, if he wills
it, when they add that this is achieved by the help of grace,
which, however, is revealed and imparted through the Incarnation of the only-begotten Son, it seems that this statement can be tolerated; still, since a difficulty can reasonably

---

52 Charus, a deacon in Palestine, but by birth a citizen of Hippo.

arise as to where and when it is accomplished in us by the said grace that we should thenceforth be sinless, and whether it is in this life, when 'the flesh lusteth against the spirit,'[53] or in that other life 'when this saying that is written shall come to pass: 'O death, where is thy victory? O death, where is thy sting? Now the sting of death is sin.'[54] This should be examined more carefully because of some other persons who have had the erroneous idea and have published it in their writings, that even in this life it is possible for man to be sinless, not from the time of his birth, but from that of his conversion from sin to righteousness, and from a bad life to a good one.[55] This is the meaning they give to what is written of Zachary and Elizabeth that ' they walked in all the justifications of the Lord without blame.'[56] This expression, 'without blame,' they took to mean 'without sin'; not, indeed, that they deny the assisting grace of our Lord—on the contrary, they piously admit it, as we find in other passages of their writings that this help is not derived from the natural spirit of man but comes originally from the Spirit of God. It seems that they have not paid sufficient attention to the fact that Zachary was a priest, and that all priests at that time were obliged by the Law of God to offer sacrifice first for their own sins and then for those of the people.[57] Therefore, as it is now proved by the sacrifice of prayer that we are not sinless, since we are commanded to say: 'Forgive us our debts,'[58] so it was proved then by the sacrifice of animal victims that the priests were not sinless, since they were commanded to offer the victim for their own sins.

---

53 Gal. 5.19.
54 1 Cor. 15.54-56.
55 Cf. St. Ambrose, *Expositio Evangelii Lucae* 1.17 (ed. Schenkl pp. 2-25).
56 Luke 1.6.
57 Lev. 9.7; Heb. 7.27.
58 Matt. 6.12; Luke 11.4.

But, if our circumstances are such that we do indeed make some progress in this life by the grace of the Saviour, when covetousness declines and charity increases, it is in the other life that we reach perfection, when covetousness is extinguished and charity made perfect. That saying, 'Whosoever is born of God, sinneth not,'[59] is undoubtedly meant to apply to pure charity which alone does not sin. Obviously, it is the charity which is to be increased and perfected that belongs to the birth which is of God, not the covetousness which is to be diminished and destroyed; yet, as long as this latter is in our members, it fights by a certain law of its own against the law of the mind,[60] whereas he that is born of God, who does not obey his own desires, nor yield his members as instruments of iniquity unto sin,[61] can say: 'Now it is no longer I that do it but sin that dwelleth in me.'[62]

Whatever the status of that question that, even if man is not found in this life without sin, it is stated that he can become sinless by the help of grace and the Spirit of God, and that he should strive and ask that he may become so, there is a tolerable chance of going wrong, and it is not a diabolical impiety but a human error to assert that this is something to work and pray for, even though there were no proof of what they assert—they believe it is possible because it is certainly praiseworthy to wish it. It is enough for us that no one of the faithful, in whatever advanced stage of high virtue he may be found, should dare to say that he has no need to make the petition of the Lord's prayer: 'Forgive us our debts,' or should say that he is sinless and not self-deceived so that truth is not in him, although he should now be living a blameless life. It is not merely some kind of

59 1 John 3.9; 5.18.
60 Rom. 7.23.
61 Rom. 6.12,13.
62 Rom. 7.20.

human temptation but a grave sin that brings him blame.

Your Blessedness will see, from the defense made in the report, the rest of the objections that have been made against him, and will no doubt judge them accordingly. Surely, the most gentle sweetness of your heart will pardon us for sending your Holiness a more lengthy letter than perhaps you wished. We are not pouring our little trickle back into your ample fountain to increase it, but the trial of our time is no slight one, and we pray to be delivered from it by Him to whom we say: 'Lead us not into temptation.' We wish to be re-assured by you that this trickle of ours, however scant, flows from the same fountainhead as your abundant stream, and we desire the consolation of your writings, drawn from our common share of the one grace.

178. Augustine gives greeting in the Lord to the saintly lord, his brother and fellow priest, Hilary,[1] revered in the truth of Christ (c. 416)

When our honored son, Palladius,[2] was on the point of sailing from our shore, he conferred rather than asked a favor by requesting me to commend him to your Benignity and myself to your prayers, most holy lord and brother, revered in the charity of Christ. Since I do this, your Holiness surely will do what we both rely on you to do. From the above-mentioned bearer your Holiness will hear what news there is of us, since I know your Charity is as anxious for us as we are for you. But I will tell you briefly what is most important. A new heresy, enemy of the grace of Christ, is trying to rise against

---

1 Believed to have been a bishop of Narbonne; not to be confused with Hilary of Arles, who was not a bishop before 428, or with Hilary of Sicily, the layman to whom Letters 156 and 157 are addressed.

2 He was later sent by Pope Celestine to reclaim Britain to the faith.

the Church of Christ, but has not yet broken away from the Church, namely, that one proposed by men who dare to attribute so much power to human weakness as to claim that we owe to the grace of God only the fact that we are created with free will and with the possibility of not sinning, and that we receive the commandments of God which are fulfilled by us, but that we need no divine help to enable us to keep and fulfill the same commandments. However, they say that the forgiveness of sins is necessary for us because we are not able to undo the evil deeds which we have committed in the past, but that the human will, by its natural strength, without any subsequent help of the grace of God, is adequate for avoiding and overcoming future sins and triumphing over all temptations, through its own ability; and that babies do not need the grace of the Saviour to deliver them from perdition by His baptism, because they have not inherited any contagion of damnation from Adam.

Your Reverence can see with us how opposed these teachings are to the grace of God, which has been granted to the human race by Jesus Christ our Lord, and how they aim at overturning the foundations of the whole Christian faith. So we must not fail to warn you to be on guard with pastoral care against men of that kind, whom we would certainly rather see healed in the Church than cut off from it. While writing this, we have learned that a decree of a council of bishops has been passed against them in the Church at Carthage, and is to be sent to the venerable Pope Innocent, and we of the Council of Numidia also have written in like tenor to the Apostolic See.

All of us who place our hope in Christ ought to resist this deadly impiety and unite in condemning and anathematizing it. It goes contrary to our very prayers, allowing us, it is true, to say: 'Forgive us our debts as we forgive our debtors,'[3]

---

3 Matt. 6.12; Luke 11.4.

yet so allowing it as to claim that man in this corruptible body which is a load on the soul[4] can by his own strength attain to such a height of goodness that he no longer needs to say: 'Forgive us our debts.' The words that follow: 'Lead us not into temptation,' they do not interpret to mean that we are to pray God to help us to overcome temptation, but only to keep us from being overwhelmed corporeally by on-rushing physical disaster, because, as it is left to our own power by the capacity of nature to overcome temptation, we should think it useless to ask this in prayer. It is not possible for us in one short letter to summarize all or even many of the arguments of such impious nature, all the more because, while I write, the bearers who are about to sail leave me no further time. I think I am not putting a burden on your holy feelings, but I could not refrain from telling you of the necessity of warding off this great evil with all watchfulness, by the help of the Lord.

179. Augustine gives greeting in the Lord to the holy lord, his deservedly revered brother and fellow bishop, John[1] (c. 416)

I do not in the least venture to resent the fact that I have not been honored with a letter from your Holiness; I would rather believe that you had no messenger than suspect that your Reverence held me in low esteem, saintly lord, deservedly revered brother. But now, as I have heard that Luke, a servant of God, by whom I am sending this, will return

---

4 Wisd. 9.15.

1 Bishop of Jerusalem, 386-417. He had not accepted the decrees of the Council of Carthage against Pelagius and Caelestius, but had held his own synod in 415. Another synod at Diospolis in 416 favored Pelagius but was later reversed.

shortly, I shall give hearty thanks to the Lord and to your Benignity, if you will be so kind as to visit me by letter. As to Pelagius, our brother and your son, whom I hear you hold in great affection, I suggest that you show him this affection in such wise that people who know him and who have listened to him with attention may not imagine that your Holiness is being deceived by him.

Some of his disciples, in fact, young men of very good birth, well-versed in the liberal arts,[2] gave up their worldly prospects at his urging and devoted themselves to the service of God. But when they noticed certain teachings opposed to the sound doctrine contained in the Gospel of the Saviour, and formulated in the preaching of the Apostles, that is, when they found that they were arguing against the grace of God which makes us Christians, by which 'we in spirit, by faith, wait for the hope of justice,'[3] they began to return to the truth through our warnings and they gave me a book which they said was written by the same Pelagius, asking that I should rather be the one to answer it.[4] Seeing that it was my duty to do this, in order to remove that hateful error more completely from their hearts, I read it and replied to it.

In that book he calls the grace of God nothing but our nature through which we are endowed with free will. As for that grace which holy Scripture commends in innumerable passages, teaching that by it we are justified, that is, made holy, and helped by the mercy of God to perform or complete every good work—something which even the prayers of the saints manifest very clearly, for they ask of the Lord what the Lord commands—this grace he not only passes over in silence, but also makes many statements against. He asserts and strongly insists that human nature,

---

2 Timasius and James; cf. Letter 168 and 177.
3 Gal. 5.5.
4 *De natura;* cf. Letter 177 n. 20.

through its free will alone, is competent to do the works of justice and to keep all the commandments of God. Anyone can see, after reading that book, how he attacks the grace of God of which the Apostle says: 'Unhappy man that I am, who shall deliver me from the body of this death? The grace of God by Jesus Christ our Lord.'[5] No room would be left for divine help which we are in duty bound to ask, saying: 'Lead us not into temptation,'[6] and the Lord would seem to have spoken to no purpose when He said to the Apostle Peter: 'I have prayed for thee that thy faith fail not,'[7] if all this is accomplished in us by the sole power of our will, with no help from God.

So, by these perverted and wicked arguments, he goes counter not only to the prayers by which we ask of the Lord whatever we read and believe that the saints asked, but it even nullifies our blessings, whenever we pray over the people, asking and begging of the Lord 'that he would make them abound in charity towards one another and towards all men,'[8] that he would grant them, according to the riches of his glory, to be strengthened by his spirit with might unto the inward man,'[9] 'that he fill them with all joy and peace in believing, and that they may abound in hope and in the power of the Holy Spirit.'[10] Why should we ask those things which we know the Apostle asked of the Lord for his people, if, even now, our nature, created with free will, can furnish itself with all this by an act of its own will? Why, too, does the same Apostle say: 'As many as are led by the Spirit of God, they are the sons of God,'[11] if we are

5 Rom. 7.24,25.
6 Matt. 6.13; Luke 11.4.
7 Luke 22.32.
8 1 Thess. 3.12.
9 Eph. 3.16.
10 Rom. 15.13.
11 Rom. 8.14.

led by the spirit of our own nature to become the sons of God? Why is it likewise said: 'The Spirit helpeth our infirmity,'[12] if our nature is so made as not to need the help of the Spirit to perform works of justice? Why is it written: 'But God is faithful who will not suffer you to be tempted above that which you are able, but will make also with temptation issue that you may be able to bear it,'[13] if we are now so endowed that by the strength of our free will we are able to overcome all temptations merely by bearing them?

Why should I draw this out any further for your Holiness when I am well aware that I am tiresome, especially as you hear my letter through an interpreter?[14] If all of you love Pelagius, may he love you in return, or, rather, may he deceive himself and not you. For, when you hear him admitting the grace of God and the help of God, you imagine he means the same as you do, who are well versed in the Catholic rule of faith, because you do not know what he has written in his book; for this reason I am sending his book and my own in which I refuted him, so that your Reverence may see what grace or help of God he speaks of when he is charged with opposing the grace and help of God. Therefore do you show him by teaching, by exhorting, and by praying for his salvation, which must needs be in Christ, how to confess that grace of God which the saints of God confessed, as has been proved, when they asked of the Lord the strength to do those things which He commanded them to do, since these commands would not be made except to show that we have a will, and strength would not be asked unless the weakness of our will were helped by Him who gave the command.

Let him be questioned publicly on whether he agrees that we must pray to the Lord to keep us from sin. If he disagrees,

12 Rom. 8.26.
13 1 Cor. 10.13.
14 His own language was Greek.

have the words of the Apostle read in his ears, where he says: 'Now we pray God that you may do no evil';[15] if he agrees, let him openly preach the grace by which we are helped, so that he himself may be kept from doing much evil. This grace of God through Jesus Christ our Lord delivers all who are delivered, since no one can be delivered in any other way than by that grace. For that reason it is written: 'As in Adam all die, so also in Christ all shall be made alive,'[16] not that no one will be damned, but that no one will be delivered in any other way, since none are sons of men except through Adam, just as none are sons of God except through Christ. Thus, all can become sons of men only through Adam and all can become sons of God only through Christ. Let him also express his views openly on this: Whether he agrees that little children, not yet able to choose or reject goodness, yet because of one man through whom 'sin entered into the world and by sin death, and so death passed upon all men in whom all have sinned,'[17] are delivered by the grace of Christ; whether he believes that the blood of Christ which was certainly shed for the remission of sin, was shed for them, also, because of original sin. Concerning these points in particular we wish to be informed about him: what he believes, what he holds as true, what he confesses and preaches with assurance. In the other objections, however, which may be raised against him, even if he is proved to be wrong, he can be borne with more tolerably until he accepts correction.

I ask you to be so kind as to send us the minutes of the Church council[18] which show that he was cleared. I ask this

---

15 2 Cor. 13.7.
16 1 Cor. 15.22.
17 Rom. 5.12.
18 Held at Diospolis (ancient Lydda) in 415. On receipt of these minutes, Augustine wrote his *De gestis Pelagii* to give a true account of the proceedings in the East.

at the joint desire of many bishops, who, like me, have been troubled by the unsubstantiated report about this affair, but I have written this in my own name because I did not want to lose the opportunity of a messenger who is making a quick journey from here, and who, I hear, will be able to return to us shortly. Instead of these minutes, or any part of them, Pelagius had sent us some kind of defense[19] he wrote, in which he said he had replied to the charges made by the Gauls.[20] In it, to pass over other points, he replied to the objection made to him that he had said man can live without sin and can keep the commandments of God, if he wills it, by saying: 'I said that God gave man this power; I did not say that anyone could be found who had never committed a sin from infancy to old age, but that a man converted from sin by his own effort and helped by the grace of God can live without sin, and his having sinned will not make him incorrigible for the future.'

In this reply of Pelagius, your Reverence can observe that he made this admission, that the early life of man, that is, from his infancy, cannot be free of sin, but that he can be converted to a sinless life by his own effort helped by the grace of God. Why, then, did he say in the book which I have answered that Abel had lived a life entirely without sin? These are his words on this point: 'This,' he says, 'can rightly be said of those of whose good or evil deeds Scripture makes no mention: that, as it recorded their goodness, it would undoubtedly have recorded their sins, if it had known that they did sin. But granted,' he says, 'that in other ages Scripture neglected to describe the sins of all, because of the numerous throng of men, right at the very beginning of the world, when there were only four people alive, what reason can we give,' he says, 'for its failure to record the misdeeds

19 Cf. Letter 177 n. 52.
20 Heros and Lazarus, Gallic bishops; cf. Letter 175 n. 4.

of all? Was it because of a great multitude which did not yet exist? Or was it because it remembered only those who committed sin, but could not remember those who had not committed any? Certainly,' he says, 'at the beginning of time, there were Adam and Eve, of whom Cain and Abel were born—four persons only are reported as existing. Eve sinned, Scripture tells us this; Adam also sinned, the same Scripture does not fail to mention it. Scripture also testifies further that Cain sinned as well. It points out not only their sins, but the nature of their sins. But if Abel, too, had sinned,' he says, 'without doubt the Scripture would have mentioned it; but it does not mention it; therefore, he did not sin.'

I have quoted these passages from his book—your Holiness will be able to find them in the volume itself—that you may understand what kind of reliance you may put on his denial of other points also; unless, perhaps, he says that Abel himself did not commit sin, but that he was not thereby without sin, and so could not be compared to the Lord, who alone of mortal flesh was sinless, because in Abel there was the original sin derived from Adam, but no sin committed by himself personally—would that at least he would say this that we might for the present get from him a clear statement about infant baptism!—or unless he says, perhaps, since he used the words 'from infancy to old age,' that Abel did not sin because it is shown that he did not live to old age. His words do not indicate this; he said that from the beginning the early part of life was sinful; the later part could be sinless. He claims that he did not say that anyone could be found who had not sinned from infancy to old age, but that after turning away from sin by his own effort, helped by the grace of God, he could live without sin. For, when he says: 'turning away from sin,' he shows that the earlier part of life is lived in sin. Let him admit, then, that Abel did sin, since his early life was lived in the world and that part he admits is not without sin; and let him look again into his own book, where it is clear that he did say what he denies having said in his defense.

If he says that this book, or this passage in the book, is not his, I have on my side competent witnesses, men of honor and integrity, and unquestioned friends of his own, on whose evidence I can clear my reputation, that they gave me this same book, and therein that statement can be read; they said it was the work of Pelagius and that evidence is enough to keep anyone from saying that it has been written or forged by me. Now, let each one choose among these which one he will believe; it does not devolve on me to discuss this question any further. I ask you to be sure to convey to him, if he denies that those views are his, the objection made against him that he is opposed to the grace of Christ. Indeed, his defense is so plausible that we shall be very glad and thankful if he has not deceived you, who are unacquainted with his other writings, by some of his ambiguous expressions, but we do not much care whether he never held those perverse and wicked views, or was sometime converted from them.

180. Augustine gives greeting in the Lord to Oceanus,[1] his deservedly cherished lord and brother, worthy of esteem in the members of Christ (End of 416)

I have received two letters together from your Charity, in one of which you mention a third which you say was dispatched before the other two. I do not recall having received it; in fact, I am quite sure I have not received it. For those I have received, however, I return hearty thanks for your kindness to us. My reason for not answering them at once is

---

1 Cf. Letter 165.

that I have been distracted by one task after another. But now I am taking advantage of a little drop of free time, choosing rather to give you some kind of answer than to maintain a long silence toward your very sincere Charity, and thus become more unmannerly by too little than by too much talk.

I know now what holy Jerome thinks about the origin of souls, and I have, in fact, read the very words which you quoted from his book in your letter. But this does not raise the troublesome question which disturbs some, how God can justly give souls to adulterous conceptions, because not even their own sins, much less those of their parents, can harm good-living persons, and those who have turned to God with faith and piety. But, if it is true that new individual souls are created from nothing for new individuals at birth, it is a question worth asking how such unnumbered souls of infants which God knows will leave their bodies without baptism before the age of reason, before they know right from wrong, can with justice be given over to damnation by Him with whom above all there is no injustice.[2] There is no need for me to say more on this subject, since you know what I wish, or rather, what I do not wish to say. I think I have said enough for a wise man. However, if you have read anything, or heard anything from his mouth, or if the Lord has given some light to your mind on this point, by which this problem could be solved, share it with me, I beg of you, and I will give you even more heartfelt thanks.

In that matter of the officious or useful lie[3] which you thought could be settled by the example of the Lord saying that the Son knows not the day nor the hour of the end of the world,[4] I was pleased to read this product of your in-

---

2 Rom. 9.14.
3 For the classification of lies, cf. Letter 40.
4 Matt. 24.36; Mark 13.32.

genuity, but I am quite sure that a figurative expression cannot rightly be called a lie. For it is not a lie to say that the day is joyful because it makes people joyful, and that a lupine seed is sad because it lengthens the face of the eater because of its bitter taste; so also we say that God 'knows' something when he makes a man know it—you yourself recalled that this was said to Abraham.[5] None of these is a lie, as you can easily see for yourself. Consequently, when the blessed Hilary[6] threw light on an obscure point by this kind of figurative expression, making us understand that in proportion as he made others ignorant by concealing his meaning he admitted his own lack of knowledge, he did not condone lying, but he proved that it was not lying to use the more common figures, or even that one which is called metaphor, a form of speech familiar to all. Will anyone call it a lie to say that vines are jewelled with buds, or that a grain-field waves, or that a man is in the flower of his youth, because he sees in these objects neither waves nor precious stones, nor grass, nor trees to which these expressions would literally to applied?

Accordingly, with your keen and learned mind, you can notice easily how different are these expressions from what the Apostle said: 'When I saw that they walked not uprightly unto the truth of the gospel, I said to Peter before them all: If thou, being a Jew, livest after the manner of the gentiles, and not as the Jews do, how dost thou compel the gentiles to live as the Jews do?'[7] There is here no figurative obscurity of speech; these are the proper words of direct speech. Here the Doctor of the Gentiles[8] spoke either truth or falsehood to those of whom he was in labor until Christ should be

---

5 Gen. 22.12.
6 Bishop of Poitiers (315-368), author of *De Trinitate* (trans. by Stephen J. McKenna, C.SS.R., as Vol. 25 in this series).
7 Gal. 2.14.
8 1 Tim. 2.7.

formed in them;[9] if falsehood, which God forbid, you notice what follows and you shrink from both alternatives,[10] but he gives us evidence of truth, and in the Apostle Peter there is an admirable example of humility.

But why do I dwell any longer on this point which has been adequately treated in the letters[11] between me and the aforementioned brother Jerome? In his most recent work against Pelagius,[12] which he published under the name of Critobulus, he held the same opinion of that episode, and the words of the Apostle, which we followed as being that of blessed Cyprian.[13] In that other question of the origin of the soul which I think it wise to explore, not because of the matter of adulterous conceptions, but because of the damnation of the innocent, which God forbid, if you have learned anything from that great and grand man which can be used to answer those in doubt, I beg you not to refuse to share it with us. Indeed, you appear to me so learned and charming in your letters that it is worth while conversing by letter with you. I ask you not to delay sending us a book—I do not know its name—of the same man of God, which the priest Orosius brought back and gave to your Charity to copy. In it he gains praise for his discussion of the resurrection of the body. But we do not ask it of you at once, because we think it needs copying and correcting, both of which we realize require ample time. As you live, remember us with God.

---

9 Gal. 4.19.
10 A lacuna is suggested in the text at this point. Augustine seems not to follow up the true-false alternative.
11 Letters 28, 40, 71, 75, and 82.
12 Jerome, *Dialogus adverus Pelagium* 1.8, in *PL* 23.502.
13 Cyprian, Letter 71.3 (ed. Hartel, pp. 773-774).

181. Innocent gives greeting in the Lord to Aurelius and all the holy bishops his beloved brothers who took part in the Council of Carthage (January 27, 417)[1]

In your inquiries into the things of God, which require to be treated by priests with great care, especially when there is question of a true, just, and Catholic council, you have kept the precedents of ancient tradition, being mindful of ecclesiastical discipline, and you have added strength to our religion, not only now in your council, but before it when you made your pronouncement according to right reason, and when you voted to submit the matter to our judgment, knowing well what is owing to the Apostolic See, since all of us who are placed in this position desire to follow the Apostle himself, from whom the very episcopate and the whole authority of its name are derived. Following in his footsteps, we know equally how to condemn what is evil and to approve what is praiseworthy, as for example, the fact that you keep the customs of the fathers with priestly zeal, that you do not think they should be trampled underfoot. Because it has been decreed by a divine, not a human, authority that whenever action is taken in any of the provinces, however distant or remote, it should not be brought to a conclusion before it comes to the knowledge of this See, so that every just decision may be affirmed by our complete authority. Thus, just as all waters come forth from their natural source and flow through all parts of the world, keeping the purity of their source, so all the other Churches may draw from this source knowledge of what they are to teach, whom they are to absolve, and

---

1 This is an answer to Letter 175. Innocent I, Pope from 401 to 417, active against Novatianists, Manichaeans, Donatists, Priscillianists and Pelagians, strongly supported St. John Chrysostom, defended the authority of the Holy See against encroachments from the East, and restored many points of Church discipline.

from whom the waters, intended only for pure bodies, should be withheld as being soiled with indelible filth.

Therefore, I thank you, dearest brothers, for sending us letters by our brother and fellow priest, Julius, in which you show that while administering the Churches of which you have care, you have an interest in the welfare of all, and on behalf of the Churches of the whole world, in union with all, you ask a decree that may be for the good of all. Thus, a Church, supported by its own rules and strengthened by the decretals of a legitimate pronouncement, may not have to be exposed to those against whom it should be on guard: men instructed or, rather, destroyed by the perverse subtleties of words, who pretend to argue for the Catholic faith yet breathe out deadly poison so as to corrupt the hearts of right-thinking men and drag them down, seeking to overthrow the whole system of true dogma.

Therefore, the remedy must be applied quickly, that this hateful disease may not make a further attack on the minds of men, in the same way as a doctor, when he sees some weakness in this earthly body, thinks it a great proof of his skill to save from a fatal outcome a patient who is despaired of, or who examines an infected sore and applies poultices or other remedies which may avail to draw out what has developed in it; but, if it persists and cannot be healed, he cuts out the harmful part with a knife lest it infect the whole body with its poison, and so he preserves the body whole and sound. Therefore, this poison is to be cut out, which, like a sore, has crept into a clean and wholly sound body, lest if it is removed too late it may settle in the very vitals from which it may not be possible for the corruption of this evil to be drawn off.

Shall we not, then, think it right to act thus toward those minds which think they owe their goodness to themselves, and take no thought of Him whose grace they daily receive?

But such men no longer receive the grace of God, because they rely on themselves for the power to accomplish as much without Him as those who ask and receive His grace can scarcely profess to do. Could anything be so unjust, so barbaric, so oblivious of all religion, so inimical to Christian minds as to deny that you owe to God whatever you achieve by your daily deeds, while admitting that you owe Him the fact of your existence—meaning that you will be more successful in providing for yourself than He who brought you into being can be for you!—and while you think you owe Him your existence, how can you think you do not owe it to Him that you live in such a manner by receiving His daily grace? And you who deny that we need His divine help, as if we were provided against everything by our own strength, do we refrain from calling His help upon us because we can be such by our own effort?

When anyone denies the help of God, I should like to ask him why he says that: Is it because we do not deserve it? Or is He unable to give it? Or is there no reason why anyone should ask it? Our very works bear witness that God can do this. We cannot deny that we need daily help. For, if we are living a good life, we ask that we may live a better and holier one; if we have turned away from good by wicked thoughts, we need His help even more. Nowhere can we find anything so deadly, so prone to make us fall, so exposed to all dangers as the thought that it can be enough for us to have received free will at birth, and so we should ask nothing more of the Lord, that is, of the Author of our being. This is to deny His power in order to show ourselves free, as if He who made us free at our birth could give us nothing more! This is to refuse to know that, unless His grace comes down upon us in answer to earnest prayer, it will be useless for us to try to overcome the aberrations of earthly corruption and a perishable body, since it is not free will but the help of God that alone can make us fit to resist.

For, if he contends that he has need of divine help and does not seek it honestly because his free will is a greater help to him—while that blessed man who was already elect of the Lord prayed thus to God, saying: 'Be thou my helper: forsake me not nor despise me, O God, my Saviour,'[2] do we call free will to our help while he calls on God as his helper? Do we say that it is enough for us that we are born, while he begs God not to forsake him? I ask, do we not learn clearly what we should ask when that saintly man, as I said above, begs so earnestly not to be despised? Those who assert such things must needs use that argument. David could not be accused of being ignorant of prayer and unaware of his own nature; if he knew that so much power resided in his nature he nevertheless called on God as his helper, his constant helper; and even this constant help does not satisfy him, but, lest God should at any time despise him, he calls upon Him in abject prayer, and through the whole collection of the Psalms he proclaims his need and cries it aloud. If, therefore, this is something so important to know that he kept saying it constantly, and if he confessed that it is so necessary to teach, how can Pelagius and Caelestius discard every refutation of it in the Psalms, and repudiate all similar teaching, and then believe they can convince some persons that we do not need the help of God, and ought not to ask it, while all the saints bear witness that they can do nothing without it?

Long since there was one[3] who had experience of his free will, making a careless use of its goods and falling into a flood of error where he would have been drowned; since he could find no means of raising himself, deceived as he was

---

2 Ps. 26.9.
3 This description fits Augustine's own conversion; cf. his *Contra duas epistulas Pelagianorum* 2.6 (Migne, *PL* 44.575).

forever by his own liberty, he would have been sunk in overwhelming ruin if the coming of Christ had not raised him afterwards by means of his grace, washed away every past sin in the font of his baptism through the purification of a new birth, and strengthened his steps that he might advance more surely and more steadily: never afterwards did he deny God's grace. And although Christ had redeemed man from his past sins, He knew that man could sin again, and for that reason He kept many remedies in reserve to heal him, so that He could amend those later offenses. He offers those remedies daily, and, unless we make use of them with faith and confidence, we shall never be able to overcome human failings. It necessarily follows, then, that as we overcome by His help, so we are in turn overcome without His help. I could say more, but it is evident that you have said all the rest.

Therefore, whoever appears to be in agreement with this statement which declares that we have no need of divine help shows himself an enemy of the Catholic faith, and an ingrate to the goodness of God. They are unworthy of our communion, which they have polluted by such preaching. They have voluntarily fled from the true religion by following those who make these statements. Since this whole matter rests on our avowal, and we accomplish nothing by our daily prayer except in so far as we receive the grace of God, how can we tolerate such boasting? I ask what great error blinds their hearts which makes them fail to notice what is individually lavished on others by divine grace, but feel no grace of God themselves because they are unworthy and undeserving of it. Indeed, they fully deserve this blindness who have not left themselves the resource of believing that they can be drawn back from their wanderings by divine help. By denying this help they have robbed themselves of it, not others. They must be plucked out and removed far from the bosom of the Church, lest their error, gaining ground for a long time, should afterwards grow into something incurable. If they were to remain long unpunished they must needs draw many into their perverted state of mind, and deceive the innocent or, rather, the unwary who now follow the Catholic faith, who will think the deceivers must be right since they see them remaining in the Church.

Therefore, let the diseased sore be cut off from the sound body, and the miasma of the cruel malady be carefully removed, that thus the healthy parts may continue to live, that the flock, being cleansed, may be clear of this contagion of an infected flock. Let there be an unspotted perfection of the whole body, such as we know, from your pronouncement against them, that you follow and hold, and which we, together with you, uphold with equal assent. If, however, they call down some help of God upon themselves, as they have hitherto refused to do, and if they recognize that they need His help, in order to be set free from this corruption into which they have fallen through the subjugation of their heart, and if they are led to the light, so to speak, from this foul cloud under which they have been, by the surrender and removal of all that darkens and dims their sight, so that they cannot see the truth, let them repudiate the views they have hitherto held; let them lend their minds for a while to true arguments, and, turning from their former corruption, let them give and deliver themselves over to be healed by true counsels. If they do this, it will be in the power of the pontiffs to help them to some extent, and to offer the care for such wounds which the Church is not wont to refuse to the lapsed when they have recanted. Thus, they may be drawn back from the precipice on which they are, and led into the sheepfold of the Lord, lest, if they are left outside and deprived of the great protection afforded by the wall of faith, they may be exposed to all the dangers of being torn and eaten by the teeth of wolves, since they cannot fight them off by reason of the perverted doctrine which roused the attack against them. But this answer, furnished with abundant examples of our law, is sufficient to meet your warning, and we think that nothing remains for us to say. Since you, also, have left nothing out, it is clear that nothing has been passed over by which they may be refuted and may acknowledge their defeat. Therefore, no testimony is added here by us because this report is filled with them; it is evident that so many learned priests have said everything, and it does not befit us to believe that you overlooked anything which could advance the case. Farewell, brothers.[4]

182. Innocent gives greeting in the Lord to his beloved brothers, Silvanus elder, Valentine, and the others who attended the Synod of Milevis (January, 417)[1]

In the midst of our other cares for the Church at Rome and the duties of the Apostolic See, in the course of which we examine decrees on various subjects with faithful and curative argument, our brother and fellow priest, Julius, brought the letter of your Charity which you sent, in your close devotion to the faith, from the Council of Milevis, and, without my knowing it, he included the report of the Synod of Carthage, adding this document of similar protest. Truly the Church rejoices that her pastors display such watchful care for the flocks entrusted to them, not only that they do

---

4 In another handwriting. And along the side of the Letter as given in textual notes: Given on the fifth day of the Kalends of February, after the seventh consulship of Theodosius Augustus and Junius Quartus.

1 This is the answer to Letter 176.

not allow any to go astray, but, if the harm of herbage on the left entices any of the sheep and they persist in wandering away, they decide either to cut them off entirely, or to watch them with all the old-time care when they unlawfully disregard warnings; on guard against both extremes, lest, if they refuse the strays, others may be led away by a like example; if they cast them off at their return, they may seem to have been devoured by the teeth of wolves. Their plan of action is always prudent and full of Catholic faith. For, who could either show indulgence to an erring soul or fail to welcome him back at his conversion? As I think it is a sign of hardness to treat sinners with connivance, so I judge that it is wicked to refuse a helping hand to the converted.

You show diligence and consideration in taking thought of the apostolic honor, of that concealed honor, I mean, of him whom 'besides those things which are without, the solicitude for all the churches'[2] weighed down; and in asking what opinion is to be held on anxious matters, following in that the form of the ancient rule, which you know has always been upheld by me throughout the whole world. But I pass over that for I believe your Prudence is well aware of it. Why did you affirm it by your action if you did not know that replies always flow from the apostolic font to petitioners in all the provinces? In particular, I think that as often as an argument on the faith is being blown about, all our brothers and fellow bishops ought to refer it solely to Peter, that is, to the one having the authority of his name and rank, as your Charity has now done, so that it may be for the common benefit of all the Churches. They must be the more on guard when they see the originators of evil cut off from communion with the Church by the enactments of our decree, in consequence of the report from a twofold synod.

Therefore, your Charity will perform a doubly good action,

---

2 2 Cor. 11.28.

for you will gain gratitude for preserving the canons of belief, and the whole world will share in the common good conferred by you. Are there any Catholic men who would be willing to join conversation hereafter with the adversaries of Christ? Would anyone want to share the common light of life with them? Surely, the authors of a new heresy should be shunned. What more bitter attack could they imagine against the Lord than to take away the reason for daily prayer, after having nullified divine assistance? This is the same as saying: 'What need have I of God?' Let the Psalmist say of them with good reason: 'Behold the men that made not God their helper!'[3] Therefore, by denying the help of God they say that man is self-sufficient, that he has no need of divine grace, the deprivation of which necessarily entangles him in the snares of the Devil[4] and makes him fall; while at the same time he claims that human liberty alone is enough to enable him to fulfill all the commandments of life.[5] O perverse doctrine of utterly depraved minds! Take note, then, how that liberty led the first man astray and made him fall into a presumptuous sin because he failed to bridle it strongly enough, and how he could not have been rescued from his state if the coming of the Lord Christ in the providence of regeneration had not reformed the condition of his original liberty. Let him listen to David saying 'Our help is in the name of the Lord' and 'Be thou my helper, forsake me not; do not thou despise me, O God, my Saviour!'[6] which according to him would be useless if what the Psalmist asked of the Lord with tearful speech rested on his own will alone.

This being so, when we read on all the divine pages nothing else than that the help of God must be added to our

---

3 Ps. 51.9.
4 1 Tim. 3.7; 2 Tim. 2.26.
5 Ezech. 33.15; Baruch 3.9.
6 Ps. 123.8; 26.9.

free will, and that, deprived of these heavenly safeguards, it can do nothing, how can Pelagius and Caelestius so obstinately defend the power of the will alone, persuading themselves of its truth, as you assert, nay, what is a subject worthy of general grief, persuading so many others? We could cite numberless examples to instruct such a group of masters, if we did not know that your Holiness is fully versed in all the divine Scriptures, especially as your report is replete with such cogent testimonies that by these alone the teachings in question could be torn apart, and there is no need of far-fetched quotations, since the heretics would neither dare nor be able to counter those which you used as coming easily to mind. Therefore, they try to deprive us of the grace of God, which we should still have to seek, even if the liberty of our original state were restored to us, inasmuch as we cannot otherwise avoid the contrivances of the Devil except by the help of the same grace.

That other doctrine which your Fraternity claims that they preach, that little children can attain the reward of eternal life without the grace of baptism, is very foolish. For, unless they eat of the flesh of the Son of man and drink His blood they will not have life in them.[7] Those who claim this for them without regeneration seem to me to wish to nullify baptism, since they teach that these children have what they believe is not to be bestowed on them in baptism even by themselves. If, then, they do not wish anything to stand in their way, let them confess that there is no need of rebirth and that the sacred stream of regeneration has no effect. But in order to disarm the vicious doctrine of vain men by the swift reasoning of truth, the Lord proclaims this in the Gospel by saying: 'Suffer the little children and forbid them not to come to me.'[8] Therefore, concerning Pelagius and

---

7 John 6.54.
8 Matt. 19.4; Mark 10.14; Luke 18.16.

Caelestius, that is, the originators of new dogmas, which, as the Apostle says, are of no profit, but tend to beget utterly vain questions, we decree, relying on the strength of apostolic authority, that they are to be deprived of communion with the Church until 'they recover themselves from the snares of the Devil, by whom they are held captives at his will';[9] that they are not to be received within the Lord's flock which they have chosen to forsake by following the path of a crooked way. 'Those who trouble us, who would pervert the gospel of Christ,' are to be cut off.[10] We likewise prescribe that if any strive to defend this teaching with similar obstinacy, they are to be bound under the same censures, 'and not only they that do these things, but they also that consent to them that do them,'[11] because I think there is not much difference between the intention of him that does something and the consent of him that agrees to it. I add more: When no one assents to the errant one he generally unlearns his error. Therefore, beloved brothers, let the aforementioned decisions stand as a fixed decree; let them be kept out of the house of the Lord; let them at least be prevented from exercising any pastoral care, lest the deadly contagion of two sheep creep in among the unwary flock, and the greedy-hearted wolf rejoice that so many flocks of sheep within the Lord's sheepfold have been scattered, because the guards have been negligent in overlooking the wounds of the two. We must be watchful then, lest, by allowing the wolves to enter, we appear to be hirelings rather than shepherds.[12]

Moreover, since Christ our Lord showed that He willed not the death of the sinner but that he should be converted and live,[13] we order that if ever these two recover a sane mind,

9 2 Tim. 2.14,23,26.
10 Gal. 1.7; 5.12.
11 Cf. Rom. 1.32.
12 John 10.12.
13 Ezech. 33.11; 2 Peter 3.9.

after having repudiated the error of their wrong teaching, and if they condemn the false statements which brought on their condemnation, the customary remedy is not to be refused them by the Church, that is, they are to be received back, lest, if we should perchance forbid their return, they might remain outside the fold and be swallowed up by the fierce jaws of their waiting enemy, which they have armed against themselves with the sharp points of their wicked arguments. Farewell, brothers.

Given on the sixth day before the Kalends of February in the consulship of the noble Honorius and the noble Constantius.[14]

183. Innocent gives greeting to Aurelius, Alypius, Augustine, Evodius, Possidius, bishops (January, 417)[1]

We have received with grateful heart the letters of your Fraternity, so full of faith, so strong with the full vigor of the Catholic religion, which you sent from the two councils by our brother and fellow bishop, Julius. Their content and the whole development of thought on the daily grace of God and the amendment of those who hold contrary views are based on right reason, so as to be well fitted to remove all error from these latter and to furnish them a worthy teacher, by citing certain precedents from our law, whom they ought to follow. However, in our previous letters in answer to your reports I think we have said enough on these points concerning what we think either of their perfidy or of your opinions. Furthermore, what may be said against them strengthens and supports your statement, and there can never

---

14 January 27, 417.

1 An answer to Letter 177.

be lacking an argument to overcome them, since this wretched and impious heresy is such that it is overcome by the strength of our faith, and, more fully, by truth itself. He who has rejected and despised the whole hope of life, confusing his own heart with his hateful and damnable argument, by which he believes that there is nothing for him to receive from God, nothing left for him to ask for his own cure—what is left for one who has bereft himself of this?

If, then, there are some whom this great perversity has forced into self-defense, who surrender and join themselves to this teaching, hoping that it is part of Catholic doctrine, whereas it is far removed from it, and is proved to be completely opposed to it, if these, infected by their words of exhortation, are led on to their ruin, they will hasten, as fast as they can, to return to the rightful path of the way, lest, if error besiege their mind too long, it may enter their senses as if it were food. For, if Pelagius, in whatever place he has stayed, has used this assertion to lead astray minds that easily and simply yield faith to an argument, whether they are here in the city[2]—and, as we do not know, we can neither affirm nor deny this, since, even if they were here, they would stay in hiding and would never dare to defend him if he preached such things, nor would they boast of them before anyone of us, and in such a great crowd of people it would not be easy for anyone to be caught, nor would it be possible for anyone to be recognized anywhere—or whether they live in any other part of the earth, we believe by the mercy and grace of God that it will be easy to convert them when they hear the condemnation of the one who has been found to be the stubborn and obstinate author of this dogma. It makes no difference where they may be, since they are to be cured wherever they can be found.

Nevertheless, we cannot be convinced that Pelagius has

---

2 Rome.

been cleared, although a report has been brought to us by some laymen or other, according to which he believes that he has been heard and absolved. We doubt that this report is true, because it did not come with any subsequent notice of that council,[3] nor have we received any letters from those before whom he stated his case on this matter. But, if he had been able to put faith in his own acquittal, we believe that what he would more probably have done would be to oblige those who gave the verdict to publish it in letters—something which was much more truly possible.[4] However, there are some points set forth in the minutes of the council which were offered as objections, and these he partly suppressed by leaving them out, partly wrapped in obscurity by twisting many words to his own advantage; other points, which were made by fallacious arguments rather than by true reasoning, as could be seen at the time, he changed by denying some and distorting others to a false meaning.

What is most to be wished is that he would turn from the error of his way to the true way of the Catholic faith, that he would wish and choose to be acquitted by considering the daily grace of God and by recognizing His help, that it may appear true to all and be proved by plain reasoning that he has been converted from the heart to the Catholic faith, not merely rectified by the publication of a document! Hence, we can neither approve nor blame the verdict of those who judged him, since we do not know whether the minutes are authentic, and in case they are authentic it is clear that he has rather escaped by evasion than cleared himself by the full truth. If he trusts and knows that he does not deserve our condemnation as he says, or that he has now rebutted the whole of what he said formerly, then he ought not so much

---

3 Of Diospolis.
4 Cf. Augustine, *De gratia Christiana et de peccato originali* 2.10 (*CSEL* 42.172.21-173.6) .

to be summoned by us as to hasten of his own accord so that he can be acquitted. But, if he still holds the same views, and if he is summoned by any kind of letter, would he ever trust himself to our judgment, knowing that he is to be condemned? On the other hand, if he were to be summoned, it would be better for it to be done through those who are nearest to him, who seem not to be separated from him by a wide range of country. Care will not be wanting if he gives a chance for healing. He can repudiate the views he held, and by sending a letter, as befits one who returns to us, can ask pardon for his error, dearest brothers.

We have, of course, gone through the book said to be his which your Charity sent us. In it we have read many statements against the grace of God, many blasphemies; nothing that pleases, nothing that is not deeply displeasing, worthy of being condemned and trampled underfoot by all; the like of which, if he did not write it, no one else would admit to his mind and hold as an opinion. We do not think it necessary in this letter to argue more extensively about the law, as if Pelagius were present and opposing us, since we are speaking to you who know the law,[5] and who rejoice in mutual agreement with us. It will be better for us to adduce examples when we deal with those who are evidently unacquainted with those matters. But to one who thinks correctly about the power of nature, about free will, and the fullness of God's daily grace, it would not be very fruitful to discuss these things. Therefore, let him repudiate those views which he holds, so that those who have fallen into error through his talks and instruction may know at length what the true faith holds. They can more easily be reclaimed when they see that these errors are condemned by their very author. But, if he chooses to persist obstinately in this impiety, action must be taken to save those who have been led astray

---

5 Rom. 7.1.

by his error, not their own, lest this remedy be lost to them, since he neither recognizes nor asks for care such as this.

May God keep you safe, dearest brothers.[6]

Given on the sixth day before the Kalends of February.

184. Innocent to Aurelius and Augustine, bishops (417)

The return of our most esteemed fellow priest, Germanus, should not be unaccompanied by some mark of our esteem. It seems to us in a sense a natural and reasonable thing to greet our dearest through those who are dear. Therefore, dearly beloved, we desire your Brotherhood to rejoice in the Lord, and we beg you to offer similar prayers for us to God, for, as you well know, we accomplish more through common and mutual prayer than we do through individual and private prayer.

184A. Augustine gives greeting in the Lord to the beloved lords, his holy sons, Peter and Abraham[1] (417)

Neither justice nor charity can or ought to belittle your holy zeal, which makes you think that I should look into many questions so that you may be well armed against the arguments of impiety, and may be strong to resist it. But one letter, however lengthy, could not contain a careful answer to all your questions. You know that in several of my works I have already answered, to the best of my ability, all or nearly all the points which you ask. If you read these—and I hear that you have undertaken a life in the service of God, so that you have leisure for reading—either the whole doctrine

---

6 In another handwriting.

---

1 Two monks. Peter was later an abbot in the province of Tripoli.

on these points will be clear to you, or not much of it will be lacking, especially as there is an inner teacher in you by whose grace you are what you are. For, how does man help man to learn anything, if we are not 'taught of the Lord'?[2] Still, in this letter, with the Lord's help, I shall not cheat your expectation of at least a short reply.

The Lord said: 'He that believeth and is baptized shall be saved, but he that believeth not shall be condemned.'[3] If, then, when little children are baptized, these are no empty words but are truthfully acted on that these little ones may be included among the believers, and if, on the lips of all Christians, they are thenceforth called a new offspring, it is certain that if they do not believe, they will be condemned, and because they have added nothing to original sin by a bad life, for this reason it can rightly be said that in their condemnation they suffer the lightest of penalties, but not that they suffer none. If anyone thinks there will not be different penalties, let him read what is written: 'It will be more tolerable for Sodom in the day of judgment than for that city.'[4] Therefore, let no middle place for infants between the kingdom and the state of punishment be sought by deceivers, but let them pass over from the Devil to Christ, that is, from death to life, lest the wrath of God[5] rest upon them; from this wrath of God nothing but the grace of God can deliver them. But what is the wrath of God if not the due penalty and vengeance inflicted by a just God? God is not stirred by any emotion, as the changeable human soul is roused to anger; what is called the wrath of God is nothing else than the just penalty of sin, and it is no wonder that this should pass down to posterity.

Now, the concupiscense of the flesh, in which men are

2 Isa. 54.13; John 6.45.
3 Mark 16.16.
4 Matt. 10.5; 11.24.
5 John 5.24; 3.36.

begotten and conceived, did not exist prior to sin, nor would it have existed at all except that the disobedience of his own flesh followed upon the disobedience of man, as a reciprocal penalty. And although the blessing of marriage makes a good use of this evil, it is a fact that without it there cannot be a marriage, that is, a licit and honorable intercourse for the purpose of begetting children; but it would have been possible without it if human nature, by not sinning, had remained in that state in which it was created. For the sex organs, like other parts of the body, could have been stimulated to perform their functions by an impulse of the will, not by the heat of passion. Who would claim that those words of God: 'Increase and multiply,'[6] were intended as a curse on sinners, not a blessing on marriage? Therefore Christ was neither begotten nor conceived in this concupiscence, because His birth of the Virgin took place far differently. But I repeat that all men who are begotten, conceived, and born in this concupiscence must necessarily be reborn if they are to escape the penalty, because, even if a man is born of parents who are regenerated, his carnal birth cannot bestow on him what a spiritual rebirth bestowed on them; in the same way, the wild olive is produced not only from a wild olive, but even from the seed of the true olive, although the olive is not a wild olive. We have spoken at length on these points in other letters of ours, and I would rather you read them than oblige me to repeat the same things.

It is a more laborious task to reply to infidels who are not bound by the authority of Christian books. Their wrong-headedness cannot be set right by the force of divine Scriptures; rather, the Scripture itself has often to be defended against them because it is too openly attacked by them. But if the Lord helps you to be persuasive, you will still make little progress among those whom you desire to see

6 Gen. 1.22.

Christians if you merely overcome their unbelief by truthful arguments, unless you beg the gift of faith for them with suppliant prayers. And faith itself, as you surely know, is a gift of God, who allots to each one his measure of faith; it is such a gift that it requires the understanding to precede it. The Prophet is not deceived when he says: 'Unless you believe, you shall not understand.'[7] And the Apostle prayed not only for the faithful but also for the unbelieving Jews, and asked only that they might believe[8] when he said: 'Brethren, the will of my heart, indeed, and my prayer to God is for them unto salvation';[9] that is to say, he prayed for those who had put Christ to death, who would have killed him, too, if the power had been theirs, for men like those whom the Lord prayed for when He was mocked as He hung on the cross,[10] and whom blessed Stephen prayed for as he was being stoned.[11]

There are two classes of those unbelievers whom we call Gentiles, or, by a more commonly used word, pagans: those of one class prefer the superstitions which they invent to the Christian religion; those of the other class are hampered by no nominal religion. I have called attention to these in certain books of the *City of God,* of which, I think notice has come to you, and the remainder of which I am now laboring to finish, if the Lord wills, in the midst of my other duties. I have finished ten books—long ones—against the first class of pagans, whom the Apostle points out when he says: 'But the thing which the heathens sacrifice, they sacrifice to devils, not to God,'[12] and whom he also certainly means when he says: 'They worshipped and served the

---

7 Cf. Isa. 7.9.
8 Goldbacher notes a lacuna here, but the text is coherent without emendation.
9 Rom. 10.1.
10 Luke 23.34.
11 Acts 7.59.
12 1 Cor. 10.20.

creature rather than the Creator.'[13] The first five volumes refute those who claim that it is necessary to worship many gods, not the one supreme and true God, in order to attain or retain earthly and temporal happiness in human affairs; the last five are directed against those who think to achieve the happiness which we hope for after this life by raising themselves up with swelling pride against the doctrine of salvation and by worshiping demons and many gods. Also, in three of the last five books we refute their well-known philosophers. The rest, as many as there will be after the eleventh— of which three are finished and the fourth in hand—will cover all that we hold and believe about the City of God, because we do not wish to give the impression of being satisfied with refuting the views of others without setting forth our own in this work. The fourth book after the first ten, that is, the fourteenth of the whole work, will have a solution, if the Lord wills, of all the questions which you have proposed in your letter.

However, with the other class of unbelievers who either believe that there is no divine power or that it has nothing to do with human affairs, I am not sure that an argument should be undertaken on any subject of dutiful devotion, although hardly anyone can be found nowadays who is so foolish as to dare to say even in his own heart: 'There is no God.'[14] But other fools are not lacking who have said: 'The Lord shall not see,'[15] that is, He does not extend His providence to these earthly affairs. Accordingly, in those books which I wish your Charity to read, along with the description of the City of God, if God wills and for whom He wills, I shall justify the belief that not only does God exist—and this belief is so ingrained in nature that hardly any impiety

13 Rom. 1.25.
14 Ps. 13.1.
15 Ps. 93.7.

ever tears it out—but that He regulates human affairs, from
governing men to rewarding the just with blessedness in the
company of the holy angels and condemning the wicked to
the lot of the bad angels.

Therefore, dearly beloved, this letter must not be loaded
down any further. We have pointed out clearly enough where
you may hope to learn what you wish to know through our
instrumentality, and if you do not yet possess those same
books, we have taken steps, in proportion to our meager
resources, to let you have them through our holy brother,
my fellow priest, Firmus,[16] who has great affection for you,
and has diligently recommended you to our affection, so
that he may give thanks for your mutual love.

185.[1] Augustine to Boniface,[2] tribune and count in Africa (417)

On the Treatment of the Donatists[3]

Chapter 1

I praise and congratulate and admire you, my beloved
son, Boniface, for your ardent desire to know the things that

---

16 A monk who had spent some time in St. Jerome's monastery, and was
the bearer of Letters 115, 134, and 194.

---

1 Goldbacher gives no title of address to this letter; it is supplied from
Migne. Augustine speaks of it in *Retractations* 2.48.
2 Governor of Africa under Honorius and Placidia.
3 In *Retractations* 2.48, Augustine says. 'At the same time I wrote a
book on the treatment of the Donatists, because of some who did not
want them to be disciplined under the imperial laws.' This Letter
represents the summary of his thought on the Donatists.

are of God, in the midst of the cares of war and arms.
Indeed, it is clear that this is what makes you serve, with
that same military valor, the faith which you have in Christ.[4]
So, then, to explain briefly to your Charity the difference
between the error of the Arians and that of the Donatists,
the Arians say that the Father, the Son, and the Holy Spirit
are different in substance, but the Donatists do not say
this; they confess one substance in the Trinity. And if some of
them say that the Son is inferior to the Father, they still do
not deny that He is of the same substance, but most of
them say that they believe of the Father, the Son, and the
Holy Spirit exactly what the Catholic Church believes. This
question does not arise with them; what they quarrel about
is union with the Church, and they stir up rebellion and
enmity against the unity of Christ by persisting in their
error. Some time ago, as we heard, some of them were trying
to win over the Goths[5] to their side, and seeing that they
could make some headway they said that they believed the
same doctrines. But they are proved wrong by the authority
of their elders, because there is no claim that Donatus
himself, to whose sect they glory in belonging, held these
beliefs.

Chapter 2

But do not be troubled by these things, my dearest son.
It has been prophesied that there will be heresies and
scandals,[1] that we may gain instruction in the midst of
enemies, and so both our faith and our love may be more

---

4 Philem. 1.5.
5 They had been won over to the Arians shortly after their conversion
from barbarism.

---

1 1 Cor. 11.19.

surely proved: our faith, of course, that we may not be deceived by them; our love, that we may provide for their amendment to the extent of our power. We must not only make an effort to free them from their abominable error and to keep them from harming the weak, but we must also pray for them that the Lord may open their minds and make them understand the Scriptures, because it is in the holy books that the Lord Christ is revealed, and His Church made manifest. In their extraordinary blindness they not only fail to know Christ Himself except in the Scriptures, they even fail to recognize the Church on the authority of the divine writings, and picture it to themselves according to the falsity of human misrepresentation.

Chapter 3

They agree with us in recognizing Christ when they read: 'They have dug my hands and my feet; they have numbered all my bones. And they have looked and stared upon me. They parted my garments and upon my vesture they cast lots'; but they refuse to recognize the Church in the verses that follow shortly after: 'All the ends of the earth shall remember and shall be converted to the Lord and all the kindreds of the Gentiles shall adore in his sight. For the kingdom is the Lord's and he shall have dominion over the nations.'[1] With us they recognize Christ when they read: 'The Lord hath said to me: Thou art my son, this day have I begotten thee,' and they refuse to recognize the Church in what follows: 'Ask of me and I will give thee the Gentiles for thy inheritance and the utmost parts of the earth for thy possession.'[2] With us they recognize Christ in what the Lord

---

1 Ps. 21.17-19,28,29.
2 Ps. 2.7,8.

Himself says in the Gospel: 'It behooved Christ to suffer and to rise again from the dead the third day,' and they refuse to recognize the Church in what follows: 'And that penance and remission of sins should be preached in his name unto all nations beginning at Jerusalem.'[3] There are other testimonies in the sacred books so numerous that I ought not to compress them into this book. And as the Lord Christ stands out in these, either as equal to the Father according to His divine nature, because, 'In the beginning was the Word and the Word was with God and the Word was God,' or in the humility of His assumed flesh, because 'The Word was made flesh and dwelt among us';[4] so His Church is manifest not in Africa alone, as the Donatists madly proclaim with their shameless pride, but as spread throughout the whole world.

Chapter 4

They prefer their quarrelsome contentions to the divine testimonies, and they have separated themselves from the Catholic Church, that is, from the unity of all nations, because of the case of Caecilian,[1] formerly bishop of the Church at Carthage, against whom they make charges which they neither could nor can prove. Yet, if the charges made by them against Caecilian had been true and could have been proved so at any time, we should have repudiated him even after his death, but we ought not thereupon, because of some man, forsake the Church of Christ which is not produced by litigious imaginations, but is based on

---

3 Luke 24.46,47.
4 John 1.1,14.

1 For an explanation of this controversy, cf. Letter 43 n. 5.

divine evidence, because 'It is good to confide in the Lord rather than to have confidence in man.'[2] For, even if Caecilian sinned—and I say this without prejudice to his innocence—Christ did not thereby lose His inheritance. It is easy for a man to believe either truth or falsehood about another man, but it is a sign of accursed shamelessness to wish to condemn the unity of the whole world because of a man's misdeeds which you cannot prove to the world.

Chapter 5

Whether Caecilian was ordained by betrayers of the divine books I do not know; I did not see it; I heard it from his enemies; it is not declared to me by the Law of God, or by the preaching of the Prophets, or by the holy Psalms, or by the Apostle of Christ, or by Christ's words. But the testimonies of the entire Scripture proclaim with one voice that the Church, with which the sect of Donatus is not in communion, is indeed spread throughout the entire world. 'In thy seed shall all the nations of the earth be blessed,'[1] said the Law of God. 'From the rising of the sun even to the going down, there is offered to my name a clean offering, for my name is great among the Gentiles,'[2] said God through the Prophet. 'He shall rule from sea to sea, and from the river unto the ends of the earth,'[3] said God in the psalm. 'Bringing forth fruit and growing in the whole world,'[4] said God through the Apostle. 'You shall be witnesses unto me in Jerusalem and in all Judea and Samaria, and even to the

---

2 Ps. 117.8.

---

1 Gen. 22.18; 26.4.
2 Mal. 1.11.
3 Ps. 71.8.
4 Col. 1.6.

uttermost of the earth,'[5] said the Son of God with His own lips. Caecilian, bishop of the Church at Carthage, is accused in human lawsuits; the Church of Christ, established among all nations, is commended by divine pronouncements. Piety itself, truth, charity do not allow us to receive against Caecilian the testimony of those men whom we do not see in the Church to which God bears witness, for those who do not follow divine testimonies have lost the power of human testimony.

Chapter 6

I add the fact that they themselves carried the case of Caecilian to the judgment of Emperor Constantine on appeal; indeed, after the bishops' verdict, they even went so far as to hale Caecilian himself—after they had failed to get him convicted—to the tribunal of this emperor before his most persistent persecutors. And they themselves did first what they now blame in us, in order to deceive the unwary, saying that Christians ought not to ask any action on the part of Christian emperors against the enemies of Christ. Even in the conference which we had with them at Carthage they did not dare to deny—on the contrary, they even dared to boast of it—that their predecessors had brought a criminal charge against Caecilian to the emperor, adding, for good measure, the lie that they had won their case and brought about his conviction. In what sense, then, are they not persecutors who persecuted Caecilian with their accusation and lost their case to him, who then tried to claim false credit for themselves by a most shameless lie, and were so far from thinking this wrong that they boasted of it as if it were to their credit, so long as they could show that Caecilian

---

5 Acts 1.8.

had been convicted by the accusation of their predecessors? It would be a long task for you, occupied as you are with other matters necessary to the peace of Rome, to read how they were vanquished at every point in that conference, because the minutes of the meeting are excessively full, but perhaps it would be possible for you to have the summary read to you, which I believe my brother and fellow bishop Optatus[1] has, or, if he has not, he can get it for you very easily from the church at Sitifis. Even so, the book, which is detailed, might prove to be a burden to you in the midst of your cares.

Chapter 7

The same thing happened to the Donatists as happened to the accusers of holy Daniel. Just as the lions were turned against the latter,[1] so the laws by which they tried to oppress the innocent were turned against the former, except that, by the mercy of Christ, those laws which seemed to be against them were rather favorable to them, since many through them have been and are daily being converted, who now give thanks both for their conversion and for their deliverance from that raging destruction. And those who hated now love, and where formerly they swore in their madness that these most salutary laws were hurtful to them, in the same measure they now rejoice over their restored sanity. They are now animated by a love like ours toward the remainder of their number with whom they were on the verge of destruction, and they urge us to put pressure on them lest they perish. The physician is hateful to the madman in a frenzy, as the father is to his rebellious son, the one because he ties him down, the

1 One of the bishops present at the Council of Zerta; cf. Letter 141.

1 Dan. 6.24.

other because he beats him, yet both do it out of love. But, if they neglected their charges and left them to destroy themselves, that would rather be a false and cruel kindness. If 'the horse and the mule that have no understanding'[2] use bites and kicks to fight against the men who are treating their wounds in order to heal them, and if these men, though often endangered and injured by their teeth and hooves, do not leave off until they have restored health by their painful and harsh remedies, how much more should man be succored by man, and brother by brother, lest he perish eternally, since he can understand, once he is set right, what a great benefit was conferred on him while he was complaining of suffering persecution!

Chapter 8

In the same way, therefore, the Apostle says: 'Let us not fail, while we have time, let us work good to all men.'[1] Let those who can do so achieve this by their sermons as Catholic preachers; let others who can do so achieve it by their laws as Catholic rulers. Thus, partly by obedience to the divine warnings, partly by compliance with the imperial decrees, all will be called to salvation, all will be called back from destruction. And the reason for this is that, when emperors pass bad laws favoring falsehood and opposing truth, staunch believers are tested and faithful champions are crowned; but, when they pass good laws favoring truth and opposing falsehood, the cruel extremists are constrained by fear and the intelligent are converted. Therefore, whoever refuses to obey the imperial laws which are passed for the protection of God's truth incurs grave punishment. For, in the times of the Prophets, all the

2 Ps. 31.8.

1 Gal. 6.9,10.

kings among the people of God who failed to annul or repeal decrees which had been passed contrary to the commandment of God are blamed, and those who did annul and repeal them receive praise beyond what others deserve. When King Nabuchodonosor was the slave of idols, he passed a sacrilegious law requiring a statue to be adored, but those who refused to obey this impious statute acted with piety and faith. Then the same king, converted by a divine miracle, published a praiseworthy law in favor of truth, that whoever should speak blasphemy against the true God of Sidrach, Misach, and Abdenago should be utterly destroyed, together with his house.[2] If any of his subjects despised this law and deservedly suffered what had been decreed, they must have said what the Donatists now say, that they were just men because they suffered persecution according to the king's law. No doubt they would have said it if they had been as mad as these are, who bring division among the members of Christ and pour scorn upon the sacraments of Christ; who boast of being persecuted because the imperial laws, enacted to protect the unity of Christ, prevent them from doing such things; who falsely vaunt their innocence and seek from men the glory of martyrdom which they cannot receive from Christ.

Chapter 9

The true martyrs are those of whom the Lord says: 'Blessed are they that suffer persecution for justice' sake.'[1] Therefore, it is not those who suffer for the sake of injustice and the impious division of Christian unity, but those who suffer persecution for justice' sake who are truly martyrs.

2 Dan. 3.5-96.

1 Matt. 5.10.

Agar suffered persecution from Sarai, yet the one who persecuted was holy and she who suffered was sinful.[2] Is that any reason for comparing the persecution suffered by Agar to that with which the wicked Saul afflicted holy David?[3] Obviously, there is a very great difference, not because David suffered, but because he suffered for justice' sake. And the Lord Himself was crucified among thieves,[4] but, though they were alike in suffering, they were different in the reason for suffering. Therefore, in the psalm we must understand the voice of the true martyr wishing to be distinguished from false martyrs: 'Judge me, O God, and distinguish my cause from the nation that is not holy.'[5] He does not say 'distinguish my punishment,' but 'distinguish my cause.' For, the punishment of the wicked can be the same but the cause of the martyrs is not the same, and their cry is: 'They have persecuted me unjustly; do thou help me.'[6] The Psalmist thinks himself worthy of being justly helped because they persecuted unjustly, for, if they persecuted justly, he would not be worthy of help but of chastisement.

Chapter 10

But, if the Donatists think that no one can persecute anyone justly, as they said at the conference that the true Church was the one that suffered, not the one that practised persecution, I forbear to say what I have said elsewhere,[1] because, if what they say is true, Caecilian belonged to the true Church when their predecessors persecuted him by bringing

---

2 Gen. 16.6.
3 1 Kings 18.8-29.
4 Matt. 27.38; Mark 15.27; Luke 23.33.
5 Ps. 42.1.
6 Ps. 118.86.

---

1 Cf. Augustine, *Ad Donatistas post conlationem* 16.20.

an accusation against him to the emperor's tribunal. The reason why we say that he belonged to the true Church was not that he suffered persecution, but that he suffered it for justice' sake, while, on the other hand, they have been estranged from the Church not because they persecuted, but because they persecuted unjustly. This, therefore, we say: that if they do not look into the reasons which induce anyone either to persecute or to suffer persecution, and if they think it is a sign of a true Christian not to persecute but to suffer persecution, without doubt they include Caecilian in that definition because he suffered persecution, he did not persecute; whereas they exclude their predecessors from their definition because they persecuted, they did not suffer persecution.

Chapter 11

But, as I said, I pass over that, and I do say this: that if the true Church is the one which suffers persecution, not the one which inflicts it, let them ask of the Apostle what Church Sara signified when she persecuted her handmaid. He says plainly that the Jerusalem which is above is free, which is our mother, that is, the true Church of God, and that it is prefigured by the woman who afflicted her handmaid. But, if we were to state the argument more correctly, it was rather she who persecuted Sara by her haughtiness than Sara who persecuted her by restraining her; the one did an injury to her mistress, the other imposed restraint on pride.[1] In the second place I ask, if the good and holy never persecute anyone but only suffer persecution, whose voice do they think that is in the psalm where we read: 'I will pursue after my enemies and overtake them, and I will not turn again until they are consumed.'[2] If, then, we are willing to speak or to

1 Gal. 4.21-31.
2 Ps. 17.38.

acknowledge the truth, there is an unjust persecution which the wicked inflict on the Church of Christ, and there is a just persecution which the Church of Christ inflicts on the wicked. She, indeed, is happy because she suffers persecution for justice' sake, but they are unhappy because they suffer persecution for injustice' sake. Therefore she persecutes out of love, they out of hatred; she to correct them, they to overturn her; she to reclaim them from error, they to hurl men into error; finally she pursues her enemies and catches them until they give up their folly and make progress in truth, but they, repaying good with evil, try to rob us of even our temporal life because we take measures to assure them eternal salvation, being so in love with murder that they even commit it on themselves when they cannot murder anyone else. While, on the one hand, the charity of the Church strives to deliver from that perdition so that none of them may die, on the other, their fury strives either to kill us in order to feed their passion for cruelty, or to kill themselves that they may not seem to have lost the power of killing men.

Chapter 12

People unfamiliar with their way of acting imagine that they have taken to committing suicide only now, when such throngs of people are being set free from their fanatical domination through the opportunity of the laws enacted in behalf of unity. But those who know how they used to act before the laws were passed are not surprised at their dying when they recall their vying with one another in evil.[1] More especially when there was idol worship, they used to come in great hordes to the crowded ceremonies of the pagans, not to break the idols, but to be killed by the worshipers of idols.

---

1 One of Augustine's puns: *Non eorum mirantur mortes, sed recordantur mores.*

If they had received authority to break the idols and tried to do it, then, if anything happened to them, they might have had some kind of shadow of the name of martyr, but they came solely to be killed, leaving the idols intact, for there were some particular worshipers of the idols, robust youths, who had the custom of dedicating to the idols as many victims as each one killed. Some, indeed, in order to be killed, mingled with armed wayfarers, making horrible threats of striking them if they were not killed by them. Sometimes, too, when judges were passing through, they used violence to extort commands from them that they should be struck down by executioners or by a court official. In this connection, a story is told of one official who tricked them by ordering them to be bound and handed over as if to blows, and then escaped their attack unhurt and unbloody. Then it was also their daily sport to kill themselves by jumping off steep crags, or by fire or water. The Devil taught them these three kinds of death, so that, when they wished to die and could find no one to frighten into killing them with a sword, they should hurl themselves from rocks or expose themselves to fire and water. For, who else was in possession of their heart, of whom else is it believable that he taught them these things except the one who suggested to our Saviour, as if it accorded with the Law, that He should cast Himself headlong from the pinnacle of the Temple?[2] They would certainly repudiate this imputation if they carried Christ in their heart. But, because they have made room instead for the Devil within them, they either perish as that herd of swine which the legion of demons rushed down the mountainside into the sea,[3] or, rescued from those deaths, they are gathered into the loving bosom of their Catholic mother, and delivered, as the Lord

---

2 Matt. 4.5-7; Luke 4.9-13.
3 Matt. 8.32; Mark 5.13.

delivered the demoniac boy whom his father brought to be healed of the demon's hold, saying that sometimes he was used to cast him into the water, sometimes into fire.[4]

Chapter 13

Consequently, a great mercy is being done them by these imperial laws by which they are first rescued, in spite of themselves, from the sect in which they have learned those evil practices through the teaching of lying demons, in order that they may afterward be healed in the Catholic fold by good teachings and may become habituated to good behavior. There are many of them whose fervent faith, piety, and charity we now wonder at in the unity of Christ, who give thanks to God with deep joy that they have been freed from that error in which they had believed that evil was good, but they would not now offer those thanks voluntarily unless they had been severed involuntarily from that abominable company. What shall be said of those who confess to us every day that they had long wanted to be Catholics, but could not be what they wanted, being overpowered with fear of those among whom they lived, because, if they had said one word in defense of the Catholic faith, both they and their homes would have been completely destroyed? No one is so mad as to say that they ought not to have been helped by the imperial decrees to escape from so great an evil, while those whom they feared are forced to fear in their turn, and by this fear are either converted themselves or at least pretend to be converted, and leave the converts in peace by whom they were formerly feared.

---

4 Matt. 17.14-18; Mark 9.16-26.

Chapter 14

But, if they tried to kill themselves to prevent those who were to be delivered from being delivered, aiming in this way to deter the devoted affection of the deliverers, and if, by creating a fear that some of the fanatics would destroy themselves, they tried to prevent any rescue from perdition of those who were either no longer willing to perish or could be saved from it by coercion, what course does Christian charity take, especially when those who madly threaten to take their own lives are very few in comparison with the throngs of those who are to be delivered? What course does fraternal love take? Surely, it does not abandon all to the eternal fires of hell because it fears the transitory fires of furnaces for a few, nor does it abandon to eternal doom so many who now wish, or will wish afterward, in spite of their weakness, to come to everlasting life through Catholic peace, because it is trying to ward off suicide from a few whose life is an obstacle to salvation for others. These do not allow men to live according to the teaching of Christ, but, according to the practice of their diabolical doctrine, they try to teach them, at any and every time, to rush into the voluntary death which is feared for themselves. Surely, the Church saves those whom it can, even if those whom it cannot save perish by their own act. It ardently longs that all may live, but toils even more ardently that all may not perish. Thanks be to the Lord that among us, not indeed everywhere, but in a great many places, as also in other parts of Africa, Catholic peace makes and has made headway without any of those deaths of madmen. But those disastrous happenings occur in the parts where the insane and useless kind of men live, who have been accustomed to act that way at other times.

Chapter 15

And indeed, even before those laws were enacted by Catholic emperors, the doctrine of the peace and unity of Christ was gradually spreading, and many a one, as he learned of it and found the inclination and ability, came over to the Church from that sect, although it is true that among them unbridled bands of abandoned men disturbed the peace of the innocent in various cases. What master was not forced to fear his own slave if once he fled for refuge to their patronage? Who would even dare to threaten a destructive servant or his instigator? Who could dismiss a wasteful warehouseman, or any debtor, if he sought their help and protection? Under fear of clubs and fires and instant death, the records of worthless slaves were torn up so that they could go free. Receipts extorted from debtors were returned. Whoever scorned their harsh words were forced by harsher blows to do what they ordered. Innocent men who had offended them had their houses razed to the ground or burned down. Some land-owners of honorable birth and gentlemanly breeding were dragged off half-dead after scourging, or were tied to a mill-stone and forced by blows to turn it as if they were beasts of burden. What help from civil laws or local authorities had any effect on them? What court officer was zealous for his duty in their presence? What tax-gatherer collected taxes from them against their will? Who would attempt to avenge the murdered victims of their beatings, unless his own madness called for punishment from them, while some were going around trying to turn men's swords against themselves by terrifying the owners under threat of death into striking them, and others were hurling themselves to self-destruction over cliffs or into water and fire, and exposing their cruel souls to the punishment brought upon themselves?

Chapter 16

A large number of those who belonged to that heretical superstition shuddered at such excesses, and when they thought their innocence was shown by their displeasure at such deeds, the Catholics said to them: 'If those evil deeds do not defile your innocence, how can you say that the Christian world was defiled by the false, or at least unknown, sins of Caecilian? How can you separate yourselves by a wicked crime from Catholic unity, as from the Lord's threshing floor, which, until the time of winnowing, must needs contain both the grain which is to be gathered into the barn and the chaff which is to be consumed in the fire?'[1] Thus to certain ones a reason is given why some came over to Catholic unity, ready to bear even the enmity of the fanatics, but many more, although they wished to, did not dare to make enemies of the men who had such scope for their cruelty. Indeed, some suffered most cruelly at their hands when they came over to us.

Chapter 17

It even happened at Carthage that, when a certain deacon of theirs, named Maximian,[1] had revolted against his bishop, some of the bishops of the same sect made a schism, split off some of the people of Carthage who were of the party of Donatus, and ordained him bishop in opposition to his own bishop. But as this displeased many of theirs, they condemned Maximian, together with twelve other bishops who had assisted at his ordination, but offered the other members of the same schismatic band the opportunity of returning to

---

1 Matt. 3.12; Luke 3.17.

---

1 Cf. Letter 43 n. 52.

them by a fixed date. But, afterward, they received back to
their clerical rank some of those very twelve, as well as others
to whom an extension of time had been granted; they did this
for the sake of peace in their own group, even though these
returned after the appointed day. In addition to that, they
did not dare to rebaptize some whom the condemned had
baptized outside their communion. This conduct of theirs
began to tell so heavily against them and for the Catholics
that their mouths were completely shut. When this circum-
stance, so fitting to win the minds of men away from
schism, was published more insistently and in every possible
direction, and when it was shown by the speeches and
arguments of Catholics that they, for the sake of peace in
Donatism, had received back their own condemned members
with rank intact, and had not dared to invalidate the baptism
given outside their church by their condemned or suspended
members, yet did dare to oppose the peace of Christ and to
charge the whole world with the defilement of some evil-doers
or other, and also to invalidate the baptism given in those
Churches from which the very Gospel came to Africa, large
numbers of their sectaries were embarrassed before the
manifest truth and began to show more frequent signs of
amendment, especially in places where freedom had a breathing spell from their cruelty.

Chapter 18

Then truly their anger blazed forth so violently, and they
were goaded on by such barbs of hatred, that hardly any of
the churches of our communion were safe from their intrigues,
their acts of violence, their bare-faced robberies; hardly any
road was safe for travel by anyone who had preached Catholic

peace as opposed to their fury, or who had shown up their madness by the clear light of truth. This went so far that not only laymen, or occasional clerics, but the very bishops themselves had to meet in some fashion their harsh alternative: either silence truth or endure their barbarity. If truth were silenced, not only would no one have been delivered by its silence, but many would be lost through their misleading doctrine. If, on the other hand, their fury were roused to savage excess by the preaching of truth, after some had been delivered and ours had been strengthened, fear would again prevent the timid from following the truth. Therefore, if anyone thinks that, after affliction had reduced the Church to these straits, we should have endured everything rather than appeal for the help of God, to be effected through Christian emperors, he overlooks the fact that no good reason could have been given for this negligence.

Chapter 19

Those who are averse to having just laws enacted against their own wicked deeds say that the Apostles did not call on the kings of the earth for such services; but they fail to notice that times were different then, and that all things have to be done at their own times. At that time there was no emperor who believed in Christ, or who would have served Him by enacting laws in favor of religion and against irreligion; it was the time when that prophetic utterance was fulfilled: 'Why have the Gentiles raged and the people devised vain things? The kings of the earth stood up and the princes met together, against the Lord and against his Christ.' Not yet had that come to pass which is spoken of a little further on in the same psalm: 'And now, O ye kings understand; receive instruction you that judge the earth. Serve ye the

Lord with fear, and rejoice unto him with trembling.'[1] How, then, do kings serve the Lord with fear except by forbidding and restraining with religious severity all acts committed against the commandments of the Lord? A sovereign serves God one way as man, another way as king; he serves Him as man by living according to faith, he serves Him as king by exerting the necessary strength to sanction laws which command goodness and prohibit its opposite. It was thus that Ezechias served Him by destroying the groves and temples of idols and the high places which had been set up contrary to the commandments of God;[2] thus Josias served Him by performing similar acts;[3] thus the king of the Ninevites served Him by compelling the whole city to appease the Lord;[4] thus Darius served Him by giving Daniel power to break the idol, and by feeding his enemies to the lions;[5] thus Nabuchodonosor, of whom we spoke above, served Him when he restrained all his subjects from blaspheming God by a terrible penalty.[6] It is thus that kings serve the Lord as kings when they perform acts in His service which none but kings can perform.

Chapter 20

Since, then, kings did not yet serve the Lord in the times of the Apostles, but were still devising vain things against Him and against His Christ, so that all the predictions of the Prophets might be fulfilled, certainly they were not then able to restrain wickedness by law, but were practising it themselves. The sequence of time was so unrolled that the

1 Ps. 2.1,2,9,10.
2 4 Kings 18.4.
3 4 Kings 23.4.20.
4 Jonas 3.6-9.
5 Dan. 14.21,41.
6 Dan. 3.96.

Jews killed the preachers of Christ, thinking they were doing a service to God,[1] as Christ had foretold, and the Gentiles raged against the Christians, and the patience of the martyrs won the victory. But after the prophetic words began to be fulfilled, as it is written: 'And all the kings of the earth shall adore him; all nations shall serve him,'[2] what serious-minded man would say to kings: 'Do not trouble to care whether the Church of your Lord is hampered or attacked by anyone in your kingdom; let it not concern you whether a man chooses to practise or to flout religion'? For it would not be possible to say to them: 'Let it not concern you whether anyone in your kingdom chooses to be virtuous or shameless.' Why, then, since free will has been divinely bestowed on man, should adultery be punished by law and sacrilege permitted? Is it a lesser matter for a soul to keep faith with God than for a woman to keep it with her husband? Or if offenses committed, not through contempt but through ignorance of religion, are to be punished more leniently, is that any reason for overlooking them altogether?

Chapter 21

Does anyone doubt that it is better for man to be led to the worship of God by teaching rather than forced to it by fear of suffering? Because the former group is preferable it does not follow that those of the latter, who are not like them, should be neglected. We have proved by experience and do still prove that it has been a blessing to many to be driven first by fear of bodily pain, in order afterward to be instructed, or to follow up in act what they have learned in words. Some objectors suggest to us the sentiment of a

---

1 John 1.62.
2 Ps. 71.11.

certain secular writer who said: 'I believe it is better to train children by feelings of self-respect and decent outlook rather than of fear.'[1] This is indeed true, but if those whom love leads are better, those whom fear restrains are more numerous. They can be answered from the same author in the passage which reads: 'You cannot do anything right unless you are compelled by fear of harm.'[2] But divine Scripture has this to say about the better group: 'Fear is not in charity, but perfect charity casteth out fear,'[3] and this about the inferior group who are more numerous: 'A hard-hearted slave will not be corrected by words, for if he understandeth he will not obey.'[4] When it said that he is not corrected by words, it did not command him to be given up, but warned silently of what needed correction; otherwise, it would not say: 'He will not be corrected by words.' In another passage it says that the unruly son, as well as the slave, is to be restrained by blows to his own great profit, in the words: 'Thou shalt beat him with the rod and deliver his soul from death;' and elsewhere it says: 'He that spareth the rod hateth his own son.'[5] Give me one who can say with upright faith and true understanding and all the strength of his soul: 'My soul hath thirsted after the living God; when shall I come and appear before the face of God?'[6] For such a one no fear will be necessary, either of temporal penalties or of imperial laws or even of hell, because to him it is so desirable a good 'to stick close to God'[7] that not only does he shrink from being separated from that happiness as from a great torture, but he feels it as a trial that it is delayed. However,

---

1 Terence, *Adelphoe* 57,58.
2 Terence, unidentified line.
3 1 John 4.18.
4 Cf. Prov. 23.14.
5 Prov. 23.14; 13.24.
6 Ps. 41.3.
7 Ps. 72.28.

before the good sons can say: 'We have a desire to be dissolved and to be with Christ,'[8] many wicked servants and worthless runaways, so to speak, are called back to their Lord by the lash of temporal scourges.

Chapter 22

Who can love us more than Christ who laid down His life for His sheep?[1] Nevertheless, although He called Peter and the other Apostles by word alone,[2] in the case of Paul, previously Saul, a dread destroyer of the Church, and afterward its great builder, He not only compelled him by words, but used His power to strike him prostrate, and in order to force him to leave off the savagery of his dark unbelief and to desire the light of his heart He afflicted him with corporeal blindness. If it had not been for that punishment, he would not have been healed of it afterward, and since he saw nothing though his eyes were open, if he had been able to see, Ananias would not have laid his hands upon him that his sight might be restored, when, as Scripture relates, there fell from his eyes, as it were, scales with which they had been closed.[3] What ground is there for the cry generally raised by schismatics: 'There is freedom to believe or not to believe: did Christ use force on anyone? did He compel anyone?' See, now they have the Apostle Paul; let them acknowledge in him Christ first compelling and afterward teaching, first striking and afterward consoling. It is a wonderful thing how he who came to the Gospel under the compulsion of bodily

8 Phil. 1.23.

1 John 10.15.
2 Matt. 4.18-22; Mark 1.16-20; Luke 5.10; John 1.35.43.
3 Acts 9.1-18.

suffering labored more in the Gospel than all the others[4] who were called by word alone, and that in him whom greater fear drove to love 'perfect charity casteth out fear.'[5]

Chapter 23

Why, then, should the Church not compel her lost sons to return if the lost sons have compelled others to be lost? And yet, even in the case of those whom they have not compelled but only enticed, if they are called back to the bosom of the Church by stern but salutary laws, their loving mother embraces them more kindly and rejoices much more over them than over those whom she has never lost. Is it no part of the shepherd's care when he has found those sheep, also, which have not been rudely snatched away but have been gently coaxed and led astray from the flock, and have begun to be claimed by others, to call them back to the Lord's sheepfold, by threats or pain of blows if they try to resist? And especially if their numbers are increased by fruitful generation in the midst of runaway slaves and bandits, has he not more authority over them because he recognizes on them the brand mark of the Lord which is not tampered with in those whom we receive back without rebaptism? The wandering of the sheep is to be remedied without destroying in it the mark of the Redeemer. But, if anyone is branded with the royal mark by a deserter who has himself been branded, and if they both find mercy and the one returns to his service, while the other begins a service which he had not yet undertaken, the mark is not erased in either of them. In fact, is it not rather recognized in both of them and accorded due honor since it is the king's mark? As the Donatists cannot prove that what

---

4 1 Cor. 15.10.
5 1 John 4.18.

they are forced to is evil, they claim that they ought not to be forced into good. But we have shown that Paul was forced by Christ; therefore, the Church imitates her Lord in forcing them, although in her early days she did not expect to have to compel anyone in order to fulfill the prophetic utterance.[1]

Chapter 24

Indeed, this is not an unreasonable deduction from that statement of the Apostle, where blessed Paul says: 'Having in readiness to revenge all disobedience when your obedience shall be fulfilled.'[1] In the same way, the Lord Himself commands the guests first to be brought in to His great supper, but afterward to be compelled, for, when the servant answered the king: 'Lord, it is done as thou hast commanded and yet there is room,' he said: 'Go out into the highways and hedges and whomsoever you find, compel them to come in.'[2] Thus, the obedience was first fulfilled in those who were first brought in gently, but the disobedience is put under restraint in those who are compelled. That is the purpose of that: 'Compel them to come in,' after he had first said: 'Bring them in,' and had been answered: 'It is done as thou hast commanded and yet there is room.' If He meant us to understand that they are to be compelled by the fear engendered by miracles, many more divine miracles were wrought for those who were invited first, especially the Jews, of whom it is said: 'The Jews require signs.'[3] Among the Gentiles, too, in the time of the Apostles, such miracles won faith in the Gospel, so that, if the command was given to

---

1 Ps. 71.11.

---

1 2 Cor. 10.6.
2 Luke 14.16-23.
3 1 Cor. 1.22.

compel them by such means, it is more reasonable to believe that the first guests were compelled to come. Consequently, if the Church, in the era of kings, exercises, as she ought, the power which she has received by a divine gift, together with religion and faith, and if those who are found in the highways and hedges, that is, in heresies and schisms, are compelled to come in, she is not to be blamed for compelling them, but they for waiting to be compelled. The banquet of the Lord is the unity of the Body of Christ, not only in the sacrament of the altar, but also in the 'bond of peace.'[4] But of the Donatists we can say with absolute truth that they compel no one to what is good; whomsoever they compel, they compel only to evil.

Chapter 25

To tell the truth, before those laws came into Africa by which they are compelled to come in, it seemed to some of the brethren—and to me among them—that, although the Donatist heresy raged everywhere, it would be better not to petition the emperors to suppress that heresy altogether by enacting a penalty for those who should persist in it, but they should rather decree that those who either preached Catholic truth by word of mouth or spread it by enactment should not have to suffer the mad violence of these men. We thought this could be accomplished to some extent in this way: if the authorities would apply directly to the Donatists—who deny that they are heretics—the law which Theodosius, of pious memory, promulgated against all heretics in general, to the effect that any bishop or cleric of theirs wherever found should pay a fine of ten pounds in gold. At the same time, not all were to be subject to that fine, but only those in

---

4 Eph. 4.3.

whose districts the Catholic Church had to suffer some form of violence at the hands of their clerics, their Circumcellions, or their people.[1] This would happen, namely, after a protest on the part of Catholics who had suffered such excesses, and it would be the duty of local officials to see that Donatist bishops or other ministers were obliged to pay the fine. Our idea was that if they were frightened in this manner, and so did not dare to commit such acts, there would be freedom for the Catholic truth to be taught and embraced, so that no one would be forced to it, but any who wished might follow it without fear, and thus we should not have any false or feigned Catholics. And despite the difference of opinion of some of the brethren, men advanced in age or impressed by the example of many cities and localities where we could see a strong and true Catholic Church founded and established on such blessings of God as were afforded by the laws of former emperors forcing men to the Catholic communion, we nevertheless carried our point, and the request I mentioned above was made to the emperors. This was decreed in our council and an embassy was sent to the court.[2]

Chapter 26

But the greater mercy of God brought it about that our ambassadors did not get what they had undertaken to secure, since He knew how necessary to the depraved and cold minds of many was the fear inspired by these laws, and a certain remedial harassment—necessary, too, to overcome that hardness of heart which cannot be influenced by words but only by some degree of disciplinary sternness. Ours were anticipated by some very serious complaints from bishops of

1 Cf. Letter 88.
2 Cf. Letter 139.

other districts, who had suffered many outrages and been turned out of their sees by the Donatists; particularly revolting and unbelievable was the maltreatment of Maximian, Catholic Bishop of Bagai. It left our embassy with nothing to transact, for a law had already been promulgated to the effect that the Donatist heresy was guilty of such monstrous conduct that to spare it seemed a greater cruelty than any perpetrated by it; that it should not only be restrained from violence but should not be allowed to exist at all under the protection of the laws. However, the death penalty was not to be invoked, because Christian moderation was to be observed even toward those unworthy of it, but fines were to be imposed and exile was decreed against their bishops and ministers.

Chapter 27

In the case of the above-mentioned Bishop of Bagai, there had been a case in the civil court, and the verdict awarded him the basilica which the Donatists had taken over, although it was Catholic. As he stood at the altar, they rushed upon him with terrifying force, and with furious cruelty they struck him inhumanly with clubs and other weapons of that sort, even with wooden beams broken from the very altar. They stabbed him in the groin with a dagger, and his life would have ebbed away with the blood from this wound if their further savagery had not saved his life. For, as they dragged him along the ground, grievously wounded as he was, the dirt clogged the bleeding vein and stopped the flow of blood which was bringing him to death. Then, when they had left him, and ours were trying to carry him away, to the accompaniment of psalms, their anger blazed forth more fiercely; they snatched him from the hands of his bearers, driving the Catholics away with kicks—an easy matter for them as they surpassed them in number and in barbarism. Finally, thinking him dead, they tossed him up into a tower and went off. But he was still living, having fallen on a heap of somethting soft. During the night he was discovered by the light of a lamp carried by some passersby, was recognized, rescued, and carried to a religious house, where he was carefully tended. After a long time he recovered from his desperate plight. However, the report that he had been killed by the Donatists had already crossed the sea; later, he arrived in person, showing himself alive, contrary to all expectation, but the sight of his scars, so numerous, so extensive, so fresh, made it seem that there had been good ground for the report of his death.

Chapter 28

He therefore asked help from a Christian emperor, not so much to avenge himself as to protect the Church entrusted to him. If he had refrained from doing so, his patience would not have been a subject of praise, while his negligence would deservedly have been a subject of blame. The Apostle Paul was not thinking of his own transitory life, but of the Church of God, when he undertook to reveal to the tribune the plot of those who had conspired to kill him, and, as a consequence, he was escorted by an armed guard to the place where he was to go, thereby escaping their ambush.[1] He had not the least hesitation in calling on Roman law by declaring himself a Roman citizen, whom it was not lawful at that time to scourge.[2] Likewise, he appealed to the help of Caesar to save himself from being given over to the Jews who were eager to kill him—and this was a Roman prince, not a

1 Acts 23.12,32.
2 Acts 22.24-29.

Christian one.[3] By this he showed clearly what the ministers of Christ were to do afterward, in times of crisis for the Church, when they should find their rulers Christian. From this it followed that, when such cases were brought to his notice, a religious and devout emperor preferred to effect a complete reformation of that impious aberration by stringent religious laws and to force those who carried the standard of Christ against Christ to return to Catholic unity, under stress of fear and compulsion, rather than merely to cut off their opportunity for savage cruelty and leave them free to go astray and be lost.[4]

Chapter 29

As soon as those laws were promulgated in Africa, there was an immediate conversion to the Church, especially of those who only wanted an opportunity or who feared the rage of rabid men, or who were timid about offending their families. Many, too, who were attached to their belief by nothing more than custom handed down by their parents, who had never before investigated the cause of the heresy, had never cared to inquire into or examine it, became Catholics without any difficulty once they began to take note of it, and found in it no adequate reason for suffering such losses. Isolation was a good teacher for those who had grown careless through immunity. Moreover, the persuasive influence of all these predecessors had many followers among those who were less capable of understanding for themselves the difference between Donatist error and Catholic truth.

---

3 Acts 25.11.
4 This was done by the Edict of Union, 405.

Chapter 30

Thus, although the true mother received great throngs of people into her bosom with rejoicing, there remained unyielding groups which persisted, with ill-fated hostility, in that deadly pestilence. Of these many pretended to conform; the rest escaped notice because of their small numbers. Those who pretended were largely converted by becoming accustomed little by little to hearing the truth preached, and this was especially true after the conference and discussion between their bishops and ours at Carthage. In some places, however, where a stubborn and unruly mob held sway, too powerful to be resisted by a minority, although these latter were well-disposed to conform, or where crowds were forced by the authority of a powerful few to follow their evil course, there was trouble for some time longer. It is among these that the trouble still exists, and in that trouble Catholics, especially bishops and clerics, have suffered unspeakable hardships which it will take too long to enumerate; some had their eyes put out; one bishop had his hands and tongue cut off; some were even massacred. I say nothing of the inhuman beatings, of looting of homes in nightly raids, of fires set not only to private houses but even to churches; and into these flames some even cast the sacred books.

Chapter 31

But the ensuing good effects consoled us after we had been afflicted with such evils. For, wherever those excesses were committed by abandoned men, there Christian unity flourished more fervently and more perfectly; there the Lord was praised more abundantly because He had deigned to grant that His servants, by their sufferings, should enrich their brothers, and by their blood should gather to the peace of eternal salvation His sheep that had been led astray by deadly error. The Lord is mighty and merciful and to Him we pray daily that He may grant 'repentance and that they may recover themselves from the snares of the devil, by whom they are held captive at his will,'[1] to the others who seek only an occasion to do us harm and to repay evil for good,[2] because they have not the mind to understand what loving sentiments we entertain for them, and how, according to the Lord's commandment, which He gave to His shepherds through the Prophet Ezechiel, we long to bring back that which was scattered and to find that which was lost.[3]

Chapter 32

But, as we have said elsewhere on occasion, these heretics refuse to take the blame for what they do to us and they lay the blame on us for what they do to themselves. Who of us would wish them to lose anything, much less that they be lost themselves? If the house of David could win peace in no other way than through the death of Absalom, David's son, in the war which he was carrying on against his father—although the latter had instructed his followers with great care to keep him safe and sound as far as it was possible for them to do so, that he might repent and receive pardon from his father's love—what was left for him but to weep over his son's loss, and find comfort for his grief in the peace thus gained for his kingdom?[1] In the same manner, then,

---

1 2 Tim. 2.25,26.
2 Ps. 34.12.
3 Ezech. 34.4-6.

1 2 Kings 18.5-15.33; 22.1-51.

our Catholic mother acts when others who are not her sons
make war on her—because it is a fact that this little branch
in Africa has been broken off[2] from the great tree which
embraces the whole world in the spreading of its branches[3]—
and although she is in labor with them[4] in charity, that they
may return to the root without which they cannot have true
life, still, if she rescues so many others by losing some,
especially when these fall by self-destruction, not by the
fortune of war as Absalom did, she solaces the grief of her
maternal heart and heals it by the deliverance of such
numbers of people. If you were to see the effects of the
peace of Christ: the joyful throngs, their eagerness to hear
and sing hymns and to receive the word of God, the well-
attended, happy meetings; the sentiments of many among
them, their great grief in recalling past error, their joy in
contemplating the known truth, their indignation at their
masters and repudiation of their lies, because they now know
what false reports these circulated about our sacraments; the
admission of many, also, that they had long wished to be
Catholics, but did not dare to brave the fury of such men—I
repeat, if you were to see in one glance these flocks of people
in many parts of Africa, now delivered from that destruction,
you would say that it would have been excessively cruel for
all these to be abandoned to eternal loss and to the torments
of everlasting fire through fear that some desperate men, not
to be compared by any standard of judgment to that unnumbered throng, should destroy themselves in flames kindled
by themselves.

Chapter 33

If two persons were living together in a house which we

2 Isa. 18.5; Rom. 11.17,19.
3 Luke 13.19; Matt. 13.32; 24.14; Mark 4.32.
4 Gal. 4.19.

knew with absolute certainty was about to collapse, and if
they refused to believe us when we forewarned them of it
and insisted on staying there, and if we were able to drag
them out, even against their will, and afterward to point
out the imminent collapse, so that they would not dare to
return again into the danger, I think that if we failed to do
so we should deserve to be called cruel. Furthermore, if one
of them were to say to us: 'As soon as you come in to
rescue us I shall kill myself on the spot,' and if the other
should refuse either to leave the house or to be pulled out,
yet dared not kill himself, what should we decide to do?
Should we leave them both to be overwhelmed in the crash,
or should we extend our compassionate help to the one at
least and leave the other to perish, not through our fault but
his own? There is no one so hapless as not to decide easily
what one should do in such cases. I have suggested in this
parable of the two men that one is lost and the other saved,
but what are we to think of the few lost and the unnumbered
throng of people saved? For, the number of those men who
perish by a self-willed death is not so great as the crowds who
are saved by these laws from that deadly and eternal destruction, on the farms, through the countryside, in the villages,
in the citadels, the towns, the cities.

Chapter 34

However, if we look carefully into this matter which we
are discussing, I think that if there were many persons in the
house doomed to collapse, and at least one could be saved,
even though the others should kill themselves by jumping
headlong while we were trying to save the one, we should
find comfort, in the safety of at least one, for our sorrow

over the others; but this would not be so if we allowed all
to perish without saving the one, because we feared that the
others would destroy themselves. What, then, is our estimate
of the work of mercy which we should practice toward men
to enable them to gain eternal life and avoid eternal torment,
if a right and kind reason obliges us to afford them help to
secure a mere temporal and brief safety, for however short a
time?

Chapter 35

As to their charging us with coveting and confiscating
their property, would that they might become Catholics and
possess jointly with us, in peace and charity, not only what
they say is theirs, but even what is ours! But they are so
blinded by their passion for false accusation that they do not
notice how they contradict themselves in what they say.
They certainly say, and they seem to make it a matter of
invidious complaint, that we force them into our communion
by the violent compulsion of law. This we would emphatically
not do if we had designs on their property. What miser looks
for a co-owner? Who that is fired with a lust of power or
puffed up with the pride of authority yearns to have a
partner? Let them at least take note of those who were
formerly their associates but are now ours, how they not
only retain their own possessions which they used to have,
but even share ours which they did not have, for, if we are
poor, our possessions are also theirs. Moreover, if we have
private property which suffices for us, the other is not ours
but the property of the poor; we are in a sense merely its
administrators, and we do not call down judgment on ourselves by usurping ownership of it.

Chapter 36

Whatever property, therefore, is held by the Donatist sect in the name of their churches, by the orders issued through the religious laws of our Christian emperors is to revert to the Catholic Church together with their churches. Since the people of the same churches are with us, and their poor, who were supported by their puny possessions, are also with us, while they remain outside, let them stop coveting the property of others; let them enter into unity as partners with us, so that we may together administer not only what they call theirs, but also what is ours. For, it is written: 'All things are yours, but you are Christ's and Christ is God's.'[1] Let us be one under that Head, in His one Body,[2] and let us deal with such things as these in the manner described in the Acts of the Apostles: 'They had one heart and one soul, neither did anyone say that aught was his own, but all things were common unto them.'[3] Let us love what we sing: 'Behold how good and how pleasant it is for brethren to dwell together in unity,'[4] that they may experience and may know how truthfully their Catholic mother calls out to them in the words written by the blessed Apostle to the Corinthians: 'I seek not the things that are yours, but you.'[5]

Chapter 37

If, however, we reflect on what is written in the Book of

---

1 Cor. 3.22,23.
2 Gal. 3.28; Eph. 1.22,23; 3.15; 5.23; Col. 1.18.
3 Acts 4.32.
4 Ps. 132.1.
5 2 Cor. 12.14.

Wisdom: 'Therefore the just took the spoils of the wicked,'[1] and likewise on what we read in Proverbs: 'But the riches of the wicked are laid up as treasure for the just,'[2] we shall see that the question is not who holds the property of heretics, but who are in the company of the just. We know, indeed, that the Donatists falsely claim such justice for themselves, that they boast not only of having it themselves but of giving it to other men. They go so far as to say that the one whom they baptize is justified by them, and the only thing left for them to say to the one who is baptized by them is that he should believe in his baptizer. And why should he not do so, when the Apostle says: 'To him that believeth in him that justifieth the ungodly, his faith is reputed unto justice.'[3] Let him therefore believe in his baptizer if he is justified by him, that his faith may be reputed unto justice. But I think they are horrified at themselves if they regard it as fitting even to imagine such things. The only just and justifying one is God.[4] But we can apply to them what the Apostle said of the Jews that, 'not knowing the justice of God and seeking to establish their own, they have not submitted themselves to the justice of God.'[5]

Chapter 38

Far be it from anyone of us to say that he is just, or to seek to establish his own justice, that is, as if it were given to him by himself, when the Apostle says to him: 'For what

---

1 Wisd. 10.19.
2 Prov. 13.32 (Septuagint).
3 Rom. 4.5.
4 2 Mach. 1.25; Rom. 8.33.
5 Rom. 10.3.

hast thou that thou hast not received?"[1] or to dare to boast
that he is without sin in this life, as they said at our conference
that they were in a Church which has not 'spot or wrinkle
or any such thing,'[2] not knowing that this is fulfilled only
in those who go out of the body either straightway after
baptism, or after the forgiveness of our debts which we pray
to have remitted in the Lord's prayer. But this will be true of
the whole Church, namely, that it should be entirely without
spot or wrinkle or any such thing, only when we can say
'O death, where is thy victory? O death, where is thy sting?
Now the sting of death is sin.'[3]

Chapter 39

If their church is like that in this life where 'the corruptible body is a load upon the soul,'[1] then let them not say
to God what the Lord taught us to pray: 'Forgive us our
debts.'[2] Since all sins are forgiven in baptism, why does the
Church make this petition if even in this life she has 'neither
spot nor wrinkle nor any such thing'? Let them also disregard
the Apostle John crying out in his Epistle: 'If we say that
we have no sin, we deceive ourselves, and the truth is not in
us. If we confess our sins, he is faithful and just to forgive us
our sins and to cleanse us from all iniquity.'[3] It is because of
this hope that the whole Church says: 'Forgive us our debts,'
that he may cleanse us, not boasting but confessing, from all
iniquity, and thus the Lord Christ may present to Himself

1 1 Cor. 4.7.
2 Eph. 5.27.
3 1 Cor. 15.55,56.

1 Wisd. 9.15.
2 Matt. 6.12.
3 1 John 1.8,9.

on that day a glorious Church not having spot or wrinkle or any such thing. This Church He now cleanses by 'the laver of water in the word,'[4] because, on the one hand, nothing of all our past sins remains unforgiven in baptism—always supposing that the baptism is not considered invalid as given outside the Church, but is either given inside, or, if it was given outside, it is not left outside with the subject—and, on the other hand, whatever guilt is contracted through human weakness by those who live on after having received baptism is forgiven by the same laver. It is of no use for the unbaptized to say: 'Forgive us our debts!

Chapter 40

Thus, He cleanses His Church by the 'laver of water in the word,' that He may then present it to Himself, having neither spot nor wrinkle nor any such thing, that is, wholly beautiful and perfect when 'death shall be swallowed up in victory.'[1] In this life, therefore, in so far as the fact that we are born of God and live by faith[2] prevails in us we are just, but in so far as we inherit the remnants of mortality from Adam we are not without sin. This saying is true: 'Whosoever is born of God committeth not sin,'[3] and this is also true: 'If we say that we have no sin, we deceive ourselves and the truth is not in us.'[4] Therefore, the Lord Christ is both the just one and the justifier, but we are 'justified freely by his grace.'[5] However, He justifies only His Body, 'which is

4 Eph. 5.26,27.

1 1 Cor. 15.54.
2 Hab. 2.4; Rom. 1.17; Gal. 3.41.
3 1 John 3.9.
4 1 John 1.8.
5 Rom. 3.24.

the Church,'[6] and thus, if the body of Christ takes the spoils
of the wicked and lays up as a treasure for the body of
Christ the riches of the wicked, the wicked ought not to
remain outside the body of Christ to their injury, but should
enter into it for their justification.

Chapter 41

Consequently, those words which are written of the day
of judgment, 'Then shall the just stand with great constancy
against those that have afflicted them and taken away their
labors,'[1] should certainly not be taken to mean that the
Chanaanite shall stand against Israel because Israel has
taken away the labors of the Chanaanite,[2] but Naboth shall
stand against Achab because Achab took away the labors of
Naboth,[3] for in this case the Chanaanite was wicked but
Naboth was just. In the same way, the pagan shall not stand
against the Christian who has taken away his labors by
despoiling or giving away the temples of the idols, but the
Christian shall stand against the pagan who took away his
labors by laying low the bodies of the martyrs. Thus, therefore, the heretic shall not stand against the Catholic who
received his labors when the laws of Catholic emperors came
into force, but the Catholic shall stand against the heretic
who took away his labors when the fury of wicked Circumcellions was in force. In truth, Scripture itself has solved
the question by saying: 'Then shall the just stand,' not 'then
shall men stand,' and therefore it will be with great constancy
because it will be with a good conscience.

---

6 Col. 1.24.

---

1 Wisd. 5.1.
2 Josue 17.12,13.
3 3 Kings 21.1-16.

Chapter 42

But no one is just by his own justice, that is, as if it were the effect of his own act, but, as the Apostle says: 'According as God hath divided to every one the measure of faith,' and he follows up and adds: 'For as in one body we have many members, but all the members have not the same office, so we being many are one body in Christ.'[1] As a consequence, no one can be just so long as he is separated from the unity of this body. For, in the same way as a member cannot retain the spirit of life if it is cut off from the body of a living man, so a man cannot possibly retain the spirit of justice if he is cut off from the body of the just Christ, although he may retain the appearance of a member which he derived from the body. Let the Donatists come, then, into the structure of this body and let them possess their labors, not with a passion for power, but with the holy desire of using them well. As has been said before, we, on our part, cleanse our will of the baseness of such passion—no matter what enemy judges us—when we strive with all our might to bring those very ones whose labors these are said to be to make use jointly with us in the Catholic community of their goods and ours.

Chapter 43

'But,' they say, 'this is what disturbs us: if we are unjust why do you seek us?' We answer them: 'We seek you in your injustice that you may not remain unjust, we seek you as lost that we may rejoice at finding you, saying: 'Our brother was dead and is come to life again, he was lost and is found.'[1]

---

1 Rom. 12.3-5.

1 Luke 15.32.

'Why, then,' says one, 'do you not baptize me to wash me from sin?' I answer: 'Because I do not dishonor the brand mark of the commander when I rectify the wandering of the deserter.' 'Why,' says he, 'do I not do penance when I join you?' 'Indeed, unless you do penance you cannot be saved, for how will you rejoice at being set right if you do not grieve at having gone astray?' 'What, then,' says he, 'do we receive when we go over to you?' I answer: 'You do not indeed receive baptism which it was possible for you to have outside the unity of the body of Christ, although it was not possible for it to profit you, but you do receive "the unity of the Spirit in the bond of peace,"[2] "without which no man shall see God,"[3] and also charity, which, as it is written, "covereth a multitude of sins."[4] The Apostle bears witness that this is so great a good that without it neither tongues of men and angels, nor knowledge of all mysteries, nor prophecy, nor faith so great as to move mountains, nor distributing to the poor of everything a man possesses, nor delivering one's body to be burned profit a man anything,[5] and, therefore, if you think this great good is little or nothing, you are in an unhappy state of error, and if you do not come over to Catholic unity, you are lost.'

Chapter 44

'If, then,' they say, 'it is our duty to repent of having been outside the Church and opposed to the Church, in order to be saved, how can we continue to be clerics or even bishops

---

2 Eph. 4.3.
3 Heb. 12.14
4 1 Peter 4.8.
5 1 Cor. 13.1-3.

after that penance?"[1] This would not happen, since we must confess as a matter of truth it ought not to happen, unless the healing of the peace of the Church effects a restoration. Let them tell themselves this, and let them grieve with great and deep humility, that those who lie prostrate in the death of such a severance can live again, in spite of such a wound inflicted on their Catholic mother. For, when a cut branch is grafted, another cut is made in the tree into which it is fitted, so that it may live by the life of the root, without which it would die; but, when the graft has become one with its host, it grows strong and produces fruit, whereas, if he does not become one with the tree, it withers away, while the life of the tree will remain. There is also a kind of grafting in which the branch which is not part of the tree is inserted without cutting off any branch belonging to it, and with some cut in the tree, but at most a very slight one. So it is, then, with them when they come to the Catholic root, although they are not deprived of the dignity of clerical or episcopal rank after they have done penance for their lapse, there is some severe effect in the bark, as it were, of the mother tree, diminishing its integrity. Nevertheless, because 'neither he that planteth is anything nor he that watereth,'[2] when their prayers are poured forth to the mercy of God, as the peace of the engrafted branches grows into unity, 'charity covereth a multitude of sins.'

Chapter 45

But when it was decreed in the Church that no one after penance should become a cleric, or return to clerical status

---

1 Agreed at the Council of Carthage, 401.
2 1 Cor. 3.7.

or remain in it,[1] this was not done through any despair of forgiveness, but for the maintenance of discipline; otherwise, there would be a challenge to the keys given to the Church, of which it is said: 'Whatsoever thou shalt loose on earth, it shall be loosed also in heaven.'[2] But lest, perchance, anyone, when his crimes have been discovered, should do penance with a mind full of pride, in the hope of ecclesiastical preferment, this more severe decree was passed that no one should be a cleric after performing penance for a mortal offense. The purpose of this was to be that the humiliation of the remedy would be more effective and more sincere when temporal rank was not to be hoped for. Holy David did penance for his mortal crimes and still retained his rank,[3] and blessed Peter certainly repented of having denied the Lord when he shed such bitter tears, but he remained an Apostle.[4] Still, not for that reason is the caution of their successors to be considered useless, by which they have added to the force of humility without removing any help to salvation: rather, salvation is thereby more safely assured. They had experience, I imagine, of the pretended repentance of some who were aiming at the power attached to rank. The experience of many diseases forces us to find many remedies. In cases of this sort, where there is question of the dread division of schism, and there is not merely danger for this or that man, but of destruction which lays low whole peoples, there has to be some reduction in severity so that a sincere charity may help to remedy greater evils.

---

1 One of the canons of the Council of Nicaea, as mentioned by Pope Innocent I in his letter to the bishops of Apulia.
2 Matt. 16.19; 18.18.
3 2 Kings 12.1-20; 24.17.
4 Matt. 26.69-75; Mark 14.66-72; Luke 22.55-62.

Chapter 46

Let them, then, have a bitter sorrow for their former detestable wrong-doing, as Peter had for his cowardly lie, and let them come to the true Church, that is, their Catholic mother, and let them be clerics or bishops in it with as much service for it as they formerly used against it. We do not begrudge it to them; on the contrary, we embrace them, we beg them, we exhort them, we compel them to come in when we find them in the highways and hedges. Even so, we do not yet persuade some of them that we seek them, not their possessions. When the Apostle Peter denied the Saviour, and wept and remained an Apostle, he had not yet received the Holy Spirit who had been promised,[2] but much less have they received Him when, severed from the unity of the body to which alone the Holy Spirit gives life,[3] they have maintained the sacraments of the Church outside the Church and in opposition to the Church, and have fought a kind of civil war, setting up our own banners and our own arms against us. Let them come; let there be peace in the strength of Jerusalem, the strength which is charity, as it was said to the holy city: 'Let peace be in thy strength and abundance in thy towers.'[4] Let them not rise up against the motherly anxiety which she had and has to gather them in, and with them so many throngs of people whom they deceive or did deceive; let them not be proud, because she thus welcomes them; let them not turn to the evil purpose of self-esteem what she does for the good purpose of peace.

---

1 Luke 14.23.
2 John 14.26; 16.13.
3 John 6.64; 2 Cor. 3.6.
4 Ps. 121.6,7.

Chapter 47

It is thus that she has been wont to succor the crowds perishing in schism and heresy. Lucifer[1] was displeased because the same thing was done in rescuing and healing those who had been lost through the poison of Arianism, and as a result of his displeasure he fell into the darkness of schism by losing the light of charity. From the beginning this was the course pursued toward these men by the Catholic Church in Africa, following the decisions of the bishops in the Roman Church when they judged between Caecilian and the sect of Donatus, who was shown to be the author of the schism. Donatus alone was condemned, but they decreed that the others, his followers, once they were converted, should be maintained in their clerical rank, even though they had been ordained outside the Church, not because it was possible for them to have the Holy Spirit while cut off from the unity of the body of Christ, but mostly for the sake of those whom they could lead astray and prevent from receiving that gift while they were established in their dissidence, and also that this more kindly treatment of their weakness might effect their cure within the Church, when obstinacy should no longer shut the eyes of their heart to the evidence of truth. What other course of action did they themselves think up when they first condemned the Maximianists[2] for their sacrilegious schism—as their council shows[3]—and ordained others in their stead; but afterward, when they saw that their flocks did not desert the Maximianists, they received them back in their respective rank, so as not to lose all of

---

1 Lucifer of Cagliari, bishop, who resented the clemency shown to repentent Arians, and gathered a schismatic group around him. Cf. *De agone Christiano* 30.
2 Cf. Augustine, *Contra Cresconum* 3.53,59; 4.10-12; *De baptismo* 1.5-7.
3 At Bagai, in 394.

them, and raised no objection or question about the baptism which they had conferred while separated from the Donatist sect by their sentence of condemnation? Why, then, do they wonder or complain or take it ill that we receive them back for the sake of the true peace of Christ, and fail to remember what they themselves did for the sake of the false peace of Donatus which is opposed to Christ? If this fact is held up before them and skillfully pressed on them, they will have no ground at all on which to make an answer.

Chapter 48

But, when they say: 'If we have sinned against the Holy Spirit by casting scorn on your baptism, what use is it for you to seek us, when it is utterly impossible for this sin to be forgiven us, in the Lord's words: "He that shall sin against the Holy Spirit, it shall not be forgiven him, neither in this world nor in the world to come," '[1] they do not observe that according to that interpretation no one should be saved. For, who does not speak against the Holy Spirit and sin against Him, whether it be he who is not yet a Christian, or a heretic Arian,[2] or a Eunomian,[3] or a Macedonian,[4] all of whom say that He is created, or a Photinian,[5] who denies Him substance entirely, saying that only the Father is God, or other heretics whom it would take too long to enumerate? Should none of them be saved? Or the Jews themselves, whom the Lord reproached that if they had believed in Him they would not have to be baptized? The Saviour did not say: 'It

---

1 Matt. 12.32.
2 Arius (4th century) held the Son and the Holy Spirit to have been created by the Father.
3 Eunomius (350-381) held the Son to be unequal to the Father.
4 Macedonius (4th century) denied the divinity of the Holy Spirit.
5 Photinus (4th century) held the three Persons of the Trinity to be merely three aspects of the divinity.

shall be forgiven in baptism,' but He said: 'It shall not be forgiven him, neither in this world nor in the world to come.'

Chapter 49

Let us, then, understand that this does not apply to every sin, but to a certain sin against the Holy Spirit, which will not be forgiven. In the same way, when He said: 'If I had not come, they would not have sin,'[1] He manifestly did not intend us to understand every sin, for indeed they were guilty of many great sins, but that, if they did not have a certain special sin, all the others which they had could be forgiven them; and that sin was that they did not believe in Him when He came—they would not have had this sin if He had not come—so also when He said: 'He that shall sin against the Holy Spirit or shall speak a word against the Holy Spirit,' it is plain that He did not mean every sin committed against the Holy Spirit by deed or word, but a certain particular sin. This sin is a hardness of heart persisted in until the end of this life, by which a man refuses to accept remission for his sins in the unity of the body of Christ, to which the Holy Spirit gives life. For, when He had said to His disciples: 'Receive ye the Holy Spirit,' He immediately added: 'Whose sins you shall forgive, they are forgiven them; whose sins you shall retain, they are retained.'[2] Therefore, whoever shall resist this gift of the grace of God, and shall oppose it or shall in any way be estranged from it until the end of this temporal life, 'It shall not be forgiven him, neither in this world nor in the world to come,' for, obviously, this is so great a sin that all other sins are comprised in it;

1 John 15.22.
2 John 20.22,23.

but it is not committed by anyone until he has left the body. As long as he lives, as the Apostle says: 'The patience of God leadeth him to do penance,' but, if the sinner remains in his persistent wickedness, then, as the Apostle adds at once: 'According to the hardness of his heart and his impenitent heart,' he treasures up for himself 'wrath against the day of wrath and revelation of the just judgment of God,'[3] and 'it shall not be forgiven him, neither in this world nor in the world to come.'

Chapter 50

Those with whom we are treating, or of whom we are treating, are not to be despaired of, for they are still in the body. But let them not seek the Holy Spirit except in the Body of Christ. It is true they have His sacrament outside the Church, but they do not hold the reality of it within, for it is His sacrament, and therefore they eat and drink judgment to themselves.[1] For, the one bread is the sacrament of unity, since, as the Apostle says: 'We being many are one bread, one body.'[2] Therefore, the Catholic Church alone is the Body of Christ; He is its head and the Saviour of His Body.[3] The Holy Spirit gives life to no one outside this body, because, as the Apostle himself says: 'The charity of God is poured forth in our hearts by the Holy Spirit who is given to us.'[4] But the enemy of unity has no share in the divine charity. Consequently, those who are outside the Church do not have the Holy Spirit, and of them it is written: 'These are they

3 Rom. 2.4,5.

1 1 Cor. 11.29.
2 1 Cor. 10.17.
3 Eph. 5.33.
4 Rom. 5.5.

who separate themselves, sensual men, having not the Spirit.'[5]
But he who pretends to be in the Church does not receive
Him either, since it is written of him: 'The Holy Spirit of
discipline will flee from the deceitful.'[6] Whoever, then, wishes
to have the Holy Spirit must beware of remaining outside the
Church; he must beware of pretending to come into it, or, if
he has made such a pretended entry, he must beware of
persisting in his pretense, so that he may truly grow into the
tree of life.

Chapter 51

I have addressed you a lengthy book; perhaps it will be
tiresome to you in the midst of your duties. But, if even parts
of it can be read to you, the Lord will give you understanding
so that you may know what to answer them for their amendment and cure. For Mother Church entrusts them to you as
to her faithful son, so that, when and as you are able, you
may amend and cure them, whether by speaking to them
and answering them yourself, or by leading them to the
doctors of the Church.

185A. To Count Boniface[1]

It is very gratifying to me that amid the tasks of your
stewardship you do not neglect to care for religion, also, and
that you wish to call back to the way of salvation and peace
men who are firmly set in schism and division.

---

5 Jude 1.19.
6 Wisd. 1.5.

---

1 A fragment found in a manuscript between Augustine's book on *The
Spirit and the Letter* and his treatise, *The Care To Be Taken for the
Dead*. It is entitled 'Here beginneth happily the letter of the same
to Count Boniface.'

*186. Alypius and Augustine, to their fellow bishop, Paulinus,[1]
their saintly lord and brother, cherished more
than words can tell, worthy of being embraced
with fraternal love in the heart of Christ*
(Mid 417)

At long last God has provided us with the most trustworthy of all letter-bearers, our justly cherished brother
Januarius.[2] Even if we did not write, your Sincerity could
learn all the news of us from him as from a living and
intelligent letter. We knew that you loved Pelagius as a servant
of God—this Pelagius, we believe, is called the Briton,[3] to
distinguish him from another Pelagius who is said to be a
Tarentine—but we do not know how you love him now. We
also not only have loved but still do love him. But the love
we have for him now is different from the love we had for
him formerly; then we loved him as one who seemed to be
of the true faith, whereas we now love him in order that, by
the mercy of God, he may be set free from those antagonistic
views which he is said to hold against the grace of God.
It was not easy to believe this about him, when the rumor
began to be circulated some time ago—for rumor is usually
a liar—but what brought it home to us and made us believe
it was a certain book of his which aims to set forth theories
intended to destroy and remove from faithful hearts any belief
in the grace of God bestowed on the human race through
the one Mediator of God and men, Christ Jesus.[4] We read
this book when it was brought to us by some servants of

---

1 Bishop of Nola.
2 It is not clear whether this is the Januarius of Letters 54 and 55.
3 Marius Mercator in his *Commonitorium,* Orosius in his *Liber Apologeticus (PL* 31), and Prosper in his *Carmen de ingratis* all name him
as Britannus or Britannicus; Jerome is supposed to insinuate the
same when he describes him as 'heavy with Scottish porridge,' in his
Praelatio ad Jeremiam (PL 24.679).
4 1 Tim. 2.5.

Christ[5] who had listened attentively to teachings such as these, and had been his followers. At their request, as we saw that it needed to be done, one of us made answer to this book in a treatise,[6] without mentioning his name, lest, if he were offended, he would not be open to correction. His book contains and asserts this view frequently and fully, as he also set it forth in certain letters sent to your Reverence,[7] where he says that he ought not to be reputed as defending free will unhelped by the grace of God, since he says that the ability to will and to do, without which we can neither will nor do any good, has been implanted by our Creator in our human nature, and that manifestly this was the grace of God as understood by the doctor of grace himself,[8] which is common to pagans and Christians, wicked and good, unbelievers and believers.

To the best of our ability, we refuted these evil views by which the coming of the Saviour is made void, to which we can say what the Apostle says of the Law: 'If justice be by nature, then Christ died in vain.'[9] Thus we aimed to pluck these views from the hearts of those who held them, and our object in making them known was that, if he were not personally attacked, he might be converted and the dignity of the man safeguarded, while the deadly infection of error might be stamped out. But later, when letters came to us from the East, giving the most open publicity to the case, we were in duty bound not to fail to use our episcopal authority, such as it is, in behalf of the Church. Therefore, reports[10] of this controversy were sent to the Apostolic See from the two Councils of Carthage and Milevis, and this was done before

---

5 Timasius and James; cf Letters 168 and 179.
6 Augustine, *De natura et gratia.*
7 Cf. Pelagius, *Liber de gratia Dei* 35.
8 St. Paul.
9 Cf. Gal. 2.21.
10 Cf. Letters 175 and 176.

the ecclesiastical minutes of the meeting, in which Pelagius is described as having been cleared before the bishops of the province of Palestine, had come into our hands or even into Africa. In addition to the reports of the councils we also wrote a personal letter[11] to Pope Innocent of blessed memory,[12] in which we dealt with the same case somewhat more at length. He answered all these communications[13] in a manner which was right and fitting for the pontiff of the Apostolic See.

You will soon be able to read all these in case none or not all of them have reached you. There you will see how, while preserving a due regard for men, not to condemn them provided they condemn their wrong views, the authority of the Church has so prohibited that new and deadly error that we wonder greatly how there could still be any who try to persist in any false view of the grace of God—that is, always supposing they have heard of these decrees—the grace of God through Jesus Christ our Lord, as the true and Catholic Church always holds, which transforms both little and great[14] from the death of the first man to the life of the second man,[15] not only by destroying sin, but also by helping those who are now able to use their free will to avoid sin and live virtuously; and this help is such that, if it is not given, we can have no trace of piety or justice either in our works or even in our very will: 'For it is God who worketh in you both to will and to accomplish according to his good will.'[16]

For, who distinguishes us from that mass and material of perdition except the One who came 'to seek and to save that

---

11 Cf. Letters 177.
12 He died on July 28, 417.
13 Cf. Letters 181, 182, and 183.
14 Apoc. 11.18.
15 1 Cor. 15.47.
16 Phil. 2.13.

which was lost'?[17] The Apostle asks this question when he
says: 'Who distinguished thee?' and if any man should say:
'My faith, my good will, my good work,' he would receive
the answer: 'But what hast thou that thou hast not received?
And if thou hast received why dost thou glory as if thou
hadst not received it?'[18] And he certainly says all this, not
that man should not glory but that 'he that glorieth may
glory in the Lord,'[19] not of works, that no man may be
puffed up';[20] not because good works are rendered useless by
that holy thought, since 'God will render to every man
according to his works and there should be glory and honor
and peace to everyone that worketh good,'[21] but because the
works come from the grace, not the grace from the works,
because 'faith that worketh by charity'[22] would have no
effect unless 'the charity of God were poured forth in our
hearts by the Holy Spirit who is given to us.'[23] And faith
itself would not be in us if God did not 'divide to every one
the measure of faith.'[24]

Therefore, it is good for a man to say truthfully and with
the full strength of his free will: 'I will keep my strength to
thee,'[25] because the man who thought he could keep it
without the help of Him who gave it went abroad into a far
country and wasted his substance, living riotously. But, worn
down by the wretchedness of a harsh slavery, he returned to
himself and said: 'I will arise and go to my father.'[26] But,
how could he have had this good thought if the most merciful
Father had not whispered it to him in secret? It was because

17 Luke 19.10.
18 1 Cor. 4.7.
19 1 Cor. 1.31.
20 Cf. Eph. 2.9.
21 Rom. 2.6,10.
22 Gal. 5.6.
23 Rom. 5.5.
24 Rom. 12.3.
25 Ps. 58.10.
26 Luke 15.12-18.

he understood this that the minister of the New Testament[27] said: 'Not that we are sufficient to think anything of ourselves as of ourselves, but our sufficiency is from God.'[28] Consequently, when the Psalmist also had said: 'I will keep my strength to thee,' lest he should attribute to himself the fact that he was keeping it, and as if he recalled to mind that 'Except the Lord keep the city, they watch in vain that keep it,'[29] and that 'He shall neither slumber nor sleep that keepeth Israel,'[30] he added the reason of his being able to keep it, or, rather, the guard by whom it is kept and said: 'For thou, O God, art my protector.'[31]

Let Pelagius then recall, if he can, his merits which would make God deign to be his protector, as if God had been protected; let him recall whether he sought or was sought by Him, I mean the One 'who came to seek and to save that which was lost.'[32] For, if a man is willing to seek for what he deserves before receiving grace, which will make him fit to receive it, he will be able to find his evil deeds, not his good ones,[33] and this would be true even if the grace of the Saviour came upon him when he had lived only one day upon earth; because, if a man does anything good by which he may merit grace, 'the reward is not reckoned according to grace, but according to debt; but if he believeth in him that justifieth the ungodly, that his faith may be reputed to justice,'[34]—for 'the just man liveth by faith'[35]—certainly before he is justified by grace, that is, made just, what else is the wicked man but wicked? If his debt followed him, what

---

27 Eph. 3.7.
28 2 Cor. 3.5.
29 Ps. 126.1.
30 Ps. 120.4.
31 Ps. 58.10.
32 Luke 19.10.
33 Job 14.5 (Septuagint).
34 Rom. 4.4,5.
35 Hab. 2.4; Rom. 1.17; Gal. 3.11; Heb. 10.38.

would he deserve to receive but punishment? 'And if by
grace, it is not now by works; otherwise grace is no more
grace.'[36] To works is given what they deserve, but grace is
given freely; that is why it is called grace.

If anyone says that faith merits the grace of doing good
works, we cannot deny it; on the contrary, we admit it most
thankfully. This is the faith we wish those brothers of ours to
have so that they may obtain charity which alone truly performs good works, for they glory much in their works, but
charity is so much the gift of God that it is called God.[37]
Therefore, those who have faith by which they win justification attain by the grace of God to the law of justice; hence
the Prophet says: 'In an acceptable time I have heard thee,
and in the day of salvation I have helped thee.'[38] Consequently, in those who are saved by the election of grace,[39]
it is God as helper 'who worketh both to will and to accomplish according to his good will,'[40] because 'to them that
love God all things work together unto good.'[41] If this is
true of all things, it is more so of that charity to which we
attain by faith, so that by His grace we love Him 'who hath
first loved us,'[42] in order to believe in Him, and by loving
Him we perform good works, but we have not performed
the good works in order to love Him.

Those, however, who expect a reward of their merits as if
it were due to them, who attribute their merits, not to the
grace of God, but to the strength of their own will, through
following after the law of justice, like carnal Israel, do not
come unto the Law.[43] 'Why so? Because they sought it not by

36 Rom. 11.6.
37 1 John 4.8.
38 Isa. 49.8; 2 Cor. 6.2.
39 Rom. 11.5.
40 Phil. 2.14.
41 Rom. 8.28.
42 1 John 4.19.
43 Rom. 9.3.

faith but, as it were, by works.' But that justice is of faith
which the Gentiles attained, of whom it is said: 'What then
shall we say? That the Gentiles who knew not justice have
attained to justice, even the justice that is of faith. But
Israel, by following after the law of justice, is not come unto
the law. Why so? Because they sought it not by faith but, as
it were, by works. They stumbled at the stumbling stone, as
it is written: Behold I lay in Sion a stumbling stone and a
rock of scandal; and whosoever believeth in him shall not
be confounded.'[44] That justice is of faith by which we
believe we are justified, that is, made just by the grace of
God through Jesus Christ our Lord, that we may be found
in Him not having our justice 'which is of the law, but that
which is of the faith of Christ Jesus, which is of God,
justice in faith';[45] certainly in the faith by which we believe
that justice is given to us from above, not made by us for
ourselves by our own strength.

Why does the Apostle call that justice his which is of the
Law and not of God? Could it be possible that the Law is
not of God? None but an irreligious man would think that.
But, because the Law commands by the letter and does not
help by the spirit, whoever listens to the letter of the Law in
such wise as to think that it is enough for him to know what
it commands or forbids, whoever trusts in the strength of his
own free will to accomplish it, and does not take refuge in
faith in order to be assisted in his approach to the Spirit that
quickeneth lest the letter find him guilty and kill him,[46] that
man has a zeal of God, but not according to knowledge. For,
not knowing the justice of God, that is, the holiness which is
given from God, and seeking to establish his own, so that
it may be uniquely of the Law, he has not subjected himself

44 Rom. 9.30-33.
45 Phil. 3.9.
46 2 Cor. 3.6.

to the justice of God, 'for the end of the law is Christ unto justice to every one that believeth.'[47] So the same Apostle says: 'That we might be made the justice of God in him,'[48] 'being justified therefore by faith, let us have peace with God through our Lord, Jesus Christ';[49] 'being justified freely by his grace,'[50] and let this faith not be proud.

Let no one say to himself: 'If it is of faith, how is it freely given? If faith earns it, why is it not rather paid than given?' Let the faithful man not say that because, when he says: 'I have faith that I may earn justification,' he is answered: 'What hast thou that hast not received?'[51] Therefore, since faith asks for and receives justification, 'according as God hath divided to every one the measure of faith,'[52] no human merit precedes the grace of God, but grace itself merits an increase, and the increase merits perfection, with the will accompanying it, not going before it; following behind it, not pointing out the way. Hence, he who said: 'I will keep my strength to thee,' gave his reason by saying: 'For thou, O God, art my protector,' and, as if asking by what merits he attained this and finding nothing in himself antecedent to the grace of God, he said: 'My God, his mercy shall prevent me.'[53] By this he means: 'However great I may think my antecedent merits to be, his mercy shall prevent me.' Therefore, by keeping to Him the strength which is attributed to Him, with God for saviour, he does not lose what he received from God as giver. In no other way does he deserve more generous gifts than by knowing through faith and piety from whom all these good things come in to him, and by knowing

---

47 Rom. 10.2-4.
48 2 Cor. 5.21.
49 Rom. 5.1.
50 Rom. 3.24.
51 1 Cor. 4.7.
52 Rom. 12.3.
53 Ps. 58.10,11.

that they do not come to him from himself, lest even this should not be in him which is not of God. Finely, indeed, does the Apostle say: 'We have received not the spirit of this world but the Spirit that is of God, that we may know the things that are given us from God.'[54] Thus, this very merit of man is a free gift, and no one deserves to receive anything from the Father of lights from whom every best gift comes down,[55] except by receiving what he does not deserve.

Much more merciful and more freely given, beyond any doubt, is the grace of God through our Lord Jesus Christ which is bestowed on infants, so that they may not suffer for their descent from Adam but may benefit by their rebirth in Christ; and this mercy of God forestalls by a long time the very consciousness of receiving it. It is certain that, if they depart from the body at this tender age, they receive eternal life and the kingdom of heaven, knowing that it is by His gift, although here they did not know it when it was beneficial to them. Certainly in their case there is nothing but the former gifts to merit the subsequent ones, and in giving them the grace of God He operates in such wise that the will of the recipients is not previously stirred or assisted, nor does it follow after, since, in fact, this great benefit is conferred on them not only without their willing it, but often in spite of their fighting against it, which would be imputed to them as a great sacrilege if the freedom of the will had any effect in them.

We have said this for the sake of those who are unable to search into the unsearchable judgments of God[56] for the reason why, of the clay of Adam, which from him alone fell wholly into condemnation, He makes one vessel unto honor, another unto dishonor,[57] yet they dare to decide that babies

---

54 1 Cor. 2.12.
55 James 1.17.
56 Rom. 11.33.
57 Rom. 9.21.

who are unable to think anything, either good or bad, are guilty of actual sins, and that they are reputed to gain either penalty or favor through their free will, whereas apostolical truth, by saying 'by one unto condemnation,'[58] shows clearly that all are born under penalty so that they may be reborn in grace, not by merit but by mercy. 'Otherwise grace is no more grace,'[59] if it is a reward for human merits, not a freely given gift of divine bounty. In this it alone differs from punishment, that punishment is from Adam and is every man's due, but grace through the one Jesus Christ is owed to none but is freely given, that it may truly be grace. The unsearchable judgments of God, as if they were God, can be the reason why He distinguishes the little ones whom no merits single out, but they cannot be unjust judgments because 'all the ways of the Lord are mercy and truth.'[60] Consequently, when the mercy of grace is bestowed on one man, he has no reason to boast of his human merit, since it is 'not of works, that no man may glory';[61] but when the truth of punishment is meted out to another he has no just ground for complaint that what is rightly owed to sin is paid to it, since it is certainly not unjust for the one in whom all have sinned to be punished even in each individual. Their punishment throws into clearer light what is conferred on the vessels of mercy[62] by a true grace which is not their due, that is, it is freely given.

Let them produce their arguments against the Apostle when he says in the clearest possible words: 'By one man sin entered into this world, and by sin death, and so death passed upon all men in whom all have sinned.'[63] As for those who

---

58 Rom. 5.16.
59 Rom. 11.6.
60 Ps. 24.10.
61 Eph. 2.9.
62 Rom. 9.23.
63 Rom. 5.12.

say that even babies commit actual sins through free will, we are tired listening to them and disgusted at having to mention them, but we are under the greater obligation to speak. For it is a mark either of indolence to avoid by silence what these great and keen minds have been able to think up, or of arrogance to pass over it through contempt. 'See,' they say, 'Esau and Jacob struggle within their mother's womb; at the time of their birth one is supplanted by the other, and by the fact that the second one came forth holding the foot of the first one in his hand,[64] this struggle is proved to be in a sense continuous. How is it possible that in infants acting thus there should be no freedom of will for good or evil, as a result of which reward or punishment should follow their previous merits?'

To this we may say that the reason why those movements and that seeming struggle of the infants were a sign of great things was because they were miraculous, not acts of free choice. We are not likely to concede that asses have the power of free will because a dumb beast of that sort, as it is written: 'used to the yoke which, speaking with man's voice, forbade the folly of the prophet.'[65] But those who claim that there were voluntary acts and not miraculous movements, accomplished by them and not through them, would be hard put to answer the Apostle who, when he saw that these twins were worthy of remembrance as a testimonial of grace, freely given, said: 'For when the children were not yet born nor had done any good or evil, that the purpose of God according to election might stand, not of works but of him that calleth, it was said to her: The elder shall serve the younger'; then, adding the testimony of a Prophet who spoke long after those events, but nevertheless declared the ancient

---

64 Gen. 25.22,25; Osee 12.3.
65 Num. 22.28-30; 2 Peter 2.16. The Prophet was Balaam.

purpose of God in this matter, he said: 'As it is written: Jacob I have loved but Esau I have hated.'[66]

Manifestly, the 'doctor of the Gentiles in faith and truth'[67] testifies that those twins, not yet born, had done neither good nor evil, in order to bring out the value of grace, so that the words 'the elder shall serve the younger' may be understood as a result 'not of works but of him that calleth, that the purpose of God according to election might stand. 'But these words do not imply the antecedent merit of each man. He does not say the election of the human will or of nature, since in each twin there was the same status of death and damnation, but without any doubt he means the election of grace which does not find men worthy of being chosen but makes them so. In a later passage of the same Epistle he treats of this again when he says: 'Even so then at this present time also there is a remnant saved according to the election of grace. And if by grace it is not now by works; otherwise grace is no more grace.'[68] This passage is in accord with the former one where he states: 'not of works but of him that calleth: the elder shall serve the younger.' What, then, is their purpose in contradicting this eminent eulogist of grace, by their impudent insistence on the free will of infants and the acts of children not yet born? Why is grace said to be preceded by merits when it would not be grace if it were allotted according to merit? Why do they attack salvation which is sent for the lost, which comes for the unworthy? However keen, however complete and well-phrased their argument, it is nevertheless hardly Christian.

'But how,' says Pelagius, 'is it possible that there is no injustice with God if He singles out by His love those whom

66 Rom. 9.11-13; Mal. 1.2,3.
67 1 Tim. 2.7.
68 Rom. 11.5,6.

no merit of good works distinguishes?' This is said to us as if the Apostle himself had not seen it, had not stated it, had not answered it. On hearing these objections, he certainly saw what human weakness or ignorance can imagine, and stating the same question to himself, he says: 'What shall we say, then? Is there injustice with God?' and he answers at once: 'God forbid.' But in giving the reason why He should forbid, that is, why there is no injustice with God, he does not say: 'For He judges the merits or works of infants even though they are still enclosed in their mother's womb—for how could he say this when he had already said of the unborn and of those who had not yet done either good or evil that 'not of works but of him that calleth it was said to her: The elder shall serve the younger?'—but when he wished to show why in these matters there is no injustice with God, he said: 'For he saith to Moses: I will have mercy on whom I will have mercy, and I will show mercy to whom I will show mercy.'[69] What did he here teach us but that, as death is the just due of the clay of the first man, it belongs to the mercy of God and not to the merits of man that anyone is saved, and that therein there is no injustice with God, because He is not unjust either in forgiving or in exacting the penalty. Mercy is free where just vengeance could be taken. From this it is more clearly shown what a great benefit is conferred on the one who is delivered from a just penalty and freely justified, while another, equally guilty, is punished without injustice on the part of the avenger.

Finally, he adds this when he says: 'So then it is not of him that willeth nor of him that runneth but of God that showeth mercy.' This is said of those who are justified and saved by grace. But of those on whom the anger of God rests, because God makes good use of them to teach others whom He deigns to save, he goes on and says: 'For the

69 Rom. 9.15; Exod. 33.19.

Scripture saith to Pharao: to this purpose have I raised thee that I may show my power in thee; and that my name may be declared throughout all the earth.' Then, making a conclusion to both passages, he says: 'Therefore he hath mercy on whom he will and whom he will he hardeneth.'[70] Obviously, He treats neither of these with injustice, but both with mercy and truth; in spite of that there is an uprising of insolent weakness on the part of those who attempt to comprehend the unsearchable depth of the judgment of God[71] according to the interpretations of the human heart.

The Apostle refutes this view when he says: 'Thou wilt say therefore to me: Why doth he then find fault? for who resisteth his will?'[72] Let us imagine this as said to us. What other answer should we make than the one he made? If such ideas disturb us also because we, too, are men, we all have need to listen to the Apostle saying: 'O man, who art thou that repliest against God? Shall the thing formed say to him that formed it: Why hast thou made me thus? Or hath not the potter power over the clay, of the same lump to make one vessel unto honor, another unto dishonor?'[73] If this lump of clay were of such indifferent value that it deserved nothing good any more than it deserved anything evil, there would be reason to see injustice in making of it a vessel unto dishonor; but when, through the free will of the first man alone, condemnation extended to the whole lump of clay, undoubtedly if vessels are made of it unto honor, it is not a question of justice not forestalling grace, but of God's mercy; if, however, vessels are made of it unto dishonor, it is to be attributed to the judgment of God, not to His injustice—far be from us the thought that there could be any such with

70 Rom. 8.16-18; Exod. 9.16.
71 Rom. 11.33.
72 Rom. 9.19.
73 Rom. 9.20-21; Isa. 45.9; 29.16.

God! Whoever is wise in this matter with the Catholic Church does not argue against grace in favor of merit, but he sings mercy and judgment to the Lord,[74] that he may not ungratefully deny His mercy or unjustly upbraid His judgment.

But that other lump is different, of which the same Apostle says: 'For if the first fruit be holy so is the lump also, and if the root be holy, so also are the branches.'[75] That lump is of Abraham, not of Adam; it is of the communion of the sacrament and of the likeness of faith, not of mortal generation; whereas the former paste or, as we read in several versions, lump, is wholly given over to death, since 'by one man sin entered into the world and by sin death and so death passed upon all men in whom all have sinned.'[76] Consequently, it is through mercy that one vessel is made unto honor, but through judgment that another is made unto dishonor. In the first case merit does not precede the grace of deliverance; in the second, sin does not escape the punishment of justice. In earlier ages this does not stand out so clearly against the objectors where those who argue for the merits of man are protected by a certain obscurity. But it was against their objection that the Apostle found those others among 'children not yet born, who had not yet done any good or evil; not of works but of him that calleth it was said: The elder shall serve the younger.'

Therefore, since the judgments of God are exceedingly deep and incomprehensible and His ways unsearchable, let man meanwhile hold that there is no injustice with God; let him confess that as man he does not know with what justice God has mercy on whom He will and hardens whom He will. In virtue of the unshaken belief which he holds that there is no injustice with God, he knows that although no one is

---

74 Ps. 100.1.
75 Rom. 11.16.
76 Rom. 5.12.

justified because of antecedent merits, so no one is hardened unless he deserves it. Piety and truth make us believe that God saves harmful and wicked men by justifying them from the penalties which were their due, but if we believe that God condemns anyone who does not deserve it and who is not subject to any sin, we make God out to be not free from injustice. When the undeserving one is saved, his gratitude ought to be greater in proportion to the justice of his penalty, but when the undeserving is condemned neither mercy nor truth is maintained.

'How is it,' they say, 'that Esau was not deservedly condemned, if it was "not of works but of him that calleth it was said: The elder shall serve the younger"? For, just as there were no antecedent good works of his to call for grace, so there were no evil works to call for punishment.' Certainly there were no acutal works, either good or evil, in either of them, but both of them were subject to the one in whom all have sinned, that all should die in him. However many descendants there were to be from that one, in him they were then all one. Therefore, that sin would have been his alone if no other had descended from him, but henceforth no one who had a share in the common nature was to be immune from his sin. If, then, those twins, who had not performed any works of their own, either good or bad, were nevertheless born with the original guilt, let the one who is saved praise His mercy, the one who is chastised not blame His judgment.

If upon this we were to say: 'How much better if both had been saved!' there will be no more appropriate answer for us than: 'O man, who art thou that repliest to God'? For, He surely knows what He is doing and how great a number there should be, first of all men, secondly of the saints, as He knows it of the stars, of the angels; and, to speak of earthly things, as He knows it of beasts, of fishes, of birds, of trees and plants, and, to sum up, of leaves and of our hairs. We, with our human thought, can still say: 'Since all the things which He has made are good, how much better it would be if He had doubled or multiplied them, so that there would be many more than there are! If the world could not hold them, could He not make it as much bigger as He wished?' Yet, however far He went in making things more numerous, or the world larger and more spacious, the same could still be said about increasing them, and there would be no limit to unbounded thought.

But, as far as that goes, this can also be said: If there is a grace by which the unjust are justified, of which we are not allowed to doubt; if, as some claim, grace is always antecedent to free will, while punishment or reward are always subsequent to merit, what reason is there at all for God to create souls of whom He foresees that they will inevitably sin so as to be worthy of condemnation to eternal fire? For, although He has not created the sins, who but God created the very natures which are undoubtedly good in themselves, but in which there are bound to be defects leading to sin by reason of their freedom of will, and, in many, there would be such defects that eternal penalty would be their due? Why, except that He willed it? As to why He willed it, 'Who art thou, O man, that repliest against God? Shall the thing formed say to him that formed it: Why hast thou made me thus? Or hath not the potter power over the clay, of the same lump to make vessel unto honor, and another unto dishonor?'

And that we may now say what follows: 'What if God, willing to show his wrath and to make his power known, endured with much patience vessels of wrath, fitted for destruction, that he might show the riches of his glory on the vessels of mercy?'[77] Here is the account given to man as far as it is owed to man—if, indeed, he who argues for the

---

77 Rom. 9.22,23.

liberty of his own free will, subject to the slavery of such weakness, accepts even that account—here are the reasons set forth in words: 'Therefore, who art thou that repliest against God, if God is willing to show his wrath and to make his power known?' because, being perfect, He is able to make good use of the wicked, provided we understand that they are wicked, not through any divine enactment but through a nature vitiated by the malice of its own will, a nature which was good when formed by God the Creator, 'who endured with much patience vessels of wrath fitted for destruction.' But it is not true that the sins of angels or men are necessary to Him any more than the justice of any creature is necessary to Him; His purpose was 'that He might show the riches of his glory on the vessels of mercy,' that they might not pride themselves on their good works as if done by their own strength, but should humbly acknowledge that if the grace of God, not owed but freely given, had not delivered them, they would have seen as the reward of their merits just what was awarded to others of the same clay.

There is, therefore, in the foreknowledge of God a predetermined limit and number of saints, who love God as He has given them to do through the Holy Spirit poured forth in their hearts,[78] and for them 'all things work together unto good to such as according to his purpose are called; for whom he foreknew he also predestinated to be made conformable to the image of his Son; that he might be the first-born among many brethren. And whom he predestinated, them he also called.'[79] Here we have to get the undertone of 'according to his purpose.' For there are others called but not chosen,[80] because they are not called 'according to his purpose.' But 'whom he called,' that is, 'according to his purpose,' 'them

---

78 Rom. 5.5.
79 Rom. 8.28-30.
80 Matt. 20.16; 22.14.

also he justified, and whom he justified them also he glorified.'[81] These are 'the children of the promise';[82] these are the chosen who are saved by 'the election of grace,' as it is said: 'But if by grace it is not now by works, otherwise grace is no more grace.'[83] These are the vessels of mercy in whom God makes known the riches of His glory by means of the vessels of wrath. Through His Holy Spirit He makes of them 'one heart and one soul,'[84] which blesses the Lord and does not forget all His recompenses; who forgiveth all its iniquities and healeth all its diseases; who redeemeth its life from destruction; who crowneth it with mercy and compassion,'[85] because 'it is not of him that willeth nor of him that runneth, but of God that showeth mercy.'[86]

But the rest of men who do not belong to that fellowship, although the goodness of God made their soul and body and whatever their nature possesses except sin, which the rebellion of a proud will inflicted on them, have been created by a foreknowing God that He might show in them what the free will of a deserter is worth without His grace, and that the vessels of mercy who have been set apart from that mass of clay, not through the merits of their own works, but by the grace of God, freely given, may learn, by the just and due penalties of the others, what has been bestowed on them, 'that every mouth may be stopped,'[87] and 'that he that glorieth may glory in the Lord.'[88]

'If any man teach otherwise and consent not to the sound words of our Lord Jesus Christ,'[89] who said: 'The Son of

81 Rom. 8.30.
82 Rom. 9.8.
83 Rom. 11.5,6.
84 Acts 4.31,32.
85 Cf. Ps. 102.1-4.
86 Rom. 9.16.
87 Rom. 3.19.
88 1 Cor. 1.31; 2 Cor. 10.17.
89 1 Tim. 6.3.

man is come to seek and to save that which was lost,'[90]—for
He did not say: 'which would have been lost,' but 'which was
lost,' and what else does that show but that the nature of
the whole human race was lost by the sin of the first man?—
whoever, then, teaches otherwise and consents not to that
doctrine which is according to godliness defends human
nature against the grace of the Saviour and the blood of the
Redeemer, yet claims to be rated in name as a Christian.
What will such a one have to say about the selection of infants,
why one is admitted to the life of the second Man, while the
other is left in the death of the first man? If he says that the
merits of free will were antecedent to grace, the Apostle
answers what we quoted above about children not yet born,
who have done neither good nor evil; but if he says what is
still maintained in the books which Pelagius is reported to
have published quite recently—although at the episcopal trial
in Palestine it now appears that he repudiated those who say
that the sin of Adam injured him alone and not the human
race—that is, if he says that both babies were born without
sin and inherited no condemnation from the first man, certainly, as he does not dare to deny that the one who was
regenerated in Christ is admitted to the kingdom of heaven,
let him answer what happens to the other one who, through
no fault of his own, is cut off by a temporal death without
baptism. We do not think he will say that God will condemn
to eternal death an innocent soul, without original sin, before
the age at which it could commit actual sin; he is therefore
forced to answer as Pelagius did at the episcopal trial, when,
in order to be considered some kind of Christian, he was
forced to repudiate the doctrine that infants, even though
unbaptized, possess eternal life. And when this has been
denied, what will remain but eternal death?

Thus, he will also argue against the sentence of the Lord

90 Luke 19.10; Matt. 18.11.

when He said: 'Your fathers did eat manna in the desert and are dead; this is the bread which cometh down from heaven, that if any man eat of it he may not die,'[91] for He was not speaking of the death which even those who eat of the same Bread must necessarily undergo; and shortly afterward, when He said: 'Amen, amen, I say unto you: Except you eat the flesh of the Son of man and drink his blood, you shall not have life in you,'[92] He meant that life which will follow after death. The objector will also argue against the authority of the Apostolic See which cited this testimony from the Gospel, while treating of the matter, to show that we should not believe unbaptized children can possess eternal life.[93] And he will contradict the very words of Pelagius himself as he pronounced them before the bishops who were hearing his case, in which he repudiated those who hold that unbaptized infants possess eternal life.

We have repeated all this because, if what we hear is true, there are some among you, or rather in your city, who support that error with such obstinacy that they say they would sooner forsake and contemn Pelagius in his repudiation of those who hold these views than give up what seems to them the truth of this opinion. But, if they submit to the Apostolic See, or, rather, to the Master and Lord of the Apostles Himself, who says that they will not have life in them unless they eat the flesh of the Son of man and drink His blood, which they certainly cannot do unless they are baptized, doubtless at some time they will admit that unbaptized children cannot possess life, and that, although it will be more bearable for them than for all who commit actual sins as well, they will nevertheless pay the penalty of eternal death.

---

91 John 6.49,50.
92 John 6.54.
93 Cf. Letter 182.

This being so, let them dare to argue and strive to convince those whom they can that a just God, with whom there is no injustice, would sentence to eternal death children innocent of actual sin if they were not bound by and involved in the sentence laid on Adam. But, if this is altogether absurd and thoroughly repugnant to the justice of God, no one who remembers that he is a Christian of the Catholic faith denies or doubts that children who have not received the grace of regeneration in Christ, who have not eaten His flesh or drunk His blood, have no life in them and are consequently subject to the penalty of everlasting death, and it certainly remains true that though they themselves have done neither good nor evil, the penalty of their death is just because they die in him in whom all have sinned, since they are alive in Him alone by whom original sin could not be bequeathed or actual sin committed.

'He hath called us not only of the Jews but also of the Gentiles,'[94] since He gathered together the children whom He would of that Jerusalem which refused Him, which killed the Prophets and stoned those who were sent to her,[95] and this He did before His Incarnation in the case of the Prophets themselves, and after 'the Word was made flesh'[96] in the Apostles and the thousands of men who laid down the price of their goods at the feet of the Apostles.[97] All these were manifestly children of a Jerusalem unwilling that they should be gathered together, yet they were gathered together at His will, of whom He says: 'If I by Beelzebub cast out devils, by whom do your children cast them out? Therefore they shall be your judges.'[98] Of these the prophecy had been made: 'If the number of the children of Israel be as the sand of the

---

94 Rom. 9.24.
95 Matt. 23.37; Luke 13.34.
96 John 1.14.
97 Acts 4.34.
98 Matt. 12.37; Isa. 10.22; Osee 1.10.

sea, a remnant shall be saved.'[99] The word of God cannot miscarry,[100] 'God hath not cast away his people which he foreknew,'[101] 'even so, there is a remnant saved according to the election of grace. But if by grace,' as we must so often say, 'it is not now by works, otherwise grace is no more grace.'[102] These are plainly the words of the Apostle, not ours. Therefore, what He called out to Jerusalem unwilling for her children to be gathered together, this we call out against those who are unwilling for their children to be gathered to the Church, although they themselves are willing. Those men have not even been converted after the trial which was held of that very Pelagius in Palestine, from which he would have issued condemned if he had not himself condemned what he could not cover up, namely, the objectionable words spoken by him against the grace of God.

Besides this, there were other teachings brought against him which he had dared to defend with such reasoning as he could, and if he had not repudiated them without any shadow of evasion he would himself have been subject to anathema. He was accused of saying that Adam was created mortal and that he was destined to die whether he sinned or not; that his sin injured only himself and not the human race; that infants just born are in the state in which Adam was before the fall; that the whole race of men does not die through the death or fall of Adam, or does the race of men rise again through the Resurrection of Christ; that infants, even though not baptized, have eternal life; that, if the rich who are baptized do not renounce all things, they cannot be credited with any good they may have seemed to do, nor can they possess the kingdom of God; that the grace and help of God

---

99 Rom. 9.27.
100 Rom. 9.6.
101 Rom. 11.2.
102 Rom. 11.5,6.

are not given for individual actions but reside in the free will, or in the Law and the doctrine; that the grace of God is given according to our merits; that none can be called children of God unless they have become entirely sinless; that free will does not exist if it needs the help of God, since each one has it in his own will to do or not to do something; that our victory is not through the help of God but through our free will; and that pardon is not given to the repentant according to the grace and mercy of God but according to the merit and effort of those who deserve mercy through their repentance.[103]

All these assertions Pelagius repudiated so thoroughly, as the official reports plainly show, that he left no ground to support any defense of them in any way. It results as a consequence that whoever follows the authority of that episcopal trial and the confession of Pelagius himself is obliged to believe what the Catholic Church has always held: that Adam would not have died if he had not sinned; that his sin injured not only himself but the human race; that newborn infants are not in the state in which Adam was before the fall and that the brief pronouncement of the Apostle does apply to them: 'By one man came death and by one man the resurrection of the dead, and as in Adam all die, so also in Christ all shall be made alive.'[104] Whence it happens that unbaptized infants not only cannot attain the kingdom of heaven but cannot even possess eternal life. Let the believer confess also that the rich who are baptized cannot be deprived of the kingdom of heaven if they are such as the Apostle describes to Timothy when he says: 'Charge the rich of this world not to be high-minded nor to trust in the uncertainty of riches, but in the living God who giveth us abundantly all things to enjoy; to be rich in good works, to give easily, to communicate to others, to lay up in store for them-

---

103 Cf. Augustine, *De gestis Pelagii* (*CSEL* 43, pp. 76-121).
104 1 Cor. 15.21,22.

selves a good foundation against the time to come, that
they may lay hold on the true life.'[105] Let him confess that
the helping grace of God is given to individual acts, and that
it is not given according to our merits, that it may be truly
grace, that is, freely given by the mercy of Him who said:
'I will have mercy on whom I will have mercy and I will
show mercy to whom I will show mercy.'[106] Let him confess
that they who say daily: 'Forgive us our debts,' can be called
the children of God, for they obviously could not say it with
truth if they were entirely sinless. Let him confess that the
will is free even though it has need of divine help. Let him
confess that when we make war on temptations and unlawful
passions, although our own will is engaged in the fight, our
victory does not result from that but from the help of God;
otherwise the Apostle's words would not be true: 'Not of
him that willeth nor of him that runneth, but of God that
showeth mercy.'[107] Let him confess that pardon is granted to
the repentant according to the grace and mercy of God, not
according to his merits, since it is that very repentance which
the Apostle called the gift of God when he said of certain
ones: 'Lest peradventure God may give them repentance.'[108]
If anyone agrees to the authority of the Catholic Church
and the words of Pelagius himself as quoted in the ecclesiastical records, let him confess all these truths straightforwardly,
without any evasions. For there is no reason to believe that
the statements which are contrary to these have been truthfully repudiated unless these statements, their contraries, are
held with upright heart and made public with open admission.

But, in the more recent books which the same Pelagius is
said to have published since the trial it is not quite clear
what he thinks on this point, although he appears to accept

---

105 1 Tim. 6.17-19.
106 Rom. 9.15; Exod. 33.19.
107 Rom. 9.16.
108 2 Tim. 2.25.

the idea of divine grace as a help. Sometimes he balances the
power of the will with such equal weight in a poised scale
that he defines it as having as much power to avoid sin as
it has to sin. But, if this is so, no scope is left for the help of
grace, without which, we say, the free will is not able to
avoid sin. Sometimes he admits that we are fortified by the
daily help of God's grace, although we have a free will
strong and firm enough to avoid sin, whereas he ought to
have confessed that our will is weak and feeble until all the
maladies of our soul are cured. The Psalmist was not praying
to be cured of weakness of body when he said: 'Have mercy
on me, O Lord, for I am weak; heal me, O Lord, for my
bones are troubled,' for by way of showing that he was
praying for his soul he went on: 'And my soul is troubled
exceedingly.'[109]

It seems, therefore, that he thinks the help of grace can be
conceded as something extra, that is, that even if it is not
granted we still have a will strong and firm enough to avoid
sin. We do not wish to be thought guilty of rash suspicion
about him, and in case someone should say that he holds
the free will strong and firm enough to avoid sin, although
it cannot fulfill this without God's grace, in the way we say
that healthy eyes are strong enough to see, but cannot possibly
do so if the help of light is lacking, it is a fact that in another
place he shows more plainly what he said or thought, when
he says that the grace of God is given to men in this sense
that what they are commanded to do by their free will they
can accomplish more easily with the help of grace. Now,
when he says 'more easily,' what else does he want us to
understand except that, even if grace is lacking, the divine
commandments can be accomplished by the free will either
with ease or with difficulty?[110]

---

109 Ps. 6.3,4.
110 Cf. Augustine, *De gratia Christi* 8.27 (*CSEL* 42, pp. 131-148).

Where does he say: 'What is man that thou art mindful of him?'[111] Where, again, are those evidences which, as we read in the records, the Bishop of Jerusalem relates that he cited to the said Pelagius when he was informed that the latter had said it is possible for man to be sinless without the grace of God?[112] These are the three texts he cited, very strong ones, against wicked presumption of this kind: where the Apostle said: 'I have labored more abundantly than all they, yet not I, but the grace of God with me,'[113] and 'not of him that willeth nor of him that runneth, but of God that showeth mercy,'[114] and 'Except the Lord build the house, they labor in vain that build it.'[115] How, then, is God's commandment accomplished, even with difficulty, without His help, since, if the Lord does not build, the builder is said to have labored in vain; and since it is not written: 'It is indeed of him that willeth and runneth, but it is more easily of God that showeth mercy,' but it is written: 'Not of him that willeth nor of him that runneth but of God that showeth mercy,' not because man does not will and run, but because he can do nothing unless God shows him mercy; and since the Apostle did not say: 'And I,' but 'not I but the grace of God with me,' not because the Apostle did nothing good, but because he would have done nothing at all if grace had not helped him? Yet, that balancing of the power of free will, equally poised in the scale toward good and evil, leaves no scope for that ease which he seems at least to have admitted by saying: 'they could accomplish it more easily with grace,' for, if good is accomplished more easily with grace, evil is committed most easily without grace, in which case that possibility is not balanced on an even scale.

---

111 Ps. 8.5.
112 Cf. Aug. *De gestis Pelagii,* 37 (*CSEL* 42, pp. 93-94).
113 1 Cor. 15.10.
114 Rom. 9.16.
115 Ps. 126.1.

What more is there to say? Not only should we take care
to avoid these persons, but, if they allow it, we should even
not be slothful in teaching and warning them. We do them
a greater service if we unhesitatingly pray for their conversion, lest, with such great abilities, they should either be
lost themselves, or destroy others by their damnable presumption, because 'they have a zeal of God but not according to
knowledge, for they, not knowing the justice of God,' that is,
the justice which comes from God, 'and seeking to establish
their own, have not submitted themselves to the justice of
God.'[116] Certainly, as they are called Christians, they are
more bound to observe this than were the Jews to whom the
Apostle said it, that they might not stumble at the stumbling-
stone,[117] by defending nature and free will as noisily as the
philosophers of this world did, trying hard to be thought or to
think themselves able to achieve happiness by the efficacy of
their own will. Let them take care, then, not to make void the
cross of Christ by wisdom of speech,[118] lest this be to them a
way of stumbling at the stumbling-stone. For, even if human
nature had remained in the integrity in which it was created,
it would have been utterly impossible for it to preserve itself
so without the help of its Creator. Therefore, as it could not,
without the grace of God, guard the salvation which it had
received, how can it recover, without the grace of God, that
salvation which it has lost?

But we should not refrain from praying for these heretics
on the ground that their failure to amend is chargeable to
their will, since they refuse to believe that they need the
Saviour's grace for this very amendment, holding that it
derives from their own will alone. In this matter they are
exactly like the Jews to whom the Apostle said that, 'not

116 Rom. 10.2.3.
117 Rom. 9.32.
118 1 Cor. 1.17.

knowing the justice of God and seeking to establish their own, they have not submitted themselves to the justice of God,' because it is clear that they did not believe in the deficiency of their own will. For, they were not forced against their will to become unbelievers, but by their refusal to believe they become responsible for the crime of unbelief. Yet, because the will is not sufficient to move man to believe the truth unless God helps him with His grace, as the Lord Himself said when He spoke of unbelievers: 'No man cometh to me unless it be given him by my Father,'[119] for that reason, although the Apostle was preaching the Gospel to them constantly, he saw that he would accomplish little unless he also prayed for them to believe. So he said: 'Brethren, the will of my heart indeed and my prayer to God is for them unto salvation,' and then he added the words which we have quoted: 'For I bear them witness that they have a zeal of God, but not according to knowledge,'[120] and the rest. Let us therefore pray for them, holy brother.

No doubt you are one with us in seeing what an evil error holds them, for your letters are fragrant with the genuine perfume of Christ, and in them you stand out as an intimate lover and defender of grace itself. But the reason why we have thought it well to speak with you at such length on this matter is first, because our delight is so great in doing it, for what could be more delightful to the sick than the grace which heals them, or to the sluggish than the grace which helps them? In the second place, if we were able with God's help to accomplish anything by our arguments, we aimed to support, not your faith, but your profession of the faith against such men, as we also have been helped to this opportunity by your Fraternity's letters.

For, what is more fruitful or more filled with the truest

119 John 6.66.
120 Rom. 10.1,2.

confession than that passage in one of your letters in which you humbly bewail the fact that our nature did not remain as it was created, but was debased by the father of the human race? In it you said: ' "But I am poor and sorrowful,"[121] I, that am still hardened in the filth of an earthly image, having in me more of the first Adam than of the second, still give my attention to the senses of the flesh and to earthly acts. How shall I dare to depict myself when earthly corruption proves that I deny my heavenly image? I blush to paint what I am, I do not dare to paint what I am not. But what good will it do me, wretched as I am, to hate iniquity and to love virtue,[122] when I do rather what I hate and am too sluggish to strive to do what I love? I am torn asunder, fighting with myself in an interior warfare, while "the spirit lusteth against the flesh and the flesh against the spirit,"[123] and the law of my body under the law of sin fights against the law of my mind.[124] Unhappy I that have absorbed the poisonous taste of that hateful tree, not the wood of the cross! The ancestral poison hardens in me, from Adam the father, who by his fall has undone the whole race.'[125] These and many other things you said, groaning over your misery and expecting the redemption of your body, knowing yourself saved by hope, if not yet in fact.[126]

But perhaps you transformed another into yourself when you said this, and you do not now suffer these hateful and importunate motions of the flesh lusting against the spirit, although you do not admit it. But, in any case, you, or whoever else suffers these ills, are also awaiting the grace of Christ through which you are delivered from 'the body of

121 Ps. 68.30.
122 Ps. 44.8.
123 Gal. 5.17.
124 Rom. 7.23.
125 Paulinus of Nola, *Ep.* 30.2 (*CSEL* 29).
126 Rom. 8.23,24.

this death.'[127] You do not see it openly in yourself but as it was hidden in that man when the forbidden food was touched and desired, and destruction would have fallen far and wide over all men, if He who was not lost had not come 'to seek and to save that which was lost.' How fervent your letter is in praying and asking with groans for help in advancing and in living well! What part of your letter is not sprinkled over with tender sighs such as we utter in the Lord's prayer: 'Lead us not into temptation'?[128] Let us then console and encourage each other in all these ways, and let us help each other as much as the Lord grants us to do. Your Holiness will hear from our mutual friend[129] what we have heard and about whom, which causes us much grief, but which we find it hard to believe. When he comes back safe, by the mercy of God, we hope to be informed about everything.

187. Augustine, bishop, to his beloved brother, Dardanus[1] (Mid 417)

On the Presence of God

Chapter 1

I confess that I have been slower than I should have been in answering our letter, my dearest brother, Dardanus, whom I hold in higher esteem for the charity of Christ than for your worldly rank. But please do not ask the reasons for my

---

127 Rom. 7.24.
128 Matt. 6.13; Luke 11.4.
129 Januarius, the bearer of the letter.

---

1 Prefect of the province of Gaul.

delay, for I should only cause you more annoyance by my long-winded excuse than you have already suffered by my tardy reply, and I would rather you gave an easy pardon to my offense than a verdict on my defense. Whatever those reasons may have been, believe me that not any of them could have involved my holding you in slight esteem. On the contrary, if I had had no respect for you I should have answered you immediately. But my reason for answering you at long last is not because at long last I have composed something at least worth your perusal, something which can deserve to be dedicated under your name; as a matter of fact, I have chosen to answer you now rather than allow the summer to pass, leaving me still in your debt for this courtesy. And it was not your high position which intimidated me and made me hold back, for your kindly manner attracts more than your rank repels me. But because I love you so much I find it proportionately difficult to measure up to the great eagerness of your religious affection.

Chapter 2

Moreover, in addition to that flame of mutual charity which makes us love even those whom we have never seen, provided they have what we love—in which you outstrip me and make me fear to fall short of your opinion and expectation of me—in addition to that, you have asked me such questions in your letter that if they were proposed by anyone else they would present no slight task for the free time which is lacking to me. But when they are proposed by you, with your mind accustomed to probing into profound truths, a summary solution of them would be utterly insufficient. Besides, they have been propounded to a very busy man who is besieged and beset by an army of cares, so it is for your

Prudence and Benevolence to figure out how I may appease
you either for not answering for so long or for not answering
even now in accord with the intensity of your interest.

Chapter 3

You ask, then, in what manner the 'Mediator of God and
men, the man, Christ Jesus,'[1] is now believed to be in heaven,
when, hanging on the cross and at the point of death, He
said to the believing thief: 'This day thou shalt be with me
in paradise.'[2] You say that from this we are to understand,
perhaps, that paradise is established in some part of heaven,
or that, because God is everywhere, the man also who is
in God is present everywhere. From this, no doubt, you wish
to deduce that He who is everywhere could also be in paradise.

Chapter 4

At this point I inquire, or rather I recognize, in what way
you understand Christ as man. Surely not as certain heretics
do who assert that He is the Word of God with a body, but,
that is, without a human soul, the Word serving as soul for
His body;[1] or, as the Word of God with a soul and a body
but without a human mind, the Word of God serving as
mind to His soul.[2] You certainly do not understand Christ as
man in this sense, but, as you expressed it above when you
said that you accepted Christ as almighty God, with this

---

1 Tim. 2.5.
2 Luke 23.43.

---

1 The Arians.
2 The Apollinarists.

formula of belief that you would not believe Him God if you had not believed Him perfect man. Obviously, when you say perfect man, you mean that the whole human nature is there, for a man is not perfect if either a soul is lacking to the body or a human mind to the soul.

Chapter 5

If, then, we think He said: 'This day thou shalt be with me in paradise,' according to the human nature which God the Word assumed, we cannot conclude from these words that paradise is in heaven, for the man Christ Jesus was not to be in heaven that day, but in hell as to His soul, in the tomb as to His body. And the Gospel is absolutely clear about His body being placed that day in the tomb;[1] while apostolic teaching reveals that His soul descended into hell, since blessed Peter bears witness to this fact from the Psalms, where he shows that the following prophecy was made of Him: 'Because thou wilt not leave my soul in hell, nor wilt thou give thy holy one to see corruption.'[2] The first part of this was said of His soul, because it was not left there, but returned from there very quickly; the second part refers to His body, which was not able to suffer corruption because of its speedy resurrection. But no one thinks that paradise was in the tomb. If anyone were so foolish as to try to justify that opinion because the tomb was a garden,[3] he would certainly find it untenable, because the one to whom Christ said: 'This day thou shalt be with me in paradise' was not with Christ in the tomb on any day. Moreover, the burial of his body, unconscious alike of joy or sorrow in death, would

---

1 Matt. 27.60; Mark 15.46; Luke 23.53; John 19.41,42.
2 Ps. 15.10; Acts 2.27.
3 *Paradisus.*

not have been offered to him as the great reward of his faith, when he was thinking of that rest where his conscious being would go.

Chapter 6

It remains, then, that if the words, 'This day thou shalt be with me in paradise,' were spoken in a human sense, paradise would be understood to be in hell, where Christ was to be that day in His human soul. But I would find it hard to say whether the bosom of Abraham where the wicked rich man, from the torments of hell in which he was, saw the poor man reposing is to be included under the term paradise, or considered as belonging to hell. Of the rich man, indeed, we read the words: 'But the rich man also died and was buried,' and 'when he was in the torments of hell.' In the case of the death or repose of the poor man there is no mention of hell, but it says: 'It came to pass that the begger died and was carried by the angels into Abraham's bosom.' After that, Abraham says to the rich man in the flame: 'Between us and you there is fixed a great chaos,'[1] as if it were between hell and the abodes of the blessed, for it is not easy to find the word hell used in a good sense anywhere in the Scriptures. Hence, the question is usually raised how we can reverently believe that the soul of the Lord Christ was in hell, if the word is not taken in any but the penal sense. A good answer to this is that he descended there to rescue those who were to be rescued. Consequently, blessed Peter says that he loosed the sorrows of hell in which it was 'impossible that he should be held.'[2] Besides, if we are to believe that there are two regions in hell, one of the suffering and one of the souls at rest, that is, both a place where the rich man was tormented and one

1 Cf. Luke 16.22-26.
2 Acts 2.24.

where the poor man was comforted, who would dare to say
that the Lord Jesus came to the penal parts of hell instead
of only among those who rest in Abraham's bosom? If He
was there, then, we must understand that as paradise which
He deigned to promise to the soul of the thief on that day.
In that case, the word paradise is a general term meaning a
state of living in happiness. But the fact of the place where
Adam lived before the fall being called paradise did not
prevent Scripture from calling the Church paradise, also, with
the fruit of apples.

Chapter 7

However, Christ may be assumed to have said: 'This day
thou shalt be with me in paradise,' in a much easier sense
and one free of all these subtleties, if He said it not as man
but as God. Manifestly, the man Christ was to be that day
in the tomb as to His body, in hell as to His soul, but as God,
Christ Himself is always everywhere present. For He is the
light which shines in the darkness although the darkness does
not comprehend it.[1] He is the strength and wisdom of God
of which it is written that 'it reacheth from end to end
mightily and ordereth all things sweetly,'[2] and that 'it
reacheth every where because of its purity and nothing defiled
cometh to it.'[3] Therefore, wherever paradise may be, whoever is blessed is there with Him who is everywhere.

Chapter 8

Since, then, Christ is God and man—God, as He tells us in

---

1 John 1.5.
2 Wisd. 8.1.
3 Cf. Wisd. 7.24,25.

the words: 'I and the Father are one,'[1] man, as He says in
'The Father is greater than I'[2]—but equally son of God,
Only-begotten of the Father,[3] and Son of man 'of the seed
of David according to the flesh,'[4] we must take account of
both these natures in Him when He speaks or when Scripture
speaks of Him, and we must mark in what sense anything is
said. For, just as a single man is rational soul and body, so
the single Christ is Word and man. Therefore, in what
pertains to the Word, Christ is creator: 'All things were made
by him,'[5] but as man Christ was created 'of the seed of David
according to the flesh' and 'made in the likeness of men.'[6]
Likewise, because man is a duality, soul and body, according
to the soul, He was sorrowful unto death; according to the
flesh, He suffered death.[7]

Chapter 9

Nevertheless, when we say that Christ is the Son of God we
do not separate His humanity from Him, nor when we say
that the same Christ is the Son of man do we lose sight of
His divinity. For, as man He was on earth, not in heaven
where He now is, when He said: 'No man ascendeth into
heaven but he that descended from heaven, the Son of man
who is in heaven,'[1] although in His nature as Son of God He
was in heaven, but as Son of man He was still on earth and
had not yet ascended into heaven. In like manner, although

1 John 10.30.
2 John 14.28.
3 John 1.14.
4 Rom. 1.3.
5 John 1.3.
6 Phil. 2.7.
7 Matt. 26.38; Mark 14.34.

1 John 3.13.

in His nature as Son of God He is the Lord of glory, in His nature as Son of man He was crucified, since the Apostle says: 'For if they had known it they would never have crucified the Lord of glory.'[2] Thus, the Son of man as God was in heaven and the Son of God as man was crucified on earth. As, then, it could rightly be said that the Lord of glory was crucified, although His Passion belonged to His humanity alone, so He could rightly say: 'This day thou shalt be with me in paradise,' since, although in terms of His human lowliness He was going to be in the tomb as to His body, in hell as to His soul, in terms of His divine immutability He had never left paradise because He is always everywhere present.

Chapter 10

Do not doubt, then, that the man Christ Jesus is now there whence He shall come again; cherish in your memory and hold faithfully to the profession of your Christian faith that He rose from the dead, ascended into heaven, sitteth at the right hand of the Father,[1] and will come from no other place but there to judge the living and the dead; and He will so come, on the testimony of the angel's voice, as He was seen going into heaven,[2] that is, in the same form and substance of flesh to which, it is true, He gave immortality, but He did not take away its nature. According to this form, we are not to think that He is everywhere present. We must beware of so building up the divinity of the man that we destroy the reality of His body. It does not follow that what is in God is in Him so as to be everywhere as God is. The

---

2 1 Cor. 2.8.

1 Mark 16.19; Luke 26.69; Col. 3.1; Heb. 1.3; 10.12.
2 2 Tim. 4.1; Acts 1.10,11.

Scripture says, with perfect truth: 'In him we live and move and are,'[3] yet we are not everywhere present as He is, but man is in God after one manner, while God is in man quite differently, in His own unique manner. God and man in Him are one Person, and both are the one Jesus Christ who is everywhere as God, but in heaven as man.

Chapter 11

Although in speaking of Him we say that God is everywhere present, we must resist carnal ideas and withdraw our mind from our bodily senses, and not imagine that God is distributed through all things by a sort of extension of size, as earth or water or air or light are distributed—for in each of these the part is less in extent than the whole—but, rather, in the way in which there is great wisdom in a man whose body is small, so that, if there were two wise men of whom one is taller in stature but neither one wiser than the other, there would not be greater wisdom in the taller one and less in the smaller, nor less in one than in the two, but as much in one as in the other and as much in each one as in both; for, if both are absolutely equally wise, the two together are not wiser than each one separately. In the same way, if they are equally immortal, the two do not live longer than each one individually.

Chapter 12

Finally, the very immortality of body which Christ first experienced and which is promised to us at the end of the world is indeed a great thing, but it is not great in size, for, although it is corporeally possessed, it is an incorporeal per-

3 Acts 17.28.

fection. So, although the immortal body is less in one part than in the whole, its immortality is as complete in the part as in the whole, and, although some members are larger than others, it does not follow that some are more immortal than others. In the same way, in this life, when we are in good health in every part of us, according to the present mode of well-being in our body, we do not say that because the whole hand is larger than the finger the health of the whole hand is greater than that of the finger, but it is equal in these unequal members. Thus, when smaller things are compared to larger ones, it can happen that one thing may not be as large as another, but it can be as healthy. There would be greater health in larger members if the larger were more healthy; since this is not so, but the larger and smaller are equally healthy, there is obviously a disparity of size in the dimensions of the members coinciding with a similarity of health in the dissimilar.

Chapter 13

Since, then, the body is a substance, its quantity is in the greatness of its bulk, whereas its health is not a quantity but a quality of it. Thus, the quantity of the body could not attain what its quality could. Quantity is found in the separate parts which cannot be together in the same place, since each one occupies its own space, the smaller ones less and the larger ones more, and it could not be entire, or even as great, in the several parts; but it is larger in the larger parts and less in the smaller ones, and in no part as great as it is in the whole body. On the other hand, a quality, such as we say health is, is as great in the smaller parts as in the larger ones when the whole body is in health, and the parts which are less extensive are not thereby less healthy nor are the larger parts more healthy. God forbid, then, that a quality which can be found in a created body would not exist in the very substance of the Creator.

Chapter 14

Therefore, God is poured forth in all things. He Himself says by the Prophet: 'I fill heaven and earth,' and, as I quoted a short time before of His wisdom: 'He reacheth from end to end mightily and ordereth all things sweetly.'[2] It is likewise written: 'The Spirit of the Lord hath filled the whole world,'[3] and one of the Psalms has these words addressed to Him: 'Whither shall I go from thy Spirit, or whither shall I flee from thy face? If I ascend up into heaven, thou art there; if I descend into hell thou art there.'[4] Yet God so permeates all things as to be not a quality of the world, but the very creative substance of the world, ruling the world without labor, sustaining it without effort. Nevertheless, He is not distributed through space by size so that half of Him should be in half of the world and half in the other half of it. He is wholly present in all of it in such wise as to be wholly in heaven alone and wholly in the earth alone, and wholly in heaven and earth together; not confined in any place, but wholly in Himself everywhere.

Chapter 15

Thus He is as the Father, thus as the Son, thus as the Holy Spirit, thus as the Trinity, one God. They did not divide the world among them into three parts, each One filling a sep-

---

1 Jer. 23.24.
2 Wisd. 8.1.
3 Wisd. 1.7.
4 Ps. 138.7,8.

arate part, as if the Son and the Holy Spirit would not have any part to be in if the Father had occupied the whole. A truly incorporeal and immutable divinity does not exist on those terms. They are not bodies, so that the Three together should be larger than each One separately; They do not hold places by Their extension so as not to be able to be in different places at the same time. For, if our soul, established in our body, not only does not feel crowded but even finds a sort of breadth, not of physical space, but of spiritual joys, when it happens as the Apostle says: 'Know you not that your bodies are the temple of the Holy Spirit who is in you, whom you have from God?'[1] and it would be the height of foolishness to say that there is no room for the Holy Spirit in our body because our soul fills it all up, how much more foolish to say that the Trinity could be prevented by crowding from being anywhere, so that the Father and the Son and the Holy Spirit could not be everywhere at the same time!

Chapter 16

Here is something much more remarkable: although God is everywhere wholly present, He does not dwell in everyone. It is not possible to say to all what the Apostle says, or what I have just said, or even this: 'Know you not that you are the temple of God and that the Spirit of God dwelleth in you?'[1] Hence, of some the same Apostle says the opposite: 'Now if any man have not the Spirit of Christ, he is none of his.'[2] Who, then, would dare to think, unless he were completely ignorant of the inseparability of the Trinity, that the

---

1 1 Cor. 6.19.

---

1 1 Cor. 3.16.
2 Rom. 8.9.

Father or the Son could dwell in someone in whom the Holy
Spirit does not dwell, or that the Holy Spirit could be present
in someone in whom the Father and the Son are not present?
Hence it must be admitted that God is everywhere by the
presence of His divinity, but not everywhere by the grace of
His indwelling. It is because of this indwelling, in which the
grace of His love is recognized with certainty, that we do
not say: 'Our Father, who art everywhere,' but 'Our Father
who art in heaven,'[3] so that in our prayer we recall His
temple which we ought to be ourselves, and the measure of
our being such is the measure of our belonging to His
fellowship and His family of adoption.[4] For, if the people
of God, not yet made equal to the angels,[5] and still absent
from the Lord,[6] is called His temple, how much more true is
it that His temple is in heaven where the people of His angels
dwell, to whom we are to be joined and made equal, when,
after our pilgrimage, we attain to what has been promised!

Chapter 17

Therefore, He that is everywhere does not dwell in all,
and He does not even dwell equally in those in whom He
does dwell. Otherwise, what is the meaning of the request
made by Eliseus that there might be in him double the Spirit
of God that was in Elias?[1] And how is it that among the
saints some are more holy than others, except that they have
a more abundant indwelling of God? How, then, did we
speak the truth when we said above that God is everywhere

3 Matt. 6.9.
4 Rom. 8.15; Gal. 4.5.
5 Luke 20.36.
6 2 Cor. 5.6.

1 4 Kings 2.9.

wholly present if He is more amply present in some, less in others? But it should be noticed with care that we said He is everywhere wholly present in Himself, not in things of which some have a greater capacity for Him, others less. He is said to be present everywhere because He is absent from no part of the universe, and wholly present because He does not give one part of Himself to one half of creation and another part to the other half, in equal shares, or less to a smaller part and more to a larger one; but, He is not only wholly present to the whole universe, He is equally so to each part of it. Those who have become wholly unlike Him by sinning are said to be far from Him; those who receive His likeness by a virtuous life are said to draw near to Him, just as it is correct to say that eyes are farther from the light of day the more blind they are, for what is so far from light as blindness, even though the light of day be near at hand and shine upon sightless eyes? But it is correct to say that eyes draw near to the light when they advance to a recovery of sight through improvement in health.

Chapter 18

However, I see that a more careful explanation is needed of my reason for adding 'in Himself' to my statement that God is everywhere wholly present, because I think this could be taken in an ambiguous sense. How is He everywhere if He is in Himself? Everywhere, of course, because He is nowhere absent; in Himself, because He is not dependent on the things in which He is present, as if He could not exist without them. Take away the spatial relations of bodies, they will be nowhere, and because they are nowhere they will not be at all. Take away bodies from the qualities of bodies, there will be no place for them to be, and, as a necessary consequence, they will not exist. For, even when a body is

equally healthy throughout its whole mass, or equally handsome, neither its health nor its beauty is greater in any part
than in any other, nor greater in the whole than in the part,
since it is evident that the whole is not any more healthy or
more handsome than the part. But, if it should be unequally
healthy or unequally handsome, it can happen that there
might be greater health or beauty in a smaller part when
the smaller members are more healthy or more beautiful than
the larger ones, because what we call great or small in
qualities does not depend on size. However, if the size itself
of the body, however great or small it may be, should be
taken away entirely, there will be nothing in which its
qualities can subsist. But, in the case of God, if less is received
by the one in whom He is present, He is not thereby lessened.
For He is entire in Himself, and He is not present in any
such way as to need them, as if He could not exist except in
them. Just as He is not absent from the one in whom He
does not dwell, but is wholly present even though this one
does not possess Him, so He is wholly present in the one in
whom He does dwell, although this one does not receive Him
wholly.

Chapter 19

He does not divide Himself among the hearts or bodies of
men in order to dwell in them, giving one part of Himself to
this one, another to that one, like the sunlight coming through
the doors and windows of houses. He is rather to be compared
to sound, although it is a corporeal and transitory thing,
which a deaf man does not receive at all, a partly deaf one
does not receive entirely, and of those who hear and are
equally near it, one receives more than another in proportion
as his hearing is keener, another less according as he is harder
of hearing, yet the sound itself does not vary from more to

less, but in the place where all of them are it is equally present to all. How much more perfect than this is God, whose nature is incorporeal and unchangeably living, who cannot be prolonged and divided like sound by intervals of time, who does not need airy space as a place in whch to exist, so as to be near to those who are present, but who remains eternally steadfast in Himself, who can be wholly present to all and to each, and although those in whom He dwells possess Him in proportion to the diversity of their own capacity, some more, some less, He builds up all of them by the grace of His goodness as His most beloved temple![1]

Chapter 20

The expression 'diversities of graces' is used as if they were parts and members of one body in which we are all one temple taken together, but individually we are individual temples, because God is not greater in all than He is in each, and it often happens that the many receive Him less, the one more. When the Apostle said: 'There are diversities of graces,' he at once added: 'But the same Spirit.'[1] Likewise, when he had listed these same diversities of graces, he said: 'But all these things one and the same Spirit worketh, dividing to every one according as he will';[2] dividing, therefore, but not Himself those diversities are spoken of as members in the body, because the ears have not the same function as the eyes, and, so, divided, because He Himself is one and the same. Thus, different duties are harmoniously allotted to the different members. However, when we are in good health, in spite of

---

1 1 Cor. 3.16; 6.19; 2 Cor. 6.16.

---

1 1 Cor. 12.4.
2 1 Cor. 12.11.

these members being different, they rejoice in a common and equal health,[3] all together, not separately, not one with more, another with less. The head of this body is Christ,[4] the unity of this body is proved by our sacrifice, which the Apostle refers to briefly when he says: 'For we being many are one bread, one body.'[5] Through our Head we are reconciled to God, because in Him the divinity of the only-begotten Son shared in our mortality, that we might be made sharers in His immortality.

Chapter 21

This mystery is far removed from the hearts of the prideful wise, but not from Christian hearts; consequently, not from the truly wise. By those other wise I mean the ones who have known God, 'because when they knew God,' as the Apostle says, 'they have not glorified him as God or given thanks.'[1] But you know in what sacrifice the words occur: 'Let us give thanks to the Lord our God.'[2] The pride and pretention of such men as these are far removed from the humility of this sacrifice. So, it is remarkable how God dwells in some souls who do not yet know Him and does not dwell in those who do. These latter do not belong to the temple of God, 'who knowing God have not glorified him or given thanks,' yet little children, sanctified by the sacrament of Christ and regenerated by the Holy Spirit, do belong to the temple of God, although it is certain that they cannot yet know God because of their age. Thus, the one group have been able to know God but not to possess Him; the other have been able to

---

3 1 Cor. 12.26.
4 Col. 1.18.
5 1 Cor. 10.17.

---

1 Rom. 1.21.
2 Words found in the Preface of the Mass.

possess Him before they knew Him. But most blessed are those to whom knowing God is the same as possessing Him, for that is the most complete, true, and happy knowledge.

Chapter 22

It is now time to take up that question which you added to your letter after you had signed it: 'If infants are still without knowledge of God, how was it possible for John, even before his birth, to leap for joy in his mother's womb, at the coming and in the presence of the Mother of the Lord?' After mentioning that you had read my book, *On the Baptism of Infants,* you added these words: 'I should like to know what you think about pregnant mothers, when the mother of John the Baptist answered in her son's name for the faith of his belief.'

Chapter 23

These are certainly the words of Elizabeth, mother of John: 'Blessed art thou among women and blessed is the fruit of thy womb. And whence is this to me that the Mother of my Lord should come to me? For behold, as soon as the voice of thy salutation sounded in my ears, the infant in my womb leaped for joy.'[1] But, in order that she might be able to say this, the Evangelist forewarns us that 'she was filled with the Holy Spirit,'[2] and it is clear that she knew by His inspiration what that leaping of her infant signified, that is, the coming of the Mother of Him whose forerunner and announcer he was to be. It was possible for that to be a sign of a great happening which the older people should know, but not of something known by the infant. For, in the

1 Luke 1.41-44.
2 Luke 1.41.

introductory part of this narration in the Gospel it did not
say: 'The infant believed in her womb,' but 'he leaped'; and
she did not say: 'The infant leaped for faith in my womb,'
but 'he leaped for joy.' We see instances of this leaping not
only in children but even in animals, although certainly not
for any faith or religion or rational recognition of someone
coming; but this case stands out as utterly uncommon and
new, because it took place in a womb, and at the coming of
her who was to bring forth the Saviour of men. Therefore,
this leaping, this greeting, so to speak, offered to the Mother
of the Lord is miraculous, it is to be reckoned among the
great signs, it was not effected by human means by the infant,
but by divine means in the infant, as miracles are usually
wrought.

Chapter 24

Yet, even if the use of reason and will were so advanced
in the child that he was able, from within his mother's womb,
to recognize, believe, and assent to what in other children
has to await the proper age, even this is to be considered
among the miracles of divine power, not adduced as an
example of human nature. For, when God willed it, even a
dumb beast spoke rationally,[1] yet not for this are men advised
to expect the counsel of asses in their deliberations. Therefore,
I neither reject what happened to John, nor do I set it up as a
norm of what is to be thought of infants; on the contrary, I
pronounce that in him it was miraculous, because I do not
find it in others. There is something similar to it in that
struggle of the twins in the womb of Rebecca, but this was
such a prodigy that the woman consulted the divine oracle
and learned that two nations were prefigured by those two
infants.[2]

---

1 Num. 22.28.
2 Gen. 25.22,23. Balaam and the ass.

Chapter 25

However, if we wish to show by words that infants do not know divine things—in fact, they do not yet know human things—I fear that we may seem to do an injury to our own senses, since our persuasion is done by speaking, in which all the force and function of speech easily overpower the evidence of truth. Do we not see that even when infants begin to utter any syllables at all of articulate speech, and pass from infancy[1] to the beginning of speech, they still think and say such things as would make anyone but a fool not hesitate to call them fools if they remained persistently in that state as they advanced in years? Unless, perhaps, it remains for us to believe that infants were wise in the wailing of infancy or in the silence of the womb, but, after they began to speak to us, they came, as they grew up, to that degree of ignorance which we deride. You see how absurd it is to think that, for, when the consciousness of children issues in any kind of words, it is almost nothing in comparison with what its elders know, but, compared to the state in which children are born, it can be called intelligence. Why, in that safeguard of salvation, when Christian grace is made available to them, although they struggle against it with all their might by voice and movement, are they not held responsible for it, and why has all that effort of theirs no effect until the sacrament is completed in them, by which the guilt derived from the original damnation is expiated, unless because, in so far as they do not know what they are doing, they are not judged for doing it? Besides, what Christian does not know that if they had the use of reason and free will, which would require assent to the sanctifying act, what an evil it would be to resist so great a grace, and how useless the act performed would be to them, or even what an increase of guilt it would bring?

1 *Infantia* means, literally, 'speechlessness.'

Chapter 26

We say, then, that the Holy Spirit dwells in baptized children although they do not know it. They are unconscious of Him although He is in them, just as they are unconscious of their own mind, and the reason in them which they cannot yet use is like a covered spark waiting to be enkindled by oncoming age. And this ought not to seem strange in the case of infants, since the Apostle says to some of their elders, also: 'Know you not that you are the temple of God and that the Spirit of God dwelleth in you?' And, shortly before, he had said: 'But the sensual man perceiveth not these things that are of the Spirit of God.'[1] Such as these he also calls little ones, not in carnal but in spiritual age.[2] Thus, their understanding did not recognize the Holy Spirit who dwelt in them, and they were still carnal, not spiritual, in spite of the indwelling of the Holy Spirit in them, because their understanding could not recognize His indwelling Spirit.

Chapter 27

He is said to dwell in such as these because He works in them secretly that they may be His temple, and He perfects His work in them as they advance in virtue and persevere in their progress. 'For we are saved by hope,'[1] as the Apostle says, and he repeats in another place: 'He saved us by the laver of regeneration.'[2] Therefore, when he says: 'He saved us,' as if salvation itself had already been given us, he explains

1 1 Cor. 2.14.
2 1 Cor. 3.1.

1 Rom. 8.24.
2 Titus 3.5.

how this is to be understood when he says: 'For we are saved by hope. But hope that is seen is not hope, for what a man seeth why doth he hope for? But if we hope for that which we see not, we wait for it with patience.'[3] Thus, many things are spoken of in the divine Scriptures as if they were accomplished, but we understand that they are still a subject of hope. Hence, that other saying of the Lord when He spoke to the disciples: 'All things whatsoever I have heard of my Father I have made known to you,'[4] which is so manifestly said of what is to be hoped for that He said to them afterward: 'I have many things to say to you but you cannot bear them now.'[5] Therefore, in the mortals in whom He still dwells He carries on the building of His dwelling which He does not perfect in this life, but in another after this one, when 'death shall be swallowed up in victory,' and shall hear these words: O death, where is thy victory? O death, where is thy sting?'—and what is the sting of death but sin?[6]

Chapter 28

Although we are now reborn of water and the Spirit,[1] and all our sins are washed away in the cleansing of that laver, both the original sin of Adam, in whom all have sinned, and our own sins of deeds, words and thoughts, we still remain in this human life which is a warfare upon earth,[2] and therefore we have good reason to say: Forgive us our debts.' This prayer is also said by the whole church which the Saviour

---

3 Rom. 8.24,25.
4 John 15.15.
5 John 16.12.
6 Cf. 1 Cor. 15.54-56.

---

1 John 3.5.
2 Job 7.1.

cleansed 'by the laver of water in the word, that He might present it to himself glorious, not having spot or wrinkle or any such thing';[3]—at that future time, of course, when it shall be perfected in deed where now it walks forward in hope. In this life it is plainly not without spot or wrinkle or any such thing, either in all men who belong to it, who have the use of reason and free will and who carry the burdens of mortal flesh, or, at least, as our objectors must necessarily admit, in many of its members; so how can it say otherwise than with truth: 'Forgive us our debts'?

Chapter 29

Since, then, of the mortals in whom He dwells He justifies the proficient in goodness more and more as they are renewed from day to day, hears them when they pray, cleanses them when they confess their sins, that He may present them to Himself as a pure and everlasting temple, it is right to say that He does not dwell in those who 'knowing God have not glorified him as God or given thanks.' For, by worshiping and serving the 'creature rather than the Creator,'[1] they have not wished to be a temple of the one true God, and thus, by wishing to have Him along with many other things, they have been more successful in not having Him at all than in joining Him to many false gods. And He is rightly said to dwell in those whom He has called according to His purpose, and whom He has received in order to justify and glorify them even before they are able to know His incorporeal nature, as far as it can be known 'in part, through a glass, in a dark manner,'[2] by man in this life, although he has made

3 Eph. 5.26,27.

1 Rom. 1.25.
2 1 Cor. 13.12.

great progress. There are some in whom He dwells who are like those to whom the Apostle says: 'I could not speak to you as unto spiritual but as unto carnal. As unto little ones in Christ I gave you milk to drink, not meat, for you were not able as yet; but neither indeed are you now able.' And to these words he added this: 'Know you not that you are the temple of God; that the Spirit of God dwelleth in you?'[3] Even if such as these are overtaken by the last day of this life before they attain to that spiritual age of mind when they will be fed solid food instead of milk, the One who dwells in them will perfect whatever they have lacked of understanding here, since they have not withdrawn from the unity of the body of Christ, who has become our way,[4] nor from their membership in the temple of God. In order not to withdraw from it, they hold steadfastly to the rule of faith which is common to little and great in the Church; they walk in Him whereunto they are come, and until God reveals to them that they are otherwise minded,[5] they do not make dogma of their carnal thoughts, because they are not hardened by clinging to contentious excuses; but walking in a certain way, that is, the way of advancement, they struggle with their understanding, winning clear sight by their pious faith.

Chapter 30

This being so, those two phenomena, birth and rebirth, which occur in a single man, belong to two men, one to the first Adam, the other to the second Adam who is called Christ. 'Yet that was not first,' says the Apostle, 'which is spiritual, but that which is natural; afterwards that which is

---

3 1 Cor. 3.1,2,16.
4 John 14.6.
5 Phil. 3.15,16.

spiritual. The first man was of the earth, earthly, the second man from heaven, heavenly. Such as is the earthly such also are the earthly; and such as is the heavenly such also are they that are heavenly. As we have borne the image of the earthly, let us bear also the image of him who is from heaven.'[1] He says, likewise: 'By one man came death and by a man the resurrection of the dead. For as in Adam all die, so also in Christ all shall be made alive.'[2] He says 'all' in both places because no one comes to death but by the first, no one to life but by the second: in the first the power of man's will to cause death was made evident; in the second, the value of God's help for life. To sum up: The first man was only man, but the second was God and man; sin was committed by forsaking God, justice is not achieved without God. Thus we should not have to die if we had not come from his members by carnal generation, nor should we live if we were not His members by spiritual incorporation. Therefore, for us there was need of birth and rebirth, but for Him need only of birth for our sake; we pass from sin to justice by rebirth, but He passed to justice without any sin. By being baptized He gave a higher commendation to the sacrament of our regeneration through His humility, signifying our old man by His Passion, our new one by His Resurrection.

Chapter 31

The revolt of concupiscence which is rooted in mortal flesh, by which it happens that its members are stirred to action even against the movement of the will, is brought into such control that those who stand in need of regeneration are lawfully begotten by the intercourse of parents. However,

1 Cf. 1 Cor. 15.46-49.
2 1 Cor. 15.21,22.

Christ did not will that His flesh should come into being by this kind of meeting of male and female, but in His conception of the Virgin, without any such human passion, He took on 'the likeness of sinful flesh'[1] for us, that the flesh of sin in us might be purified. 'For, as by the offense of one,' the Apostle says, 'unto all men to condemnation, so also by the justice of one unto all men to justification of life.'[2] No one is born without the intervention of carnal concupiscence which is inherited from the first man who is Adam, and no one is reborn without the intervention of spiritual grace which is given by the second man who is Christ. Therefore, if we belong to the former by birth, we belong to the latter by rebirth; as no one can be born again before he is born, it is clear that Christ's birth was unique in that He had no need to be born again because He did not pass over from sin, to which He was never subject. He was not conceived in iniquity nor did His Mother nourish Him in her womb in sin,[3] because the Holy Spirit came upon her and the power of the Most High overshadowed her; therefore, the Holy that was born of her is called the Son of God.[4] He does not destroy the good of marriage, but He curbs the evil of rebellious members, so that when carnal concupiscence has been tamed it may at least become conjugal chastity. But the Virgin Mary, to whom the words were said: 'And the power of the Most High shall overshadow thee,' burned with no heat of this concupiscence in conceiving her holy offspring under such a shadow. Therefore, with the exception of this cornerstone,[5] I do not see how men are to be built into a house of God, to contain God dwelling in them,[6] without being born again, which cannot happen before they are born.

---

1 Rom. 8.3.
2 Rom. 5.18.
3 Ps. 50.7.
4 Luke 1.35.
5 Isa. 28.16; 1 Peter 2.6; Eph. 2.20.
6 2 Cor. 6.16.

Chapter 32

Furthermore, whatever opinion we may hold about pregnant mothers, or even about men still sheltered within their mother's womb, whether or not they can be endowed with some kind of sanctification, either because of John who leaped for joy, though he had not yet come forth to the light of day—and who would believe this could happen without the action of the Holy Spirit?—or because of Jeremias to whom the Lord said: 'Before thou camest forth out of the womb I sanctified thee,'[1] it is a fact that the sanctification by which we become temples of God individually, and form one temple of God all together, takes place only in the reborn, which men cannot be unless they are first born. No one will make a good end of the life into which he is born unless he is born again before he ends it.

Chapter 33

But if anyone says that a man is already born even when he is still in his mother's womb, and offers as proof from the Gospel the words to Joseph about the Virgin Mother of the Lord, then with child: 'For that which is born in her is of the Holy Spirit,'[1] is that any reason why a second nativity should follow on this one? Otherwise, it will not be the second but the third. When the Lord was speaking on this point He said: 'Unless a man be born again,'[2] counting that

1 Jer. 1.5.

1 Matt. 1.20. This objection arose from the version of Scripture used by St. Augustine. The Vulgate obviates it by using 'conceived' instead of 'born.'
2 John 3.3.

the first nativity, of course, which happens when a mother gives birth, not when she conceives or becomes pregnant; birth is what happens from her, not what happens in her. We do not say that a man is reborn when his mother brings him forth, as if he were born a second time after being born once in the womb, but, not counting that as a birth which makes a woman pregnant, a man is said to be born when he comes forth, so that he may be born again 'of water and the Holy Spirit.'[3] The Lord is said to have been born at Bethlehem of Juda[4] according to the time of His birth from His Mother. If, then, a man can be regenerated in the womb by the grace of the Spirit, since he still has to be born, he is reborn before he is born, which is absolutely impossible. Therefore, it is not by the works of justice which they are about to perform that men are born into the totality of the body of Christ as into a living structure of the temple of God which is His Church, but, by being born again through grace, they are carried over as from a ruinous mass into the foundation of the building. Outside this building which is raised up to be made blessed as an eternal dwelling of God, the whole life of man is unhappy and is rather to be called death than life. Whoever, therefore, has God dwelling in him, that the anger of God may not rest on him, will not be hostile to this Body, this temple, this birth. But whoever is not reborn is hostile to it.

Chapter 34

Moreover, our Mediator, when revealed to us, wished the sacrament of our regeneration to be manifest. But for the just men of old it was something hidden, although they also were to be saved by the same faith which was to be revealed

3 John 3.5.
4 Matt. 2.1.

in its own time. For we do not dare to prefer the faithful of our own time to the friends of God by whom those prophecies were to be made, since God so announced Himself as the God of Abraham, the God of Isaac, the God of Jacob,[1] as to give Himself that name forever. If the belief is correct that circumcision served instead of baptism in the saints of old, what shall be said of those who pleased God before this was commanded, except that they pleased Him by faith, because, as it is written in Hebrews: 'Without faith it is impossible to please God'?[2] 'But having the same spirit of faith,' says the Apostle, 'as it is written: I believed, for which cause I have spoken, we also believe for which cause we speak also.'[3] He would not have said 'the same' unless this very spirit of faith were theirs, also. For, just as they, when this same mystery was hidden, believed in the Incarnation of Christ which was to come, so we also believe that it has come. And both we and they expect His future coming to judgment, for there is no other mystery of God[4] except Christ in whom all who have died in Adam are to be made alive, because 'as in Adam all die, so also in Christ all shall be made alive,'[5] as we have explained above.

Chapter 35

Therefore, God, who is everywhere present and everywhere wholly present, does not dwell in all men, but in those only whom He has made into His most blessed temple or temples, delivering them 'from the power of darkness,' and translating them 'into the kingdom of the Son of his love,'[1] which began

---

1 Exod. 3.15.
2 Heb. 11.6.
3 2 Cor. 4.13; Ps. 115.10.
4 Apoc. 10.7.
5 2 Cor. 15.22.

---

1 Col. 1.13.

with their regeneration. But His temple has one meaning
when it is built by the hands of men, of inanimate materials,
as the Tabernacle, made of wood, tapestries, skins and other
movables of that sort; as also the Temple built by King
Solomon, of stone, wood and metal; and another meaning
for that true temple which was symbolized by those meanings.
Hence the words: 'Be you also as living stones, built up, a
spiritual house';[2] hence it is also written: 'For we are the
temple of the living God, as God saith: I will dwell in them
and I will be their God and they shall be my people.'[3]

Chapter 36

Yet we ought not to be disturbed because some who do not
belong or do not yet belong to this temple, that is, among
whom God does not or does not yet dwell, perform some
works of power, as happened to him who cast out devils in
the name of Christ; although he was not a follower of Christ,[1]
Christ ordered that he be allowed to continue because it gave
a useful testimony of His name to many. He said also that
many would say to Him at the last day: 'In thy name we
have done many miracles,' to whom He would certainly not
say: 'I know you not,'[2] if they belonged to the temple of
God, which He makes blessed by His indwelling. The centurion Cornelius also saw the angel that was sent to him
and heard him saying that his prayers had been heard and his
alms accepted, even before he was incorporated into this
temple by regeneration.[3] God does these things as One everywhere present, even when He acts through His holy angels.

2 1 Peter 2.5.
3 2 Cor. 6.16; Lev. 26.12.

1 Mark 9.37-39.
2 Matt. 7.22,23.
3 Acts 10.1-4.

Chapter 37

In the case of that sanctification of Jeremias before he came forth from the womb,[1] some take it that he was a type of the Saviour, who had no need of regeneration; however, even if it is taken literally, it can also be appropriately understood in the sense of regeneration; as the Gospel calls sons of God those not yet regenerated, when, after Caiaphas had said of the Lord: 'It is expedient for you that one man should die for the people and that the whole nation perish not,' the Evangelist goes on and adds: 'This he spoke not of himself, but being the high priest of that year, he prophesied that Jesus should die for the nation, and not only for the nation, but to gather together in one the children of God that were dispersed.'[2] In addition to the Hebrew race, he obviously calls children of God men included in all other races who were not yet among the faithful, not yet baptized. How else can he call them sons of God except in the sense of their predestination, in which sense, also, the Apostle says that God chose us in Christ before the foundation of the world?[3] That very gathering together in one would have made them children of God. And by the words 'in one' he would not have meant any corporeal place, since the Prophet made this prophecy of a similar calling of the Gentiles: 'They shall adore him every man from his own place; all the islands of the Gentiles,'[4] but 'gathered together in one' refers to the one Spirit and one body of which the Head is Christ.[5] Such a gathering together is the building of the temple of God; such a gathering together is not effected by carnal generation, but by spiritual regeneration.

1 Jer. 1.5.
2 John 11.50-52.
3 Eph. 1.4.
4 Soph. 2.11.
5 Col. 1.18; Eph. 1.22,23.

Chapter 38

Therefore, God dwells in each one singly as in His temples, and in all of them gathered together as in His temple. As long as this temple, like the ark of Noe, is tempest-tossed in this world, the words of the psalm are verified: 'The Lord dwelleth in the flood,'[1] although, if we consider the many people of the faithful of all races whom the Apocalypse describes under the name of waters,[2] they can also be appropriately meant by 'The Lord dwelleth in the flood.' But the psalm goes on: 'And the Lord shall sit king forever,'[3] doubtless in that very temple of His, established in eternal life after the tempest of this world. Thus, God, who is everywhere present and everywhere wholly present, does not dwell everywhere but only in His temple, to which, by His grace, He is kind and gracious, but in His indwelling he is received more fully by some, less by others.

Chapter 39

Speaking of Him as our Head, the Apostle says: 'For in him dwelleth all the fullness of the Godhead corporally.'[1] He does not say 'corporally' because God is corporeal, but he either uses the word in a derived sense as if He dwelt in a temple made by hands, not corporally but symbolically, that is, under prefiguring signs—for using a derived word he calls all those observances shadows of things to come,[2] for the most high God, as it is written, 'dwelleth not in temples made

---

1 Ps. 28.10. The Vulgate has: 'The Lord maketh the flood to dwell.'
2 Apoc. 17.15.
3 Ps. 28.10.

---

1 Col. 2.9.
2 Col. 2.17; Heb. 10.1.

with hand'[3]—or else the word 'corporally' is certainly used because God dwells, as in His temple, in the body of Christ which He took from the Virgin. That is why, when He said to the Jews who demanded a sign: 'Destroy this temple and in three days I will raise it up,' the Evangelist, explaining what He meant, added: 'But he spoke of the temple of his body.'[4]

Chapter 40

What then? Are we to think there is this difference between the head and the other members that divinity may dwell in any given member however outstanding, as some great prophet or apostle, yet not 'all the fullness of the Godhead'[1] as in the Head which is Christ? In our body there also is sensation innate in the individual members, but not so much as in the head, where it is clear that all the five senses are centered; for there are located sight and hearing and smell and taste and touch, but in the other members there is only touch. But perhaps, besides the fact that 'all the fullness of the Godhead' is found in that Body as in a temple, there is another difference between that Head and the perfection of any of the members. There is, indeed, in the fact that by a certain unique assumption of humanity He became one Person with the Word. Of none of the saints has it been, is it, or will it be possible to say: 'The Word was made flesh';[2] none of the saints by any supreme gift of grace received the name of only-begotten Son, so as to be called by the name which is that of the very Word of God Himself before all

---

3 Acts 17.24.
4 John 2.19,21.

---

1 Col. 2.9.
2 John 1.14.

ages, together with the humanity which He assumed. Therefore, that act of becoming man cannot be shared with any
holy men, however eminent in wisdom and sanctity. That is
a sufficiently evident and clear proof of divine grace. Who,
then, could be guilty of such sacrilege as to dare assert that
any soul, through the merit of its free will, could succeed in
becoming another Christ? How could one single soul, by
means of the free will given uniformly to all by nature, have
merited to be joined to the Person of the only-begotten Word,
unless a supreme grace had granted this, a grace which we
may lawfully extol, but of which it is forbidden us to wish
to judge?

Chapter 41

If I have been successful in treating of these matters, in
proportion to my strength and by the Lord's help, when you
set yourself to think of God everywhere present and everywhere wholly present, not distributed in different places as if
by the stretching of physical mass, turn your mind from all
corporeal images such as it is wont to fashion. That is not
how we think of wisdom or justice or, finally, of charity, of
which it is written: 'God is charity.'[1] And when you think of
His indwelling, think of the unity of the gathering of saints,
especially in heaven, where He is said to dwell in a unique
manner, because His will is done there by the perfect
obedience of those in whom He dwells; then think of Him
on earth where He dwells while building His house which is
to be dedicated at the end of time. But when you think of
Christ our Lord, the only-begotten Son of God, equal to the
Father, and likewise Son of man, in which respect the Father
is greater then He, do not doubt that as God He is everywhere wholly present, and also as God He dwells in the

1 1 John 4.8.

same temple of God; while in His true Body He is in some part of heaven.

It gives me such pleasure to talk with you that I do not know whether I have observed a due measure of speech, in my desire to compensate for my long silence by my long talk. Truly I speak to you as to a friend, so closely are you bound to my heart by the ties of religion and kindness, in which you have surpassed me. Give thanks to God whenever you know that any work of my pen has been fruitful, but if you observe my defects, pardon them as a most dear friend, with the same sincere affection, praying for my cure, as you grant me your indulgence.

188. *Alypius and Augustine give greeting in the Lord to the lady Juliana,[1] their deservedly distinguished daughter, worthy of honor, with due respect in Christ (End of 417 or beginning of 418)*

It was a pleasing and happy coincidence that the letter of your Reverence found us settled together at Hippo. This gives us an opportunity of writing you a joint reply, assuring you of our joy in hearing of your welfare and giving you news, with reciprocal affection, of our own, which we trust is dear to you, lady worthy of honor with due respect in Christ, our deservedly distinguished daughter. We know well that you know the depth of religious affection we owe you, and the great solicitude we feel for you before God and among men. Although our Lowliness came to know your family as pious Catholics, that is, true members of Christ, first by letters, and then by personal acquaintance, nevertheless as you have, through our ministry, 'received the word of

---

1 Mother of Demetrias, a consecrated virgin, who had received from Pelagius a book filled with errors.

the hearing of God,' as the Apostle says: 'you received it not as the word of men, but, as it is indeed, the word of God.'[2] And this ministry of ours has borne such fruit in your house, by the helping grace and mercy of the Saviour that, although a worldly marriage had been arranged for her, the saintly Demetrias preferred the spiritual embrace of the Spouse, 'beautiful above the sons of men,'[3] to whom virgins pledge themselves that they may gain the more abundant fruitfulness of the spirit without losing the integrity of their flesh. We should not have known how that exhortation of ours had been received by the faithful and noble girl if we had not learned the most joyful news from the truthful report of your letter, which reached us on our journey a short time after she had made profession of virginity as a consecrated nun, that this great gift of God which He plants and waters by means of His servants, but gives the increase Himself,[4] had prospered so well for His workers.

This being the case, no one will call us unmannerly if we are moved by too urgent distress in warning you to avoid teachings contrary to the grace of God. Although the Apostle warns us to be instant in preaching the word not only in season but even out of season,[5] we do not include you in the list of those persons to whom a sermon or a page of ours would seem unseasonable when we advise you to avoid carefully what is not in accord with sound doctrine. That is the reason why you have received our warning in so grateful a spirit that you say in the letter which we are now answering: 'Indeed I return fervent thanks to your Reverence for the loving warning you gave us not to lend our ears to the men who often corrupt our venerable faith by lying treatises.'

---

2 1 Thess. 2.13.
3 Ps. 44.3.
4 1 Cor. 3.5,6.
5 2 Tim. 4.2.

But what presses us more and more urgently not to refrain from speaking to you about those who are trying to distort even those teachings which are sound is the sentence which you add when you say: 'But your Priesthood knows that I and my little household are far removed from persons of that kind; all our family follow the Catholic faith so closely that we have never fallen into any heresy, nor ever lapsed into any sect which seems to have even small errors, much less those which are outside the pale.' We count your house as no small Church of Christ. Similarly, it is no small error on the part of those who think that we have of ourselves whatever justice, continence, piety, and chastity there is in us, because God has made us so that He gives us no further help beyond a revelation of knowledge, which makes us do, with love, what we know through learning that we ought to do; in short, who define nature and doctrine as being the only form of grace and help given us by God that we may live justly and up-rightly. They will not admit that we are divinely helped to-ward the possession of a good will on which depends the very fact that we live justly, or of charity itself, which is so eminent among all the gifts of God that it is said to be God,[6] by which alone any fulfillment of the divine law and teaching there may be in us is accomplished; but they say that we are sufficient of ourselves and of our own will to accomplish such fulfillment. It ought to seem no slight error to us that Christians should profess such belief and refuse to listen to the Apostle of Christ who said: 'The charity of God is poured forth in our hearts,' and, lest anyone think he has it through his will alone, he at once adds: 'by the Holy Spirit who is given to us.'[7] You understand how greatly and how irreme-diably anyone errs who no longer admits that this great grace

6 1 John 4.8,16.
7 Rom. 5.5.

is from the Saviour who 'ascended on high, led captivity captive and gave gifts to men.'[8]

We would like to know, preferably through your reply, how, owing you such affection, we could have refrained from warning you to beware of such teaching, after we had read the book which a certain one[9] addressed to the saintly Demetrias, or even whether it reached you. If it is right and proper, let the virgin of Christ read what may make her believe that her virginal sanctity and all her spiritual riches come to her from herself alone, and thus, before she reaches full beatitude, let her learn to be ungrateful to God—which God forbid! These are the words written in that same book addressed to her: 'You have here,' he says, 'the reason why you are preferred to others; nay, you have here much more, for your physical beauty and the wealth of your family will not be attributed to you, but of your spiritual riches, no one but you could bestow them on you. For these, then, you are deservedly praised, for these you are deservedly preferred to others, because they can be found only in you and of you.'[10]

You see, of course, the destructive effect of these words. Certainly, when he says: 'These good things cannot be found except in you,' he speaks well and truly: these words are food; but when he says: 'They come only from yourself,' this is all poison. God forbid that these words should find a willing hearing from the virgin of Christ who lovingly understands the natural poverty of the human heart and knows therefrom that her only adornment is in the gifts of her Spouse. Let her listen, rather, to the Apostle when he says: 'I have espoused you to one husband that I may present you as a chaste virgin to Christ; but I fear lest, as the serpent seduced Eve by his subtlety, your minds should be corrupted

8 Eph. 4.7,8; Ps. 67.19.
9 Pelagius.
10 *Pelagii Liber ad Demetriaden* 11 (*PL* 33.1107.3-36).

from the chastity that is in Christ.'[11] Therefore, let her not listen to the one who says of her spiritual riches: 'No one but yourself could bestow them on you,' and 'they can be found only in you and of you,' but let her listen to the one who says: 'We have this treasure in earthen vessels, that the excellency may be of the power of God and not of us.'[12]

Concerning this same sacred virginal continence, also, which is not of herself but is a gift of God, although it is given to one who believes and desires it, let her listen to the same truthful and pious teacher who said, in treating of this subject: 'I would that all men were even as myself; but everyone hath his proper gift from God; one after this manner and another after that.'[13] Let her listen to what is said of such chastity and integrity by Him who is the sole Spouse of the whole Church as well as her own: 'All men take not this word but they to whom it is given,'[14] and let her learn from it that she has such a great and excellent gift that she ought to give thanks to our God and Lord rather than listen to the words of, we do not say a cajoling flatterer lest we seem to judge rashly of men's secret motives, but at least of a deluded admirer who tells her that she has this from herself. As the Apostle James says: 'Every best gift and every perfect gift is from above, coming down from the Father of lights.'[15] This is the source of the holy virginity in which your daughter surpasses you, to your joy and satisfaction; after you in age, before you in conduct; of you by birth, before you in honor; inferior to you in years, excelling you in holiness. In her you begin to have for yours what you could not have in yourself. She, indeed, did not contract a carnal marriage and as a result she was spiritually enriched more than you, yet not

11 2 Cor. 11.2,3.
12 2 Cor. 4.7.
13 1 Cor. 7.7.
14 Matt. 19.11.
15 James 1.17.

only for herself but for you; though you are inferior to her, in this you are made equal to her that your marriage was the cause of her birth. These are gifts of God, and they are yours also, but they are 'not of yourselves,'[16] for you have this treasure in earthly and still frail bodies, as 'in earthen vessels that the excellency may be of the power of God and not of you.'[17] Do not be surprised that we say it is both yours and not of you, for when we speak of our daily bread, we say' Give us,' lest it be thought to be 'of us.'

Therefore, as it is written: 'Pray without ceasing; in all things give thanks,'[18] for you pray that you may have it continually and increasingly; you give thanks because you do not have it of yourselves. Who set you apart from that clay[19] of Adam, that lump of death and damnation? Was it not He who 'is come to seek and to save that which was lost'?[20] On the other hand, when a man hears the Apostle saying: 'Who hath distinguished thee?' will he answer: 'My good will, my faith, my justice,' and not listen to the words immediately following: 'For what hast thou that thou hast not received? And if thou hast received it, why dost thou glory as if thou hadst not received it?'[21] Thus, when the consecrated virgin hears or reads: 'No one but yourself can bestow spiritual riches on you; for these you are deservedly praised, for these you are deservedly preferred to others, because they can be found only in you and of you,' we do not wish her thereupon to glory as if she had not received them. Let her say: 'In me, O God, are vows to thee which I will pay, praises to thee';[22] but because they are in her but not of her, let her remember to say: 'O Lord, in thy favor thou givest strength to my

16 Eph. 2.8.
17 Cf. 2 Cor. 4.7.
18 1 Thess. 5.17,18.
19 Rom. 9.21.
20 Luke 19.10; Matt. 18.11.
21 1 Cor. 4.7.
22 Ps. 55.12.

beauty,'[23] because even though they may be of her because of her free will, without which we perform no good work, yet it is not true, as he said: 'They could come only from her.' There can be no good will in man unless the free will is helped by the grace of God. The Apostle says: 'For it is God who worketh in you both to will and to accomplish, according to his good will,'[24] not, as they think, by a mere revelation of knowledge so that we may know what we ought to do, but also by breathing His charity into us so that we do with love what we have learned by our knowledge.

Surely, the wise man knew how great a good continence was when he said: 'And as I knew that no one can be continent except God give it.' Therefore, he not only knew how great, how desirable, how much to be coveted this good is, but also that it could not exist unless God gave it, for wisdom had taught him this. When he also said: 'And this also was a point of wisdom to know whose gift it was,' his own wisdom did not supply him with it, but he said: 'I went to the Lord and besought him.'[25] Thus, God's help does not consist only in this, that we know what is to be done, but also in our doing with love what we have learned by our knowledge. Therefore, no one can be either learned or continent unless God give it. Consequently, when he had the knowledge he prayed to have the continency, that it might also be in him, because he knew that it was not of himself; or if by reason of his free will it was to some extent of himself, it was not exclusively of himself, 'because no one can be continent unless God give it.' But when Pelagius speaks of spiritual riches, among which that shining and beautiful continence is certainly included, he does not say: 'They can be in you and of you,' but 'They can be only of you and in you.'

23 PS. 29.18.
24 Phil. 2.13.
25 Wisd. 8.21.

Consequently, he believes that as they cannot be found elsewhere than in her, so they can have no other source than herself, and therefore—may the merciful Lord avert it from her heart!—let her so glory as if she had not received them.

Our opinion, however, of the training and Christian humility of the saintly virgin in which she was nourished and brought up makes us think that when she read those words, if indeed she did read them, she groaned and humbly struck her breast, perhaps wept, also, and faithfully prayed God, to whom she is consecrated and by whom she is sanctified, that, as those words are not hers but another's so her faith should not be such that she would believe she has anything which would make her glory in herself and not in the Lord. Her glory, indeed, is in herself, not in another's words, as the Apostle says: 'But let every one prove his own work and so he shall have glory in himself and not in another.'[26] But God forbid that she should be her own glory and not He to whom it is said: 'My glory and the lifter up of my head.'[27] Thus, it is safe for that glory to be in her when God who is in her is Himself her glory; from whom she has all the good things by which she is good, and will have all things by which she will be better, in so far as she can be better in this life; and by which she will be made perfect when divine grace, not human praise, has made her perfect. For, 'in the Lord shall her soul be praised,'[28] 'who hath satisfied her desire with good things,'[29] because He has Himself inspired this desire, lest His virgin should glory in any good as if she had not received it.

Inform us about this in your answer and let us know whether we are wrong about her state of mind. For we know one thing very well, that you and all your household are and

---

26 Gal. 6.4.
27 Ps. 3.4.
28 Cf. Ps. 33.3.
29 Cf. Ps. 102.5.

have been worshipers of the undivided Trinity. But this is not the only source from which human error steals upon us, namely, that we should have heterodox views of the undivided Trinity, for there are also other points in which it is possible to fall into error, such as the one we have spoken of in this letter, more at length, perhaps, than was needful for your faithful and chaste prudence. Still, if anyone says that the good which is of God is not of God, we do not know whom else he insults except God, and thereby also the undivided Trinity. May this evil be far from you, as we believe it has been. God forbid utterly that this book—from which we have thought it advisable to quote some passages to make their meaning more clear—should leave any such impression in your mind, and we do not mean yours only or that of the consecrated virgin, your daughter, but even the mind of any one of your male or female servants of however long service.

But if you will look into it more carefully, you will find that even what he seems to say there in favor of grace or of the help of God is ambiguous, and can be referred either to nature or knowledge or the remission of sins. As to their being forced to admit that we ought to pray lest we enter into temptation, they can apply it in this sense so as to answer that we are helped to it to this extent that when we ask and knock,[30] our intellect is opened to truth by which we learn what we ought to do, but not to the extent that our will receives strength to make us do what we have learned. And when they say that the Lord Christ is set before us as a model of virtuous living, and that this is the grace or help of God, they go back to the same idea of grace as knowledge, because obviously we learn by His example how we ought to live; but they refuse to admit that we are helped to do with love what we know through what we have learned.

Find some passage in the same book, if you can, where he

30 Cf. Matt. 7.7,8; Luke 11.9,10.

admits that such help from God is something else except nature or free will, which belongs to the same nature, or the remission of sins and revelation of knowledge, or that it is such as the wise man confessed when he said: 'As I knew that no one can be continent except God give it, and this also was a point of wisdom to know whose gift it was, I went to the Lord and besought him.'[31] In answer to that prayer, he did not wish to receive the nature in which he was created, nor was he exercised about the natural freedom of will with which he was created, nor did he long for the remission of sins, since he rather sighed after continence that he might not sin, nor did he long to know what he had to do, since he has already admitted that he knew whose gift it was, but undoubtedly he wished to receive from the spirit of wisdom such strength of will, such ardor of love as would make him fit to attain the great virtue of continence. If, then, you can find anything of that sort in his book, we will give you hearty thanks if you will be so kind as to point it out to us in your answer.

It is impossible to express how much we long to find in the writings of those men, who are read by many because of their keenness and fluency, an open admission of that grace which the Apostle praises so strongly, who even says that God has divided to everyone the measure of faith itself,[32] without which it is impossible to please God, by which the just man lives,[33] which 'worketh by charity,'[34] before which and without which no good works can be imagined in anyone, since 'all that is not of faith is sin';[35] and not the claim that we are helped by God to live piously and justly by the sole

---

31 Wisd. 8.21.
32 Rom. 12.3.
33 Heb. 11.6; Rom. 1.17; Gal. 3.11; Heb. 10.38.
34 Gal. 5.6.
35 Rom. 14.24.

revelation of knowledge, which puffs us up without charity;[36] whereas He does it by breathing charity itself into us, charity which is the fulfilling of the law,[37] and which edifies our heart so that charity may not puff us up. But thus far we have been unable to find any such statement anywhere in their writings.

We should wish most of all that this had been in the book from which we have quoted the above selected passages, where, after praising the virgin of Christ as if no one but herself could bestow spiritual riches on her, and as if they could not exist except as coming from her, he does not wish her to glory in the Lord, but to so glory as if she had not received them. Although he has not mentioned in this book the name of your Reverence or that of your daughter, he does say that he was asked by the girl's mother to write to her. However, the same Pelagius, in a certain letter of his to which he openly signed his own name, and in which he does not fail to mention the name of the consecrated virgin, says that he has written to her and tries to prove by the testimony of the same work that he makes open confession of the grace of God, which he is reputed to ignore or deny. We beg you to be so kind as to inform us in your answer whether the book in question is the one in which he used those expressions about spiritual riches, or whether it has reached your Holiness.

---

36 1 Cor. 8.1.
37 Rom. 13.10.

*189. Augustine gives greeting in the Lord to the noble lord,
his deservedly distinguished and honorable son,
Boniface[1] (c. 418)*

I had already written an answer to your Charity and I was
looking for an opportunity of forwarding it to you, when my
dear son Faustus arrived on his way to your Excellency.
After receiving the letter which I had already written for
delivery to your Benevolence,[2] he gave me to understand that
you greatly desired me to write you something which might
edify you and help you to win eternal salvation, of which your
hope is in our Lord Jesus Christ. And although I am so busy,
he insisted that I should not put off doing it, and you know
how great is his urgency because he loves you so sincerely.
Therefore, to accommodate myself to his haste, I have chosen
to write something hurried rather than disappoint your
religious craving, noble lord, deservedly distinguished and
honorable son.

All that I can say, then, in brief is this: 'Thou shalt love
the Lord thy God with thy whole heart and with thy whole
soul and with thy whole strength' and 'thou shalt love thy
neighbor as thyself.'[3] This is the compendium which the Lord
gave upon earth when He said in the Gospel: 'On these two
commandments dependeth the whole law and the prophets.'[4]
Do you, then, advance daily in this love both by prayer and
good works, so that, with the help of Him who endows and
bestows it on you, it may be fostered and increased until,

---

1 Count or Governor of Africa under Honorius and Placidia. Unjustly
disgraced through the treachery of his rival Aetius, he allied himself
with Genseric and the Vandals whom he invited into Africa in 429.
Later, vindicated and restored to favor, he fought the invaders. St.
Augustine died during the siege of Hippo, one of the results of the
invasion. Boniface died in Italy in battle in 432.
2 There is some doubt whether this was Letter 185.
3 Matt. 22.37,39; Mark 12.20,31; Luke 10.27; Deut. 22.37; Lev. 19.18.
4 Matt. 22.40.

being perfected, it may perfect you. This is the charity which, as the Apostle says, 'is poured forth in our hearts by the Holy Spirit who is given to us';[5] this is the charity of which he likewise says: 'Love is the fulfilling of the Law';[6] this is the charity by which faith works, of which he says again: 'For neither circumcision availeth anything nor uncircumcision but faith that worketh by charity.'[7]

In this charity all our holy fathers and patriarchs and prophets and apostles have been pleasing to God. In it, all true martyrs have striven against the Devil unto blood,[8] and because it has not grown cold or fallen away in them they have won the victory. In it, all good faithful souls daily progress in their desire to attain, not a mortal kingdom but the kingdom of heaven; not a temporal but an eternal inheritance;[9] not gold and silver but the incorruptible riches of the angels; not the goods of this world which fill life with fear, and which no one can take with him when he dies, but the vision of God.[10] The sweetness and bliss of this vision surpass the beauty not only of terrestrial creatures but even of celestial ones; it exceeds all the loveliness of souls however good and holy; it exceeds all the splendor of the highest angels and heavenly powers; it exceeds not only all that can be said but even what can be thought. And let us not despair of the fulfillment of this great promise, because it is so exceedingly great, but, rather, let us believe that we shall receive what is promised because He who has promised it is exceedingly great. Thus, blessed John the Apostle says: 'We are the sons of God and it hath not yet appeared what we shall be. We

---

5 Rom. 5.5.
6 Rom. 13.10.
7 Gal. 5.6.
8 Matt. 24.12.
9 Matt. 4.21; Heb. 9.15.
10 Matt. 5.8.

know that when he shall appear we shall be like to him because we shall see him as he is.'[11]

Do not imagine that no one can please God while he is
engaged in military service. Among such was holy David to
whom the Lord gave such high testimony. Among such were
many just men of that time. Among such, also, was that
centurion who said to the Lord: 'I am not worthy that thou
shouldst enter under my roof, but only say the word and my
servant shall be healed. For I also am a man, subject to
authority, having under me soldiers, and I say to this one:
Go, and he goeth, and to another: Come, and he cometh;
and to my servant: Do this, and he doth it'; of him the Lord
said: 'Amen I say to you I have not found so great faith in
Israel.'[12] Among such, also, was that Cornelius to whom the
angel was sent, who said: 'Cornelius, thy prayer is heard and
thy alms are accepted,' when he advised him to send to the
blessed Apostle Peter, to hear from him what he ought to do.
And to summon the Apostle to him he sent a religious
soldier.[13] Among such, also, were those who came for baptism
to John, the holy precursor of the Lord and friend of the
bridegroom, of whom the Lord said: 'There hath not arisen
among them that are born of women a greater one than
John the Baptist.'[14] When they asked him what they ought
to do, he answered them: 'Do violence to no man, neither
calumniate any man, and be content with your pay.'[15]
Obviously, he did not forbid them to serve in the army when
he commanded them to be satisfied with their pay.

Those who serve God with the highest self-discipline of
chastity, by renouncing all these wordly activities, have a

11 1 John 3.2.
12 Matt. 8.8-10; Luke 7.6-9.
13 Acts 10.1-8; 30-33.
14 Matt. 11.11.
15 Luke 3.12-14.

more prominent place before Him: 'But everyone hath his proper gift from God, one after this manner and another after that.'[16] Thus, some fight for you against invisible enemies by prayer, while you strive for them against visible barbarians by fighting. Would that one faith were found in all, for there would be less striving and the Devil and his angels would be overcome more easily! But as it must needs be in this world that citizens of the kingdom of heaven are troubled by temptations in the midst of the erring and the godless, so that they may be tested and tried as gold in the furnace,[17] so we should not wish to live before the time with the holy and upright only, that we may deserve to receive this reward in its own time.

Think first of this, then, when you are arming for battle, that your strength, even of body, is a gift of God, for so you will not think of using the gift of God against God. When your word is pledged, it must be kept even with the enemy against whom you wage war, how much more with the friend for whom you are fighting! Your will ought to hold fast to peace, with war as the result of necessity, that God may free you from the necessity and preserve you in peace. Peace is not sought for the purpose of stirring up war, but war is waged for the purpose of securing peace. Be, then, a peacemaker even while you make war, that by your victory you may lead those whom you defeat to know the desirability of peace, for the Lord says: 'Blessed are the peacemakers for they shall be called the children of God.'[18] Yet, if human peace is so sweet as a means of assuring the temporal welfare of mortals, how much sweeter is divine peace as a means for assuring the eternal welfare of angels! Therefore, let it be necessity, not choice, that kills your warring enemy. Just as violence is

---

16 1 Cor. 7.7.
17 Wisd. 3.5,6.
18 Matt. 5.9.

meted out to him who rebels and resists, so mercy is due him who is defeated or captured, especially where no disturbance of peace is to be feared.

Let chastity in the marriage bond be the adornment of your character, let sobriety and moderation be its adornment, for it is exceedingly disgraceful that lust should conquer one whom man cannot conquer, and that he who cannot be captured by the sword should be laid low by wine. If earthly riches are lacking to you, do not seek them in the world by evil deeds; if they fall to your lot, let them be laid up in heaven by good works. A manly Christian soul ought neither to be elated at acquiring them nor cast down when they leave him. Let us, instead, reflect on what the Lord says: 'Where thy treasure is, there will thy heart be also,'[19] and surely when we hear that we should lift up our hearts, the answer which you know we make should not be a lie.[20]

I know in truth that you are very zealous in these matters, I take great pleasure in your good reputation, and I congratulate you heartily in the Lord. Let this letter serve you as a mirror in which you see yourself as you are rather than learn what you ought to be. However, if you find either in this letter or in holy Scripture that something is lacking to you for a good life, be instant in work and prayer that you may attain it. For what you have give thanks to God, as to a fount of goodness, from whom you have it, and in all your good deeds give the glory to God, keep humility for yourself. For, as it is written: 'Every best gift and every perfect gift is from above, coming down from the Father of lights.'[21] But whatever progress you make in the love of God and your neighbor, as well as in true piety, do not believe that you

---

19 Matt. 6.21; Luke 12.34.
20 *Sursum corda: Habemus ad Dominum,* one of the responses at the Preface of the Mass.
21 James 1.17.

are free from sin as long as you are in this life; on which point we read in the holy Writ: 'Is not the life of man on earth a warfare?'[22] Consequently, since it will always be necessary for you, as long as you are in this body, to say in the prayer which the Lord taught: 'Forgive us our debts as we also forgive our debtors,'[23] remember to forgive quickly if anyone sins against you and asks pardon, so that you may say this prayer sincerely and may be able to win pardon for your own sins.

I have written this hurriedly for your Charity, as the haste of the bearer put pressure on me. But I give thanks to God that I have in some measure complied with your laudable desire. May the mercy of God ever protect you, noble lord, deservedly distinguished and honorable son.

190. Augustine gives greeting in the Lord to the holy lord, his brother and fellow bishop, Optatus,[1] cherished with sincere affection (418)

Although I have not received any letter from your Holiness, addressed to me personally, I read one which you sent to Caesarea in Mauretania, which came while I was there. An urgent matter connected with the Church took me to that city at the bidding of the venerable Pope Zozimus,[2] Bishop of the Apostolic See, and your letter was given me to read by the holy servant of God, Renatus,[3] a brother most dear to us in Christ. It is at his request, in fact at his vehement insistence,

---

22 Cf. Job 7.1.
23 Matt. 6.12; Luke 11.4.

---

1 A bishop of Mauretania Tingitana (modern Tangier) .
2 Pope in 417 and 418.
3 A priest of Caesarea and champion of Augustine against one Vincent who had attacked him.

that I am impelled, though busy with other matters, to answer
your letter to him. Additional force was given to my decision
by the arrival, in the above-mentioned town where we were
staying, of another holy brother of ours, whose name I speak
with due respect, Muresis,[4] a kinsman of yours, as I learned
from him. He brought me another letter which your Reverence had sent him on this subject, and he consulted me
on it, asking that I should let you know, either by my answer
or his, what I think about it; that is, whether souls are
propagated like bodies, and are derived from the first one
which was created for the first man, or whether the all-power-
ful Creator, who undoubtedly 'worketh until now,'[5] creates
new ones for individual persons, without any root-stock.

Before I advise your Sincerity on this matter, I wish you
to know that in my numerous works I have never ventured
to commit myself to a definite opinion on this subject, and I
consider it lacking in modesty to put into letters designed for
the instruction of others what I have not clearly expressed.
It would take too long to set forth in this letter the motives
and reasons which influence me so that my mind inclines to
neither of these theories, and I still balance between them,
but the necessity of this decision is not so imperative that we
cannot pass it over and carry on a satisfactory discussion
which may serve to ward off temerity if not to remove doubt.

The truth, then, on which the Christian faith especially
rests is that 'by a man came death and by a man the resurrection of the dead; for as in Adam all die, so also in Christ
all shall be made alive';[6] and that 'by one man sin entered
into this world, and by sin death, and so death passed upon
all men in whom all have sinned'; and that 'judgment
indeed was by one unto condemnation, but grace is of many

---

4 A Mauretanian priest.
5 John 5.17.
6 1 Cor. 15,21,22.

offenses unto justification'; and that 'by the offense of one
unto all men to condemnation, and by the justice of one
unto all men to justification of life.'[7] If there are any other
testimonies, they assert that no one is born of Adam without
being bound under the fetters of sin and damnation; that no
one is delivered therefrom except through rebirth in Christ,[8]
and this we must hold with such unshaken faith as to know
that whoever denies this does not belong to the faith of
Christ, or to that grace of God which is given through Christ
to little and great. Thus, if the origin of the soul is an obscure
question, there is no danger so long as the doctrine of
Redemption is clear, for we do not believe in Christ in order
to be born, but in order to be born again, whatever may
have been the mode of our first birth.

Thus far, then, we say without risk that the origin of the
soul is an obscure question, provided we believe that the
soul is not a part of God but a creature; not born of God
but made by Him to be adopted into sonship with Him, by
a marvellous condescension of grace, not by a likeness or
worthiness of nature; that it is not body but spirit; not the
Creator, obviously, but the thing created; that the reason
why it comes into this corruptible body which is a load upon
it[9] is not because it is being driven there in punishment for
a previous life badly spent among celestial beings or in some
other parts of the universe; for, when the Apostle speaks of
the twin sons of Rebecca, he says that they had not yet done
any good or evil, so that not of works, in which one was not
distinguished from the other, but of Him that calleth was it
said that the elder should serve the younger.[10]

Therefore, when we have firmly established these points,

---

7 Rom. 5.12,16,18.
8 John 3.3.
9 Wisd. 9.15.
10 Rom. 9.11,12; Gen. 25.23.

if it is something so withdrawn and hidden in the secret works of God that even the divine Scriptures do not declare in plain words whether we are to believe that these children had as yet done nothing good or evil because they received their soul individually, not propagated from others, but created from nothing at that instant, or whether it was because they themselves had no existence by which they could lead their own lives while they were in embryo in their parents, we must nevertheless hold firmly to that faith by which we believe that no one born of man, whether a person of great age or an infant just born, is freed from the contagion of the primal death and the bond of sin which is contracted at birth except through the one Mediator of God and men, the Man, Christ Jesus.[11]

Those just men also were saved by their salutary faith in Him as man and God who, before He came in the flesh, believed that He was to come in the flesh.[12] Our faith is the same as theirs, since they believed that this would be, while we believe that it has come to pass. Hence, the Apostle Paul says: 'But having the same spirit of faith, as it is written: I believed for which cause I have spoken: we also believe for which cause we speak also.'[13] If, then, those who foretold that Christ would come in the flesh had the same faith as those who have recorded His coming, these religious mysteries could vary according to the diversity of times, yet all refer most harmoniously to the unity of the same faith. It is written in the Acts of the Apostles that the Apostle Peter said: 'Now therefore why tempt you God to put a yoke upon the neck of the disciples which neither our fathers nor we have been able to bear? But by the grace of the Lord Jesus Christ we believe to be saved in like manner as they

---

11 1 Tim. 2.5.
12 1 John 4.2; John 1.7.
13 2 Cor. 4.13; Ps. 115.1.

also.'[14] If, therefore, they, that is, the fathers, being unable to bear the yoke of the Old Law, believed that they were saved through the grace of the Lord Jesus, it is clear that this grace saved even the just men of old through faith, for 'the just man liveth by faith.'[15]

'Now the law entered in that sin might abound,'[16] that grace might superabound through which the abounding of sin might be healed. 'For if there had been a law given which could give life, verily justice should have been by the law.' Still, he indicates for what good purpose the Law was given when he adds: 'But the Scripture hath concluded all under sin, that the promise by the faith of Jesus Christ might be given to them that believe.'[17] Therefore, the Law had to be given to reveal man more clearly to himself, lest the proud human spirit should think it could be just by its own effort, and 'not knowing the justice of God,' that is, what comes to man from God, 'and seeking to establish its own,' that is, as if it had been won for it by its own strength, 'should not submit to the justice of God.'[18] For it was fitting that, in addition to the commandment which is thus expressed: 'Thou shalt not covet,'[19] there should come upon the proud sinner the charge of prevarication, so that, convinced of his weakness which was not cured by the Law, he should seek the remedy of grace.

Consequently, since all the just, that is, the true worshipers of God, whether before the Incarnation or after the Incarnation of Christ, neither lived nor live except by faith in the Incarnation of Christ, in whom is the fullness of grace, certainly the words which are written that 'there is no other

---

14 Acts 15.10,11.
15 Rom. 1.17; Gal. 3.11; Heb. 10.38; Hab. 2.4.
16 Rom. 5.20.
17 Gal. 3.21,22.
18 Cf. Rom. 10.3.
19 Exod. 20.17; Deut. 5.21; Rom. 7.7.

name under heaven whereby we must be saved,'[20] were effective for saving the human race from the time when the human race was tainted in Adam. 'For as in Adam all die, so also in Christ all shall be made alive,'[21] because as no one is in the kingdom of death but through Adam, so no one is in the kingdom of life but through Christ; as by Adam all are men, so by Christ all are just men; as by Adam all mortals become children of the world in their punishment, so by Christ all immortals become children of God in grace.

And with a brevity as concise as his authority is compelling, the blessed Apostle explains the reason for the creation of those also of whom the Creator knows that they are to belong to damnation, not to grace. He says that 'God, willing to show his wrath and to make his power known, endured with much patience vessels of wrath fitted for destruction, that he might show the riches of his glory on the vessels of mercy,' having described Him above as a potter using 'clay of the same lump to make one vessel unto honor, and another unto dishonor.'[22] But it would seem unjust that vessels of wrath should be made unto destruction if the whole lump of clay had not been condemned in Adam. The fact that men become vessels of wrath at birth is due to the penalty deserved, but that they become vessels of mercy at their second birth is due to an undeserved grace.

Therefore, God shows His wrath, not indeed as a disturbance of mind, which is what the wrath of men is called, but as a fixed and settled decree of punishment, because the root-stock of disobedience produces the offshoot of sin and doom. 'Man born of woman,' as it is written in the Book of Job, 'is short-lived and full of wrath.'[23] For he is a vessel of that of which he is full; hence they are called vessels of

---

20 Acts 4.12.
21 1 Cor. 15.22.
22 Rom. 9.22,23,21.
23 Job 14.1 (Septuagint).

wrath. He shows His power, also, of which He makes a good use by bestowing many natural and temporal goods even on the wicked, adapting their malice to make trial of the good and warning them by a comparison of their state, so that they may learn to thank God for having distinguished them from these others by His mercy, not for any merit of theirs, since they were equally vessels of the same clay. This is especially manifest in the case of infants, some of whom are born again by the grace of Christ, and if they end their lives at that tender age pass on to an eternal and blessed life. Yet it cannot be said that they are distinguished because of their free will from other infants who die without this grace in the damnation of that clay.

But if the only ones created from Adam were those who were to be recreated through grace, and no other men were born but those who are adopted as sons of God, the fact that bounty is bestowed on the unworthy would be obscured, because the due punishment would not be inflicted on any who come of the same doomed stock. When 'He endured with much patience vessels of wrath fitted for destruction,' He not only 'showed his wrath and made known his power' by meting out punishment and making a good use of the wicked, but He also made known 'the riches of his glory on the vessels of mercy.' Being thus freely justified, man learns what is bestowed on him when he is distinguished from the condemned, not by his own merit, but by the glory of God's most bountiful mercy, though he himself deserved damnation and was of the same original justice.

By creating so many He willed that those should be born of whom He foreknew that they would have no part in His grace, so that by their countless multitude they might outnumber those whom He deigned to predestine to the kingdom of His glory as sons of promise. Thus, also, He willed to show by this very multitude of the castaways how the mere

number, whatever it may be, of the justly damned is of no
account with a just God; and thus, also, those who are
ransomed from that damnation may understand that this
fate, which they see meted out to so large a part, is owed to
the whole lump of clay. And in this part are included not
only those who add many sins to the original sin by the free
choice of an evil will, but even many infants, bound only
by the fetter of original sin, who are carried off from this
life without the grace of the Mediator. Doubtless, the whole
mass of clay would have received its due of just damnation,
if the potter, not only just but merciful, had not made of it
vessels unto honor, according to grace, not according to their
due, when He both succors the little ones who have no
merits to be recorded, and forestalls their elders that they
may have some merits.

This being so, you will be right if your statement does.
not lead you to say that newly created souls, because of the
innocence of their new state, cannot be subject to original
damnation before they make use of their free will to commit
sin, but if you admit that, in accord with Catholic faith, if
they leave the body at that tender age, they will go to eternal
loss unless they are freed by the sacrament of the Mediator
who 'came to seek and to save that which was lost.'[24] Inquire,
therefore, where or whence or when they began to deserve
damnation, if they are newly created, so long as you do not
make God, or some nature which God did not create,
responsible either for their sin or for the damnation of the
innocent. And if you discover what I advise you to seek out,
which, I confess, I have not yet discovered myself, defend it
as vigorously as you can, and proclaim this newness of souls
of such sort as not to be derived from any root-stock, and in
your brotherly affection share what you have discovered with
us.

---

24 Luke 19.10; Matt. 18.11.

But if you do not discover why or how infant souls become sinful, and why they are obliged to derive the source of their damnation from Adam, though they have no evil in themselves, since you believe that they are included in the flesh of sin though not propagated from that first sinful soul, but created new and blameless, do not let your inclination lead you rashly to that other opinion, to make you believe that they are derived from that primal one by propagation, lest, perhaps, another make the discovery which you cannot, or you might sometime discover what you cannot now find out. For those who claim that souls are begotten from one which God gave to the first man, and who say that they are derived from their parents, if they follow the opinion of Tertullian,[25] they certainly hold that such souls are not spirits but bodies, and are produced from corporeal seed—and what more perverted view could be expressed? But it is not surprising that Tertullian was dreaming when he thought this, since he even thought that God the Creator was not spirit but body.

Any Christian who rejects this madness with heart and lips, and confesses that the soul is not body but spirit, as indeed it is, and that it is nevertheless transmitted from parents to children, in one respect at least is not involved in difficulties, because the true faith teaches that all souls, even of infants whom the Church baptizes, not indeed to a feigned but to a real remission of sins, inherit the original sin committed by the free will of the first man and transmitted by generation to all his descendants, which sin can be cleansed away only by the second birth. But when anyone begins to consider and examine into what is here said, it is a wonder that any human perception can understand in what manner a soul is produced in the offspring from the soul of the parent, as light is kindled from light, and a second flame comes into existence without loss to the first; whether the

---

25 Tertullian, *Adv. Praxean* 7; Augustine *De Genesi ad litteram* 10.25,26.

incorporeal seed of the soul flows up by its own secret and invisible way from the father to the mother when conception takes place in a woman, or, which is still harder to believe, whether it is latent in the bodily seed. But, when seed flows out uselessly without any conception, the question is whether the seed of the soul does not issue forth at the same time, or whether it returns, with the greatest speed in an instant of time, to the place from which it came, or whether it is destroyed. If it is destroyed, we ask how the soul whose seed is mortal is itself immortal, or if it receives its immortality when it is formed that it may live, as it receives justice when it is formed that it may be wise; and how God fashions it in man, even if soul is derived from soul by seed, as He fashions the members of the body in man, although body is derived from body by seed. For, if the spiritual being were not formed by God, these words would not have been written: 'Who formeth the spirit of man in him,'[26] and also this that we read: 'He hath made the hearts of men, every one of them';[27] if by hearts we mean souls, who could doubt that they can be formed? But the question remains whether each soul is formed from that of the first man, as He forms the faces of men singly, but from the one body of the first man.

Since many questions of this kind are raised on this matter, such as cannot be investigated by any human sense, are far removed from our experience and hidden in the most secret recesses of nature, it is no shame for a man to admit that he does not know what he does not know, lest by pretending that he does know he should deserve never to know. Who would deny that God is the creator and maker not only of one soul but of every soul, except the man who is most openly opposed to His word? He speaks through the Prophet without any ambiguity when He says: 'I have made every

26 Zach. 12.1.
27 Ps. 32.15.

breath,'[28] evidently intending us to understand souls, as the
subsequent words show. For He did not breathe only the
one breath into the first man made from the earth, but He
made every breath, as He still does. Nevertheless, there is
question whether He makes every breath from that one breath,
as He makes each body of man from that first body, or
whether He makes new bodies from that one, but new souls
from nothing. Who is it that makes from seeds various kinds
of things appropriate to their origins, except He who made
the very seeds without seeds? When a thing naturally obscure
surpasses our limited intelligence, and there is no assistance
from a clear passage of sacred Scripture, human conjecture
is rash in presuming to define any opinion on it. Speaking in
terms of the life which they begin to have as their own we
say that men are new-born, whether of soul or body, but in
terms of original sin they are born old, and therefore they
are made new by baptism.

I have therefore found nothing certain about the origin of
the soul in the canonical Scriptures. Those who assert that
souls are created anew without any root-stock rely on certain
testimonies by which they seek to prove it, among which are
the two which I quoted awhile ago: 'Who formeth the spirit
of man in him,' and 'He hath made the hearts of men, every
one of them.' You see how these can be used by those who
oppose this view, for it is not certain whether, when He
forms it, He forms it from another or from nothing. The one
outstanding evidence seems to be the one which occurs in
the Book of Ecclesiastes by Solomon: 'And the dust shall
return into its earth from whence it was, and the spirit return
to God who gave it.'[29] But the rebuttal to this is easily found:
The body returns to the earth from which the first human
body was made and the spirit to God by whom the first

28 Isa. 57.16 (Septuagint).
29 Eccle. 12.7.

human soul was made; for, as they say, just as our body, although propagated from that first body, returns to that element from which the first body was made, so our soul, although propagated from that soul, does not return to nothing, because it is immortal, but to Him by whom that first soul was made. Therefore, this passage which was written about the soul of every man that 'it returns to God who gave it', does not solve this very obscure question, because, whether the soul came from that first one or from no other, it is true that God gave it.

Likewise, those who rashly and inconsiderately defend the theory of the propagation of souls, in offering evidence which they imagine supports their case, think they can produce no clearer or more explicit text on their side than this passage from Genesis: 'And all the souls that went with Jacob into Egypt and that came out of his thighs.'[30] From this apparently clear testimony it is possible to believe that souls are transmitted to sons by parents, since it seems to be quite plainly stated that the souls and not only the bodies of his sons came out of the thighs of Jacob; and in the same way they want to understand the whole for the part in what Adam said when his wife was presented to him: 'This is now bone of my bones and flesh of my flesh,'[31] for he did not say: 'and soul of my soul'; but it could be possible by naming the flesh to imply both, just as in the former passage the writer named the souls yet wished the bodies of the sons to be understood.

But this testimony, seemingly clear and direct, would not suffice to disentangle this knotty point, even if in the clause, 'who (*qui*) came out of his thighs' we were to read '*quae*' (which) in the feminine gender so as to refer it to souls, since it is proved that under the name of soul the body alone can be designated by a certain figure of speech in which the

---

30 Gen. 46.26 (Septuagint).
31 Gen. 2.23.

thing contained is signified by the container. Thus, the poet says: 'They wreathed the wine,'[32] although it was the wine-cups that were wreathed: the wine is the thing contained, the cup the container. So also we call a basilica, in which the people are contained, a church; yet it is the people who are rightly called the church;[33] and so, by the name of church, that is, of the people who are contained, we designate the place which contains them. Thus, as souls are contained in bodies, the bodies of the sons can be understood under the name of souls. An even better interpretation is that of the Law, which says that a man is unclean who goes in to a dead soul,[34] that is, the corpse of a dead man, by the words 'dead soul' meaning to designate the dead body which formerly contained the soul. And so, too, when the people, that is, the church, are not present, the place of assembly is nonetheless called a church. This answer could be made, as I said, if the feminine gender had been used in: 'that came out of the thighs of Jacob,' that is, the souls that came out. But now, since the masculine gender has been used, that is, 'who (*qui*) came out of the thighs of Jacob', anyone might prefer to interpret it thus: 'All the souls of those who came out of his thighs,' that is, the souls of men. Thus it would be possible to understand that men came out of the thighs of their father according to the body only, but theirs were the souls according to the number of which so many were designated.

I should like to read the treatise of yours which you mentioned in your letter, in case you have collected there some unambiguous evidence. But when a friend,[35] who is very dear to me and very well versed in sacred literature, asked me my opinion on this subject, and I had confessed

---

32 Vergil, *Aeneid* 1.724.
33 *Ecclesia* literally means 'assembly.'
34 Num. 9.6-10.
35 Marcellinus; cf. Letter 143.

to him without human respect my uncertainty and ignorance, he wrote from there to a very learned man,[36] far across the sea. He answered advising him rather to consult me, not knowing that he had already done so and had not been able to get a certain or definite answer from me. However, in his brief letter he indicated that he inclined to the belief that souls are created separately rather than propagated, although he warned his correspondent that the Western Church generally—he is in the East—holds to the belief in the propagation of souls. Upon this I took advantage of a favorable opportunity and wrote him a long book,[37] asking his advice and begging him to instruct me first and then send me others to instruct.

This book, which is not the work of a teacher but of an inquirer, or, rather, of one desiring to learn, can be read at my house, but ought not to be sent anywhere or given to anyone outside, until I receive an answer and find out what he thinks, for I am ready and willing to defend him, if he succeeds in teaching me how it happens that souls do not descend from Adam, yet inherit from him the just doom of damnation unless they attain by a second birth a remission of sin. But far be it from us to believe either that the souls of little children receive an apparent cleansing from sin in the baptismal font, or that God, or some nature which God did not create, is the source of the defilement from which they are cleansed. Therefore, until either he writes me an answer, or I myself, if God wills, find out in some fashion what is the cause of the soul's incurring original sin if it does not derive its origin from that first sinful soul, I would not dare to make any such statement, because that sin must necessarily exist in all infants, and God does not drive the guiltless soul

---

36 St. Jerome; cf. Letter 165.
37 Letter 166.

into it, because He is not the author of sin, nor does any nature of evil do it because nothing of that sort exists.

If you will bear with me willingly and patiently, dearest brother, I warn you not to rush heedlessly into this new heresy which is trying to undermine the solid foundations of the ancient faith by arguing against the grace of God, lavished by the Lord Christ with indescribable bounty on little and great. When Pelagius and Caelestius were found to be the authors, or, at least, the keenest and best-known promoters of this heresy, they were condemned by the watchful care of councils of bishops, as well as by two venerable prelates of the Apostolic See, Pope Innocent and Pope Zozimus, and by the whole Christian world, and were ordered to amend their lives and do penance. We have copies of recent letters from the above-mentioned Apostolic See, both those sent in particular to Africa, and those issued in general to all the bishops, and in case they have not yet reached your Holiness, we have made it a point to have them sent by the brothers to whom we are giving this letter to deliver to your Reverence. The reason why those two are heretics is not because they hold that souls do not derive their origin from that first sinful one, which could either be asserted as true with some semblance of reason, or could be ignored without offense to faith, but they are judged to be most openly heretical because on this foundation they try to build up the theory that the souls of infants inherit no evil from Adam which needs expiation in the baptismal font. The argument of Pelagius, which is included among others of his condemned statements in the letters of the Apostolic See, runs thus: 'If the soul,' he says, 'is not from a root-stock, but if only the flesh belongs to the parent stock of sin, then the flesh alone deserves the penalty. For it is unjust that a soul, born today and not formed of the clay of Adam, should bear the consequences of so ancient a sin committed by another, because reason does not concede that God, who pardons a man's own sins, should impute to him another's sin.'

If, then, you can affirm the theory of newly created souls, not propagated from another, so as to show by a right reason, not inconsistent with the Catholic faith, that they are, even so, subject to the sin of the first man, affirm what you think as best you can. But if you cannot find any argument against the propagation of souls without making them free from every bond of sin, refrain entirely from discussion of this kind. For the remission of sins given to infants in baptism is not a pretended one nor is it confined to words only; it is truly effected in them. To quote the words which we read in the letter of the blessed Pope Zozimus: 'The Lord is faithful in his words,'[38] and His baptism has the same fulfillment in fact and in words, that is, indeed, by a true confession and remission of sins in every sex, age, and condition of the human race. No one is set free but he who is the slave of sin, and no one can be called ransomed but he who was formerly made captive by sin, as it is written: 'If the Son shall make you free, you shall be free indeed.'[39] Through Him we are spiritually born again, through Him we are crucified to the world, by His death the decree of death that was brought upon all of us by Adam, and transmitted to every soul by its descent, is torn down; but there is no single one of his children who is not held subject to this decree before he is set free by baptism.'[40] In these words of the Apostolic See the Catholic faith stands out as so ancient and so firmly established, so certain and so clear, that it would be wrong for a Christian to doubt it.

Since, then, the decree of death, brought upon not one or some but every human soul by its descent, is torn down by

---

38 Ps. 144.13.
39 John 8.36.
40 Fragment of a *tractoria* or papal brief of Pope Zozimus, not otherwise extant.

the death of Christ, if you can defend the theory of souls free of this descent, yet so that they may be proved by strict reasoning to be bound by this decree which is to be torn down only by the death of Christ, and if you can show that they owe this just debt to their flesh if not to their own descent, defend it without hindrance from anyone, and show us how we may defend it with you. But if you cannot affirm what you think regarding the new creation of souls without claiming either that they are not involved in the sin of the first man, or that innocent souls become sinful not through their own origin but through that of the body, with God or some evil nature as the cause, then it would be better for the origin of the soul to remain unknown—so long as we do not doubt that it is created by God—rather than have it said that God is the author of sin, or that some evil nature opposed to God should be introduced into the discussion, or that the baptism of infants should be called useless.

However, in order that your Charity may hear something definite from me on this question, something not to be lightly esteemed, but, on the contrary, something necessary and memorable, it is not allowable to believe that the soul of the Mediator contracted any sin from Adam, and that holds true no matter what view we take of the origin of souls, whether they are propagated from the first one or from no other. For, if no soul is propagated from another, while all souls are enclosed in flesh descended from sinful flesh, how much less credible is it that His soul could have come by propagation from a sinful woman, whereas his flesh came from a virgin and was not conceived in lust, that He might be 'in the likeness of sinful flesh,'[41] not in sinful flesh! Now, if all other souls are held in bondage to the sin of the first sinful soul because they are derived from it, then, manifestly, the soul which the Only-begotten prepared for Himself either

41 Rom. 8.3.

did not derive any sin from it or it was not derived from it at all. He who freed us from our sins was able to derive for Himself a soul without sin, and He who created a new soul for the body which He made from the earth without parents was equally able to create a soul for the body which He took of a woman without the co-operation of man.

I have written this answer as best I could to the letter of your Holiness, addressed, it is true, not to me but to my very dear brothers. What is lacking in skill must be supplied by anxious affection. If you receive it kindly and keep my brotherly and useful warning by not going astray on this question, but by considering it prudently in the peace of the Church, I give thanks to God. But if you wonder that I do not yet know these things, or even if you do not wonder and do not refuse with mutual love to teach me something certain about the origin of the soul, provided our faith, which is most certain and most clear, is not attacked, I will give even more abundant thanks to God.

Live always in the Lord and remember me, most saintly lord, brother cherished with sincere affection.

191. Augustine gives greeting in the Lord to the revered lord, Sixtus,[1] his holy brother and fellow priest, cherished in the charity of Christ (418)

The letter which your Benignity sent me by our holy brother, the priest Firmus,[2] reached Hippo while I was away, and I was able to read it on my return only after the bearer had departed, but this earliest and most welcome opportunity of answering is afforded by our very dear son, the acolyte,[3]

---

1 Afterwards Pope Sixtus III (432-440).
2 A faithful letter-bearer; cf. Letters 115 and 134.
3 He was a personal attendant of his bishop, having received some of the minor orders.

Albinus. Although your letter was addressed jointly to both
of us, we were not together when it arrived, and that accounts
for your receiving a letter from each of us instead of a single
one from both. The bearer of this letter, after leaving me,
will pass by my revered brother and fellow bishop, Alypius, so
that he may write another one to your Holiness, and he is
taking with him your own letter which I have finished reading. As to the great joy which your letter roused in me, why
should a man try to express what is inexpressible? I imagine
you do not adequately appreciate how much good you have
done us by writing as you did, but take our word for it; just
as you are witness to your own soul, so we are to ours of the
depth to which we have been moved by the transparent
sincerity of your letter. For, if our joyful eagerness was so
great as we copied out that very short letter on the same
subject, which you sent by the acolyte, Leo,[4] to the saintly
elder, Aurelius, and if we read it with great zeal to all whom
we could reach—the letter in which you explained to us your
views on that altogether deadly doctrine, and, contrariwise,
on the grace of God which He bestows on little and great, to
which this doctrine is diametrically opposed—how great do
you think was our joy in reading this longer letter of yours,
how great our care to have it read by all to whom we have
been able or are still able to offer it? What more welcome
statement could be read or heard than so perfect a defense
of the grace of God against its enemies, pronounced by one
whom those same enemies had previously boasted of as an
influential authority on their side? Or is there anything which
should make us give more grateful thanks to God than the
fact that His grace is so well defended by those to whom it is
given against those to whom it is either not given or who
resent its being given because by a secret judgment of God
it is not given to them to receive it gratefully?

---

4 Afterwards Pope Leo the Great (440-461).

Therefore, revered lord and holy brother, cherished in the love of Christ, although you perform an excellent service in writing on this subject to the brothers among whom those men are in the habit of boasting of your friendship, a greater duty awaits you, not only of using a wholesome severity in punishing those who dare with too great boldness to prate of that error so utterly hostile to the name of Christ, but also, for the sake of the weaker and more simple-minded of the Lord's sheep, of directing your pastoral vigilance to the erection of most careful safeguards against those who do not cease to whisper this error, more moderately, it is true, and more covertly, 'creeping into houses,'[5] as the Apostle says, and with practised impiety doing the other things which he goes on to mention. And those are not to be overlooked who through fear conceal what they think under a deep silence, but do not cease to hold the same perverted views. Some of them, indeed, may have come to your notice before that pestilence was condemned by a most explicit decree of the Apostolic See, and you may observe that they have suddenly lapsed into silence, making it impossible to discover whether they have been cured of it, unless they not only refrain from proclaiming those false doctrines but also defend the true and contrary views with the same zeal they showed in promoting error. These, however, ought surely to be treated more gently, for what need is there of frightening them when their very silence shows that they are already frightened enough? At the same time they are not to be passed over by your remedial care as if they were sound, merely because their wound is hidden. While they are not to be frightened, they must still be taught, and in my opinion this can be done more easily while their fear of severe measures aids the teacher of truth. Thus, with the Lord's help, by uttering what they have learned and loved of His grace, they may refute what they no longer dare to affirm.

---

5 2 Tim. 3.6-8.

192. Augustine gives greeting in the Lord to his revered lord, holy brother and greatly desired fellow deacon, Celestine[1] *(418)*

The letter which your Holiness sent me by the cleric, Projectus, reached Hippo while I was far away. As soon as I read it at my return and realized that I had become your debtor, I began to look for a chance to pay my debt, when lo! a most welcome opportunity presented itself in the unexpected departure from us of Albinus,[2] the acolyte of our very dear brother. I take pleasure, therefore, in your good health as in the fulfillment of my dearest desire, and I return to your Holiness the greeting which I owe you. But I always owe you love, the only thing which leaves us still in debt even when it has been repaid. For it is repaid when it is expended, but it is owed even after it has been repaid, since there is never a time when it does not have to be expended. Yet, when it is repaid it is not lost, but is rather increased by repayment, for it is repaid by retaining it, not by being without it. And since it cannot be repaid unless it is retained, so it cannot be retained unless it is repaid; nay, rather, when it is paid out by a man it increases in him, and the more generously he pays it out the more of it he gains. But how can we refuse to friends what we owe even to enemies? We pay it out to enemies, however, with reserve, but to our friends with ready trust. Nevertheless, the heart makes a strong effort to recover what it expends, even from those to whom it is returning good for evil. That is because we wish to have as a friend the one whom we sincerely love as an enemy, for we do not love him unless we wish his good,

---

1 Afterwards Pope Celestine I (422-432). He sent Germanus of Auxerre and Palladius to reclaim the Britons from Pelagianism.
2 Cf. Letter 191 n. 3.

which certainly he cannot have unless he lays aside the evil of enmity.

Therefore, love is not expended like money. For, besides the fact that the one is diminished by being expended and the other increased, they also differ in this that we show greater good will toward anyone, if we do not seek to recover the money we have given him; but no one can be a true spender of love unless he is also a kindly collector of it. When money is received, it is a gain to the recipient but a loss to the giver; love, on the other hand, not only grows in the one who asks it back from the object of his love, even if he does not receive it, but the one from whom he receives it only begins to possess it when he pays it back. Therefore, my lord and brother, I willingly pay you and gladly receive back from you the love we owe each other; what I receive I still claim, what I repay I still owe. For we ought to hearken submissively to the one Master whose fellow pupils we are, who instructs us by His Apostle, saying: 'Owe no man anything but to love one another.'[3]

193. Augustine gives greeting in the Lord to the beloved lord, Mercator,[1] a son worthy to be praised among the members of Christ with sincere affection (418)

I received the former letter sent by your Charity while I was at Carthage, and it gave me such pleasure that when your second letter came I even bore graciously your indignant reproach at my failure to answer. But, of course, your in-

---

3 Rom. 13.8.

1 Author of some newly published tracts against the Pelagians. He was at this time residing at Rome.

dignation was a sign of affection, not a beginning of enmity. What kept me from writing you at Carthage was not a lack of opportunity to send a letter, but other urgent matters which were a cause of great preoccupation and strain to us up to the time when we left. Moreover, on leaving there we went straight to Caesarea in Mauretania on exigent matters connected with the Church. And while we traveled through all those lands, many distractions assailed our senses and diverted our attention this way and that, but there was no insistent monitor to remind me to write to you, no opportunity offered by a bearer. At my return, I found at home the letter from your Sincerity, with its sharp note of complaint, and a book filled with proofs from the pages of holy Writ, directed against the new heretics. After reading them, and even running through your first letter, I found myself impelled to reply because of the opportune occasion offered by the return of our very dear brother Albinus, an acolyte of the Church at Rome.

Therefore, my very dear son, God forbid that I should treat you carelessly when you write to me or send me your writings to examine, or that I should look down on you with lofty scorn, especially as the pleasure you have given me is greater for being unexpected and unforeseen; for, I admit, I did not know you had made such progress. We ought to have no dearer wish than that there should be many men able to refute those who attack the Catholic faith with their deadly errors, and lay snares everywhere for the weak and ignorant among the brethren; men who can staunchly and faithfully defend the Church of Christ against 'the profane novelties of words,'[3] according to the passage: 'The multitude of the wise is the welfare of the whole world.'[4] Therefore, to the

---

2 Goldbacher indicates a lacuna here, but the sense is complete as it stands.
3 1 Tim. 6.20.
4 Wisd. 6.26.

best of my ability I have looked into your heart, as revealed
in your writings, and I have found that I must embrace it and
encourage it to press forward with untiring zeal to what lies
before you, with the help of the Lord who has given you your
ability that He may foster it.

Some whom we are trying to call back to the way from
which they have strayed are not far from the truth on the
question of the baptism of infants when they claim that an
infant of however recent birth makes its act of faith through
those by whom it is offered for baptism. For, when they say,
as you write, that infants do not believe in the remission of
sins in the sense that remission is made to them—since it is
believed that they have no sin—but because they also receive
the same cleansing through which remission is made in those
who do receive it, they believe that what does not happen in
them happens in others, and since they say 'they do not
believe in one sense but they do believe in another' they admit
that these do manifestly believe. Let them, then, hearken to
the Lord: 'He that believeth in the Son hath life everlasting;
but he that believeth not the Son shall not see life, but the
wrath of God abideth on him.' Therefore, infants who became
believers through others by whom they are offered for
baptism become equally unbelievers through them, if they
are in the hands of such as believe they are not to be offered
for baptism because it does them no good. Consequently, if
they believe through believers and have everlasting life, no
doubt they disbelieve through unbelievers and will not see
life, but the wrath of God abides on them. It does not say
'comes upon them,' but 'abides on them,' because it has been
on them since the beginning and cannot possibly be lifted
from them except by 'the grace of God by Jesus Christ our
Lord.'[6] Of this wrath we read in the Book of Job: 'Man

---

5 John 3.36.
6 Rom. 7.25.

born of a woman, living for a short time and full of wrath.'
Whence, then, comes the wrath of God upon the innocence
of an infant except from the lot and taint of original sin?
In the same Book we read again that the infant is not free of
this, 'whose life is of one day upon earth.'[7]

Thus, he accomplished something among them by refuting
them with ready arguments and making Catholic words echo
in their ears, since, although they were trying to argue against
the sacraments of the Church, they nevertheless admitted that
infants believe. But let them not promise life to these without
baptism, for to what other life do these words refer: 'he that
believeth not the Son shall not see life'? And let them not
admit that these have no part in the kingdom of heaven, while
at the same time they defend them from damnation, for what
else but damnation is meant by the wrath which, as the Lord
bears witness, abides on him who does not believe? That
admission brings them at once close to our side and the
case is ended without wrangling over trifles. For, if they grant
that infants believe, no doubt this statement applies to them:
'Unless a man be born again of water and the Holy Spirit,
he cannot enter into the kingdom of heaven,'[8] as well as this
one: 'He that believeth and is baptized shall be saved, but
he that believeth not shall be condemned.'[9] Therefore, since
these men confess that infants become believers when they are
baptized, let them not doubt that if they are unbelievers they
are damned; and let them dare to say, if they can, that beings
who inherit no evil from their origin and have no taint of
sin are damned by a just God.

I do not understand what help it is to them in the present
issue to bring against us, as you mentioned in your letter, the
case of Enoch and Elias, who did not die but were removed

---

7 Job 14.1,5 (Septuagint).
8 John 3.5.
9 Mark 16.16.

in their bodies from contact with men. I pass over the general belief that they will meet death later, for several interpreters of John's Apocalypse[10] refer to the two Prophets what he says without mentioning their names, namely, that they will then appear in the bodies in which they now live so that they, too, may die, as other martyrs have died, for the truth of Christ; but, I repeat, I pass over that, and postponing that question, I ask you, what help is the status of these two Prophets to them? They derive no proof from these that physical death is not a punishment of sin. For, if God, who remits their sins to so many of His faithful, has willed to remit the punishment of death to certain ones, who are we that reply against God[11] as to why He treats 'one after this manner and another after that?'[12]

We say, therefore, what the Apostle says very plainly: 'The body indeed is dead because of sin, but the spirit liveth because of justification. And if the Spirit of him that raised up Christ from the dead dwell in you; he that raised up Christ from the dead shall quicken also your mortal bodies because of his Spirit that dwelleth in you.'[13] When we say this, we do not mean to deny that God can do now for some, according to His will, without death what we have no doubt He will do for so many after death; not for this will the Apostle's words be falsified when he says: 'By one man sin entered into this world and by sin death, and so death passed upon all men.'[14] This is said because there would have been no death if death had not entered by sin. So, also, when we say 'all are sent to hell because of sin,' is our saying falsified because not all men are sent to hell? That statement is true, because no one is sent there except as a punishment of sin,

10 Apoc. 11.3-7.
11 Rom. 9.20.
12 1 Cor. 7.7.
13 Rom. 8.10,11.
14 Rom. 5.12.

not because everybody is sent there. This other opposite statement is of the same kind: 'By the justice of one unto all men to justification of life,'[15] for all men do not attain to the justification of Christ, but no one is justified except by Christ.

Not without reason does the question puzzle us why the penalty of death remains, although the sin does not remain— that is, if bodily death is also a punishment of sin; but it is much more of a question why an infant dies after it has been baptized than why Elias did not die after he had been justified. In the former case, what puzzles us is why the penalty of sin follows after the sin has been destroyed; in the latter, we ought not to be puzzled if the penalty of sin does not follow after the sin has been destroyed. To the best of my ability, and with the Lord's help, I have settled that question about the death of baptized children—that is, why some penalty of sin follows even after the destruction of sin— in my books on the baptism of infants,[16] which I am sure are well known to you. But we should not be troubled by that other question, 'Why did the just Elias not die if death is the penalty of sin?' any more than if one said, 'Why did the sinner Elias not die if death is the penalty of sin?'

But if they raise one difficulty from another and say: 'If Enoch and Elias were so sinless that they did not suffer death, which is the penalty of sin, how does that tally with the teaching that no one lives in this world without sin?' the probable answer to them would be: 'Because God willed them to live after they had done with sin, they were not permitted to live here, since here no one can live without sin.' But this and other arguments of the same sort could be brought against them if it could be proved with certainty from any source that those two will never die. But, since they cannot teach

15 Rom. 5.18.
16 *De peccatorum meritis et remissione et de baptismo parvulorum.*

this it is better to believe that Enoch and Elias will die at the
end of the world, and since it is better to believe that they
will meet death, there is no reason why these should wish to
make an objection to us of men who will not support their
case at any point.

On the other hand, those whom the Apostle mentions when
he speaks of the resurrection of the dead: 'Then we who are
alive, who are left, shall be taken up together with them in
the clouds to meet Christ, into the air, and so we shall be
always with the Lord,'[17] do indeed raise something of a
difficulty, but it concerns themselves, not our objectors. Even
if these survivors are not themselves going to die, I see no
way in which their case helps these objectors, since it is
possible to make the same comments on these as were made
on the other two. As a matter of fact, as far as the words of
the blessed Apostle are concerned, he seems to state that
certain persons, at the end of the world, when the Lord comes,
when the resurrection of the dead is to take place, will not
die, but, being found alive, are to be suddenly transformed
into the immortality which is given to the rest of the saints,
and to be taken up together with them, as he says, in the
clouds; as often as I think over these words, they seem to me
to mean nothing else but that.

But I should be better pleased to hear more competent
teachers on this point; otherwise, those who think that some
persons, having received life without previously dying, are
to pass to everlasting life, may find the Apostle saying to
them: 'Senseless man, that which thou sowest is not quickened
except it die first!' For, if we do not all die, how can there
be a fulfillment of what we read in many texts: 'We shall all
rise again?'[18] Obviously, there is no resurrection without a
preliminary death. And the fact that some texts have the

17 1 Thess. 4.16.
18 1 Cor. 15.36,51.

words: 'We shall all fall asleep,' makes this much easier and plainer to understand. And every other similar passage found in holy Writ seems to force us to conclude that no man will attain immortality without first passing through death. Consequently, when the Apostle says: 'And we who are alive, who remain unto the coming of the Lord shall not prevent them who have slept. For the Lord himself shall come down from heaven with commandment and with the voice of an archangel and with the trumpet of God, and the dead who are in Christ shall rise first. Then we who are alive, who are left, shall be taken up together with them in the clouds to meet Christ, into the air, and so we shall be always with the Lord';[19] as I said, I should like to hear more competent teachers comment on these words, and if they can only be interpreted so that it is possible to understand from them that all men who are now alive or who are to live after us will die, I wish to correct a different view which I formerly held. We who are teachers ought not to be intractable, and it is certainly better for a little man to be set right than for an obdurate one to be broken, since by our writings our own deficiency and that of others may be trained and taught, yet not in such wise as to set up in them anything like canonical authority.

If no other meaning can be found for these words of the Apostle, and it is clear that he intended them to mean what the words themselves seem to cry aloud, that is, that at the end of the world and the coming of the Lord there will be some who will be clothed with immortality without being stripped of their bodies, 'that that which is mortal may be swallowed up by life,'[20] undoubtedly that will agree with the words which we profess in the Creed, namely, that the Lord will come to judge the living and the dead. In this sense we

---

19 1 Thess. 4.14-16.
20 2 Cor. 5.4.

will not take the living to mean the righteous and the dead the ungodly, although both righteous and ungodly are to be judged, but by living we shall understand those who, at His coming, have not yet gone out of their bodies, and by the dead those who have gone out from them long since. If that interpretation stands, we shall have to examine carefully into these passages: 'that which thou sowest is not quickened except it die first,' and 'we shall rise again,' or 'we shall all fall asleep,' so as to understand them in a manner consistent with this view which holds that some will enter into eternal life in their bodies without first tasting death.

But whichever one of these interpretations turns out to be truer or clearer, what good does it do the case of our objectors whether all men are bound by the debt of death, or some are spared its necessity, when it is still a fact that there would have been no subsequent death of soul or body if sin had not come first, and that it is a more remarkable effect of grace for the just to rise from death to eternal happiness than for them not to experience death? This will have to be enough to answer those of whom you wrote me, although I do not imagine they are now saying that Adam would have died, at least in body, even if he had not sinned.

However, as far as the question of resurrection is concerned, because of the belief that some will not die but will pass from mortal life to immortality without any intervening death, there is need of a more careful examination into it. If you have either read or heard anything certain and definite on it, anything based on a reasonable and satisfactory argument, or even if you have been able to think it out for yourself, or if in future you are able to hear or read or think it out, I beg you not to refuse to share it with me. For I must confess to your Charity, I like much better to learn than to teach. We are also advised to this by the words of the Apostle

James: 'Let every man be swift to hear but slow to speak.'[21] Therefore, the sweetness of truth should invite us to learn where the necessity of charity forces us to teach. In this case it is the more to be desired that this necessity which causes man to teach man anything may pass away that we may 'all be taught of God',[22] although we are this when we learn what belongs to true godliness, even when man seems to teach it, because 'neither he that planteth is anything nor he that watereth, but God that giveth the increase.'[23] Since, then, the Apostles would have accomplished nothing by planting and watering if God had not given the increase, how much more true is this of you or me or any men of our time who fancy themselves as teachers!

194. Augustine gives greeting in the Lord to his holy brother and fellow priest, Sixtus,[1] his lord most beloved in the Lord of lords (418)

In the letter[2] which I sent by our very dear brother, the acolyte, Albinus, I promised to send a longer one by our holy brother and fellow priest, Firmus. He had brought us a letter from your Sincerity, showing forth the candor of your faith, which filled us with a joy so great that we can more easily contain than describe it. We had been exceedingly sad when rumor spread abroad the news that you sided with the enemies of Christian grace. But several developments erased this sadness from our hearts: first, the same rumor made it known that you were the first to pronounce anathema on

21 James 1.19.
22 John 6.45; Isa. 54.13.
23 1 Cor. 3.7.

1 Cf. Letter 191 n. 1.
2 Letter 191.

them before a large crowd; second, your letter to the venerable elder, Aurelius, came with the letter sent by the Apostolic See to Africa concerning their condemnation, and although yours was short it gave sufficient evidence of your strong repudiation of their error; and finally, now that your faith speaks more openly and comprehensively against that dogma, stating your views to us and to the Roman Church, to which the blessed Apostle Paul spoke so frequently and variously about the 'grace of God by Jesus Christ our Lord,'[3] not only has every shadow of sadness fled from our hearts, but such a brilliance of happiness shines there that the former sorrow and fear seem to have intensified the glowing warmth of the joys that were to come.

Therefore, dearest brother, although we do not see you with the eyes of the flesh, nevertheless in spirit, in the faith of Christ, in the grace of Christ, in the members of Christ, we hold you, we embrace you, we kiss you, and we are taking advantage of the return of that most holy and faithful bearer of our mutual communications, whom you wished us to have as the narrator and witness of your deeds, as well as the carrier of your writings, to send you our answer and to hold a somewhat longer conversation with you, encouraging you to follow up by instructing those in whom you have begun, as we hear, to instill an adequate fear. There are some who think it a mark of the liberal mind to defend the impious doctrine which has been most justly condemned; there are some who 'creep into houses,'[4] in secret, and propagate actively but in secret what they fear to preach openly; there are some who have been forced by great fear into complete silence, but who still keep in their hearts what they dare not utter with their lips, and these can be well known to the brethren from their former defense of this doctrine.

3 Rom. 7.25.
4 2 Tim. 3.6.

Therefore, some are to be restrained by severe measures; some to be investigated with care; some to be treated more gently but instructed more diligently, and, although there may be fear of their doing harm, there should be no backwardness in saving them from harm.

When they think they are being deprived of their free will if they admit that man has no good will of his own without the help of God, they do not understand that they are not thus strengthening human free will but puffing it up so that it is carried off into empty space, not anchored on the Lord as on an immovable rock, for 'the will is made ready by the Lord.'[5]

And when they affect to believe that God is a respecter of persons,[6] because without any antecedent merits of theirs 'He hath mercy on whom he will,'[7] and calls whom He deigns to call and makes righteous whom He will, they overlook the fact that a deserved penalty is meted out to the damned, an undeserved grace to the saved, so that the former cannot complain that he is undeserving nor the latter boast that he is deserving. Where one and the same clay of damnation and offense is involved, there can be no respect had of persons, so that the saved may learn from the lost that the same punishment would have been his lot, also, if grace had not rescued him; if it is grace, it is obviously not awarded for any merit, but bestowed as a pure act of bounty.

'But,' they object, 'it is unjust in one and the same case for this one to be saved and that one to be punished.' That means it is just for both to be punished. Would anyone deny this? Then let us give thanks to the Saviour when we see that we have not received what we recognize as our due from the damnation of our fellow men. If both were saved, then what

---

5 Prov. 8.35 (Septuagint).
6 Acts 10.34; 2 Paral. 19.7; Rom. 2.11; Eph. 6.9; 1 Peter 1.17; Col. 3.25.
7 Rom. 9.18.

is justly due to sin would not be apparent; if no one were saved, we would not know the free gift of grace. Therefore, in this very difficult question, let us rather use the words of the Apostle: 'God, willing to show his wrath and to make his power known, endured with much patience vessels of wrath, fitted for destruction, that he might show the riches of his glory on the vessels of mercy.' And the thing formed cannot say to Him: 'Why hast thou made me thus? Since He has power of the same lump to make one vessel unto honor, another unto dishonor.'[8] For, when the whole lump of clay is justly doomed to destruction, justice awards it the dishonor it deserves, while grace bestows an undeserved honor, not for any privilege of merit, not through any inevitability of fate, not through any chance stroke of fortune, but through 'the depth of the riches of the wisdom and of the knowledge of God,' which the Apostle does not reveal to us, but marvels at as something hidden, crying out: 'O the depth of the riches of the wisdom and of the knowledge of God! How incomprehensible are his judgments, how unsearchable his ways! For who hath known the mind of the Lord? or who hath been his counsellor? or who hath first given to him and recompense shall be made him? For of him and by him and in him are all things: to him be glory forever!'[9]

But they do not wish the glory of justifying the sinful by His freely given grace to be given to Him, because, not knowing His justice, they seek to establish their own,[10] and even when influenced by the clamorous words of religious and godly men, they admit to receiving some divine help in attaining justice or performing its works, they claim some previous merit of their own, as if they were first willing to give that recompense might be made to them by Him of

8 Rom. 9.22,23,20,21.
9 Rom. 11.33-36.
10 Rom. 10.3.

whom it is said: 'who hath first given to him and recompense shall be made him?' Thus they think their merits precede His action of whom they hear, or, rather, refuse to hear that 'of him and by him and in him are all things.' From those riches which are the depth of His wisdom and His knowledge come also the riches of His glory toward the vessels of mercy whom He calls to adoption; these riches He also wills to make known even through the vessels of wrath which are fitted for destruction. And what are His ways which are unsearchable, if not those which are praised in the Psalm: 'All the ways of the Lord are mercy and truth'?[11] His mercy, therefore, and His truth are unsearchable, because 'He hath mercy on whom he will,' not through justice but the mercy of grace; and 'whom he will he hardeneth,' not through injustice but the truth of retribution. Nevertheless, mercy and truth meet so harmoniously, as it is written: 'Mercy and truth have met each other,'[12] that mercy does not hinder truth when the one who deserves it is cast down, nor does truth hinder mercy when the one who does not deserve it is saved. What merits of his own has the saved to boast of, when, if he received his just deserts, he would be damned? But, have the just no merits at all? Certainly they have, since they are just; only, there were no previous merits to make them just. They became just when they were justified, but, as the Apostle says, 'They are justified freely by his grace.'[13]

Although these men are dangerous opponents of this grace, those who say that the grace of God is given according to our merit were anathematized by Pelagius at the ecclesiastical trial in Palestine—otherwise, he could not have come off unscathed. But no other statement is found in their subsequent

11 Ps. 24.10.
12 Ps. 84.11.
13 Rom. 3.24.

controversy except that merit regulates grace, of which the
Epistle to the Romans speaks in such high terms and which
was afterward preached throughout the world, coming down,
so to speak, from the head of the world. It is grace that
justifies the wicked, that is, he who was formerly wicked
thereby becomes just. Therefore, the reception of this grace
is not preceded by any merits because the wicked deserve
punishment, not grace, and it would not be grace if it were
awarded as something due and not freely given.

But, when these men are asked what kind of grace Pelagius
thought was given without any antecedent merits, since he
anathematized those who say that the grace of God is given
according to our merit, they answer that grace without any
antecedent merit is the human nature in which we have been
created, for, before we existed, it was not possible for us to
merit existence. Let Christian hearts reject that fallacy. No,
a thousand times no! The grace which is praised by the
Apostle is not that by which we were created and became men,
but that by which, being sinful men, we were made just.
That grace is given by Jesus Christ our Lord. Christ did not
die for some that they might be created, but for sinful men
that they might be made just. It was a man, indeed, who
said: 'Unhappy man that I am, who shall deliver me from
the body of this death? The grace of God by Jesus Christ our
Lord.'[14]

They can indeed say that the remission of sins is a grace
which is given without any antecedent merit, for what good
merits can sinners have? Yet, even that remission of sins is
not without some merit, if faith asks and obtains it. There
is some merit in faith, that faith which made the publican
say: 'O Lord be merciful to me, a sinner. And he went down
justified'[15] by the merit of humble faith, because 'he that

14 Rom. 7.24,25.
15 Luke 18.13,14.

humbleth himself shall be exalted.'[16] It remains, then, that
faith itself, from which all justice derives its origin—and
that is why these words of the Canticle of Canticles are
addressed to the Church: 'Thou shalt come and shalt pass
over from the beginning of faith'[17]—it remains, I repeat, that
faith itself is not to be attributed to the human free will
which these men extol, nor to any antecedent merits, since
any good merits, such as they are, come from faith; but we
must confess it as a free gift of God, if we are thinking of
true grace without merit, because we read in the same
Epistle: 'God hath divided to every one the measure of
faith.'[18] It is true that good works are performed by man,
but faith is imparted to man, and without it no good works
are done by any man: 'For all that is not of faith is sin.'[19]

Therefore, the very act of prayer should not take credit to
itself, even if help is granted to him who prays to overcome
his covetousness of temporal things and to love eternal goods
and God Himself, the source of all goods, for it is faith that
prays, faith which is given to him who does not pray, for, if it
were not given he could not pray. 'How then shall they call
on him in whom they have not believed? or how shall they
believe him of whom they have not heard and how shall they
hear without a preacher? Faith then cometh by hearing and
hearing by the word of Christ.'[20] Consequently, the 'minister
of Christ,' the preacher of this grace, 'because of the grace
which is given to him,'[21] is the one who plants and waters.
'For neither he that planteth is anything, nor he that watereth,
but God that giveth the increase,'[22] 'who divideth to every
one the measure of faith.' Therefore, in another place he

---

16 Luke 14.11; Matt. 23.12.
17 Cant. 4.8 (Septuagint).
18 Rom. 12.3.
19 Rom. 14.23.
20 Rom. 10.14,17.
21 Rom. 15.15,16.
22 1 Cor. 3.7.

says: 'Peace be to the brethren and charity with faith,' and that they may not attribute it to themselves he adds: 'from God the Father and the Lord Jesus Christ,'[23] because not all those who hear the word have faith, but those to whom God allots the measure of faith, just as all seeds, which are planted and watered, do not sprout but those to which God gives the increase. The reason why one believes and another does not believe, although both hear the same thing, and, if a miracle is worked in their sight, both see the same thing, is hid in the depth of the riches of the wisdom and of the knowledge of God whose judgments are unsearchable,[24] and with whom there is no injustice, when He 'has mercy on whom He will and whom He will He hardeneth,'[25] for His judgments are not unjust because their meaning is hidden.

But then, unless the Holy Spirit dwells in the clean house after the remission of sins, does not the unclean spirit return with seven other spirits and will the last state of that man not be worse than the first?[26] And in order that the Holy Spirit may dwell there, does He not breathe where He will,[27] and is not the charity of God, without which no one lives a good life, 'poured forth in our hearts by the Holy Spirit who is given to us'?[28] This is the faith which the Apostle defined when he said: 'For neither circumcision availeth anything, nor uncircumcision, but faith that worketh by charity.'[29] And that is obviously the faith of Christians, not of demons. 'For the devils also believe and tremble,'[30] but do they love? If they had not believed, they would not have said: 'Thou

23 Eph. 6.23.
24 Cf. Rom. 11.33.
25 Rom. 9.14,18.
26 Matt. 12.43-45; Luke 11.24-26.
27 John 3.8.
28 Rom. 5.5.
29 Gal. 5.6.
30 James 2.19.

art the holy one of God' or 'Thou art the Son of God,'[31] but if they had loved, they would not have said: 'What have we to do with thee?'[32]

Faith, therefore, draws us to Christ, and if it were not given to us from above as a free gift, He Himself would not have said: 'No man can come to me except the Father, who hath sent me, draw him.'[33] And shortly after this He said: 'The words that I have spoken to you are spirit and life. But there are some of you that believe not.' And the Evangelist adds: 'For Jesus knew from the beginning who they were that believed and who it was that would betray him.' And lest anyone should think that His foreknowledge concerned believers in the same way as unbelievers, that is, not in the sense that faith itself was given them from above, but only that their will was foreseen, the Gospel at once added the words: 'And he said: Therefore did I say to you that no man can come to me unless it be given him by the Father.'[34] This explains why some of those who heard Him speak of His flesh and His blood were scandalized and went away,[35] while some remained steadfast in their belief, because no man could come to Him unless it were given him by the Father, and consequently also by the Son Himself and by the Holy Spirit. There is no separation in the gifts and works of the inseparable Trinity; when the Son thus honors His Father He does not give us proof of any separation, but He does offer us a great example of humility.

Here, again, if those defenders of free will, nay rather, those deceivers, because they are puffed up, and they are puffed up because they are presumptuous, were to speak, not against us but against the Gospel, what else would they say

---

31 Luke 4.41,34; Mark 3.11,12.
32 Matt. 8.29; Mark 5.7; Luke 8.28.
33 John 6.44.
34 John 6.64-66.
35 John 6.53,61,62,67.

but what the Apostle proposes as an objection to himself, as if it were said by such men: 'Thou sayest therefore to me: Why doth he then find fault? for who resisteth his will?' He put this objection to himself as if from another, in the very words of those who refuse to accept what he had said before: 'He hath mercy on whom he will and whom he will he hardeneth.' Let us therefore say with the Apostle to such men—for we cannot find anything better than that to say— 'O man, who art thou that repliest against God?'[36]

What we seek to know is how this hardening is deserved, and we find it to be so because the whole clay of sin was damned. God does not harden by imparting malice to it, but by not imparting mercy. Those to whom He does not impart mercy are not worthy, nor do they deserve it; rather, they are worthy and do deserve that He should not impart it. But when we seek to know how mercy is deserved we find no merit because there is none, lest grace be made void if it is not freely given but awarded to merit.

If we say that faith goes before and that the merit of grace is in it, what merit does a man have before faith so as to receive faith? For, what has he that he has not received? And if he has received it, why does he glory as if he had not received it?[37] Just as a man would not have wisdom, understanding, counsel, fortitude, knowledge, piety, and fear of God unless, according to the Prophet's words, he had received 'the spirit of wisdom and of understanding, of counsel and of fortitude, of knowledge and of godliness, and of fear of God,'[38] and just as he would not have power and love and sobriety, except by receiving the Spirit of whom the Apostle speaks: 'We have not received the spirit of fear but of power and of love and of sobriety,'[39] so also he would not have faith

36 Rom. 9.19,18,20.
37 Cf. 1 Cor. 4.7.
38 Isa. 11.2,3.
39 2 Tim. 1.7.

unless he received the spirit of faith of which the same Apostle says: 'But having the same spirit of faith, as it is written: I believed for which cause I have spoken, we also believe for which cause we speak also.'[40] Thus, he shows very plainly that faith is not received because of merit but by the mercy of Him who has mercy on whom He will,[41] when he says of himself: 'I have obtained mercy to be faithful.'[42]

If we say that prayer produces antecedent merit so that the gift of grace may follow, it is true that prayer, by asking and obtaining whatever it does obtain, shows clearly that it is God's gift when a man does not think that he has grace of himself, because if it were in his own power, he would assuredly not ask for it. But, lest we should think that even the merit of prayer is antecedent to grace, in which case it would not be a free gift—and then it would not be grace because it would be the reward which was due—our very prayer itself is counted among the gifts of grace. As the Doctor of the Gentiles says: 'We know not what we should pray for as we ought, but the Spirit himself asketh for us with unspeakable groanings.'[43] And what does 'asketh for us' mean but that He makes us ask? It is a very sure sign of one in need to ask with groaning, but it would be monstrous for us to think that the Holy Spirit is in need of anything. So, then, the word 'ask' is used because He makes us ask, and inspires us with the sentiment of asking and groaning, according to that passage in the Gospel: 'For it is not you that speak, but the Spirit of your Father that speaketh in you.'[44] However, this is not accomplished in us without any action on our part, and therefore the help of the Holy Spirit is described by saying that He does what He makes us do.

---

40 2 Cor. 4.13; Ps. 115.10.
41 Rom. 9.18.
42 1 Cor. 7.25.
43 Rom. 8.26; 1 Tim. 2.7.
44 Matt. 10.20.

The Apostle himself makes it quite clear that our spirit is not meant when he says it 'asketh with unspeakable groanings,' but the Holy Spirit by whom our infirmity is helped. He begins by saying: 'The Spirit helpeth our infirmity'; then he goes on: 'For we know not what we should pray for as we ought,' and the rest.[45] And indeed he speaks even more plainly of this Spirit in another place: 'For you have not received the spirit of bondage again in fear, but you have received the spirit of adoption of sons, whereby we cry: Abba, Father.'[46] Notice that he does not here say that the Spirit Himself cries in His prayer, but he says: 'whereby we cry: Abba, Father.' However, in another passage he says: 'Because you are sons, God hath sent the Spirit of his Son into your hearts, crying: Abba. Father.'[47] Here he does not say 'whereby we cry,' but he preferred to represent the Spirit Himself as crying, which has the effect of making us cry, as in the other two passages: 'The Spirit himself asketh with unspeakable groanings,' and 'The Spirit of your Father that speaketh in you.'

Therefore, as no one has true wisdom, true understanding; no one is truly eminent in counsel and fortitude; no one has a pious knowledge or a knowledgable piety; no one fears God with a chaste fear unless he has received 'the spirit of wisdom and understanding, of counsel and fortitude, of knowledge and piety and fear of God;'[48] and as no one has true power, sincere love, and religious sobriety except through 'the spirit of power and love and sobriety,'[49] so also without the spirit of faith no one will rightly believe, without the spirit of prayer no one will profitably pray; not that there are so many spirits, 'but all these things one and the same Spirit worketh,

45 Rom. 8.26.
46 Rom. 8.15.
47 Gal. 4.6.
48 Isa. 11.2,3.
49 2 Tim. 1.7.

dividing to every one according as he will,'[50] because 'the Spirit breatheth where he will.'[51] But it must be admitted that His help is given differently before and after His indwelling, for before His indwelling He helps men to believe, but after His indwelling He helps them as believers.

What merit, then, has man before grace which could make it possible for him to receive grace, when nothing but grace produces good merit in us; and what else but His gifts does God crown when He crowns our merits? For, just as in the beginning we obtained the mercy of faith, not because we were faithful but that we might become so, in like manner He will crown us at the end with eternal life, as it says, 'with mercy and compassion.'[52] Not in vain, therefore, do we sing to God: 'His mercy shall prevent me,' and 'His mercy shall follow me.'[53] Consequently, eternal life itself, which will certainly be possessed at the end without end, is in a sense awarded to antecedent merits, yet, because the same merits for which it is awarded are not effected by us through our sufficiency, but are effected in us by grace, even this very grace is so called for no other reason than that it is given freely; not, indeed, that it is not given for merit, but because the merits themselves are given for which it is given. And when we find eternal life itself called grace, we have in the same Apostle Paul a magnificent defender of grace: 'The wages of sin,' he says, 'is death. But the grace of God life everlasting in Christ Jesus our Lord.'[54]

Notice, please, how concisely and how exactly he has chosen his words; a careful examination of them will throw some light on the obscurity of this question. After he had said: 'The wages of sin is death,' anyone would have agreed

---

50 1 Cor. 12.11.
51 John 3.8.
52 Ps. 102.4.
53 Ps. 58.11; 22.6.
54 Rom. 6.23.

that he could have made a most consistent and logical conclusion if he had said: 'But the wages of justice is eternal life.'
And it is true, because eternal life is awarded as if it were
the wages which justice deserves, just as death is the wages
which sin deserves. Or if he had not said 'justice' he might
have said 'faith,' since 'the just liveth by faith.'[55] Hence, the
word 'pay' is also used in many passages of the holy Scriptures,
but neither justice nor faith is ever called pay, because the
pay is made to justice or faith. What pay is to the workman,
that wages is to the soldier.

But the blessed Apostle was speaking against pride, which
is always trying to steal into great souls, when he said of
himself on that account that an angel of Satan had been
given to him by whom he was buffeted lest he should lift up
his head in presumption;[56] and it was in his vigilant warfare
against this bane of pride that he said: 'The wages of sin is
death.' Rightly does he say 'wages,' because it is owed, because
it is rendered according to a man's deserts. But after that he
did not make the contrary statement: 'the wages of justice
is eternal life'; instead he said: 'the grace of God, life everlasting,' so that justice might not be based on human merit
in the same way that sin is undoubtedly the cause of evil
retribution. And in order that eternal life might not be sought
in any other way than through the Mediator, he added: 'in
Christ Jesus our Lord,' as if he were saying: 'Having heard
that the wages of sin is death, why do you try to exalt yourself, O human justice, who are truly pride under the name
justice? Why do you try to exalt yourself and demand eternal
life, the opposite of death, as if it were due you as wages?
That to which eternal life is owed is true justice, but if it is
true justice, it does not originate in you, 'it is from above,

---

55 Rom. 1.17; Gal. 3.11; Heb. 10.38; Hab. 2.4.
56 2 Cor. 12.7.

coming down from the Father of lights.'[57] In order to have it, if you do have it, you must have received it, for 'what good hast thou that thou hast not received?'[58] Therefore, O man, if you are to receive eternal life, it is indeed the wages of justice, but for you it is a grace just as justice itself is a grace. It would be paid as something due to you if the justice to which it is due had its origin in you. But now, 'of his fulness we have received,' not only the grace by which we now live uprightly and in labors unto the end, but also 'grace for this grace,'[59] that afterward we may live in repose forever. Faith has no more salutary doctrines to believe than this because the understanding finds none more true, and we should hearken to the Prophet saying: 'If you will not believe, you shall not understand.'[60]

The objector says to this: 'But men who refuse to live uprightly and faithfully will excuse themselves by saying: 'What wrong have we done by leading a bad life, since we did not receive grace to lead a good life?' They cannot possibly say with truth that they have done no wrong in living a bad life, for if they do no wrong they lead a good life; but if they lead a bad life the wrong is of their own doing, either the original sin which they inherited or the sin they have added over and above. But, if they are 'vessels of wrath, fitted for destruction,' let them impute this to themselves as something owed and paid to them, because they are made of the clay which God deservedly and justly condemned on account of the sin of one man, in whom all have sinned, but if they are 'vessels of mercy,' fashioned of the same clay on which God did not will to inflict the punishment due, let them not be puffed up, but give the glory to Him who has

---

57 James 1.17.
58 1 Cor. 4.7.
59 John 1.16.
60 Isa. 7.9 (Septuagint).

shown them an undeserved mercy,[61] and, if they are 'otherwise minded, God himself will reveal this to them also.'[62]

After all, how will they excuse themselves? No doubt, in the manner briefly mentioned[63] by the Apostle when he raised an objection for himself in their supposed words: 'Why doth he then find fault? for who resisteth his will?' This is the same as saying: 'Why is fault found with us that we offend God by an evil life, since no one can resist His will, and He has hardened us by not giving us His grace?' If they are not ashamed to offer this excuse, not against us but against the Apostle, why should we tire of saying to them again and again what the Apostle said: 'O man, who art thou that repliest against God? Shall the thing formed say to him that formed it: Why hast thou made me thus? or hath not the potter power over the clay, of the same lump,' justly and deservedly damned, 'to make one vessel unto honor,' through the undeserved grace of mercy, 'another unto dishonor,' which is due because of His just wrath, and 'that he might make known the riches of his glory on the vessels of mercy,' by showing what is bestowed on them, while the vessels of wrath receive the punishment which is equally due to all? Let it be enough at present for the Christian still living by faith and not yet seeing that which is perfect, but knowing it in part,[64] to recognize or believe that God saves no one except by a freely given mercy through our Lord Jesus Christ, and condemns no one except by the most just truth through the same Lord Jesus Christ. Let him who is able search out His reason for saving or not saving this one or that, but let him also beware of the deep abyss of His judgments. 'Is there

61 Rom. 9.22,23; 5.12.
62 Cf. Phil. 3.15.
63 Rom. 9.19-23.
64 1 Cor. 13.9,10.

injustice with God? God forbid!' but 'His judgments are incomprehensible and his ways are unsearchable.'[65]

In earlier ages it could at least be said with justice: 'They would not understand that they might do well,'[66] but the men of our time are worse; they have understood and have not obeyed, because, as it is written: 'A stubborn slave will not be corrected by words, for if he understand he will not obey.'[67] And what makes him disobey but his own evil will? A heavier punishment is due him by divine justice: 'And unto whomsoever more is given, of him more shall be required.'[68] Indeed, the Scripture says they are inexcusable who know the truth and persist in ungodliness. The Apostle says: 'For the wrath of God is revealed from heaven against all ungodliness and injustice of those men that detain the truth of God in injustice; because that which is known of God is manifest in them, for God hath manifested it unto them. For the invisible things of him from the creation of the world are clearly seen, being understood by the things that are made; his eternal power also and divinity, so that they are inexcusable.'[69]

If, then, he calls those inexcusable who were able to see and understand the invisible things of Him by the things that are made, yet did not obey the truth but persisted in their wickedness and ungodliness—for they did know, but, he says, 'knowing God they have not glorified him as God or given thanks,'[70]—how much more inexcusable are those who are confident that they are leaders of the blind, who teach others and do not teach themselves, who preach that men should not steal, yet they themselves steal,'[71] and the

---

65 Rom. 9.14; 11.33.
66 Ps. 35.4.
67 Prov. 29.19 (Septuagint).
68 Cf. Luke 12.47,48.
69 Rom. 1.18-20.
70 Rom. 1.21.
71 Cf. Rom. 2.18,19,21.

other things which the Apostle says of them! That is why
he says to them: 'Wherefore thou art inexcusable, O man,
whosoever thou art that judgest. For wherein thou judgest
another thou condemnest thyself; for thou doest the same
things which thou judgest.'[72]

The Lord Himself also says in the Gospel: 'If I had not
come and spoken to them, they would not have sin, but now
they have no excuse for their sin.'[73] Surely He does not mean
that they have no sin, when they are full of many great sins,
but He wishes us to know that, if He had not come, they
would not have had this sin of having heard Him and not
having believed in Him. He protests that they lack the excuse
which would let them say: 'We have not heard, therefore
we have not believed.' Human pride, presuming on the
strength of free will, thinks it is excused when its sin seems
to come from ignorance, not from a deliberate choice.

Referring to this excuse, divine Scripture says those are
inexcusable who are proved to sin knowingly. Nevertheless,
the just judgment of God does not spare those either who
have not heard: 'For whosoever have sinned without the law,
shall perish without the law.'[74] And although they think they
have an excuse, God does not accept this excuse, because He
knows that He made man right[75] and gave him a commandment to obey, and that this sin, which passed upon his
descendants, came from his having made a bad use of his free
will. And we cannot say that those who have not sinned are
damned, since that first sin passed upon all from one, in
whom all sinned together before they committed any separate
sins of their own. Thus, every sinner is inexcusable by reason
either of the original guilt or of the added sin of his own will,
and this is true whether he knows or not, whether he judges

---

72 Rom. 2.1.
73 John 15.22.
74 Rom. 2.12.
75 Eccle. 7.30.

or not, because that ignorance in those who refused to know is assuredly a sin; even in those who were unable to know it is the penalty of sin. Therefore, in either case there is no just excuse, but there is a just condemnation.

The reason why holy Scripture says that those are inexcusable who sin, not in ignorance but knowingly, is because they now have no excuse for their ignorance, and there is no longer any justice on which the self-sufficiency of their will can presume, and these words are to make them see that they are inexcusable even by the verdict of their own pride, which makes them rely heavily on the strength of their own will. But he to whom the Lord granted the grace of knowing and obeying said: 'By the law is the knowledge of sin,'[76] and 'I did not know sin but by the law, for I had not known concupiscence if the law did not say: Thou shalt not covet.'[77] He does not mean the man ignorant of the Law which commands but the one in need of the grace which redeems when he says: 'I am delighted with the law of God according to the inward man,' and also when he speaks later on not only of this knowledge but also of delight in the Law, saying: 'Unhappy man that I am who shall deliver me from the body of this death? The grace of God by Jesus Christ our Lord.'[78] Therefore, man is delivered from the wounds of that murder by the grace of the Saviour alone, and those sold into sin are delivered from the bonds of captivity by the grace of the Redeemer alone.

For this reason, a most just punishment falls on those who try to make excuses for their sins and wickedness, whereas grace alone delivers those who are delivered. If their excuse were valid, it would not be grace but justice that redeemed them. But, since only grace redeems man, it finds nothing just

---

76 Rom. 3.20.
77 Rom. 7.7; Exod. 20.17; Deut. 5.21; 17.25.
78 Rom. 7.22,24,25.

in him whom it redeems, neither will, nor act, nor, least of all, that excuse, for if it were a just excuse the one using it would not truly be redeemed by grace. We know that the grace of Christ does redeem some of those who say: 'Why doth he then find fault? for who resisteth his will?'[79] If this excuse is valid, men are no longer redeemed by a freely given grace, but through the validity of their excuse. But, if it is grace that redeems, doubtless this excuse is not valid, for it is truly grace that redeems man if it is not awarded him as something owed in justice. Therefore, in those who say: 'Why doth he find fault? for who resisteth his will?' nothing is effected but what is expressed by the Book of Solomon: 'The folly of a man supplanteth his steps; he fretteth in his mind against God.'[80]

Thus, although God makes 'vessels of wrath fitted for destruction,' that He may show His wrath and make known His power, which He exercises even over the wicked, 'that he may show the riches of his glory on the vessels of mercy,' which He makes unto honor, not as something due to their condemned clay, but as granted by the bounty of His grace, nevertheless, in those same vessels of wrath made unto a dishonor due to their clay,[81] that is, in men created for natural goods, but doomed for their sins to punishment, He knows that He is condemning injustice which truth rightly rejects; He does not commit it. Human nature as coming from His will is unquestionably worthy of praise; sin, as coming from man's will, is an object of reprobation to all. This will of man either transmitted a hereditary taint to the descendants whom he had within him when he sinned, or each one acquired other guilt by living sinfully within himself. But, neither from that sin which is derived from man's

---

79 Rom. 9.19.
80 Prov. 18.22 (Septuagint); cf. 19.3 (Vulgate).
81 Rom. 9.21-23.

origin, nor from those which each one accumulates as his own, either by not understanding, or by not wishing to understand their evil, or even by increasing them through his instruction in the law by an added act of malice, is anyone redeemed or justified except by 'the grace of God by Jesus Christ our Lord.'[82] This is effected not only by the remission of sins, but first by the inspiration of faith itself and of the fear of God, when His love has been graciously imparted to us by the operation of prayer, until He heals all our diseases and redeems our life from destruction and crowns us with mercy and compassion.[83]

But, for those who think that God becomes a respecter of persons[84] if, for one and the same reason, His mercy comes upon some while His wrath remains on others, all the force of human reasoning comes to naught in the case of infants. I pass over for the present the fact that infants, however lately come from their mother's womb, are not alone in being subject to the penalty of which the Apostle says: 'By the offense of one unto all men to condemnation,' from which there is no deliverance except through the One alone of whom the same Apostle says: 'By the justice of one unto all men to justification of life.'[85] I repeat, I shall pass over this for the present and I shall say of infants only what they themselves concede without any objection, terrified as they are by the authority of the Gospel, or, rather, overawed by the perfect agreement in that belief of Christian peoples, namely, that no infant enters the kingdom of heaven unless it is born again of water and the Holy Spirit.[86] I ask, then, what reason they will offer why one is so treated as to go out of life after baptism while another is given over to the

---

82 Rom. 7.25.
83 Ps. 102.3,4.
84 Acts 10.34.
85 Rom. 5.18.
86 John 3.5.

hands of unbelievers or even of believers and dies before it is brought by them to be baptized? Will they attribute it to fate or chance? I do not think they will rush into such madness, if they have even a slight desire of retaining the name of Christian.

Why, then, will no infant enter into the kingdom of heaven without receiving the 'laver of regeneration'?[87] Surely, it did not chose to be born of unbelieving or careless parents? What is to be said of the innumerable unexpected and sudden deaths by which children of pious Christians are often carried off and prevented from being baptized, while on the other hand children of wicked parents, enemies of Christ, come somehow into Christian hands and do not leave this life without the sacrament of regeneration? What answer will they make to this, those who claim that some human merit precedes in order that grace may be given, lest God be a respecter of persons? What merits have preceded in this case? If you take these same infants, there are no merits of theirs; the same doomed clay is common to both. If you look at their parents, those whose children have died sudden deaths without the baptism of Christ were good; those whose children received the sacraments of the Church through some Christian influence are bad. Yet, the providence of God, by which the hairs of our head are numbered, without whose will not a sparrow falls to the ground,[88] which is neither constrained by fate, nor restrained by chance happenings, nor frustrated by any injustice, does not provide rebirth to a heavenly inheritance for all the children of His sons, yet does provide it for some children of evil men. One child born of faithful wedlock, received with joy by its parents, but suffocated in sleep by mother or nurse, becomes an outcast with no share in its parents' faith; the other, born in shame and sacrilege,

87 Titus 3.5.
88 Matt. 10.29,30.

abandoned by the cruel fear of its mother, but rescued by the compassionate charity of strangers and baptized through Christian care, becomes a partaker and sharer in the eternal kingdom. Let them think of these things, let them examine into them, and then let them dare to say that God is a respecter of persons, or that He bestows His grace as a reward for antecedent merits.

Even if they try to seek out some form of deserving, either good or bad, on the part of those of mature age, what will they say of these two cases of infants of whom one could not, by any evil deeds of his own, draw on himself the violent death of suffocation, nor the other, by any good deeds, deserve the care of his baptizer? They are men of excessive vanity and blindness if, after examining these facts, they still refuse to cry out with us: 'O the depth of the riches of the wisdom and of the knowledge of God! How incomprehensible are his judgments and how unsearchable his ways!'[89] They will not thereby frustrate the freely given mercy of God by their obstinate madness. Let them permit the 'Son of man to seek and to save that which was lost,'[90] but let them not dare to judge why, in His incomprehensible judgments, His mercy comes upon one, and in one and the same case His wrath remains on the other.

Who are these that reply to God, when He says to Rebecca, who had twin sons of one conception of Isaac our father, 'when the children were not yet born nor had done any good or evil (that the purpose of God according to election might stand)'—the election, namely, of grace not of merit, the election by which He does not find but makes elect—'that it was not of works but of him that calleth, that the elder should serve the younger'?[91] To this sentence the blessed Apostle adds

89 Rom. 11.33.
90 Matt. 18.11; Luke 19.10.
91 Rom. 9.10-12.

the testimony of a Prophet who came long afterward: 'Jacob I have loved, but Esau I have hated,'[92] to give us to understand plainly by the latter utterance what was hidden in the predestination of God by grace before they were born. For what did He love but the free gift of His mercy in Jacob, who had done nothing good before his birth? And what did He hate but original sin in Esau, who had done nothing evil before his birth? Surely, He would not have loved in the former a goodness which he had not practised, nor would He have hated in the latter a nature which He himself had created good.

It is strange, when they are entangled in such straits, to see into what an abyss they hurl themselves through fear of the nets of truth. 'The reason,' say they, 'why He did not yet hate one of the children and love the other was because He foresaw their future deeds.' Who would not be surprised that this very subtle reasoning escaped the Apostle? Of course he did not see this, when he did not make this answer, so brief, so plain, and, as they think, so true and absolute, to the hypothetical question made him by an objector. For, when he had set forth the amazing fact how, of children not yet born, not having done any good or evil, it could rightly be said that God loved the one and hated the other, he makes an objection expressing the feeling of his hearer: 'What shall we say then? Is there injustice with God? God forbid!'[93] this would have been the place for him to say what these men say: 'God foresaw their future deeds when He said that the elder should serve the younger.' But the Apostle does not say this; rather, he wishes what he says to redound to the praise of the grace and glory of God, that no one may dare to glory in the merits of his own acts. For, when he had said: 'God forbid that there should be injustice with God,' as if we had said to him:

92 Mal. 1.2,3.
93 Rom. 9.14.

'How do you prove this when you state that it is not of works but of Him that calleth that the elder shall serve the younger?' he goes on to say: 'For he saith to Moses: I will have mercy on whom I will have mercy, and I will show mercy to whom I will show mercy. So then it is not of him that willeth nor of him that runneth but of God that showeth mercy.'[94] Where, now, are the merits, where the works, either past or future, as if they had been or were to be performed by the strength of free will? Did the Apostle not make this plain statement in praise of free grace, that is, true grace? 'Hath not God made foolish the wisdom'[95] of heretics?

But what was the issue that made the Apostle say this, that made him cite the example of the twins? What point was he trying to make? What did he wish to drive home? Doubtless, this, which the madness of heretics attacks, which the proud do not accept, which they do not wish to understand: who, 'not knowing the justice of God and seeking to establish their own, have not subjected themselves to the justice of God.'[96] Clearly, the Apostle was treating of that very grace, and that is why he commended the children of promise. What God promises no one but God performs; and while there is some reason and truth in saying that man promises and God performs, it is a reprobate sentiment of impious pride for a man to say that he performs what God has promised.

Therefore, by commending the children of promise, he showed the first prefiguring of this in Isaac, the son of Abraham. The action of God appears much more plainly in him who was not begotten in the ordinary course of nature, but in a womb that was sterile and worn out by age, that it might be a sign of a divine, not a human activity, among

94 Rom. 9.15,16.
95 1 Cor. 1.20.
96 Rom. 10.3.

the sons of God whose coming was foretold. 'In Isaac,' he says, 'shall thy seed be called, that is to say, not they that are the children of the flesh are the children of God, but they that are the children of the promise are accounted for the seed. For this is the word of promise: According to this time will I come, and Sara shall have a son. And not only she,' he says, 'but Rebecca also had conceived at once of Isaac our father.'[97] What significance was there in his adding 'at one conception,' except that Jacob was not to boast of his own merits nor of those of other parents, much less of his own father, as if his will had somehow been changed for the better, saying that he was loved by the Creator because, when his father begot him, he was rewarded for his superior conduct? He says 'of one conception'; consequently, there was one merit of their father in begetting them, one merit of their mother in conceiving them, because, although their mother carried them shut up in her womb until she brought them forth, and perhaps varied in her will and affection, she certainly did not vary for one but for both whom she carried equally in her womb.

We must, then, look into the meaning of the Apostle and note how, in his zeal for extolling grace, he does not want him of whom it was said 'Jacob I have loved' to glory except in the Lord; and, although they were of the same father, the same mother, the same conception, before they had done anything good or evil God loved the one and hated the other, so that Jacob might understand that he was of the same clay of original sin as his brother, with whom he shared a common origin, and thus he sees that he is distinguished from him by grace alone. 'For when the children were not yet born, he says, 'nor had done any good or evil (that the purpose of God according to election might stand), not of

---

97 Rom. 9.7-10.

works but of him that calleth it was said to her: The elder shall serve the younger.'[98]

In another passage, the same Apostle shows most plainly that the election of grace is effected without any antecedent merits, when he says: 'Even so, then, at this present time also, there is a remnant saved according to the election of grace. But if by grace it is not now by works, otherwise grace is no more grace.'[99] And applying thereupon the testimony of the Prophet to this grace, he says: 'Jacob I have loved but Esau I have hated,' and goes on to say: 'What shall we say then? is there injustice with God? God forbid!' But why 'God forbid'? Was it because He foresaw the future deeds of the twins? God forbid this even more! 'For he saith to Moses: I will have mercy on whom I will have mercy, and I will show mercy to whom I will show mercy. So then it is not of him that willeth, nor of him that runneth, but of God that showeth mercy.'[100] So also in the case of the vessels which are fitted for destruction, a consequence of their doomed clay, let the vessels made of the same clay unto honor recognize what the divine mercy has bestowed on them. For he says: 'The Scripture saith to Pharao: And therefore have I raised thee that I may show my power in thee and my name may be spoken of throughout all the earth.' Finally, he concludes both passages with the words: 'Therefore he has mercy on whom he will and whom he will he hardeneth.'[101]

But let the self-conceit of the proud unbeliever or the excuse of the object of final punishment say: 'Why then doth he find fault? for who resisteth his will?' Let him say it and hear in reply what man deserves: 'O man, who art thou that repliest against God?' and the remaining words on which

98 Rom. 9.11,12.
99 Rom. 11.5,6.
100 Rom. 9.13-18.
101 Exod. 9.16; 33.19.

I have commented long enough and often enough, to the best of my ability. Let him hear this and not despise it. If he does despise it, let him find himself hardened so that he may despise it; if he does not despise it, let him believe himself helped that he may not despise it; but the hardening is his due, the help is a free gift.

Since we have now shown what blindness it is for anyone to say, in the case of the twin sons of the patriarch Jacob, that God foresaw their future deeds because they lived and grew old, and therefore He loved Jacob but hated Esau, it is even more impossible for anyone to say the same in the case of infants who are destined to die, namely, that God foresees their future deeds, therefore He does not provide that one should receive baptism, but does provide that the other should; for how can anyone speak of future deeds for those who will have none?

'But,' they say, 'in the case of those whom He takes away, God foresees how each one would have lived if he had lived, and therefore He causes one to die without baptism, thus punishing in him, not the evil deeds he did, but those he would have done.' Now, if evil deeds which have not been committed are punished by divine decree, let these objectors observe how illusory is their promise that infants who die without baptism will not suffer damnation, if the reason why they lack baptism is the evil life they would have lived if they had lived, and if even probable evil deeds are subject to damnation. In the second place, if provision is made for the reception of baptism on the part of those of whom God knows that they would have lived a good life if they had lived, why are not all maintained in a life which they are likely to adorn with their good works? And why do some of those who are baptized live long and wickedly and eventually come to apostasy? Why, since He certainly knew that they were going to sin, did He not expel that very first pair of sinners from paradise before they could commit there an act so unworthy of that holy place—that is, if it is just to punish sins not yet committed? Again, what benefit is it to the one who 'is taken away lest wickedness should alter his understanding or deceit beguile his soul?'[102] if it is just to punish acts which he has not committed, but which he might have committed by living longer? Finally, why is provision not made for the one who would have lived a bad life, if he had lived, to receive the laver of regeneration[103] before his imminent death, so that the sins he was going to commit may be forgiven in baptism? Is anyone so irrational as to deny that these sins can be forgiven by baptism if he says that they can be punished without baptism?

In our debate against those who try, even though refuted at every point, to present God as the avenger of uncommitted sins, we run the risk of being thought to imagine such things about them, whereas they are not to be supposed so stupid as either to believe or to try to make others believe them. If I had not heard them say these things, I should not have thought them worthy of rebuttal. Confronted by the authority of divine writings as well as by the rite of baptism, handed down from antiquity and firmly adhered to in the Church, in which it is plainly shown that infants are freed from the power of the Devil both by the exorcism and by the renunciation pronounced for them by the sponsors who carry them, and not finding any way out of their dilemma, these heretics plunge headlong into fatuity because they will not change their opinion.

Doubtless, some imagine they have a clever rebuttal when they say: 'How does the sin of faithful parents pass to their children when we are sure this sin of the parents was forgiven in their baptism?' as if carnal birth cannot have what spiritual

---

102 Wisd. 4.11.
103 Titus 3.5.

rebirth alone takes away. Or does it happen in baptism that the weakness of concupiscence in the flesh is immediately healed as its guilt is immediately removed? This is the effect of the grace of rebirth, not a condition of birth. Anyone born of this concupiscence, even of a regenerated parent, will undoubtedly suffer its effects unless he is likewise regenerated. But, however great the difficulty in this question, it does not prevent the workers in the field of Christ from baptizing infants unto the remission of sins whether they are born of unbelievers or of believers, just as it is no obstacle to farmers engaged in grafting wild olives upon olive trees not to know whether the grafts originated from wild olives or from olive trees. If you put this question to a country man—why nothing but a wild olive will grow from the seed of either species, although there is a difference between olive and wild olive— he may not be able to answer the question, but he does not for that give up his work of grafting; otherwise, if he thought that seedlings springing up from the seed of the olive were olives, the sloth due to his mistake would make the whole field run wild with unproductive sterility.[104]

As to that theory they think up when overpowered by the weight of truth, that 'the Lord is faithful in his words,'[105] and therefore His Church does not act hypocritically when it baptizes children for the remission of sin, but that what is done is effected through faith—for, certainly, what is pronounced is effected—what Christian would not laugh at them, however subtle this trumped-up doctrine appears, when the very manifest body of truth is weighted against them? They say that infants truly answer by the lips of their sponsors that they believe in the remission of sins, not because their own sins are remitted but because they believe there is remission in the Church or in baptism for those in whom sin

104 Cf. Rom. 11.24.
105 Ps. 144.13.

is found, but not for those who have no sins. Consequently, they do not want them baptized for the remission of sins, as if such remission took place in them whom they claim to be without sin, but they say that, when they are baptized, even though sinless, by that baptism the effect is a remission of sin in those who are sinners.

It is possible that, with more time, this crafty subtlety could be refuted with more detail and greater penetration. But that cleverness of theirs does not find an answer to the fact that infants are exorcized and breathed upon in baptism. Undoubtedly, this is an illusory practice if the Devil has no power over them, but, if he has power over them, and if the exorcism and breathing are not illusory, where does he get his power if not through the primal sin of all sinners? Hence, if they now blush and shrink from saying that these ceremonies in the Church are spurious, let them confess that even among infants Christ came to seek that which was lost. For, that which was lost by sin alone cannot be sought, cannot be found, but by grace alone. But, thank God, when they argue against the remission of sins, lest anyone should believe that it is effected in children, now at least they admit that children profess their belief in it through the lips of their elders. Therefore, as they hear the Lord saying: 'Unless a man be born again of water and the Holy Spirit, he cannot enter into the kingdom of heaven,'[106] and thereupon admit that children should be baptized, let them hear the same Lord saying: 'He that believeth not shall be condemned,'[107] since they admit that children are reborn through the ministry of the baptizer, just as they profess their faith through the hearts and lips of their sponsors. Let them, then, dare to say that the innocent are condemned by a just God if they are bound by no fetters of original sin.

106 John 3.5.
107 Mark 16.16.

If this treatise is a long and burdensome one in the midst of your busy life, grant me your pardon because I was induced by your own letter to write this to you, and the kindness you there expressed made me want to have this conference with you. Indeed, it has been a forcible interruption of my own cares. If you hear that they have thought up other attacks on the Catholic faith, and if you develop any arguments against them, lest they lay waste the weak members of the Lord's flock, in your faithful and truly pastoral charity share them with us. Thus our own effort is roused from slothful sleep by the restlessness of heretics, forcing us to examine the Scriptures more carefully, lest they use them to harm the flock of Christ. And so, by the manifold grace of the Saviour, God turns to our help what the enemy plots for our destruction, because 'to them that love God all things work together unto good.'[108]

195. Jerome to the saintly lord and blessed father,[1] Augustine (c. 418)

I have always revered your Blessedness with the respect which befits you and I have loved the Lord our Saviour dwelling in you, but now we add something to the heap, and, if that is possible, we fill up what was full, so as not to allow one single hour to pass without mention of your name; because the ardor of your faith has stood firm against the blasts of the wind, and you have chosen, in so far as it rests with you, to be delivered from Sodom rather than to remain there with the doomed.[2] Your Prudence knows what I mean.

---

108 Rom. 8.28.

---

1 He uses the word *papa,* 'pope.'
2 Gen. 19.14.

Bravo to your valor! Your fame is world-wide; Catholics revere you and accept you as the second founder of the ancient faith, and—which is a mark of greater fame—all the heretics hate you, and pursue me, too, with equal hatred; they plan our death by desire if they cannot achieve it by the sword. May the mercy of Christ our Lord keep you safe and mindful of me, revered lord, most saintly father.

196. Augustine gives greeting in the Lord to his saintly brother and fellow bishop, Asellicus[1] (End of 418)

The letter which your Holiness sent to our venerable senior, Donatian,[2] containing a discussion of the necessity of avoiding Jewish practices, has been forwarded by him to me, with the urgent request, or command, that I answer it. Not wishing to show him disrespect, I am answering it as best I can, with the Lord's help, in the belief that by writing to you I am giving pleasure to your Charity, also; besides, I could not refuse to comply with the request of one whom we both esteem for his good qualities.

The Apostle Paul teaches that Christians who have been Gentiles should not have to practice the Jewish law, when he says: 'I said to Peter before them all: If thou being a Jew livest after the manner of the Gentiles and not as the Jews do, how dost thou compel the Gentiles to live as do the Jews?' and he added at once: 'We by nature are Jews and not of the Gentiles, sinners. But knowing that man is not justified by the works of the law, but by the faith of Jesus Christ, we also believe in Christ Jesus that we may be justified by the

---

1 Probably an African bishop.
2 Bishop of Byzacena, found in the list of bishops who signed the report of the Council of Carthage; cf. Letter 175.

faith of Christ and not by the works of the law, because by the works of the law no flesh shall be justified.'[3]

Not only are those works of the Law which are found in the ancient observance no longer practiced by Christians since the revelation of the New Testament, such as circumcision, the Sabbath rest from worldly activity, abstinence from certain foods, the offering of animals in sacrifice, new moons, unleavened bread, and other such customs, but even the commandment which is found in the Law, 'Thou shalt not covet,'[4] which no one doubts is addressed to Christians, too, does not justify a man except by the faith of Jesus Christ and 'the grace of God by Jesus Christ our Lord.'[5] The same Apostle likewise says: 'What shall we say then? Is the law sin? God forbid! But I did not know sin but by the law, for I had not yet known concupiscence if the law did not say: Thou shalt not covet. But sin, taking occasion by the commandment, wrought in me all manner of concupiscence. For without the law sin was dead. And I lived some time without the law, but when the commandment came sin revived. And I died and the commandment that was ordained to life was found to be unto death to me. For sin, taking occasion by the commandment, seduced me and by it killed me. Wherefore the law indeed is holy and the commandment holy and just and good. Was that then which is good made death unto me? God forbid! But sin, that it may appear sin, by that which is good, wrought death in me; that sin by the commandment might become sinful above measure. For we know that the law is spiritual, but I am carnal, sold under sin. For that which I work I understand not, for I do not that good which I will, but the evil which I hate, that I do. If then I do that which I will not, I consent to the law that is good.'[6]

---

3 Gal. 2.14-16; Rom. 3.20.
4 Exod. 20.17; Deut. 5.21; 7.25; Rom. 7.7.
5 Rom. 7.25.
6 Rom. 7.7-16.

We see, therefore, from these words of the Apostle, that not only is the Law not sin, but that it is even holy, and that the commandment which says 'Thou shalt not covet' is holy and just and good. But sin seduces under the appearance of good and thus kills those who think, even though they are carnal, that they can fulfill the spiritual Law by their own strength. Thus, they become not only sinners, which they would be even if they had not received the Law, but also transgressors, which they would not be if they had not received the Law. So the Apostle says in another passage: 'Where there is no law, neither is there transgression,'[7] and elsewhere he testifies that 'the law entered in that sin might abound, and where sin abounded grace did more abound.'[8]

This, then, is the useful function of the law, that it shows man to himself, that he may know his own wickedness and see how his carnal concupiscence is increased rather than healed by prohibition. Forbidden things are more eagerly sought after when carnal nature is forced to practice what is spiritually commanded.[9] Man must be spiritual to observe a spiritual law; he does not become so by the law but by grace, that is, not by a commandment but by a free gift, not by the impulsion of the letter but by the impulse of the Spirit. Now, a man begins to be renewed in the inward man according to grace, provided he carries out what he loves in his mind and does not consent to the urging of the flesh which he hates; this does not mean that he has no evil desires at all, but that he does not go after his lusts.[10] This, however, is so great a thing that, if it were perfectly accomplished, and if we yielded no assent to any of the enticements of sin, although they are still present in us as long as we are in

7 Rom. 4.15.
8 Rom. 5.20.
9 2 Cor. 4.16.
10 Eccli. 18.30.

'the body of this death,'[11] there would be no occasion for us to say to our Father who is in heaven: 'Forgive us our debts.'[12] Yet we should not for that be such now as we shall be when 'this mortal hath put on immortality,'[13] for then not only shall we not obey any enticement of sin, but there will be no such enticements of the kind we are commanded not to obey.

So, then, when the Apostle says: 'It is no more I that do it but sin that dwelleth in me,'[14] he is speaking of the lust of the flesh which stirs its impulses in us even when we do not obey them, so long as sin does not reign in our mortal body to obey its lusts, and we do not yield our members as instruments of iniquity unto sin.[15] By progressing constantly in that justice which is not yet perfected we shall eventually come to its perfection where the lust of sin does not have to be curbed and bridled, for it does not then exist at all. The Law lays down this obligation in the words: 'Thou shalt not covet,'[16] not that we are able to do this, but that we should strive for it. And this is accomplished not by the law which imposes, but by the faith which implores; not by the letter through which the commandment is given, but by the Spirit through which help is given; not, therefore, by the merits of man's striving, but by the grace of the Saviour's bestowing. The value of the Law is that it shows a man his own weakness and forces him to beg for the remedy of grace which is in Christ. 'For whosoever shall call upon the name of the Lord shall be saved. How then shall they call upon him in whom they have not believed? or how shall they believe him of whom they have not heard?' Therefore he adds a little further on:

11 Rom. 7.24.
12 Matt. 6.9,12; Luke 11.4.
13 1 Cor. 15.54.
14 Rom. 7.17.
15 Rom. 6.12,13.
16 Exod. 20.17; Deut. 5.21; Rom. 7.7.

'Faith then cometh by hearing and hearing by the word of Christ.'[17]

From this it is clear that the Apostle is speaking of those who rejoice in being Israelites according to the flesh, and who glory in the Law more than in the grace of Christ, when he says that 'not knowing the justice of God and seeking to establish their own, they have not submitted themselves to the justice of God.'[18] Notice that he says 'the justice of God,' which comes to man from God, and 'their own,' by which they think they have strength in themselves to fulfill the commandments without the help and gift of Him who gave the Law. There are some like these who indeed profess to be Christians, but are so hostile to the very grace of Christ that they think they can fulfill the divine commandments by their own human strength, and thus they, too, 'not knowing the justice of God and seeking to establish their own, have not submitted themselves to the justice of God.' These are not Jews in name, but they become so by their error. This group of men have found leaders for themselves in Pelagius and Caelestius, passionate preachers of this impiety, who have recently been deprived of communion with the Catholic Church by the judgment of God through His careful and faithful servants,[19] and who still persist with impenitent heart in their own damnation.

Whoever seeks to be a stranger to that carnal and animal Judaism which is justly repudiated and condemned must first consider as alien to himself those ancient observances which have clearly ceased to be necessary now that the New Testament has been revealed, and the things which were prefigured by those others have come to pass, and he is not to be judged 'in meat or in drink or in respect of a festival day, or of

17 Rom. 10.13,14,17; Joel 2.32; Acts 2.21.
18 Rom. 10.3.
19 They were excommunicated by Pope Innocent I in 417.

the new moon, or of the sabbaths, which are a shadow of things to come.'[20] On the other hand, he must receive, embrace, and observe, without any reserve, those commandments in the Law which help to form the character of the faithful, such as that 'denying ungodliness and worldly desires, we should live soberly and justly and godly in this world,'[21] and this one: 'Thou shalt not covet,' chosen by the Apostle as the part of the Law worthy of the greatest commendation; and the commandments about loving God and our neighbor, as set forth in the Law without any figure or mystery—on which two commandments the Lord Christ Himself said the whole Law depends[22]—but whatever progress he makes in them he must not attribute it to himself but to 'the grace of God by Jesus Christ our Lord.'

However, when anyone has become by that means a true and full-fledged Christian, the question may reasonably be asked whether he is also to be called a Jew or an Israelite. This term is understood, of course, in a spiritual, not a carnal, sense; even so, he should not give himself this name in ordinary conversation—though he may retain it in his spiritual consciousness—because daily speech does not distinguish this twofold meaning and he might seem to take credit for something inimical to the name of Christian. The same blessed Apostle solves and settles this question for us—whether one who is a Christian can also be considered a Jew or an Israelite—when he says: 'Circumcision profiteth indeed if thou keep the law; but if thou be a transgressor of the law, thy circumcision is made uncircumcision. If then the uncircumcised keep the justices of the law, shall not his uncircumcision be counted for circumcision? And shall not that which by nature is uncircumcision, if it fulfil the law, judge

---

20 Col. 2.16,17.
21 Titus 2.12.
22 Matt. 22.37-40; Mark 12.30-31; Luke 10.27; Deut. 6.5; Lev. 19.18.

thee who by the letter and circumcision art a transgressor of
the law? For not he is a Jew that is so outwardly, nor is that
circumcision which is outward in the flesh; but he is a Jew
that is one inwardly, and the circumcision is that of the heart,
in the spirit, not in the letter, whose praise is not of men but
of God.'[23] Thus, when we hear the Apostle of Christ commending for us the Jew who is one inwardly, by the circumcision, not of the flesh but of the heart, in the spirit, not in the
letter, what is he but a Christian?

So, then, we are Jews not in the flesh but in the spirit,
just as we are the seed of Abraham, not according to the flesh
like those who boast proudly of the carnal name, but according to the spirit of faith which they lack. We know that
we were the ones promised when God said to him: 'I have
made thee a father of many children.'[24] We know, too, how
much the Apostle has to say on this theme: 'For we say,' he
says, 'that unto Abraham faith was reputed to justice. How,
then, was it reputed? When he was in circumcision or uncircumcision? Not in circumcision, but in uncircumcision. And
he received the sign of circumcision, a seal of the justice of
the faith, which he had being uncircumcised; that he might
be the father of all them that believe, being uncircumcised,
that unto them also it may be reputed to justice; and might
be the father of circumcision, not to them only that are of
the circumcision, but to them also that follow the steps of
the faith, that is, in the uncircumcision of our father,
Abraham.' And a little further on he says: 'Therefore it is
of faith that, according to grace, the promise might be firm
to all the seed, not to that only which is of the law, but to
that also which is of the faith of Abraham, who is the father
of us all. As it is written: I have made thee a father of many
nations.'[25] Likewise, in Galatians he says: 'As Abraham

---

23 Rom. 2.25-29.
24 Gen. 17.5.
25 Rom. 4.9-12,16,17.

believed God and it was reputed to him unto justice, know
ye therefore that they who are of the faith, the same are the
children of Abraham. And the Scripture, foreseeing that
God justifieth the Gentiles by faith, told unto Abraham before: In thee shall all nations be blessed. Therefore they
that are of faith shall be blessed with faithful Abraham.'[26]
And somewhat further on in the same Epistle he says:
'Brethren, I speak after the manner of man, yet a man's
testament, if it be confirmed, no man despiseth nor addeth to
it. To Abraham were the promises made and to his seed.
He saith not: And to his seeds, as of many, but as of one:
And to thy seed, which is Christ.' And again a little further
on he says: 'You are all one in Christ Jesus, but if you be
Christ's then are you the seed of Abraham, heirs according
to the promise.'[27]

Thus, in accord with that definition of the Apostle, there
are found to be some that are Jews but not Christians, who are
not the sons of Abraham, although they are descendants of
Abraham according to the flesh. For, when he says: 'Know
ye therefore that they who are of the faith the same are
the children of Abraham,' he certainly means that those who
are not of the faith are not the children of Abraham. Consequently, if Abraham is not a father to the Jews in the same
way as he is to us, what good does it do them to have been
his descendants in the flesh, and to have borne a name without
value? But, when they come to Christ and begin to be the
children of Abraham who are of the faith, then they will be
Jews, not outwardly, but inwardly; by the circumcision of
the heart, in the spirit, not in the letter; whose praise is not
of men but of God. But those who are strangers to this faith
will be counted among the branches broken from that olive
tree into whose root the same Apostle says that the wild olive,

---

26 Gal. 3.6-9; Gen. 12.3; 15.6; 22.18; 26.4; Rom. 4.3; James 2.23; Acts 3.25.
27 Gal. 3.15,16,27,28.

that is, the Gentiles, are ingrafted,[28] which certainly is not accomplished by the flesh but by faith; not by the law but by grace; not by the letter but by the spirit; by the circumcision of the heart not of the flesh; not outwardly but inwardly; with praise from God, not from men. Thus, as every Christian is a child of Abraham not carnally but spiritually, so he is a Jew not carnally but spiritually, and an Israelite not carnally but spiritually, for the Apostle speaks of that name in these words: 'For all are not Israelites that are of Israel; neither are all they that are the seed of Abraham children; but in Isaac shall thy seed be called; that is to say not they that are the children of the flesh are the children of God; but they that are the children of the promise are accounted for the seed.'[29] Is it not a great marvel and a deep mystery that many who are born of Israel are not of Israel, and many are not children although they are the seed of Abraham? How is it that they are not his children but we are, except that they are not the children of the promise who belong to the grace of Christ, who boast an idle name? Therefore, they are not of Israel as we are, nor are we of Israel as they are. Our claim is that of a spiritual rebirth; theirs, of a carnal birth.

We must note, then, and distinguish two Israels: one which receives the name because of the flesh, the other, by the spirit, has attained to the reality which is signified by the name. The Israelites are not descended from Agar the handmaid of Sara, are they? Was not Ishmael her son and did he not beget the race of Ishmaelites, not Israelites? Israel descended from Sara by Isaac, who was born to Abraham according to promise.[30] Still, although that is the manner of the fleshly descent, we find, when we come to the spiritual meaning, that

---

28 Cf. Rom. 11.17-24.
29 Rom. 9.6-8; Gen. 21.12; Heb. 11.18.
30 Gen. 18.10.

the carnal Israelites do not belong to Sara, although they trace their fleshly origin to her; and those who are sons of the flesh, not according to Ishmael but according to Isaac, are the children of promise, not because they belong to the carnal seed of Isaac, but to a spiritual mystery. In this sense the Apostle speaks thus to the Galatians: 'Tell me, you that desire to be under the law, have you not heard the law? For it is written: that Abraham had two sons, the one by a bond-woman, and the other by a free woman. But he who was of the bondwoman was born according to the flesh, but he of the free woman was of promise, which things are said by an allegory. For these are the two testaments, the one from Mount Sina engendering unto bondage, which is Agar; for Sina is a mountain in Arabia, which hath affinity to that Jerusalem which now is, and is in bondage with her children. But that Jerusalem which is above is free, which is our mother. For it is written: Rejoice thou barren that bearest not, break forth and cry thou that travailest not; for many are the children of the desolate, more than of her that hath a husband. Now we, brethren, as Isaac was, are children of promise. But as then he that was born according to the flesh persecuted him that was after the spirit, so it is now. But what saith the Scripture? Cast out the bondwoman and her son, for the son of the bondwoman shall not be heir with the son of the free woman. So then, brethren, we are not children of the bond-woman but of the free, by the freedom wherewith Christ hath made us free.'[32]

See how, according to this spiritual meaning of the Apostle, we belong to the free woman, Sara, although we trace no carnal descent from her, while the Jews, who do trace their descent from her, are shown to belong rather to Agar, the bondwoman, from whom they do not trace their

---

31 Gal. 4.21-5.1; Gen. 16.15; 21.2.
32 Gal. 4.21-31; Gen. 16.15; 21.2; Isa. 54.1.

descent. This great and profound mystery is also found in the grandsons of Abraham and Sara, that is, the sons of Isaac and Rebecca, the twins Esau and Jacob, who was afterward called Israel. In speaking of this, the same Apostle stated that the sons of promise through Isaac are those who belong to the grace of Christ, when he said: 'Not only she, but when Rebecca also had conceived at once of Isaac our father. For when the children were not yet born, nor had done any good or evil, that the purpose of God according to election might stand, not of works but of him that calleth, it was said to her: the elder shall serve the younger, as it is written: Jacob I have loved but Esau I have hated.'[33] This apostolic and Catholic doctrine certainly shows quite clearly that the Jews, that is, the Israelites, belong to Sara, and the Ishmaelites to Agar, according to carnal descent, but according to the spiritual mystery Christians belong to Sara, Jews to Agar; likewise, the race of Idumeans, according to carnal descent, belong to Esau who was also called Edom,[34] and the race of Jews to Jacob who was also called Israel;[35] but according to the spiritual mystery the Jews belong to Esau, the Christians to Israel. In this way we see the fulfillment of the pronouncement: 'The elder shall serve the younger,' that is, the Jewish people, born first, shall serve the Christian people, born later. This is how we are of Israel, boasting of a divine adoption, not a human kinship; Jews inwardly, not outwardly; not in the letter, but in the spirit; by the circumcision of the heart, not of the flesh.

This being the case, we ought not to upset the usage of human speech by an ill-chosen manner of speaking, nor introduce common terms with a distorted meaning into matters that need to be carefully distinguished; as if someone

---

33 Rom. 9.10-13; Gen. 25.23; Mal. 1.2,3.
34 Gen. 25.30.
35 Gen. 32.28.

should affect to call Jews those who are Christians and are
most commonly called Christians, using the word in a far-
fetched sense; or as if he should both be and be called a
Christian but should take greater pleasure in the name of
Jew. It is a sign of foolish inexperience, and, if I may say so,
of ignorant knowledge, to introduce into the ordinary speech
of everyday a term which ought to be taken in a mystical
sense and rarely uttered by the tongue. Surely, the Apostles,
from whom we learn these things, were not ignorant of the
manner in which it is rather we who are the seed of Abraham,
heirs of the promise according to Isaac, Jews in spirit, not in
the letter, by the circumcision of the heart, not of the flesh;
Israel not according to the flesh, but the Israel of God.
Naturally, they knew all that much more truly and surely
than we do, yet in their mode of speaking they called Jews
and Israelites those who come of the stock of Abraham according to the flesh, and who are universally called by that
name.

The Apostle Paul says: 'The Jews require signs and the
Greeks seek after wisdom, but we preach Christ crucified;
unto the Jews indeed a stumbling-block but unto the Gentiles foolishness; but unto them that are called both Jews
and Greeks, Christ the power of God and the wisdom of
God.'[36] Those whom he called Greeks he also referred to
by the name of Gentiles, because the Greek language was
prevalent among the Gentiles; but he called Jews only those
to whom all give that name. If the Christians themselves are
Jews, then Christ crucified is a stumbling-block to the
Christians, since it is said: 'To the Jews indeed a stumbling-
block.' Anyone who is not completely out of his mind can
see that. He also says: 'Be without offense to the Jews and
to the Gentiles and to the church of God.'[37] How could he

---

36 1 Cor. 1.22-24.
37 1 Cor. 10.32.

make that distinction if it were proper to call the Church of
God Jews in the ordinary meaning of daily speech? Again he
says: 'Even us whom also he hath called, not only of the
Jews but also of the Gentiles.'[38] How did He call them 'of the
Jews' if, instead, He called them of the non-Jews to be Jews?
He says similarly of the Israelites: 'What then shall we say?
That the Gentiles who followed not after justice have attained
to justice, even the justice that is of faith. But Israel by fol-
lowing after the law of justice, is not come unto the law
of justice. Why so? Because they sought it not by faith but as
it were by works; for they stumbled at the stumbling-stone.'[39]
Again: 'But to Israel what doth he say? All day long have
I spread my hands to a people that believeth not and contradicteth me.'[40] And he goes on to say: 'I say then: Hath
God cast away his own people? God forbid. For I also am
an Israelite of the seed of Abraham and of the tribe of
Benjamin. God hath not cast away his people which he foreknew.'[41] How can the Apostle call Israel a people that believeth not and contradicteth if Christians are Israel; or how
could he call himself an Israelite? Was it because he had become a Christian? Certainly it was not for that reason, because according to the flesh he was 'of the seed of Abraham,
of the tribe of Benjamin,' whereas we are not that according
to the flesh, although we are the seed of Abraham and therefore Israel according to faith. But there is a difference between
what the mind acknowledges as part of a higher mystery
and what the usage of everyday speech means by the word.

Finally, there is that obscure person named Aptus, of
whom you wrote that he is teaching Christians to become
Jews, and likewise, as your Holiness claimed, calls himself
Jew and Israelite in order to forbid the use of those foods

---

38 Rom. 9.24.
39 Rom. 9.30-32.
40 Rom. 10.21.
41 Rom. 11.1,2.

which the Law, given through the holy servant of God, Moses,
forbade in accordance with the circumstances of that time;
and to advocate the observances of that time,[42] now abolished
and dispensed with among Christians, which the Apostle calls
shadows of things to come,[43] thereby showing that they are
to be understood prophetically and that their observance has
now been made void. From this it seems clear why that Aptus
wishes to be called an Israelite and a Jew, not in a spiritual
sense, but in an absolutely carnal sense. We, however, are not
bound by those observances which have been made void by
the revelation of the New Testament, but we have learned
and we teach that the commandments of the Law which are
obligatory at this time, such as: 'Thou shalt not commit adultery; thou shalt not kill; thou shalt not covet; and if there
be any other commandment it is comprised in this word:
Thou shalt love thy neighbor as thyself,'[44] are to be observed
by us not by our own strength, as if we were establishing our
own justice, but through the 'grace of God by Jesus Christ
our Lord,' in that justice which comes to us from Him. Yet,
we do not refuse to be called the seed of Abraham, as the
Apostle says: 'You are the seed of Abraham';[45] or Jews
inwardly, of whom he also says: 'For not he is a Jew that is
so outwardly, nor is that circumcision which is outward in
the flesh; but he is a Jew that is so inwardly, in the spirit
not in the letter; whose praise is not of men but of God';[46]
or spiritual Israelites, belonging manifestly to him of whom it
was said that the elder should serve the younger. But we do
not apply those terms to ourselves improperly; we restrict
their use to the mystical meaning; we do not fill the air with
novelties of language.

---

42 Lev. 11.1-32; Deut. 14.3-21.
43 Col. 2.16,17.
44 Rom. 13.9; Exod. 20.14,13,17; Luke 10.27; Gal. 5.14; James 2.8.
45 Gal. 3.29.
46 Rom. 2.28,29.

197. Augustine[1] to Bishop Hesychius,[2] on the end of the world (End of 418)

I am availing myself of the return to your Holiness of your son, our fellow priest, Cornutus, from whom I received the letter of your Reverence in which you were so kind as to visit my insignificance, and I am finally paying my debt of the answer, as well as the long-due courtesy of returning your greeting, recommending myself to your acceptable prayers to the Lord, my lord and brother. But regarding the prophetic words, often uttered, on which you wished me to write something, I thought it better to refer you to the interpretation of those same words done by holy Jerome, a man of great learning, and in case you did not have them at hand, I have had extracts copied from his works, which I am sending to your Beatitude. However, if you have them, and they do not satisfy your inquiry, I ask you to please write me what you think of them, and how you yourself understand the prophetic oracles. I think that the phrase of Daniel about the weeks should be taken to refer to time already past; but as to the coming of the Saviour at the end of the world, I do not venture to calculate the time, and I do not think that any Prophet has defined the number of years in that matter, but that special weight is to be given to what the Lord Himself said: 'It is not for you to know the times and moments which the Father hath put in his own power.'[3]

In another place He says: 'But of that day and hour no one knoweth,'[4] and there are some who take this to mean that they can calculate the time, but what no one knows is merely the day and hour. Here I shall pass over the manner in which Scripture uses 'day' and 'hour' in the sense of time.

---

1 There is no title of address in the text; another reading gives this one.
2 Bishop of Salona in Dalmatia. Cf. *De civ. Dei* 20.5.
3 Acts 1.7.
4 Matt. 24.36; Mark 13.32.

It is clear that the former quotation speaks very plainly of not knowing the time, for it was when He was questioned on this point by His disciples that He said: 'No one can know the times which the Father hath put in his own power.' He did not say 'day' or 'hour,' but 'times,' a word not ordinarily used of a short lapse of time, as 'day' and 'hour' are, especially if we examine the Greek version, from which, as we know, the same book has been translated into our tongue, although it is not possible to distinguish the terms adequately in Latin. In Greek, we read *chrónous* or *kaírous,* but we call both words 'times,' whether *chrónous* or *kaírous,* although there is a significant difference between the two. The Greeks use the word *kaírous* not for time as a succession of eras, but for time as it is felt in human happenings as either suitable or unsuitable for doing something, such as harvest, vintage, heat, cold, peace, war, and the like; the actual passing of time they call *chrónous.*

Certainly, the Apostles did not ask their question as if they wanted to know the final day or hour—that is, a small part of a day—but they asked if the time was suitable for restoring the kingdom of Israel. It was then they heard: 'No one can know the times which the Father hath put in his own power,' that is, *chrónous* or *kaírous.* If this were translated into Latin by 'times' and 'occasions' (*opportunitates*), and not as it now is, it would be clearly expressed, because when times are spoken of as suitable or unsuitable they are called *kaíroi.* But when we mean to calculate time, the word is *chrónous.* Hence, to wish to know when the end of the world will come and when the Lord will appear is, it seems to me, what He says no one can know.

The suitable occasion for that time will certainly not come until the 'Gospel shall be preached in the whole world for a testimony to all nations,' for the statement of the Saviour on this point as we read it is very clear: 'And this Gospel of the kingdom shall be preached in the whole world for a testimony to all nations, and then shall the consummation come.'[5] What else does 'then it shall come' mean but that it will not come before then? How long after that it will come is unknown to us, but, obviously, we ought not to doubt that it will not come sooner. Therefore, if the servants of God were to undertake the labor of traveling all over the earth so as to gather in as many as they can, we could certainly estimate how long a time remains before the end of the world by the remaining number of nations to whom the Gospel has not yet been preached. But, if anyone believes that it is not possible for the servants of God to travel over the whole earth because some regions are inaccessible and inhospitable, and therefore a truthful report cannot be made on the number and importance of the nations still deprived of the Gospel of Christ, I think it is much less possible to understand from the Scriptures how much time there will be before the end, since we read in them: 'No one can know the times which the Father hath put in his own power.' Hence, if someone were to announce to us now, with complete certainty, that the Gospel had been preached to all nations, not even so could we say how much time remains before the end, but we could reasonably say that we are coming nearer and nearer to it. Someone might answer to this that, by the preaching of the Gospel with such speed, the Roman nations and many barbarian ones, as well as some whose territory we now occupy, would have been converted to the faith of Christ suddenly, not gradually, so that it might not be beyond the bounds of probability that in a few years, not, perhaps, in the lifetime of us elders, but certainly in that of young men who will grow old, all the remaining nations will be completely accounted for. If that happens, it will be easier to prove it by experience than by reading about it before it happens.

5 Matt. 24.14.

I have been impelled to say this by the opinion of one exegete whom the priest Jerome charges with rashness because he has dared to apply the weeks of Daniel to the future coming of Christ, not to His first one.[6] However, if the Lord has revealed or will reveal anything better to the holy humility of your heart, as you deserve, I ask you to share it with us and to receive this letter as coming from a man who would rather have knowledge than ignorance of these matters of which you inquire; but, as that cannot yet be, I choose rather to confess a cautious ignorance than to profess a false knowledge.

198. Hesychius[1] gives greeting in the Lord to the saintly lord, Augustine, his brother and fellow bishop, revered with the most sincere affection (End of 418)

Our holy fellow priest, Cornutus, has satisfied my longing and expectancy by bringing me the letter of your Blessedness, and it has given me joy that you so kindly remembered me and that you outlined in passing in a few words of the very language of your holy mind what I had asked. You also added some extracts from the works of our holy fellow priest, Jerome, so that I could complete the answer to my question by reading his work on the holy Scriptures. As you were so kind as to ask me to set forth in a letter to your most sincere Charity what I think on those questions, I am adding it to what I have read as far as the limited intelligence of my mediocrity can either think or understand.

All things are governed by the will and power of Almighty God, the Creator of the universe; both those things that have

---

6 Jerome, *Commentary on Daniel* 9 (*PL* 25.548.14-549.5).

1 The text edition gives no heading: another reading gives this one. The writer is the recipient of Letter 197.

happened and those that are about to happen are made known by the words of the holy Prophets who have followed the divine will in announcing future happenings to men before they happened. In this there is matter for sufficient wonder whether God determined that the prophecies which He wished made should not be able to penetrate deeply into the understanding of men, according to the passage in which the Lord spoke to the blessed Apostles, saying: 'No one can know the times which the Father hath put in his own power,' especially as it is not written 'no one can' in the earliest texts of the Church, but it is written: 'It is not for you to know the times and moments which the Father hath put in his own power,' a fashion of speech which is logically completed by what follows: 'But . . . you shall be witnesses unto me in Jerusalem and Samaria and even to the uttermost part of the earth.'[2] He wishes us to understand, therefore, that the Apostles were to be witnesses of His name and His resurrection, not of the end of the world.

In this matter of knowing the times, the Lord Himself warns us thus: 'Who, thinkest thou, is a faithful and wise servant whom his lord hath appointed over his family to give them meat in season? Blessed is that servant whom when his lord shall come he shall find so doing!'[3] The family of Christ is fed by the word of preaching, and the faithful servant is the one who furnishes this necessary meat in season to believers who are awaiting their lord. But the evil servant is thus rebuked: 'But if the evil servant shall say in his heart: My lord is long a-coming, his lord shall come in a day that he knoweth not and an hour that he thinketh not,'[4] and the rest. Likewise, He shows why this time is not known by saying:

---

2 Acts 1.7,8. The second version given by the writer is that found in the Vulgate. It is possible to surmise that St. Augustine had put together two passages in Letter 197, Acts 1.7 and Matt. 24.36, and that Hesychius is tactfully setting him right.
3 Matt. 24.45,46.
4 Matt. 24.48-50; Luke 12.45,46.

'You hypocrites, you know how to discern the face of heaven, how is it that you do not discern this time?'[5] The Apostle also says: 'In the last days shall come on dangerous times,'[6] and the rest. And again the Apostle says: 'But of times and moments we have no need to write to you; for yourselves know perfectly that the day of the Lord shall so come as a thief in the night. For when they shall say: Peace and security, then shall sudden destruction come upon them, as the pains upon her that is with child, and they shall not escape.'[7] Again, the Apostle says: 'Remember you not that when I was yet with you I told you these things? And now you know what withholdeth that he may be revealed in his time. For the mystery of iniquity already worketh; only that he that now holdeth do hold until he be taken out of the way. And then that wicked one shall be revealed whom the Lord Jesus shall kill with the spirit of his mouth.'[8] In like manner in the Gospel the Lord thus reproaches the Jews: 'If thou also hadst known . . . the time of thy visitation,' perhaps thou shouldst have remained, 'but now these things are hidden from thy eyes.'[9] And the Lord made this prediction to the Jews: 'The time is accomplished; do penance; believe in the Gospel.'[10] Rightly did He tell the Jews that their time was accomplished, because their time came to an end after His preaching and the thirty-five or forty years of His life. In Daniel we read: 'Until the beast was slain and the body thereof was destroyed and given to the fire to be burnt; and the power of the other beasts was taken away and the times of life were appointed them for a time'—which in Greek is called both *chrónos* and *kaíros*. And he goes on: 'Behold the son of man coming with the clouds of heaven.'[11]

---

5 Luke 12.56.
6 2 Tim. 3.1.
7 1 Thess. 5.1-3.
8 2 Thess. 2.5-8; Isa. 11.4.
9 Cf. Luke 19.42,44.
10 Mark 1.15. These words were spoken by St. John the Baptist.
11 Dan. 7.11-13.

The second point is that the coming of the Lord is to be loved and expected. For it is a great bliss for those who love His coming, as the blessed Apostle Paul bears witness: 'As to the rest there is laid up for me a crown of justice which the Lord, the just judge, will render to me in that day. And not only to me but to them also that love his coming.'[12] And the Lord says in the Gospel: 'Then shall the just shine as the sun in the kingdom of their Father.'[13] The Prophet also says: 'For behold darkness shall cover the earth and a mist the people, but the Lord shall arise upon thee and his glory shall be seen upon thee';[14] and again the Prophet: 'But they that hope in the Lord shall renew their strength, they shall take wings as eagles; they shall run and not be weary; they shall walk and not faint.'[15] Many other such passages may be found showing the happiness of those who love the Lord's coming.

It is evident that no one can deduce the exact length of the time. In fact, the Gospel says:[16] 'Of that day and hour no one knoweth'; and I say, with due regard for the limitations of my mind, that neither the day nor the month nor the year of that coming can be known, but by noticing and believing the existing signs of the coming, it befits me to hope for it and to distribute this food to believers that they may hope for and love the coming of Him who said: 'When you shall see all these things, know ye that it is nigh, even at the doors.' Therefore, the signs which are given in the Gospel and in prophecy and which are fulfilled in us show forth the coming of the Lord. For, those who seek to know or to traduce seek in vain to understand the days and the years by computation, since it is written: 'And unless those days

---

12 2 Tim. 4.8.
13 Matt. 13.43.
14 Isa. 60.2.
15 Isa. 40.31.
16 Matt. 24.36,33,22.

had been shortened no flesh should be saved, but for the sake of the elect those days shall be shortened.' Certainly, there is no computation for a time which is to be shortened by the Lord who has established the times, but we know that the coming is at hand by the fact that we see the fulfillment of certain signs of that coming which have been accomplished. Again He says: 'But when these things begin to come to pass, be revived and lift up your heads because your redemption is at hand.'[17] The signs which He told them to look for are listed in the Gospel of Saint Luke: 'Jerusalem shall be trodden down by the Gentiles till the times of the nations be fulfilled.' This has happened and no one doubts that it has happened. And He goes on: 'And there shall be signs in the sun and in the moon and in the stars and upon the earth distress of nations.' Our very suffering forces us to admit, if our will refuses, that we are suffering these things, for it is well known that at one and the same time signs are seen by men in heaven[18] and distress of nations is suffered on earth. And he goes on: 'Men withering away for fear and expectation of what shall come upon the whole world.'[19] It is plain that there is no country, no place in our time which is not harassed or humbled according to the words 'for fear and expectation of what shall come upon the whole world,' and all the signs which the Gospel describes in the earlier verses[20] have in large measure been accomplished.

As to the words, 'And this Gospel shall be preached in the whole world and then shall the consummation come,'[21] this was rather[22] a promise made by the Lord that the Apostles should be witnesses of His name and resurrection 'in Jeru-

---

17 Luke 21.28.
18 A possible reference to an eclipse of the sun on July 19, 418, which was followed by a severe drought.
19 Luke 21.24-26.
20 Luke 21.8-12,16-26.
21 Matt. 24.14.
22 Goldbacher indicates a lacuna here, but the sense is complete.

salem and in Judea and in Samaria and even to the uttermost part of the earth,'[23] and the Apostle teaches by this authority: 'But I say: have they not heard? Yes, verily, their sound hath gone forth into all the earth and their words unto the ends of the whole world.'[24] Again he says: 'For the hope that is laid up for you, which you have heard before in the word of truth of the Gospel, which is come unto you, as also it is in the whole world and bringeth forth fruit and groweth.'[25] But the faith introduced by the Apostles among the Gentiles had many persecutors and, although retained, it was slower in growing strong, giving the fulfillment of the words: 'But before all these things they will lay hands on you and persecute you, delivering you up to the synagogues and into prisons, dragging you before kings and governors for my name's sake,'[26] and that word also shall be fulfilled: 'And thou shalt quickly be rebuilt by those by whom thou hast been destroyed.'[27] For, as soon as we began, by the will of God, to have most clement Christian emperors, the faith which had previously increased slowly because of persecution grew from age to age, and under Christian kings the Gospel of Christ little by little made its appearance everywhere.

As to the *Commentary* on the weeks of blessed Daniel,[28] although it was made by our holy fellow priest, Jerome, in the manner handed down by the learned men of the churches, it leaves the reader hanging in the air.[29] If our fellow priest, learned man that he is, says it is dangerous to judge among opinions of the masters in the churches,[30] how much less possible is it for the reader to do what the master shrinks

---

23 Acts 1.8.
24 Rom. 10.18; Ps. 18.5.
25 Col. 1.5.6.
26 Luke 21.12.
27 The origin of this quotation is unknown.
28 Dan. 9.24-27.
29 A manifest lacuna after *lectorem* has been supplied by the editors with *suspendit*.
30 Jerome, *Commentary on Daniel* 9.24, in *PL* 25.542.34-36.

from doing! But we believe what the Lord says: 'that heaven and earth shall pass but one jot or one tittle shall not pass of the law till all be fulfilled.'[31] I wonder, then, how the mystery of weeks is accomplished by the time of the birth and Passion of Christ, since the Prophet, speaking thus of the half of the week, says: 'In the half of the week my sacrifice and supplication shall be taken away and the abomination of desolation shall last until the sacrifice.'[32] If, then, this abomination has come to pass, how does the Lord warn us, saying: 'When you shall see the abomination of desolation which was spoken of by Daniel the prophet, standing in the holy place, he that readeth let him understand'?[33]

I have written your Charity this statement of what I think, not wishing to show disesteem of the request of your Blessedness. Be so kind when you answer as to instruct and rejoice us more fully with the word of your grace.

199. Augustine gives greeting in the Lord to the blessed lord, Hesychius,[1] his brother and fellow bishop, worthy of respect and esteem (c. 419)

On the End of the World

Chapter 1

I have received the letter of your Reverence in which you urge on us the great good of loving and longing for the

---

31 Matt. 5.18.
32 Cf. Dan. 9.27.
33 Matt. 24.15; Mark 13.14; Dan. 9.27.

1 Cf. Letter 197 n. 2. This letter is an answer to Letter 198.

coming of our Saviour. In this you act like the good servant of the master of the household who is eager for his lord's gain and who wishes to have many sharers in the love which burns so brightly and constantly in you. Examining, therefore, the passage you quoted from the Apostle where he said that the Lord would render a crown of justice not only to him but to all who love His coming,[2] we live as uprightly as he and we pass through this world as pilgrims while our heart constantly expands with this love, and whether He comes sooner or later than He is expected, His coming is loved with faithful charity and longed for with pious affection. Doubtless, that servant who says: 'My lord is long a-coming,' and who strikes his fellow servants and eats and drinks with drunkards, does not love His coming; his mind is shown by his behavior.[3] The good master was careful, however briefly, to explain this conduct, that is, pride and riotous living, lest his saying 'My lord is long a-coming' be attributed to a longing for his Master in the same way as the Psalmist longed for Him when he said: 'My soul hath thirsted after the living God; when shall I come and appear before the face of God?'[4] For, by saying 'When shall I come?' he showed his impatience at the delay, because, even though it be quickened in time, it seems slow to his longing. But, how is His coming slow or how is it far in the future when the very Apostles, while they were still in the flesh, said: 'It is the last hour,'[5] although they heard the Lord say: 'It is not for you to know the times'? Therefore, they did not know this any more than we know it —I am speaking for myself and for those who share this lack of knowledge with me—yet, those to whom He said: 'It is not for you to know the times which the Father hath

---

2 2 Tim. 4.8.
3 Matt. 24.48,49.
4 Ps. 41.3.
5 1 John 2.18.

put in his own power,'[6] loved His coming and gave their fellow servants meat in due season; did not strike them by lording it over them, nor revel with the lovers of the world, saying: 'My lord is long a-coming.'[7]

Chapter 2

Therefore, not to know the times is something different from decay of morals and love of vice. For, when the Apostle Paul said: 'Be not easily moved from your mind nor be frighted, neither by word nor by epistle as sent from us, as if the day of the Lord were at hand,'[1] he obviously did not want them to believe those who thought the coming of the Lord was already at hand, but neither did he want them to be like the wicked servant and say: 'My lord is long a-coming,' and deliver themselves over to destruction by pride and riotous behavior. Thus, his desire that they should not listen to false rumors about the imminent approach of the last day was consistent with his wish that they should await the coming of their Lord fully prepared, with their loins girt and lamps burning.[2] He said to them: 'But you, brethren, are not in darkness that that day should overtake you as a thief, for all you are the children of light and children of the day; we are not of the night nor of darkness.'[3] On the other hand, the one who says: 'My lord is long a-coming,' and then strikes his fellow servants and eats and drinks with drunkards, is not of light but of darkness, and therefore that day will overtake him as a thief, because everyone ought to fear the last day of his life here. In whatever state his own

6 Acts 1.7.
7 Matt. 24.45,49,48.

1 2 Thess. 2.2.
2 Luke 12.35,36.
3 1 Thess. 5.4.5.

last day finds each one, in that state the last day of the
world will overtake him; such as he is on the day of his
death, such each one will be judged on that last day.

Chapter 3

What is written in the Gospel of St. Mark has a bearing
on this: 'Watch, for you know not when the lord of the
house cometh, at even or at midnight or at the cock crowing
or in the morning, lest coming on a sudden he find you sleeping. And what I say to you, I say to all: Watch.'[1] Who are
the 'all' to whom He says this if not His elect and His beloved,
the members of His body which is the Church?[2] Therefore,
He said if not only to those who then heard Him speaking,
but also to those who came after them and before us, as well
as to us and to those who will come after us until His final
coming. Is that day going to find all in this life or is anyone
likely to say that these words are also addressed to the dead,
when He says: 'Watch, lest coming on a sudden he find you
sleeping?' Why, then, does He say to all what concerns only
those who will then be living, unless it concerns all in the
way I have explained it? For that day will come to every
single one, when the day comes for him to go out of life, such
as he is, to be judged on the last day. For this reason, every
Christian ought to watch lest the coming of the Lord find him
unprepared. But that day will find unprepared anyone whom
the last day will find unprepared. This at least was certainly
clear to the Apostles, that the Lord was not likely to come
in their times, while they were still living here in the flesh,
yet who would doubt that they watched most carefully and
observed what He said to all, lest coming on a sudden He
find them unprepared?

1 Mark 13.35-37.
2 Col. 1.24.

Chapter 4

I do not quite understand how one ought to take what your Holiness wrote of the reason why the Lord said to the Apostles: 'It is not for you to know the times or moments which the Father hath put in his own power,' because He added at once: 'But you shall be witnesses unto me in Jerusalem and in Judea and in Samaria and even to the uttermost part of the earth.' You explain the meaning of this passage of Scripture by saying: 'He wished us to understand, therefore, that the Apostles were to be witnesses of His name and His resurrection, not of the end of the world.'[1] It is true He did not say: 'It is not for you to announce the times' but 'it is not for you to know.' If you want us to understand His saying: 'It is not for you to know' as if He had said: 'It is not for you to let others know,' that is, it is not for you to teach this, who of us would dare to teach or presume to know what neither God the Master taught the disciples by whom He was questioned face to face, nor the holy and great doctors have been able to teach the Church?

Chapter 5

Will you answer that the Apostle did not teach this, but the Prophets did? You said the things that are about to happen are made known by the words of the holy Prophets who have followed the divine will, as you say, 'in announcing future happenings to men before they happened.' But, if your Reverence says: 'In this there is sufficient matter for wonder whether God determined that the prophecies which He wished made should not be able to penetrate deeply into the understanding of man,' how much greater matter for

---

1 Cf. Letter 198.

wonder there would be if the Apostles were prevented from
knowing or teaching what the Prophets spoke to men! How
would it be possible for the Apostles not to understand the
teachings of the Prophets regarding those times now under
discussion if they are understood by us? Or, if the Apostles
did understand the prophecy of the length of time, how
could they fail to teach what they understood, when it is
through their preaching that the Prophets themselves, who
taught these things in their books, have become known?
Therefore, as they learned these matters from previous writings, others among the Gentiles to whom the Apostles commended the authority of the Prophets could learn them from
the same writings. Why were they told: 'It is not for you to
know'—or if it must be taken to mean it is not for you to
teach—'the times which the Father hath put in his own
power,' when they were teaching them and when those
writings through which these things are learned were becoming known through them? Hence, it is better to believe,
not that God was unwilling to make known what He wished
to have preached, but that He did not wish to have preached
what He saw was not useful for us to know.

Chapter 6

'Why, then,' you say, 'in this matter of knowing the times,
does the Lord Himself warn us when He says: "Who, thinkest
thou, is a faithful and wise servant whom his lord hath
appointed over his family to give them meat in season," '
and the rest? Indeed, He does not warn the good servant to
know the end of time, but to watch at all times by his good
works because he knows not the end of time; He does not
warn us to outdo the Apostles by searching into the 'times
which the Father hath put in his own power,' but to imitate

the Apostles by preparing our heart, because we know not when the lord cometh. But on this I have already said enough above. He censured the Jews for not knowing the time when He says: 'You hypocrites, you know how to discern the face of heaven', and the rest, because they did not know the time which He wished to know, that is, the time of His first coming, so that they might believe in Him and so await His second coming by watching for Him whenever that coming should be. Whoever does not recognize the first coming of the Lord cannot prepare himself for the second by believing in Him and watching faithfully lest that day overtake him in darkness as a thief,[1] whether He comes later or sooner than He is expected.

Chapter 7

As you note, the Apostle Paul says: 'In the last days shall come dangerous times,' and the rest. He surely is not here referring to the 'times which the Father hath put in his own power,' and he is not giving anyone to understand how long or how short those times will be which are admittedly to be the last. We should recall how long ago the Apostles said: 'Little children, it is the last hour.'[1]

Chapter 8

Again you remind us that the same Apostle said: 'But of times and moments you need not that I should write to you, for yourselves know perfectly that the day of the Lord shall

1 1 Thess. 5.4; 2 Peter 3.10.

1 1 John 2.18.

so come as a thief in the night. For when they shall say: Peace and security, then shall sudden destruction come upon them as the pains upon her that is with child and they shall not escape.' Here he did not say how much time would elapse before this happens, that is, he did not give the length or brevity of the age, but whatever interval and space of time intervenes this last evil will not come upon them until they have said: 'Peace and security.' By these words the Apostle seems to have removed either the hope or the fear of that last day from our times, for we do not see the lovers of this world, on whom destruction will come suddenly, now saying: 'Peace and security.'

Chapter 9

The Apostle himself shows quite clearly what it is enough for us to know when he says: 'Of times and moments we have no need to write to you' or, as other manuscript readings have it: 'You need not that we should write to you.'[1] He did not go on and say: 'For you yourselves know perfectly how much time remains,' but he said: 'For you yourselves know perfectly that the hour of the lord shall so come as a thief in the night.'[2] Those who do not wish to be overtaken by that hour as by a thief in the night have need to know this, that they may strive to be children of light and watch with well-prepared hearts. If it were necessary to know the length of time in order to avoid this misfortune, that is, of the hour of the Lord coming upon us unprepared like a thief, the Apostle would not have said that he had no need to write this, but, like a far-sighted teacher, he would rather

---

1 The latter is the Vulgate version.
2 1 Thess. 5.1,2.

have judged that he ought to write it to them. But now he shows that this is not needful for them, for whom it was enough to know that the hour of the Lord would come like a thief upon sleepers and the unready; and by knowing this they would themselves be ready and watchful however long a time He would be in coming. He also kept his own place, and, Apostle though he was, he did not presume to teach others what He knew the Lord had forbidden the Apostles: 'It is not for you to know.'

Chapter 10

You also quote what the same Apostle said: 'Remember you not that when I was yet with you I told you these things? And now you know what withholdeth that he may be revealed in his time. For the mystery of iniquity already worketh, only that he that now holdeth do hold until he be taken out of the way. And then that wicked one shall be revealed whom the Lord Jesus shall kill with the spirit of his mouth.'[1] Would that you had not only quoted but had also deigned to expound these words, for, though they are so obscure and so mystical in meaning, it does not appear that he said anything about fixed time or that he revealed any length or interval of time. He says: 'that he may be revealed in his time,' but he does not say how long it will be before this happens. What the mystery of iniquity is is variously understood by one and another, but how long it will work is a secret. The Apostle did not say this as a man outside the number of those to whom it was said: 'It is not for you to know the times,' for, although he was not yet among them when this was said to them, we do not doubt that he is their colleague and a member of their group.

---

1 2 Thess. 2.5-8.

Chapter 11

Likewise, in what follows: 'Only that he that now holdeth do hold until he be taken out of the way, and then that wicked one shall be revealed whom the Lord Jesus shall kill with the spirit of his mouth,' he teaches us openly that Antichrist will come, and although he seems to have described him in somewhat clearer terms as due to be killed by the breath of the mouth of the Lord Jesus Christ, he does not say, even obscurely, how long it will be before this happens. Who he is 'that now holdeth,' or what he holds, or what is meant by 'taken out of the way,' each one can work out for himself so as to understand or have some inkling of it, according as he reads what is written in one way or another; but how long he holds or how long it will be before he is taken out of the way is wholly wrapt in secrecy.

Chapter 12

You also say: 'In like manner, the Lord, in the Gospel, reproaches the Jews, saying: "If thou also hadst known . . . the time of thy visitation, perhaps thou shouldest have remained, but now these things are hidden from thy eyes." ' But this refers to the time of the first coming of the Lord, not of the second which is now in question. Obviously, it was of His second coming, not of the first, that He said: 'It is not for you to know the times,' for the Apostles had asked Him about the coming they hoped for, not the one they then witnessed. If the Jews had known His first coming, 'they would never have crucified the Lord of glory,'[1] and thus they could have escaped destruction and might have remained. As to His words to them: 'The time is accomplished, do penance,

---

1 1 Cor. 2.8.

believe in the Gospel,' you yourself have affirmed that they were said of the time of the Jews which was to come after a few years, and we now know that it is past by the destruction of the city in which their realm had been established.

Chapter 13

From what your Reverence next quoted from Daniel about the slaying of the beast, and the power of the other beasts, and the Son of man coming with the clouds of heaven in the midst of these happenings, it is plain that you speak to those who are versed in the Scripture. But, if you will be so kind as to explain how those passages have any bearing on our knowledge of the length of time which is to elapse before the Saviour's coming, I will confess with great thankfulness that the Lord's words, 'It is not for you to know,' were addressed only to the Apostles, not to their followers who are to know.

Chapter 14

According to your holy advice, the Lord's coming is to be loved and hoped for, and, as you say, the happiness of those who love it is great, as shown by the testimony of the Apostle whose words you thus quote: 'As to the rest, there is laid up for me a crown of justice which the Lord, the just judge, will render to me in that day. And not only to me but to them also that love the Lord's coming.' And then, also, as you recite from the Gospel, 'the just shall shine as the sun in the kingdom of their Father,' and, as the Prophet says, 'For behold darkness shall cover the earth and a mist the people, but the Lord shall arise upon thee and his glory shall be seen upon thee'; he likewise says: 'But they that hope in the

Lord shall renew their strength; they shall take wings as eagles, they shall run and not be weary, they shall walk and not faint.'

Chapter 15

All this you repeat with great piety and truth, praising the happiness of those who love the coming of the Lord. But those to whom the Apostle said: 'Be not easily moved from your mind . . . as if the day of the Lord were at hand,'[1] evidently loved the Lord's coming, and the purpose of the Doctor of the Gentiles in saying this was not to break them away from the love which burned in them; rather, he did not want them to put their faith in those from whom they heard that the day of the Lord was at hand, lest, perhaps, when the time had passed within which they had thought He would come, and they saw that He had not come, they might think the other promises made to them were also false, and might despair of the mercy of faith itself. Therefore, it is not the one who asserts that He is near nor the one who asserts that He is not near who loves the coming of the Lord, but the one who waits for Him, whether He be near or far, with sincere faith, firm hope and ardent love. For, if love of the Lord is in proportion to the belief and profession that He will come soon, then those who said that His coming was at hand loved Him more than those whom the Apostle warned not to believe them, or even than the Apostle himself who manifestly did not believe it.

Chapter 16

If my weakness is not troublesome to your Holiness, I beg you not to refuse to explain more clearly how you could say

---

1 2 Thess. 2.2.

that 'no one can deduce the exact length of the time,' as
this might not mean the same to me as it does to your
Charity, and any one of us might look in vain to be enlightened by the other. After saying that, you went on and
said: 'In fact, the Gospel says: "of that day and hour no one
knoweth," but I,' you say, 'with due regard for the limitations
of my mind, say neither the day nor the month nor the year
of that coming can be known.' That sounds as if we cannot
know in what year He will come, but we can know in what
week or decade of years, as if it were possible to assign it
with certainty to this or that period of seven years, this or
that period of ten years. But, if not even this can be known,
I ask whether at least the time of His coming can be defined
so as to say that He will come, for instance, in the next fifty
or a hundred years, or any other number of years more or less,
but that we do not know in which of these years He will come.
If that is how you have understood it, it is a great thing to
understand. What I ask is that you would kindly impart your
knowledge to us, citing the proper sources from which you
have been able to work it out; if you do not claim this
knowledge, then your opinion is the same as mine.

Chapter 17

All of us who believe see that those times are indeed the
last by the appearance of many signs in nature which we
read that the Lord foretold. If we take a period of a thousand
years,[1] and if the end of that period were the end of the
world, we could say that it was the ultimate end of time or
also the last day because it is written: 'For a thousand years
in thy sight are but as one day,'[2] so that anything that was
done during that thousand years could be spoken of as done

---

1 Apoc. 20.4-7.
2 Ps. 89.4; 2 Peter 3.8.

at the end of time or on the last day. I repeat what must
often be said on this question: let us recall how long ago
the blessed Evangelist, John, said: 'It is the last hour.'[3] If
we had been alive then and had heard this, how could we
have believed that so many years would pass after it, and
would we not rather have hoped that the Lord would come
while John was still present in the body? For he did not say:
'It is the last of time, or the last year or month or day,' but
'It is the last hour', and see what a long hour it is! He did
not lie, however, but we must understand that he used the
word 'hour' instead of 'time.' Some explain this by setting up
a period of 6,000 years as one day, and they divide it into
twelve parts like hours, so that the last hour seems to consist
of the last 500 years, and they say that John was speaking of
these years when he said it was the last hour.

Chapter 18

But knowing something and surmising it are two different
things. If 6,000 years is to be taken as one day, why is one
hour a twelfth of it and not rather a twenty-fourth, that is,
not 500 but 250 years? For the whole day is more truly spoken
of as the whole course of the sun, not from east to west but
from east to east where it rises again after the whole day is
over; that is, in twenty-four hours. According to that reckoning, the last hour is found to be past by at least seventy years[1]
from the time John said that, and the end of the world has
not yet come. Besides, if we look carefully into Church history,
we find that the Apostle John died long before the completion
of 5,500 years from the beginning of the human race. It was

3 1 John 2.18.

1 It works out to sixty-eight years, which is near enough; St. John wrote
his Epistle in A.D. 99.

not yet the last hour if the twelfth part of 6,000 years, that is, 500 years, is taken as the length of one hour. Moreover, if we follow the Scriptures and take a thousand years as one day, then the last hour of so long a day is even further past, I do not say if we take one-twenty-fourth of it, which is a little over forty, but if we suppose a twelfth part of it which has twice as many years. Therefore, it is more consistent to believe that the Apostle used 'hour' for 'time,' but how long that hour is we do not know, because it is not for us to 'know the times which the Father hath put in his own power,' although we certainly know that last hour much better than those who preceded us, from the time when it began to be the last hour of the day.

Chapter 19

I do not understand what your Reverence means by saying that the exact time cannot be computed, so as to define in what year the end will come, because, according to the promise of the Lord, those days will be shortened. If they will be so shortened as to become fewer rather than more, I ask you, according to what truth would they have been more if they had not been shortened? You think that the weeks of holy Daniel do not refer to the first coming of the Lord, as the majority do, but to the second. Will they then be shortened so that there will be one less week in that number, thus falsifying the prophecy which had defined the number of weeks so carefully that it said a certain event would occur even in the middle of a week? I find it surprising that the prophecy of Daniel is annulled by the prophecy of Christ. What sort of prophecy is that which makes us think that Daniel, or, rather, the angel from whom he learned it, did not know that the Lord would shorten those days and erred in what he said, or that he did know it indeed, but lied to the one whom he was instructing? If that is nonsense, why do we not rather believe that Daniel prophesied so many weeks according to the reckoning that the Lord would shorten those days, if that number of years does refer to the second coming of Christ? But I do not see how that can be proved.

Chapter 20

Finally, if those weeks foretell the coming of the Lord, it is much surer and safer to say that it will occur within seventy or, at most, within a hundred years. There are 490 years in seventy weeks, but from the birth of the Lord down to the present we count about 420; from His Resurrection or Ascension, 390, more or less. Thus, if we count from His birth, there are seventy years left; if from His Passion, about one hundred remain, within which all those weeks of Daniel will be completed if they are a prophecy of His final coming. Hence, if anyone says: 'It will happen within so many years,' he will be wrong if it happens beyond them; but because the times will be shortened, it will be possible for them to be less, not more. Therefore, it is correct to say: 'It will happen within such a time,' because it will be true however much the time is shortened; for, if that shortening is understood in the sense of fewer years, it does not allow of the day of the Lord coming after that time, but it is more and more true of the shortened time the fewer those years will be. Hence, that shortening does not disturb the computer who defines it so as to say that the day of the Lord will come within so many years; it helps him, instead, because the greater the reduction in the number of those days, the more the coming will occur within them and will not possibly occur beyond them. Thus, what is so defined will be true if we say: 'It will happen within so many years,' although we do not know the year in which it will happen.

Chapter 21

Consequently, the whole question comes down to this: whether the weeks of Daniel were fulfilled by the first coming of the Lord, or foretold the end of the world, or refer to both; for there are some authorities, well versed in this matter, who say that they were fulfilled at the time of the first coming of Christ and that they are to be fulfilled again by the same number to the end of the world. For my part, I see that if the first coming did not fulfill them, the second must necessarily do so, since the prophecy cannot be falsified. If it was fulfilled at the time of the first coming, there is no obligation to believe that it will be fulfilled again at the end of the world. This point of view, then, is uncertain even if it is true, and we should neither deny nor assume that it will be so. It remains, then, that if anyone wishes to insist on believing that the prophecy is to be fulfilled at the end of the world, he should exert himself to the best of his ability and prove, if he can, that it was not fulfilled at the first coming of the Lord, contrary to the teachings of so many expounders of the divine writings, who prove that it was fulfilled, not only by reckoning the time, but also by the very circumstances of it. Especially do they adduce what is written in the prophecy: 'The Saint of saints shall be anointed,' or, as the Hebrew versions of the same prophecy say more explicitly: 'Christ shall be slain and shall not be theirs,'[1] that is, He will not belong to their city because He was cast off by the Jews who did believe that He was their Saviour and Redeemer, and therefore it was possible for them to kill Him. But Christ is not to be anointed or killed at the

---

1 Dan. 9.24,26.

end of the world, which prevents us from believing that this prophecy of Daniel is not yet fulfilled but that its fulfillment is to be looked for then.

Chapter 22

Considering the signs mentioned by Gospel and prophecy which we see happening, would anyone deny that we ought to hope for the proximate coming of the Lord? Manifestly, it is nearer and nearer every day. But the exact span of the nearness, that, as we said, 'is not for you to know.' Notice when the Apostle said this: 'For our salvation is nearer than when we believed. The night is past and the day is at hand,'[1] and look how many years have passed! Yet, what he said was not untrue. How much more probable is it to say now that the coming of the Lord is near when there has been such an increase of time toward the end! Certainly, the Apostle said: 'The Spirit manifestly saith that in the last times some shall depart from the faith.'[2] Obviously, those were not yet the times of heretics such as he describes them in the same sentence, but they have now come. According to this, we seem to be in the last times and the heretics seem to be a warning of the end of the world. Likewise, he says in another place: 'Know also this: that in the last days shall come on savage times'—or, as another version has it: dangerous times —and then he describes what they will be like, saying: 'Men shall be lovers of themselves, lovers of money, haughty, proud, blasphemous, disobedient to parents, ungrateful, wicked, irreligious, without affection, slanderers, incontinent, unmerciful, without kindness, traitors, stubborn, blind, lovers of pleasures more than of God, having an appearance of godliness but denying the power thereof.' I wonder if such men

---

1 Rom. 13.11,12.
2 1 Tim. 4.1.

have ever been lacking. Finally, he goes on and speaks of them
as they then were: 'Now these avoid, for of these are they
who creep into houses.' He does not say: 'they will creep,'
as he said above: 'there will come on dangerous times,' but
he says: they creep into houses and lead captive silly women';[3]
he does not say: 'they will lead' or 'they are likely to lead,'
but they now lead.

Chapter 23

We are not to think that in this passage he used his verbs
in the present tense for the future, because, in fact, he was
warning his correspondent to avoid these persons. Yet, he
had a purpose in saying: 'In the last times shall come on
dangerous days,' and he proved that the times will be
dangerous by prophesying that men will be such, if for no
other reason than because they will be more and more
numerous as the end draws near. We see that they are numerous at present. But what does that signify if they will be
even more numerous after us and most numerous of all when
the end itself is imminent, although it is not known how far
off it is? Indeed, those last days were spoken of even in the
first days of the Apostles when the Lord's Ascension into
heaven was a recent happening; when on the day of Pentecost
He had sent the promised Holy Spirit; when some were
amazed and wondered at men speaking tongues which they
had not learned, while others mocked, saying that they were
full of new wine.[1] On that day, Peter, speaking to those who
were variously affected by this portent, said: 'For these are
not drunk, as you suppose, seeing that it is but the third
hour of the day. But know you that this is that which was

3 2 Tim. 3.1-6.

1 Acts 2.1-14.

spoken of by the Prophet: It shall come to pass in the last days, saith the Lord, I will pour out of my Spirit upon all flesh,'[2] and the rest.

Chapter 24

Therefore, there were last days even then; how much more now, even if there remained as many days to the end as have already passed from the Ascension of the Lord to this day, or even if there remain something over, more or less! Manifestly, we do not know this, because it is not for us 'to know the times which the Father hath put in his own power,' although we do know that we, like the Apostles, are living in last times, last days, a last hour, and this is much more so of those who lived after them and before us, much more so of us, and much more of those who will come after us than of us, until the time comes, so to speak, of the last, and finally of that very last moment which the Lord referred to when He said: 'And I will raise him up in the last day.'[1] But how far off that is cannot be known.

Chapter 25

The future signs, which, as your Holiness remarked, are foretold in the Gospel according to Luke, are the same as those in Matthew and Mark.[1] These three tell what the Lord said in answer to His disciples who had asked when the events which He had foretold of the destruction of the Temple would come to pass, and what was to be the sign of

2 Acts 2.15-17; Joel 2.28.

1 John 6.40.

1 Matt. 24.4-33; Mark 13.5-29.

His coming and of the end of the world.[2] There is no dis-
crepancy in the Gospels as to facts, although one tells one
detail which another passes over or describes differently;
rather, they supplement each other when compared, and
thus give direction to the mind of the reader. But it would
take too long to discuss them all now. To their questions the
Lord replied by telling what was to happen from that time
on, whether of the destruction of Jerusalem, which had given
rise to their inquiry, or of His coming in the Church in which
He does not cease to come until the end—for He is recognized
when He comes to His own, while His members are daily
born, and of this coming He said: 'Hereafter you shall see
the Son of man coming in the clouds,'[3] of which clouds the
Prophet said: 'I will command my clouds not to rain upon it'[4]
—or, finally, of the end itself at which He will appear 'to
judge the living and the dead.'[5]

Chapter 26

Since He gives the signs which refer to these three events,
that is, to the destruction of the city, to His coming in His
body which is the Church,[1] and to His coming in His own
Person as the head of the Church, it requires careful consideration to distinguish which of these signs refer to each
of these three. Otherwise, we might think that the signs
which belong to the destruction of Jerusalem are to be referred to the end of the world; or, on the other hand, we
might assert that what refers to the end of the world is a
prophecy of the destruction of the city; or we might say that

---

2 Matt. 24.1-3; Mark 13.1-4; Luke 21.5-7.
3 Matt. 26.64.
4 Isa. 5.6.
5 2 Tim. 4.1.

1 Eph. 1.22,23; Col. 1.24.

what points to His coming in His body which is the Church is a sign of His last coming in His Body which is the head of the Church; or, again, we might affirm that what refers to His final coming in person belongs to that coming which is in the Church. In all these details, some are plain, but others are so obscure that it would either be hard to distinguish them or rash to pronounce on them so long as they are not understood.

Chapter 27

Anyone can see that when He says: 'When you shall see Jerusalem compassed about with an army, then know that the desolation thereof is at hand,'[1] He refers to that city. Again, anyone can see that these words refer to the last coming of the Lord when He says: 'When you shall see these things come to pass, know that the kingdom of God is at hand.'[2] But, when He says: 'Woe to them that are with child and that give suck in those days. But pray that your flight be not in the winter or on the sabbath, for there shall be great tribulation, such as hath not been seen from the beginning of the world, neither shall be,'[3] this passage is so phrased in Matthew and Mark that it is uncertain whether it is to be understood of the destruction of the city or of the end of the world. It reads this way in Mark: 'And woe to them that are with child and that give suck in those days. But pray ye that these things happen not in winter. For in those days shall be such tribulations as were not from the beginning of the creation which God created until now, neither shall be. And unless the Lord had shortened those days, no flesh shall be saved; but for the sake of the elect

1 Luke 21.20.
2 Luke 21.31.
3 Matt. 24.19-21.

which he hath chosen he hath shortened the days.'[4] This is
not different from Matthew. But Luke has so arranged it
that it seems to refer to the destruction of that city, for it
reads thus in his Gospel: 'But woe to them that are with
child and give suck in those days, for there shall be great
distress in the land and wrath upon this people; and they
shall fall by the edge of the sword and shall be led away
captives into all nations, and Jerusalem shall be trodden down
by the Gentiles till the times of the nations be fulfilled.'[5]

Chapter 28

But in the passage which precedes this, Matthew writes
thus: 'When therefore you shall see the abomination of
desolation which was spoken of by Daniel the prophet standing in the holy place, he that readeth, let him understand.
Then they that are in Judea, let them flee to the mountains,
and he that is on the house-top, let him not come down to
take anything out of his house, and he that is in the field,
let him not go back to take his coat. But woe to them that
are with child and that give suck in those days.'[1] Mark has
it thus: 'And when you shall see the abomination standing
where it ought not, he that readeth, let him understand. Then
let them that are in Judea flee unto the mountains, and let
him that is on the house-top not go down into the house nor
enter therein to take anything out of the house, and let him
that shall be in the field not turn back to take up his garment.
But woe to them that are with child and that give suck in
those days,'[2] and the rest. But Luke, in order to show that the

---

4 Mark 13.17-20.
5 Luke 21.23,24.

---

1 Matt. 24.15-19; Dan. 9.27.
2 Mark 13.14-17.

abomination of desolation which had been foretold by Daniel, would come to pass when Jerusalem was besieged, relates the words of the Lord in the same passage: 'And when you shall see Jerusalem compassed about with an army, then know that the desolation thereof is at hand.' Thus, the abomination of desolation of which those two Evangelists had spoken appears in this connection. Finally, he continues in the same strain as they: 'Then let those that are in Judea flee to the mountains,' but, instead of saying as they do: 'He that is on the house-top, let him not go down into the house nor enter therein to take anything out of the house,' he says: 'And let those that are in the midst thereof depart out,' to show that by those words of the other Evangelists haste in flight had been commanded. And instead of what they said: 'And let him that shall be in the field not turn back to take up his garment,' he says more plainly: 'And let those who are in the countries not enter into it, for these are the days of vengeance that all things may be fulfilled that are written.' Then he continues in the same way, so that it is quite clear that this passage of the Gospel refers to the same thing in all three: 'But woe to them that are with child and give suck in those days,' and the other words which bear on this point as I have already remarked above.[3]

Chapter 29

Thus, Luke made clear what could have been uncertain, that what was said of the abomination of desolation referred to the siege of Jerusalem, not to the end of the world; and also what was said about the shortening of the days for the sake of the elect, for, although he himself did not say exactly that, he did say other things quite plainly about this, by which

---

3 Luke 21.20-23.

he showed that the other two were referring to it. We must not doubt that there were elect of God among that people when Jerusalem was destroyed, men of the circumcision who had become or were about to become believers, chosen before the foundation of the world, for whose sake those days were shortened that the evils might be bearable. Some commentators, it seems to me, have aptly held that the evils mentioned are signified by the word 'days', as days are spoken of as evil in various places of the divine Scripture;[1] not that the days themselves are evil, but that what happens on them is evil. Therefore, they were said to be shortened because when God gave endurance they were felt less, and thus what was great became brief.

Chapter 30

But, whether that shortening of days is to be taken in that sense, because either they were reduced in number or they were shortened by a swifter course of the sun—there are some who think that days will be shorter in the future, as the day became longer at the prayer of Josue,[1]—the Evangelist Luke showed that this shortening of days and abomination of desolation referred to the destruction of Jerusalem, although he did not speak of both of them, while Matthew and Mark did; and he did this by adding other details to make it plainer, whereas they had spoken more obscurely. Josephus, who wrote a history of the Jews,[2] says that the evils which then befell that people are scarcely believable. Consequently, it is correct to say that such tribulation has not been since the beginning of creation, nor shall be. Even if there shall be such, or possibly greater,

1 Cf. Ps. 40.2; 48.6.

1 Josue 10.12-14.
2 Flavius Josephus (37-94), *History of the Jewish War* 6.3.3.

tribulation in the time of Antichrist, what is here said must
be referred to the Jewish people, that such or greater
tribulation will not befall them, for, if they are the first and
foremost to receive Antichrist, that people will rather cause
than suffer tribulation.

Chapter 31

There is no reason, then, for us to think that the weeks of
the Prophet Daniel were either falsified by the shortening of
the days or were not fully completed, but that they are to be
completed at the end of the world; for they were not completed before the Passion of the Lord. Those who think this
are correctly refuted by your pronouncement in which you
said: 'If, then, the abomination has come to pass, how does
the Lord warn us, saying: "When you shall see the abomination of desolation which was spoken of by Daniel the
prophet standing in the holy place, he that readeth let him
understand"?' These words of your Blessedness ought to set
right those who say that this prophecy had been fulfilled when
the Lord spoke, even before His Passion and Resurrection.
Those who say, as the Evangelist Luke bears witness most
plainly, that it came to pass when Jerusalem was destroyed,
ought to see what answer to make to those who think it will
happen at the end of the world or near the end. However,
this abomination of desolation is such an obscure saying
that it could be understood by men in more than one way.

Chapter 32

In regard to the saying, 'He that is on the house-top, let
him not come down to take anything out of his house, and
he that is in the field, let him not go back to take his coat,'

it can be suitably taken in a spiritual sense, namely, that in
all our trials each one must take care not to be overcome or
to come down from a spiritual height to a carnal life; or
that he who had progressed should not look back by turning
toward the past or failing to reach out to the future. But, if
this is true of every trial, how much greater care must be
prescribed in a trial such as that foretold for the city: 'Such
as hath not been from the beginning, neither shall be'; and if
for that, how much more still for that final tribulation which
is to come upon the whole world, that is, the Church spread
through the whole world! It is true that Luke does not
connect this with the time when the Lord was questioned
about His coming, as Matthew and Mark do, but he puts it
in another place where the Pharisees had asked Him when
the kingdom of God would come, and he relates that the
Lord said something similar: 'In that hour,' He said, 'he
that shall be on the house-top and his goods in the house,
let him not go down to take them away, and he that shall
be in the field, in like manner let him not return back.'[1]

Chapter 33

But we are now dealing with the reckoning of time
according to the weeks of Daniel, and if they were not
completed about the time of the first coming of the Lord,
and they are to be completed at the end, who could believe
that the Apostles did not know this, or that they did know
it but were forbidden to teach it? Of course, if this is the case,
it is useful for the Gentiles not to know what the Lord forbade
those whom He chose as teachers of the Gentiles to teach
them. But, if those weeks have been completed, because the
Saint of saints has been anointed, Christ has been slain, the

1 Luke 17.31.

sacrifice has been taken away, and the anointing has been taken away,[1] then, when the Apostles asked about the end of the world, the answer given was correct: 'It is not for you to know the times which the Father hath put in his own power,' since the times which they could know from the prophecy of Daniel did not refer to the end of the world about which they had asked.

Chapter 34

Have we, then, seen greater signs in heaven and on earth than have those who came before us? If we read the history of the nations, are not such portents found to have happened in heaven and on earth that some are not even credible? To pass over others which it would take too long to go into, when have we seen two suns, as those who lived before the Lord's coming in the flesh saw and described in writing? When have we seen the sun darkened as it was darkened when the Light of the world hung upon the cross? Unless, perhaps, we are to include among celestial portents eclipses of the sun and moon which astronomers have been wont to calculate and predict, because we have seen the full moon eclipsed fairly often, but the sun more rarely and in the dark of the moon, according to their reckoning. But there was no such eclipse of the sun when Christ was crucified, and therefore it was a miraculous and portentous happening. It happened, indeed, at the Pasch of the Jews, which was celebrated only at the full moon; now, according to the calculations of the astronomers, it is an assured fact that the sun cannot be eclipsed when the moon is full, and it does not always suffer eclipse when the moon is dark, but, according to the same calculations, it never does so at any other time. Therefore, if such

---

1 Dan. 9.24,26,27 (Septuagint).

prodigies appear—if they are not rather to be taken in a spiritual sense—they will appear when the end is so near that they must necessarily appear.

Chapter 35

As to wars, when has the earth not been scourged by them at different periods and places? To pass over too remote history, when the barbarians were everywhere invading Roman provinces in the reign of Gallienus,[1] how many of our brothers who were then alive do we think could have believed that the end was near, since this happened long after the Ascension of the Lord! Thus, we do not know what the nature of those signs will be when the end is really near at hand, if these present ones have not been so foretold that they should at least be understood in the Church. Certainly, there are two nations and two kingdoms, namely, one of Christ, the other of the Devil, of which it was possible to say: 'Nation shall rise against nation and kingdom against kingdom,'[2] which has not ceased to be the case since the words were uttered: 'Do penance, for the kingdom of heaven is at hand.'[3] Notice when that was said, and how many years have passed since that time, yet it was said with perfect truth. For in those last days the Lord came by the Virgin, and that would not be called the last hour[4] unless the kingdom of heaven were at hand, and so those things which the Lord predicted would happen at the approach of His kingdom do happen throughout this whole hour. As to how long a time this hour is to last, if it was said to the Apostles: 'It is not for you to know,' how much more should any mere man

1 Emperor from 260 to 268.
2 Mark 13.8; Matt. 24.7; Luke 21.10.
3 Matt. 3.2; 4.17.
4 Cf. 1 John 2.18.

such as I am recognize his limitations: 'not to be more wise than it behooveth to be wise!'[5]

Chapter 36

But, you say, our very suffering forces us to admit that the end is at hand when there is a fulfillment of what was foretold: 'Men withering away for fear and expectation of what shall come upon the whole world.' 'It is plain,' you say, 'that there is no country, no place in our time which is not harassed or humbled according to the words, "for fear and expectation of what shall come upon the whole world." ' If, then, these evils which the human race now suffers are clear signs that the Lord is about to come now, what becomes of the Apostle's words: 'When they shall say: Peace and security'?[1] For, when the Gospel said: 'Men withering away for fear and expectation,' it went on at once: 'For the powers of heaven shall be moved. And then shall they see the Son of man coming in a cloud with great power and majesty.'[2]

Chapter 37

Let us therefore see whether, perhaps, a better understanding of the things which are foretold in those words may not show that they are not being fulfilled now but are rather to come at a time when there will be tribulation in the whole world, so as to refer to the Church which will suffer tribulation throughout the world, but not to those who will afflict the Church. For these latter will say: 'Peace and security,'

---

5 Rom. 12.3.

---

1 1 Thess. 5.3.
2 Luke 21.26,27.

so that sudden destruction will come upon them and the coming of the Lord will overtake them as a thief in the night, while, on the other hand, those who love the manifestation of the Lord will rejoice and exult. But we see that these present evils which are considered so supreme and ultimate are common to both nations and both kingdoms, that is, of Christ and of the Devil; both good and bad are afflicted by them and there is no one to say: 'Peace and security'; everywhere, disasters happen or there is fear that they will happen. Yet, in the midst of these misfortunes, there are still people crowding to luxurious banquets, drunkenness is rife, avarice plies its trade, wanton songs shrill out, there are organs, flutes, lyres, harps, dice, many and various kinds of sound and spectacles. Is this withering away with fear and not, rather, reeking with lust? But those sons of darkness shall possess goods and shall use them more amply when they shall say: 'Peace and security.'

Chapter 38

But what of the very children 'of light and children of the day, that that day should overtake them as a thief'?[1] Do they not still 'use this world as if they used it not,' because they think with pious care of the saying: 'The time is short,'[2] even though this was said many years ago, in the times of the Apostles? Do not the majority of them still set out vines, build, buy, possess, hold offices, marry wives? I speak of those 'who wait for their lord when he shall return from the wedding,'[3] and who, although they do not refrain from carnal marriage, hearken, with obedient love, to the Apostle

---

1 1 Thess. 5.4,5.
2 1 Cor. 7.31,29.
3 Luke 12.36.

teaching them how wives should live with their husbands, husbands with wives, children with parents, parents with children, slaves with masters, masters with slaves.[4] Do not all these use this world in all these ways? They cultivate land, they sail ships, they acquire goods, they beget children, they fight wars, they manage their affairs. I think they will not be doing so when, as the Gospel foretells: 'There shall be signs in the sun, and in the moon, and in the stars, and upon the earth distress of nations by reason of the roaring of the sea and of the waves; men withering away for fear and expectation of what shall come upon the whole world, for the powers of heaven shall be moved.'[5]

Chapter 39

I think it is better to apply these things to the Church so that the Lord Jesus may not seem to have predicted, for the approach of His second coming, a magnified form of what has been accustomed to happen in this world even before His first coming, and that, when we fall into a panic over present happenings as if they were the ultimate and extreme of all things, we may not be laughed at by those who have read of more and worse things in the history of the world. The Church is the sun and the moon and the stars, to which it was said: 'Fair as the moon, bright as the sun.'[1] By her our Joseph is adored in this world as in Egypt, when He is raised from humble to high estate. Certainly, his mother could not adore that other Joseph, since she died before Jacob came to his son;[2] therefore, the truth of that prophetic

---

4 Eph. 5.22-6.9.
5 Luke 21.25,26.

---

1 Cant. 6.9.
2 Gen. 35.19; 46.1-7; 37.9-11.

dream was saved for its fulfillment in the Lord Christ. But, when 'the sun shall be darkened, and the moon shall not give her light, and the stars fall from heaven, and the powers of heaven shall be moved,'[3] as this passage is given by the other two Evangelists, the Church will not be manifest; for, when impious persecutors rage beyond measure, and when the fortune of this world seems to smile upon them and fear leaves them and they say: 'Peace and security,' then the stars shall fall from heaven and the powers of heaven shall be moved, when many who seemed to shine brilliantly with grace will yield to the persecutors and will fall, and even the strongest of the faithful will be shaken. Now, according to Matthew and Mark it is said that this will happen 'after the tribulation of those days,' not because these things will happen after the whole persecution has come to an end, but because the tribulation will precede so that the falling away of some may follow, and because this will happen through all those days, it will happen 'after the tribulation of those days,' yet it will be in the same days.

Chapter 40

By the words according to Luke, 'And upon the earth distress of nations,' He wishes us to understand, not the nations belonging to the seed of Abraham, 'in whom all nations shall be blessed,'[1] but the nations which shall stand on His left,[2] when all nations shall be gathered together before the Judge of the living and the dead.[3] In all nations there

---

3 Matt. 24.29; Mark 13.24,25.

---

1 Gen. 22.18; 26.4.
2 Matt. 25.33,32.
3 Acts 10.42.

will be two groups, one which oppresses, the other which is oppressed; one which says: 'Peace and security,' the other in which the sun is darkened and the moon does not give her light, from which the stars shall fall, and in which the powers of heaven are moved.

Chapter 41

'And then shall they see the Son of man coming in a cloud, with great power and majesty.'[1] As I see it, this could be taken in two ways: one, that He will come in the Church as in a cloud, as He continues to come now according to His word: 'Hereafter you shall see the Son of man sitting on the right hand of the power of God, and coming in the clouds of heaven';[2] and He comes with great power and majesty because His greater power and majesty will appear in the saints to whom He will give great power, so that they may not be overcome by such persecution. The other way in which He will come will be in His Body in which He sits at the right hand of the Father,[3] in which, also, He died and rose again and ascended into heaven, as it is written in the Acts of the Apostles: 'And when he had said these things, a cloud received him and he was taken up from their sight.' And because the angels said thereupon: 'He shall so come as you have seen him going away,'[4] we have reason to believe that He will come not only in the same Body but also in a cloud, since He will so come as He went away, and a cloud received Him as He went.

---

1 Luke 21.27; Matt. 24.30; Mark 13.26.
2 Matt. 26.64.
3 Rom. 8.34; Mark 16-19; Col. 3.1.
4 Acts 1.9,11.

Chapter 42

It is hard to decide which of these two views is preferable. The more ready sense would make anyone who hears or reads: 'And then shall they see the Son of man coming in a cloud with great power and majesty,' immediately understand it of His coming not in the Church but in His person, when He will come to judge the living and the dead. As the Scriptures are to be closely studied, and we are not to be satisfied with a general view of them, since they yield a changed meaning to our effort and demand a deeper insight, the sequence of passages must be carefully examined. For, when He had said: 'Then shall they see the Son of man coming in a cloud with great power and majesty,' He went on and said: 'But when these things begin to come to pass, look up and lift up your heads because your redemption is at hand. And he spoke to them a similitude: See the fig-tree and all the trees, when they now shoot forth their fruit, you know that summer is nigh. So also you, when you shall see these things come to pass, know that the kingdom of God is at hand.'[1] Thus, when He says: 'When you shall see these things come to pass,' what else are we to think they are but the ones mentioned above? But among these is His prediction: 'And then shall they see the Son of man coming in a cloud with great power and majesty.' Consequently, when He is seen thus, it will not yet be the kingdom of God, but it will be near.

Chapter 43

We see that the other two Evangelists keep to the same order. In Mark, when He had said: 'And the powers that are in heaven shall be moved,' He said: 'And then shall they see

---

1 Luke 21.28-31.

the Son of man coming in the clouds with great power and glory.' Then He adds something more than Luke had said: 'And then shall he send his angels and shall gather together his elect from the four winds, from the uttermost part of the earth to the uttermost part of heaven.' Then He mentions the fig-tree alone, where Luke had spoken of the fig-tree and other trees: 'Now of the fig-tree learn ye a parable: when the branch thereof is now tender and the leaves are come forth, you know that summer is very near; so you also, when you shall see these things come to pass, know ye that it is very nigh, even at the doors.'[1] What is the meaning of 'When you shall see these things come to pass' but the things which He spoke of above? And among these is that prediction: 'And then shall they see the Son of man coming in the clouds with great power and glory.' Therefore, this will not actually be the end, but the end will then be very near.

Chapter 44

Or are we to say that not all the details mentioned above are to be included when He says: 'When you shall see these things come to pass,' but that one of them, this one, for instance, is to be excepted, when He says: 'Then shall they see the Son of man coming,' and the rest? Certainly, that will be the end; it will not then be near. But Matthew makes it clear that everything mentioned is to be included without exception, for in his Gospel, after saying: 'The powers of heaven shall be moved,' he says: 'And then shall appear the sign of the Son of man in heaven: and then shall all the tribes of the earth mourn; and they shall see the Son of man coming in the clouds of heaven with much power and

---

1 Mark 13.25-29.

majesty. And he shall send his angels with a trumpet and a great voice, and they shall gather together his elect from the four winds, from the farthest parts of the heavens to the utmost bounds of them. And from the fig-tree learn a parable: When the branch thereof is now tender and the leaves come forth, you know that summer is nigh. So you also, when you shall see all these things, know ye that it is nigh, even at the doors.'[1]

Chapter 45

Therefore, we know that He is near when we see all of these things, not some of them; among which is this that the Son of man shall be seen coming, and He will send His angels, and He gathers together His elect from the four parts of the world, that is, from the whole world. He does this during the whole of this last hour, coming in His members as in the clouds, or in the whole Church itself, which is His Body, as in a cloud, 'bringing forth much fruit and growing over the whole world.'[1] This He does ever since He began to preach and to say: 'Do penance, for the kingdom of heaven is at hand.'[2] So, perhaps, if all the details of His coming which are mentioned by the three Evangelists are carefully compared and discussed, we may find that they refer to His daily coming in His Body, which is the Church; and of this coming He said: 'Hereafter you shall see the Son of man sitting on the right hand of the power of God, and coming in the clouds of heaven';[3] with the exception of those passages in which His final coming in person, when 'He shall judge the living and the dead,' is so promised by

---

1 Matt. 24.29-33.

---

1 Col. 1.6.
2 Matt. 3.2; 4.17.
3 Matt. 26.64; Mark 14.62.

Him that it is said to be at hand; and also the place at the
end of His speech according to Matthew, where the final
coming is so very evidently described, with certain signs by
which He shows that its nearness is to be recognized. In
Matthew His speech ends thus: 'And when the Son of man
shall come in his majesty, and all the angels with him, then
shall he sit upon the seat of his majesty; and all nations shall
be gathered together before him,' and the rest, up to the
place where He says: 'And these shall go into everlasting
punishment but the just into life everlasting.'[4] No one doubts
that this is a prophecy of Christ's final coming and of the
end of the world. As to the parable of the five wise and the
five foolish virgins,[5] there are some who wish to teach—and
their contention is not to be slighted—that it refers to Christ's
present coming which is effected through the Church. These
are things not to be lightly promised, lest something arise to
offer a valid contradiction; and this is especially so because
it has pleased God to test our minds by a kind of obscurity
in the divine utterance, with the result, for those who deal
with holy Scripture in matters of probability, that one is
impressed more deeply by one passage another by another;
and it may even happen to any one of them that he has
more understanding at one time, less at another.

Chapter 46

However, I do not know whether we can discover anything
more definite on this question—supposing we can do so by
any ability of reasoning—than what I wrote in my previous
letter about the time when the whole world will be filled
with the Gospel. I have not proved by sure authorities what

4 Matt. 25.31.32,46.
5 Matt. 25.1-12.

your Reverence thinks, namely, that this has already been brought about by the Apostles themselves. For there are among us, that is, in Africa, innumerable barbarian tribes among whom the Gospel has not yet been preached. We learn this by the daily evidence before our eyes of those who are taken captive from there, and are now subjected to slavery by the Romans. Nevertheless, a few years ago, some of them, but very few and far between, made their peace and were joined to Roman territory, so that they have no kings of their own, and are governed by Roman authority through prefects who are set over them, and these same prefects began about then to be Christians. Those in the interior, however, who are not under Roman authority are manifestly not in contact with the Christian religion in any of their members, yet it cannot rightly be said that the promise of God does not concern them.

Chapter 47

The Lord did not promise the Romans but all nations to the seed of Abraham, and He did this by means of an oath. According to this promise, it has already come to pass that some nations, not held under Roman power, have received the Gospel and have been joined to the Church which brings forth fruit and grows throughout the whole world. It still has room to bring forth fruit and grow until the fulfillment of the prophecy made of Christ under the figure of Solomon: 'He shall rule from sea to sea and from the river unto the ends of the earth';[1] 'from the river,' that is, where He was baptized,[2] because from there He began to preach the Gospel; but 'from sea to sea' means the whole earth with all its

---

1 Ps. 71.8.
2 Matt. 3.13-16; Mark 1.9.

inhabitants, because the universe is surrounded by the Ocean sea. But how otherwise shall this prophecy be fulfilled: 'All the nations, as many as thou hast made, shall come and adore before thee, O Lord?'[3] For they shall not come by moving from their own lands, but by believing in God in their own lands. Doubtless, it was of believers that the Lord said: 'No man can come to me unless it be given him by my Father,'[4] but the Prophet says: 'And they shall adore him, every man from his own place, all the islands of the Gentiles.'[5] 'All the islands,' he said, as if to say 'even all the islands,' showing by this that no part of the earth is excluded from having the Church, since none of the islands is left out, some of which are found in the Ocean, and of these we have heard that some have already received the Gospel. Thus, in some single islands there is a fulfillment of what was said: 'He shall rule from sea to sea': the sea by which every single island is surrounded, as is the case of the whole world, which is, in a sense, the greatest island of all because the Ocean also girds it about. It is to some of its shores in the West that we know the Church has come, and whatever shores it has not yet reached it will eventually reach, bringing forth fruit and growing.

Chapter 48

If, then, as the prophecy of truth cannot be falsified, it must needs be that all nations, as many as God has made, should adore Him, how shall they adore Him unless they call upon Him? But, 'how shall they call upon him in whom they have not believed? how shall they believe him of whom they have not heard? And how shall they hear without a

3 Ps. 85.9.
4 John 6.66.
5 Soph. 2.11.

preacher? and how shall they preach unless they be sent?"[1]
He sends His angels and gathers together His elect from the
four winds, that is, from the whole world. Therefore, the
Church must necessarily be found among the nations where
it does not yet exist, but it does not necessarily follow that all
who live there shall believe, for the promise was of all nations,
not all men of all nations: 'for all men have not faith.'[2] Therefore, each nation believes, among all 'who have been chosen
before the foundation of the world,'[3] but among the rest
none believe and they hate the believers. How else shall the
prophecy, 'You shall be hated by all nations for my name's
sake,'[4] be fulfilled, unless in all nations there are some
who hate and some whom they hate?

Chapter 49

How, then, was that prophecy fulfilled by the Apostles,
when there are still nations, as we are well assured, in which
there is only a beginning and some in which there is not yet
a beginning of fulfillment? It was not in this sense that He
said to the Apostles: 'You shall be witnesses unto me in
Jerusalem and in all Judea and Samaria, and even to the
uttermost part of the earth,'[1] as if they alone to whom He
spoke were to carry such a task to completion; similarly, He
seemed to say to them alone the words: 'Behold I am with
you even to the consummation of the world,'[2] yet who does
not know that He made this promise to the universal Church,

1 Rom. 10.14,15.
2 2 Thess. 3.2.
3 Eph. 1.4.
4 Matt. 24.9,10,22; Mark 13.13; Luke 21.17.

1 Acts 1.9.
2 Matt. 28.20.

which will last from now even to the consummation of the world by successive births and deaths? So, also, He told them something which does not concern them exclusively, yet it was said as if it did concern them alone: 'When you shall see all these things, know ye that it is nigh, even at the doors,'[3] yet whom does it concern if not those who will be alive when all things are fulfilled? How much more is this true of what was to be in large part carried out by them, although the same activity was reserved for their successors!

Chapter 50

As to the Apostle's saying: 'Have they not heard? Their sound hath gone forth into all the earth,'[1] although he used his verbs in the past tense, he spoke of what was going to be, not of what was over and past, just as the Prophet whom he adduces as witness did not say: 'Their sound will go forth into all the earth,' but, 'it hath gone forth.' Yet, it is certain that this had not yet happened, just as in the case of that other phrase, 'They have dug my hands and feet,'[2] we know that it came to pass long afterward. Lest we should believe that those were only prophetic utterances not apostolic ones, did not the same Apostle say: 'Which is the church of the living God, the pillar and ground of the truth. And evidently great is the mystery of godliness which was manifested in the flesh, was justified in the spirit, appeared unto angels, hath been preached unto the Gentiles, is believed in the world, is taken up in glory'?[3] Surely it is clear that what he said at

---

3 Matt. 24.33; Mark 13.29.

---

1 Rom. 10.18; Ps. 18.5.
2 Ps. 21.17.
3 1 Tim. 3.15,16.

the end has not yet been fulfilled, even in our time; how much less when he said it! Manifestly, it is the Church that will be taken up in glory when He says: 'Come, ye blessed of my Father, possess you the kingdom,'[4] yet what he spoke of as if it had taken place was certainly recognized as something still to come.

Chapter 51

It is much less surprising that he used his verbs in the present tense in that passage which, as you remarked, he repeated again and again: 'For the hope which is laid up for you in heaven, which you have heard before in the word of the truth of the Gospel, which is come unto you as also it is in the whole world, and bringeth forth fruit and groweth,'[1] although the Gospel did not yet embrace the whole world, he said that it brings forth fruit and grows in the whole world, in order to show how far it would extend in bearing fruit and growing. If, then, it is hidden from us when the whole world will be filled by the Church bringing forth fruit and growing, undoubtedly it is hidden from us when the end will be, but it certainly will not be before that.

Chapter 52

So, then, that I may disclose to you as to a holy man of God and a most sincere brother what I think on this matter, there is error to be avoided on both sides—as far as it can be avoided by man—that is, whether we believe that the Lord will come sooner or later than He actually will come. However, it seems to me that a man does not go wrong when

---

4 Matt. 25.34.

---

1 Col. 1.5,6. Cf. Letter 198.

he knows that he does not know something, but only when he thinks he knows something which he does not know. Let us therefore remove from our midst that evil servant who says in his heart: 'My lord is long a-coming,' and who tyrannizes over his fellow servants and spends his time reveling with drunkards,[1] for without any doubt such a one hates the coming of his Lord. So, when we have removed this evil servant, let us set before our eyes three good servants who manage the Lord's family with care and moderation, who ardently long for the coming of their Lord with watchful care and faithful love. One of them thinks the Lord will come sooner, another later, while the third admits his own ignorance on this matter. Although all are in agreement with the Gospel because all love the manifestation of the Lord, and wait for it longingly and watchfully, let us see which one is in closest agreement.

Chapter 53

The first says: 'Let us watch and pray because the Lord will come soon'; the second says: 'Let us watch and pray because this life is short and uncertain, although the Lord delays to come'; the third says: 'Let us watch and pray because this life is short and uncertain and we do not know the time when the Lord will come'; the Gospel says: 'Take ye heed, watch and pray, for ye know not when the time is.'[1] I ask you what else do we hear the third one saying but what we hear the Gospel saying? All, indeed, in their great desire for the kingdom of God wish the first one's thought to be true, but the second one denies this, while the third does not deny either of them but confesses that he does not know which of them speaks truly. Therefore, if the first one's

---

1 Matt. 24.48,49.

---

1 Mark 13.33.

prediction comes true, the second and third will rejoice with
him, for all love the manifestation of the Lord, and because
they love Him they will rejoice at His more speedy coming.
But if it does not come to pass, and it begins to look as if the
view of the second is more likely to be the true one, there is
reason to fear that those who believed what the first had
said may be troubled at the intervening delay and may begin
to think that the Lord's coming is not so much delayed as
non-existent. You can see how much damage to souls that
means. But, if these should be possessed of such great faith
that they turn to the teaching of the second, and await the
Lord's coming, however late, with fidelity and patience,
there will still be an abundance of taunts and insults and
mockeries on the part of enemies who may turn many weak
members from the Christian faith by saying that the promise
made to them of the kingdom is as spurious as the prophecy
of His speedy coming. On the other hand, those who believe
what the second one says, that the Lord's coming will be
delayed, will not be troubled in faith if it is proved false by
the Lord's speedy coming, but they will experience an
unexpected joy.

Chapter 54

Consequently, the one who says that the Lord will come
soon speaks of what is more desirable, but he is wrong at his
peril. Would that it were true, because it will be a cause of
trouble if it is not true! But the one who says that the Lord's
coming will be delayed, and who nevertheless believes in,
hopes for, and loves His coming, is happily in error if he is
wrong about His delay. He will have greater patience if it is
so; greater joy if it is not. Thus, for those who love the
manifestation of the Lord, it is sweeter to listen to the first,
safer to believe the second. But the one who admits that he

does not know which of these views is true hopes for the one, is resigned to the other, is wrong in neither of them. I beg you not to despise me for being such a one, because I love you when you affirm what I wish to be true. At the same time I am the more anxious that you should not be deluded the more I love what you promise, and the more I see the danger if you are wrong. Pardon me if I have been irksome to your holy feelings, but because it happens so seldom I take pleasure in speaking with you at greater length, at least through letters.

200. Augustine gives greeting in the Lord to Valerius,[1] his distinguished lord and justly renowned son, most dear in the love of Christ (End of 418 or beginning of 419)

I had been feeling downcast for a long time because I had written so often and had not deserved any answer from your Highness, when suddenly I received three letters from your Benignity, one not addressed to me individually, but given to me by my fellow bishop, Vindemialis,[2] and, not long afterward, two brought by my fellow priest, Firmus.[3] That holy man, bound to us by ties of most intimate friendship, as you may have heard from him, spoke to us at length about your Excellency, and described you so truthfully, as he knows you 'in the bowels of Christ,'[4] that he surpassed not only the letters brought me from the above-mentioned bishop and by himself, but even those we had complained of not receiving. And his account of you was all the more agreeable because

---

1 Count of Africa, a devout Christian and strong defender of orthodoxy against heresy. Cf., also, Letter 206.
2 Not otherwise known.
3 Cf. Letters 113, 134, 191, and 194.
4 Phil. 1.8.

he told me things you could not write back to me even if I asked them, for fear of being a preacher of your own praises, which holy Scripture forbids.[5] In fact, I am almost afraid to write these things to you, distinguished lord, justly renowned son, most dear in the love of Christ, lest I incur the suspicion of flattering you.

Imagine, then, what pleasure and joy it was to me to hear your praises in Christ, or, rather, the praises of Christ in you, from one who could not deceive me because of his trustworthiness nor fail to know you because of his friendship. We have also heard other details from others—not such full or reliable information, but still worth while—how sound and Catholic your faith is; how devout your hope of the world to come; what love you have for God and your brothers; how lowly of mind you are in your high offices; how your hope is not in the uncertainty of riches, but in the living God; how rich in good works you are;[6] what a rest and refuge your home is for the faithful, and what a terror for evil-doers; what care you take to prevent any of His old or newer enemies from cloaking themselves with the name of Christ, yet how well you provide for the salvation of these same enemies, while fighting their error. These and other such things, as I said, I am accustomed to hear from others, also, but now I have learned them in fuller and more authentic detail from the above-mentioned brother.

Moreover, in the matter of conjugal chastity, how could I hear of that, too, so as to be able to praise and love it in you, save from someone on intimate terms with you, who knew your life inside and out? I, too, should love to speak with you more familiarly and more at length about this virtue of yours which is God's gift. I know I shall not tire you if I send you something comprehensive which may keep you

5 Prov. 27.2.
6 1 Tim. 6.17,18.

longer with me as you read it. For I have also learned that
among your many and great cares you are ready and willing to
read my modest works, and that you take considerable pleasure in them when they happen to come into your hands,
even when they are not addressed to you. How much more
likely is it that you will receive with pleasure one addressed
to yourself[7] in which I speak to you as if you were present,
and that you will kindly give it your close attention! From
this letter, then, pass on to the book which I am sending
with it; in its introduction it will inform you more adequately
both why it was written and why it is especially sent to you.

201. *The august Emperors, Honorius and Theodosius,*[1] *give
greeting to Bishop Aurelius*[2] *(June 419)*

It had been decreed some time ago that Pelagius and
Caelestius, inventors of an unspeakable doctrine, should be
expelled from the city of Rome as sources of contamination
to Christian unity, lest by their vile persuasion they should
seduce untutored minds. In this our Clemency followed the
verdict of your Holiness,[3] according to which it was evident
that they had been condemned unanimously after a just
inquiry into their teaching. Whereas the deep-rooted evil of
persistence in wrong requires a doubling of the law, we have
recently sanctioned the decree that, if anyone who knows that

---

7 Book 1 of the treatise on *Marriage and Concupiscence.* Augustine was
accused by Julian of Eclanum, a Pelagian, of denying the divine
institution of marriage. He then added a second book in refutation of
the charge.

---

1 This was Theodosius II, who had succeeded Arcadius in 408 as
Emperor of the East.
2 Archbishop of Carthage.
3 Acts of the Synods of Milevis and Carthage in 416, confirmed by Pope
Innocent I, and of the plenary Council of Carthage in 418, confirmed
by Pope Zozimus, were promulgated by Aurelius in Africa.

they are in hiding in any part of the provinces delays to expel them or to inform on them, he is to be subject to the same penalty as being party to the offense.

As a special means of curbing the obstinacy of certain bishops who either further their vile arguments by tacit consent or fail to stamp them out by public attack, it will be fitting, very dear and loving Father, that the authority of your Holiness continue as long as the Christian devotion of all is agreed on the abolition of this perverted heresy. Therefore, by the requisite written notices, your Holiness will make known to all who are to be informed that this decree has been enjoined on them by the decree of your Holiness, to the effect that all those who impiously persist in refusing to subscribe to the condemnation of the above-mentioned heretics, whereby their true mind is made known, are to be punished by the loss of their bishoprics, are to be expelled from the cities, and are to be shut off forever from communion with the Church. Whereas we ourselves, in accord with the Synod of Nicaea,[4] adore God with sincere confession, as the Creator of all things and the Source of our imperial power, your Holiness will not suffer men of that accursed sect, who draw up new and unheard of theories in secret treatises to the injury of religion, to conceal a sacrilege which has once been condemned by public authority. One and the same guilt rests on those who connive by dissembling as well as on those who give dangerous support by not condemning the heresy.

May the Divine Power keep you safe for many years, dearest and most loving Father.[5]

Given at Ravenna on the fifth day before the Ides of June.[6]

A notice to the same effect has been sent to the holy bishop, Augustine.

---

4 Council of Nice, 325: the Nicene Creed is the summary of its conclusions.
5 In another handwriting.
6 June 9.

202. Jerome[1] gives greeting in Christ to Bishops Alypius and Augustine, his truly holy lords, worthy of due respect with all affection (End of 419)

The holy priest, Innocent, who is the bearer of this missive, did not deliver my letter of last year to your Worthiness, on the ground that he had no intention of returning to Africa. However, I thank God that it happened so, because it gave you a chance to overpower my silence by your letters. Every occasion is welcome to me which allows me to write to your Reverence, calling God to witness that if it were possible I would take the wings of a dove and fly to be enfolded in your embrace. This is always my sentiment because of your virtues, but it is especially so now that the heresy of Caelestius has been given its death blow on your initiative and by your combined efforts.[2] This heresy has so deeply infected the hearts of many that, even though they see themselves defeated and condemned, they do not eject the poison from their minds, but do the only thing left to them, which is to hate us through whom they think they have lost the freedom to teach heresy.

As to your inquiry whether I have written in answer to the books of Annianus,[3] the self-styled deacon of Celenderis,[4] who feeds copiously on the worthless words of another's blasphemy so as to serve them up again, you must know that it is only a short time since I received the books, copied

1 This was Jerome's last letter to Augustine. He died the following year.
2 Unfortunately not. Although Pelagius and Caelestius drop into oblivion after this condemnation, the heresy was carried on for many more years with unabated bitterness by Julian of Eclanum and his coterie.
3 He had translated some homilies of St. John Chrysostom into Latin, giving them a heretical slant. Jerome seems to hint here that Pelagius was using him as a puppet to spread his errors after he himself had been reduced to silence.
4 A town in Cilicia.

on small sheets of paper and sent by our holy brother, the priest Eusebius,[5] and since then I have been in such grief over the increasing illness and death of your holy and venerable daughter, Eustochium,[6] that I was almost minded to cast them aside. For 'he sticks in the same old mud'[7] and says nothing new, with his tinkling words like coins given to a beggar. However, we have made a great effort to force him into the open, so that when he tries to answer my letter, he will betray himself and reveal his blasphemies to all. He makes profession in this work of everything he denied having said at the unfortunate Council of Diospolis.[8] It is no great task to answer such childish nursery rhymes. But, if the Lord grants me life, and I have a good number of secretaries, I will answer in a few carefully composed paragraphs, not for the purpose of giving a final blow to a dead heresy, but in order to show up his clumsiness and his blasphemy in my own words. It would be better for your Holiness to do this so that I may not be forced to praise my own work against the heretic. Our mutual saintly children, Albina, Pinianus and Melania,[9] send you sincere greetings. I am giving this note to the holy priest, Innocent, to deliver from holy Bethlehem. Your granddaughter,[10] Paula, begs you to remember her in her grief, and sends you cordial greetings.

May the mercy of Christ our Lord keep you safe, and mindful of me, truly holy lords, and fathers universally loved and revered.

---

5 Not the Donatist bishop of Letters 34 and 35, but possibly a priest of Jerome's religious congregation.
6 Daughter of Paula; cf. Letter 172 n. 6.
7 Terence, *Phormio* 780.
8 Ancient Lydda; cf. Letters 176 n. 19 and 179 n. 18.
9 Cf. Letters 124, 125, and 126.
10 In a purely religious sense.

202A. Augustine gives greeting in the Lord to Optatus,[1] *saintly lord, his sincerely loved and cherished brother and fellow bishop (Beginning of 420)*

The religious priest, Saturninus,[2] has brought me a letter from your Reverence in which you ask me most earnestly for something which I do not yet possess. You tell me frankly the reason why you do this, which is that you think I have had an answer long ago to my request for advice. If only I had! God forbid that I should cheat you of a share in this bounty, knowing as I do your eager anticipation. But behold, if you will believe it, my dearest brother, five years have gone by since I sent my book[3] to the East, not out of presumption but for my own information, and thus far I have not deserved an answer with the solution of the question on which you want me to give a definite pronouncement. I would have sent you both if I had both.

But it does not seem right to me to send to anyone or to publish what I have without the other which as yet I have not, lest he[4] may still possibly answer me as I greatly long to have him do, and may then be angry that my inquiry, worked out with intricate reasoning, had been passed around and become generally known without his answer, which I still do not despair of, and may think that I have acted out of boastfulness rather than of a desire to help. It would be as if I had been able to raise a question which he could not solve, when perhaps he can and should be given time in which to do it, for I know that he is engaged on other tasks of more importance, which should not suffer delay.

That your Holiness may have some idea of this, also, give

---

1 Bishop of Tingitana in Mauretania. Cf. Letter 190.
2 Cf. Letter 142.
3 Letter 166, *On the Origin of the Human Soul* (written in 415).
4 Jerome, to whom he addressed Letter 165.

your attention for a little to what he wrote me another year[5] by a return bearer through whom I had written to him.[6] I am copying from his letter into this one: 'I have,' he says, 'been going through a difficult time when it has been better for me to keep silent than to speak; consequently, my studies have fallen off and, like Appius, my speech has been a snarl. So I have not been able to seize this occasion to answer the two books which you dedicated to my name, learned books and brilliant, with the full splendor of eloquence; not that I think there is anything to criticize in them, but, according to the blessed Apostle: "Let every man abound in his own sense, one after this manner, another after that." Certainly, you have set forth and discussed with your profound mind all that can be said, drawing from the fount of sacred Scripture. But I ask your Reverence to leave me for a while to the praise of your genius. You and I carry on discussion with the intention of learning, but the envious and, especially, the heretics, if they see us holding different opinions, will conclude falsely that this comes from ill feeling between us. It is my fixed determination to love you, support you, cherish you, marvel at you, and defend your opinions as my own. Certainly, in the dialogue which I published recently I made mention of your Blessedness, as was fitting; let us, then, make a greater effort to uproot this most baneful heresy from the Churches; a heresy which is always pretending to repent so as to have the chance of teaching in the Churches, because, if it came out into the full light of day, it would be driven out and would die.'[7]

Surely you see, venerable brother, that these words sent by one very dear to me, as an answer to my query, did not refuse that reply but made an excuse of the time, because he was obliged to expend his effort on other more urgent tasks.

---

5 Letter 172, in 416.
6 Orosius: cf. Letter 166.
7 Letter 172.

You see, too, how kindly disposed he is toward me and how he warns against allowing the envious and, especially, heretics to conclude falsely that what we do for the purpose of learning—with all due regard for charity and sincere friendship—proceeds from ill feeling. Therefore, if men read the work of both of us, both the questions I raised and the answers he gave to the questions—because it is also fitting that if the same question has been adequately explained I should give thanks for being enlightened—there will be no slight advantage in having this come to the knowledge of many, so that those who come after us may not only know what they ought to think on this matter, which has been argued between us with careful discussion, but may also learn from our example, by the mercy and favor of God, how mutual discussion for the sake of inquiry may be carried on without injury to abiding charity.

But if my treatise, in which a most obscure matter is read as a question only, without his answer, in which perhaps the solution will appear, should be made public and should be spread abroad, it might even reach those who, as the Apostle says, compare themselves with themselves,[8] and fail to understand the spirit in which we do what they cannot do in the same spirit. They do not see, either, my good will toward a friend whom I honor and hold dear for his mighty merits, since they do not see it as it is, but they describe it as it pleases them and as they suspect it to be, at the suggestion of their hatred. This is certainly something we ought to avoid as far as in us lies.

But if in spite of our unwillingness the work which we do not wish to publish should become known to those whom we do not wish it to reach, what will be left to us but to bear it with resignation as the will of God? I ought not to have written to anyone what I wanted to keep secret forever. And

---

8 2 Cor. 10.12.

if, which God forbid, through some accident or exigency he
never answers it and it is circulated, it will be useful to readers
because, even if they do not find what they are seeking, they
will certainly find out how these matters are to be examined
and how things not known are not to be rashly affirmed.
And according to what they read there they will make it a
point to consult whomever they can, not with contentious
discord but with zealous charity, until they either find what
they want or so sharpen their mind by the inquiry that they
know when no further inquiry is to be made. But at present,
as long as there is hope of a reply from the friend whom I
have consulted, I do not think my consultation should be
published, as least as far as it rests with me, and I would
give the same advice to your Charity, although you not only
asked for my work but earnestly desired me to send the
appended answer of the one whom I consulted. I would
certainly send it if I had it. But if, to borrow the words of
your Holiness as you wrote in your letter, you are seeking the
luminous demonstration of my wisdom, which the Author of
light has added to my life, as you write, and you do not
mean that consultation and inquiry of mine, because you
think that the solution of the matter which I inquired of
has come to me, and you are rather asking me to send that,
I would do it if things were as you think. I admit that up to
the present I have not discovered how the soul derives its sin
from Adam, which it is not allowed us to doubt, without being
itself derived from Adam, which is something to be carefully
inquired into rather than rashly affirmed.

Your letter has a reference to several elders and men trained
by learned priests whom you were not able to bring to an
understanding of your moderation and to an acceptance of
a statement full of truth, but you do not explain what
statement full of truth this is of yours which you could not
bring the elders and the men trained by learned priests to

accept. For, if these elders held or hold to the teaching received from the learned priests, how has a rustic and ill-instructed band of clerics raised up trouble for you in the matters in which they had been instructed by learned priests? But, if these elders or the band of clerics have deviated through malice from the teaching received from the learned priests, they ought rather to be set right and to be restrained from strife and contention by their authority. Again, when you say that as a fledgling and inexperienced teacher you feared to break down the traditions of such great teachers and bishops, and that you shrank from winning men over to a better course for fear of doing an injustice to the dead, what else do you give us to understand but that those whom you wished to convert refused to assent to a fledgling and inexperienced teacher because they were unwilling to forsake the traditions of great and learned bishops now dead? For the present I say nothing of them, but I have an extreme desire to know that statement of yours which you say is full of truth, and I do not mean the statement itself but your assertion of it.

You have made it sufficiently clear to me that you disagree with those who assert that all human souls are propagated and produced by successive generation from that one which was given to the first man, but by what reasoning or what evidences from the divine Scriptures you prove that this view is false I do not know, because your letter does not indicate it. Secondly, it is not quite clear to me as I read your letter, both the one you wrote previously to the brethren at Caesarea and the one you recently sent me, what view you hold in place of the one you disapprove; the only thing I see is that you believe, as you write, that God created, creates, and will create men, and that there is nothing in heaven or on earth which does not owe its existence and continuance to His creative act. Certainly, that is so true that no one should have any doubt of it. But you still have to explain from what sources God makes the souls which you say are not derived by generation: whether from something else—and if that is so, what it is—or entirely from nothing. God forbid that you should hold that opinion of Origen[9] and Priscillian[10] or any others who have the same idea, that souls are sent into earthly and mortal bodies in accord with their merits in a previous life. Apostolic authority is quite contrary to this opinion, where it speaks of Esau and Jacob and says that before they were born they had done nothing either good or evil.[11] Therefore, your opinion on this matter is partly if not wholly known to me, but the statement of it, that is, on what ground your opinion is to be taught as true, is altogether unknown to me.

For that reason I asked you in my former letter[12] to be so kind as to send me the treatise *On Faith* which you mentioned having written, and of which you complained that some priest had deceitfully signed his name to it; and I ask it again now, as also that you tell me what Scriptural proof you were able to apply to the solution of this question. In you letter to the Caesareans you say that you were pleased that even secular judges recognized the whole approval of truth, that they were holding session in accord with a universal appeal and were scrutinizing everything that concerned the faith, and that the Divine Power, as you write, had granted them an outpouring of faith, so that they uttered a stronger protestation and assertion according to their views which your Mediocrity—in comparison with them—kept in memory with the authority of weighty evidence. It is this authority of weighty evidence which I most eagerly desire to know.

---

9 Cf. Letter 40 n. 21.
10 Cf. Letter 36 n. 65.
11 Rom. 9.11.
12 Letter 190.

Certainly you seem to have followed up only one reason by which you refute your opponents, namely, that they deny that our souls are the work of God. If they believe this, their opinion is rightly judged worthy of condemnation. If they said this even of bodies, undoubtedly they should be held worthy of correction and detestation. What Christian would deny that the bodies of all who are born are the work of God? We do not deny that they are begotten of their parents because we confess that they are fashioned by God. When, therefore, anyone says that certain unique incorporeal seed of our souls is derived from parents, yet that souls are made of it by the work of God, it is not human supposition which is needed to refute this, it is the divine Scripture which has to be adduced as proof. An abundance of evidence could be available to you from the sacred book of canonical authority by which to prove that God creates souls, and by such evidence it is possible to refute those who deny that each separate soul at birth is the work of God, but not those who admit it, although these contend that souls are formed as bodies are by the action of God, but through generation by parents. To refute these latter you will need to seek out divine testimony which is certain, or, if you have already found it, you must send it to us as a duty of mutual charity, since we have not yet found it, although we seek it most eagerly to the limit of our ability.

Your brief inquiry at the end of the letter which you wrote to the brethren at Caesarea goes this way: 'I beseech you,' you say, 'to teach me as you ought, as is worthy of you, as befits prudent priests, to answer with your information one who is your son and disciple but lately and recently come to these mysteries with the help of God, and tell me whether I ought to hold the opinion which claims that the soul is derived from a root-stock and that all other souls come by generation from the first man, Adam, upon the whole race of men by some hidden origin and secret process, or whether that other formula is to be chosen and belief awarded to it, which all your brothers and priests stationed here hold and affirm, and which testifies and believes that God is and was and will be the Creator of all things and of all men.' You wish, then, that one or other of these two opinions which you proposed in your inquiry should be chosen, and that you should be told which one, a thing it would be possible to do if these two opinions were contrary to each other, so that if one were to be chosen the other would necessarily be rejected.

But now, if someone were not to choose one of those two but should answer that both are true, that is, that all souls come by generation from the first man, Adam, upon the whole race of men, and that God nevertheless is and was and will be the Creator of all things and of all men, would you think he ought to be contradicted? Shall we say to him: 'If souls are begotten from parents, God is not the Creator of all things, because He does not create souls'? If we say that, the answer will be: 'Therefore, since bodies are begotten from parents, God is not the Creator of all things, if for this reason we say that He does not make bodies.' Who would say that God is not the Creator of all human bodies but only of that one which He first fashioned from the earth, or at least of his wife, also, because He formed her from Adam's side, but not of the bodies of others, because we cannot deny that the bodies of the rest of men have come from theirs?

Hence, if your contest in this matter is with those who affirm the begetting of souls by generation from that first one, but deny that God makes and forms them, continue to refute them, convince them, correct them as strongly as you are able with the Lord's help. But if they admit a certain origin from the first man and subsequent generation by parents, and still affirm that individual souls are created and formed for individual persons by God, the source of all things, seek the answer to be made to them from the holy Scriptures above all, and let it not be ambiguous or susceptible of another meaning, or, if you have already found it, send it to us, as I asked you above. But if this still eludes you as it does me, continue just the same with all your strength to refute those who say that s‍ ‍ls are not of divine handiwork, as you said in your letter that they had at first muttered this among their less-known aberrations, but had subsequently withdrawn from your company and the service of the Church because of this insensate and impious opinion. Do you, then, uphold and defend against them by every means the view you set forth in the same letter: that God has created, creates, and will create souls, and that there is nothing in heaven or on earth that has not been formed and does not exist by His creative power. This is most truly and most rightly believed, stated, defended, proved about every possible variety of creature. God was and is and will be the Creator of all things and of all men, as you wrote at the end of your inquiry to our fellow bishops of the province of Caesarea, wherein you exhorted them, so to speak, rather to choose this statement of belief, following the example of all their brothers and fellow priests who are with you and who hold to this.

It is one thing to ask whether God is the Creator and Maker of all souls and bodies, which is the truth, or whether anything comes into existence in nature which He does not make, which is manifestly an erroneous opinion; but it is another thing to ask whether God creates human souls by generation or without generation, while recognizing that it is not lawful to doubt that they are created by Him. In this controversy I would have you restrained and on guard not to break down the theory of the generation of souls and thereby fall into the Pelagian heresy. For, if we say—and we say it with truth—that God is the Creator of human bodies whose generation is known to all, and not only of the first man or the first pair, but of all bodies begotten from them, I think it is easy to understand that those who defend the begetting of souls do not wish to break down the idea that we have our souls from that source, since God makes souls when He makes bodies, which we cannot deny are the result of generation, but other proofs must be looked for to refute those who believe in the generation of souls, if truth says they err. If it had been possible, an inquiry on this point should have been put to those of whom you wrote in the last letter you sent me that you shrank from converting men to the better course for fear of doing an injustice to the dead. You said that those dead were such great and such learned bishops that you, a fledgling and inexperienced teacher, feared to break down their traditions. Therefore, as far as I could learn, by whatever reasoning and evidence such great and learned men maintained that opinion about the begetting of souls,[13] which in your letter addressed to Caesarea you nevertheless called a new invention and an unheard-of dogma, showing no regard for their authority, it may indeed be an error; if so, we know that it is not a new one but an old and hoary one.

However, when certain reasons force us not unjustly to doubt in a given question, we ought not to doubt whether we ought to doubt. Indeed, on doubtful matters doubt should be maintained without doubt. You see how the Apostle does not hesitate to doubt about himself, when he was rapt to the third heaven, 'whether it was in the body or out of the body; 'whether it was the latter or the former, 'I know not,' he says, 'God knoweth.'[14] Why, then, should I not be allowed to doubt, so long as I do not know, whether my soul has come into this life by generation or without generation, provided I do not doubt that in either case it was created

---

13 Goldbacher indicates a lacuna here, and the first half of the sentence does seem to require a balancing phrase.
14 2 Cor. 12.2,3.

by the supreme and true God? Why should it not be permissible for me to say: 'I know that my soul derives its existence from the work of God, and, moreover, that it is the work of God, but whether by generation like the body, or without generation like the soul that was given to the first man: 'I know not, God knoweth.' Whichever one of these you wish me to affirm, I could if I knew. And if you yourself know, then you have in me one more eager to learn what I do not know than to teach what I do know. But if, like me, you do not know, then pray as I do that whether it be through some servant of His or by Himself, the Master who said to His disciples: 'But be not you called by man, Rabbi, for one is your master, Christ,'[15] may teach us, if, however, He knows that it is expedient for us to know such things, for He knows not only what He teaches, but also what it is expedient for us to learn.

I confess my covetousness to your Charity. Indeed, I covet to know this doctrine that you are seeking, but I should be much more anxious to know, if it were possible, when 'the desired of all nations'[16] shall appear, and when the kingdom of the saints will come to pass, than I am to know whence I began to come upon this earth. Yet, when His disciples, our Apostles, asked this of Him who knows all things, they received the answer: 'It is not for you to know the times which the Father hath put in his own power.'[17] What if He knows that it is not for us to know this, also, since He surely knows what it is useful for us to know? This, indeed, I know from Him, that 'it is not for us to know the times which the Father hath put in his own power.' But, whether it is for us to know the origin of souls, which I do not yet know, that is, whether it concerns us to know it, I do not know even

15 Matt. 23.8,10.
16 Aggeus 2.8.
17 Acts 1.7.

that. If I knew at least that it is not for us to know it, I would cease not only to affirm it, as long as I do not know, but also to inquire into it. But now, although it is a matter so dark and so deep that I am more on guard against rashness in teaching it than I am eager to learn it, I would like to know it, even so, if I could. And although what the holy Prophet said is much more necessary: 'O Lord, make me know my end'[18]—he did not say 'my beginning'—would that my beginning, also, which belongs to that question, might not be hidden from me!

I am not ungrateful to my Teacher, however, that I know this much about my own beginning: that the human soul is a spirit, not a body; that it is a rational or intellectual being; that it is not the nature of God, but rather a creature, to some extent mortal, in so far as it can be turned to a lower course and can be cut off from the life of God, a sharing in which is its happiness; and to some extent immortal, since it cannot lose the consciousness through which it experiences happiness or woe after this life. I know that it is not enclosed in the flesh as a reward or punishment for acts performed before it was joined to the flesh, but not for that reason does it exist in man 'without the uncleanness of sin, even if his life on earth be but one day.'[19] From this I know that no one is born of Adam through the succession of generation without sin; hence it is necessary for babies to be reborn in Christ by the grace of regeneration. I am glad to have learned and I assert that I know these things, both numerous and important, concerning the beginning or origin of our souls, for many of these truths belong to that knowledge which supports faith. Therefore, if in this question of the origin of souls I do not know whether God creates them for men by generation or without generation—I do not doubt that they are created

18 Ps. 38.5.
19 Job 14.4 (Septuagint).

by Him—I choose to know rather than not to know; but, as
long as I cannot know, it is better for me to doubt than to
dare to assert something as certain which might be contrary
to a truth of which perhaps I ought not to doubt.

Therefore, my good brother, since you consult me and you
wish me to declare for one of these two theories: whether
other souls are derived from the first man by generation as
bodies are, or are made by the Creator individually for
each individual, without generation like that of the first man
—for we do not deny that they are created in one or other
manner—allow me to consult you on how the soul contracts
original sin from a source from which it is not itself derived.
In order not to rush horribly into the horrible heresy of
Pelagius, we admit that all souls equally derive original sin
from Adam. If you do not know what I ask, be patient and
allow me not to know two things: both what you ask and
what I ask. But, if you do know what I ask, I will answer
what you wish me to answer when you enlighten me, because
I shall no longer fear any snare. I ask you, then, not to be
angry with me because I have not been able to make the
statement which you are seeking, but I have been able to
demonstrate what you are seeking. When you find what you
are seeking, do not hesitate to defend it.

I thought this much should be written to your Holiness,
because you think that the theory of the begetting of souls is
to be condemned. But, if I were answering those who maintain
it, I would probably show how ignorant they are of what
they think they know, and how great reason they have to
shrink from daring to make this statement.

Coming now to my friend's[20] answer which I enclose in
this letter, do not be disturbed at his mentioning two books[21]
I sent which he said he had no leisure time to answer: one

20 Jerome; cf. Letter 172.
21 Letters 166 and 167.

of them is on this question, but not both; in the other I had proposed another point to be examined and treated by him. In the advice and admonition he gives that I rather apply my effort to stamping out this deadly heresy from the Churches, he refers to that same Pelagian heresy which I urge you, my brother, with all my strength, to avoid with the utmost care, whenever you either think or argue about the origin of souls, so that the belief may not steal upon you that any soul at all, save that of the unique Mediator, was free from inheritance of Adam, that original sin under which we are bound when we are begotten but from which we are freed by our second birth.

203. Augustine gives greeting in the Lord to Largus,[1] his illustrious and distinguished lord and most cherished son (420)

I have received your Excellency's letter in which you ask me to write to you. You would not desire this unless you thought that I could write you something in which you could take pleasure and satisfaction; namely, that if you coveted the vanities of this world before you had tried them, you should despise them now that they are known. For the sweetness in them is deceptive, the toil fruitless, the fear constant, and the elation dangerous; you begin without forethought, you end with regret. Thus it is with everything that is pursued with more eagerness than prudence in the sad state of mortal life. But with devout souls hope is a different thing; different, too, the fruit of their toil, different the reward of perils. In this world it is impossible not to fear, not to grieve, not to labor, not to be in danger, but it is a matter of utmost im-

---

1 Proconsul in Africa 415. 418, and 419.

portance for what reason, with what hope, for what purpose a man suffers those trials. As for me, when I look at the lovers of this world, I do not know when wisdom has the best opportunity of healing their souls. But they enjoy apparent prosperity, they scornfully reject her wholesome warnings and esteem them as an old wives' ditty; when they are pinched by adversity, they are more intent on escaping the source of their present straits than on laying hold of what may furnish a cure and a place of refuge from which anguish is completely excluded. Sometimes, however, some of them turn the ears of their heart to listen to truth, but this happens more rarely in prosperity, more often in adversity. Still, they are few, for so it was foretold,[2] but I long to see you among them, for I truly love you, illustrious and distinguished lord, and most cherished son. Let this advice be the greeting I return to you, for, although I do not wish you to suffer hereafter such trials as you have already endured, I wish still more that you may not have endured them without some change for the better in your life.

---

2 Matt. 20.16,22. A reference to the few who find the strait and narrow path.

THE FATHERS
OF THE CHURCH

(A series of approximately 100 volumes when completed)

Life of St. Cyprian by Pontius
    translated by M. M. Mueller, R. Deferrari
Life of St. Epiphanius by Ennodius
    translated by G. Cook
Life of St. Paul the First Hermit
Life of St. Hilarion by St. Jerome
Life of Malchus by St. Jerome
    translated by L. Ewald
Life of St. Anthony by St. Athanasius
    translated by E. Keenan
A Sermon on the Life of St. Honoratus by St. Hilary
    translated by R. Deferrari

OCLC 806775

Volume 16:   **SAINT AUGUSTINE**   (1952)
The Christian Life
Lying
The Work of Monks
The Usefulness of Fasting
    translated by S. Muldowney
Against Lying
    translated by H. Jaffe
Continence
    translated by M–F. McDonald
Patience
    translated by L. Meagher
The Excellence of Widowhood
    translated by C. Eagan
The Eight Questions of Dulcitius
    translated by M. Deferrari

OCLC 806731

Volume 17:   **SAINT PETER CHRYSOLOGUS**   (1953)
Selected Sermons
Letter to Eutyches
             SAINT VALERIAN
Homilies
Letter to the Monks
    translated by G. Ganss

OCLC 806783

Volume 18:   **SAINT AUGUSTINE**   (1953)

The Sacrament of the Incarnation of Our Lord
The Sacraments
translated by R. Deferrari

OCLC 2316634

Volume 45:   SAINT AUGUSTINE   (1963)
The Trinity
translated by S. McKenna

OCLC 784847

Volume 46:   SAINT BASIL   (1963)
Exegetic Homilies
translated by A–C. Way

OCLC 806743

Volume 47:   SAINT CAESARIUS OF ARLES II   (1963)
Sermons (81–186)
translated by M. M. Mueller

OCLC 2494636

Volume 48:   THE HOMILIES OF SAINT JEROME   (1964)
Homilies 1–59
translated by L. Ewald

OCLC 412009

Volume 49:   LACTANTIUS   (1964)
The Divine Institutes
translated by M–F. McDonald

OCLC 711211

Volume 50:   PAULUS OROSIUS   (1964)
The Seven Books of History Against the Pagans
translated by R. Deferrari

OCLC 711212

Volume 51:   SAINT CYPRIAN   (1964)
Letters (1–81)
translated by R. Donna

OCLC 806738

Volume 52:   THE POEMS OF PRUDENTIUS   (1965)
The Divinity of Christ
The Origin of Sin
The Spiritual Combat
Against Symmachus (two books)
Scenes from Sacred History Or Twofold Nourishment
translated by C. Eagan